Rome

A Photographic Journey

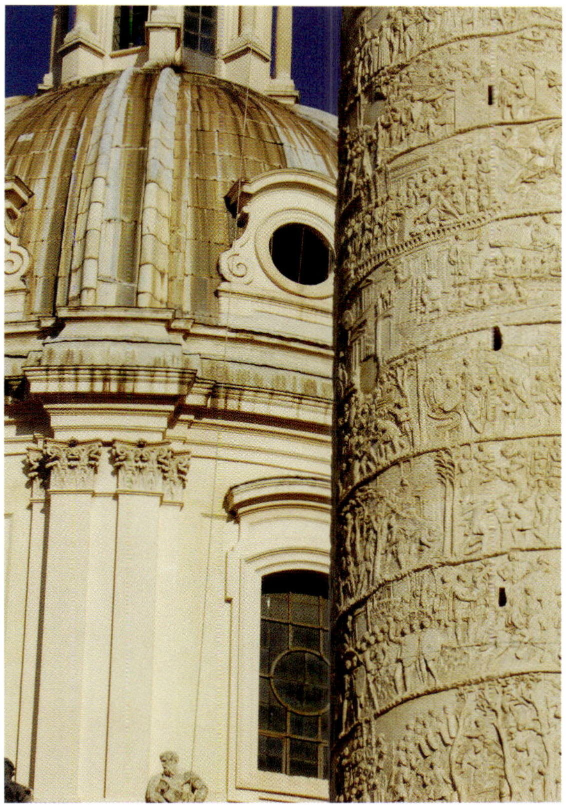

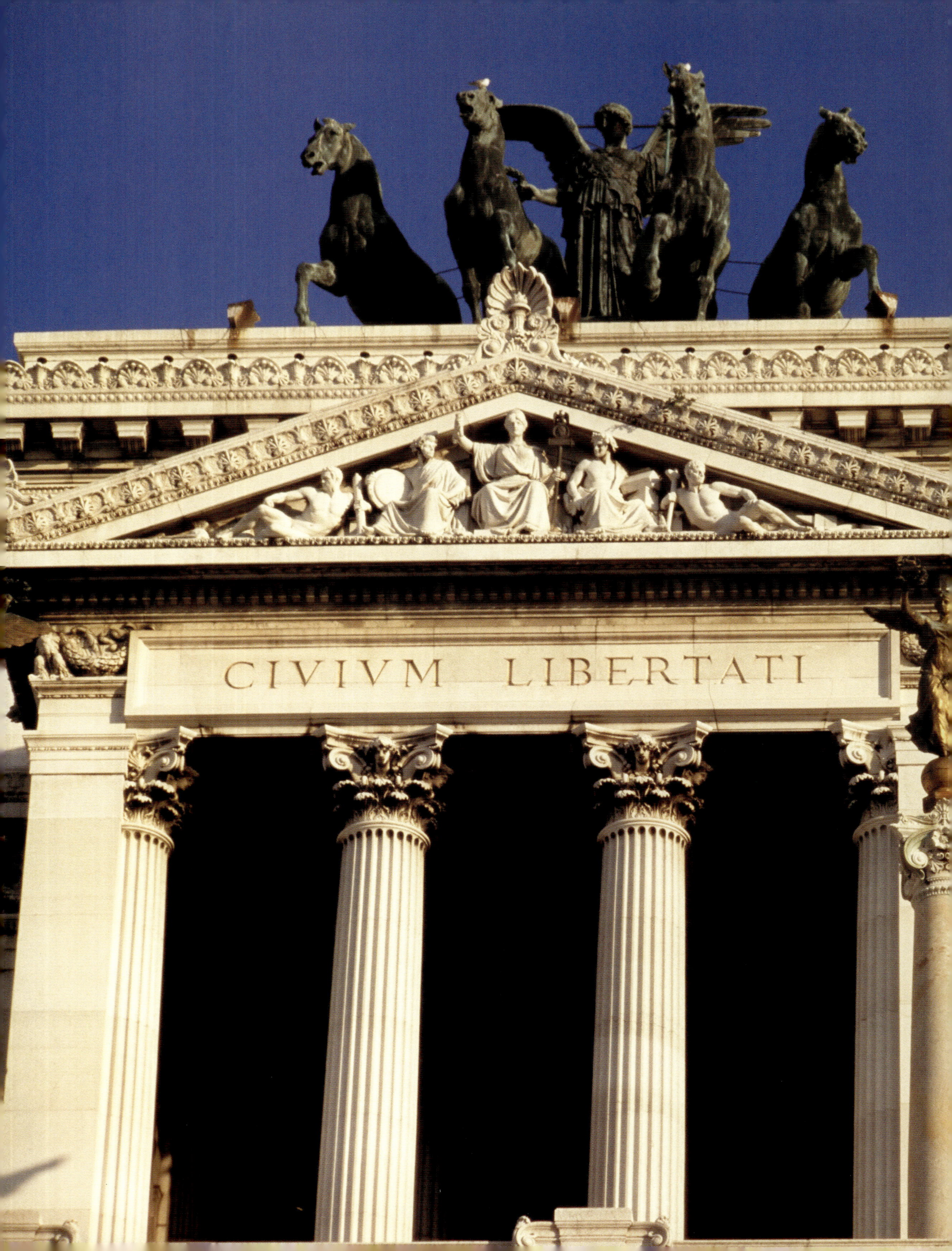
CIVIVM LIBERTATI

Rome

A Photographic Journey

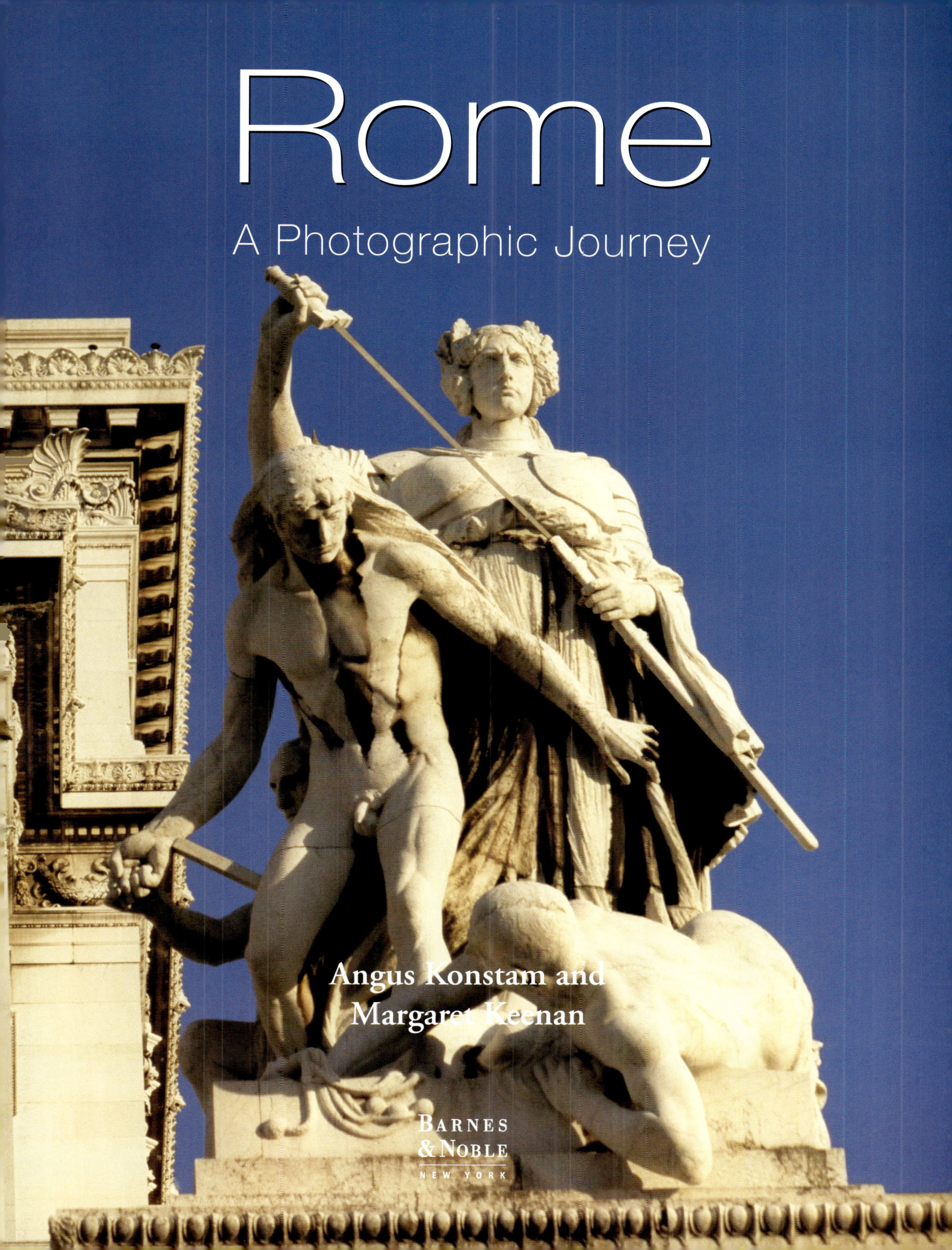

Angus Konstam and Margaret Keenan

BARNES & NOBLE
NEW YORK

This 2007 edition published by Barnes & Noble, Inc. by arrangement with Compendium Publishing Limited.

Editor: Don Gulbrandsen
Design: Danny Gillespie/Compendium Design
Map: Mark Franklin
Photographs: Thanks to Gaz de Vere for all the material unless credited otherwise either with the caption or below.
iStockphoto 6–7, 10–11, 12–13, Roberto A. Sanchez 14 (B), 21, 22, 26, 28 (B), Hedda Gjerpen 34, Yannick Luthy 39 (B), Mary Lane 40 (T), Bruce Bean 40 (B), Bruce Bean 41 (both), Hedda Gjerpen 84, 90–91 (both), Hedda Gjerpen 95 (T), 96 (both), 104 (T), 126, Steven Allan 127, Hedda Gjerpen 136, Shane Stezelberger 137, 144–145, 145 (T).
Getty Images Hiroshi Higuchi/ Photographer's Choice 8.
Library of Congress 9 (both), 18, 19, 20 (T), 27.
Fotolibra Kathryn Turner 94, Uwe Stiens 95 (B), Uwe Stiens 154–155.

2007 Barnes & Noble

ISBN-13: 978-0-7607-9117-2
ISBN-10: 0-7607-9117-1

Printed and bound in China

1 3 5 7 9 10 8 6 4 2

Page 1: The two great flowerings of Roman culture are exemplified here by Trajan's Column and the early sixteenth century church of Santa Maria di Loreto.

Pages 2–3: The Vittoriano—the Victor Emmanuel II Monument dominates the Piazza Venezia. *Nico Tondini/Robert Harding World Imagery*

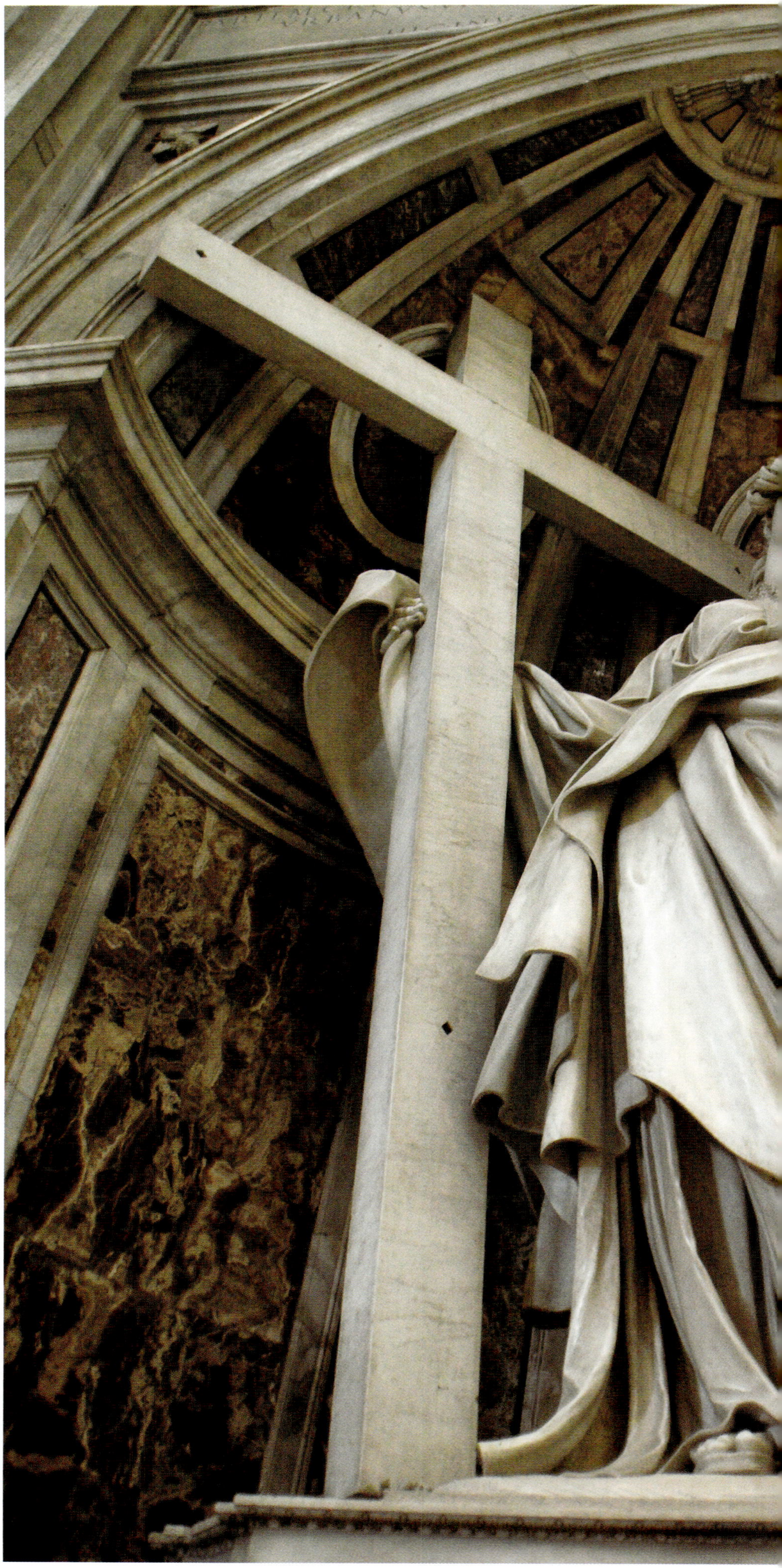

Right: St. Peter's Basilica contains the greatest collection of devotional art anywhere in the world: paintings, frescoes, and sculpture by the greatest artists of Christendom. *Bojan Vogrin/Fotolibra*

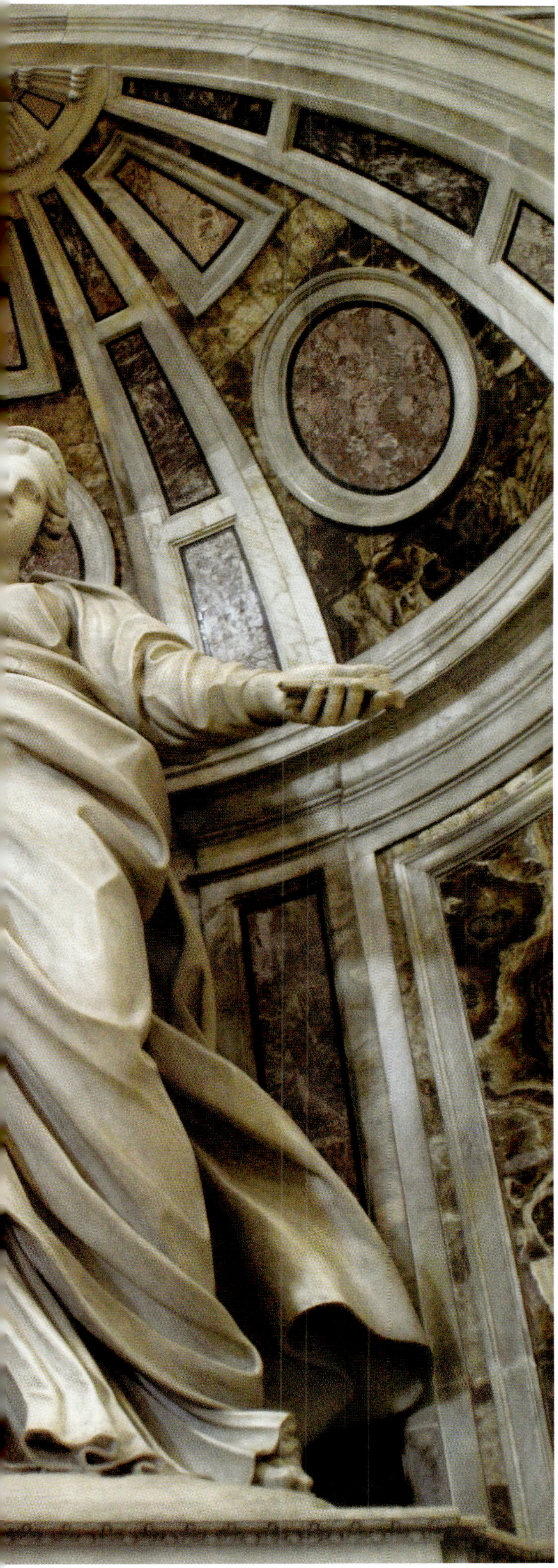

Contents

Introduction

City of the Seven Hills

Even more so than other great cities, the origins of Rome are shrouded in legend. During the reign of the Emperor Augustus the Roman historian Livy (Titus Livius) recorded these myths for posterity. He claimed that the Romans were the descendants of the great Trojan warrior Aeneas, and went on to tell the story of his grandsons Romulus and Remus, the royal twins sired by a she-wolf on the Palatine Hill, close to the banks of the River Tiber. A humble shepherd then raised the babies. When they reached manhood the brothers decided to found their own settlement, but they argued over where it should be sited. During the argument Romulus slew his brother and so his choice—the Palatine Hill—became the site for the settlement that was named Rome in his honor.

Romulus attracted other young adventurers to his side, but as Livy described it the settlement was short of women. Romulus' solution was to invite women of the neighboring tribe—the Sabines—over for a feast, then seize them, rape them, and keep them as their wives. A war between the Romans and the Sabines was prevented when the women intervened, and the two tribes formed an alliance, the first of many that saw Rome expand her influence in the area. One by one the neighboring tribes were brought into the Roman fold through conquest, treaty or assimilation, and by the sixth century B.C. the Roman kingdom controlled much of what became the province of Latium (now Lazio).

A series of six more Roman kings followed after Romulus (ca. 753–715 B.C.), including Tarquinius Priscus, the first of three Etruscan rulers. During these centuries the legends told of a string of intrigues, assassinations, conquests, and betrayal. The last of these rulers was the Etruscan tyrant Tarquin the Proud (ca. 534–509 B.C.). Although he did much to improve the city, including the building of the Temple of Jupiter on the Capitoline Hill, his rule was marked by violence. In the end, the Roman people revolted in 507 B.C. and ousted him. After driving Tarquin from the city the populace decided they had enough of kings,

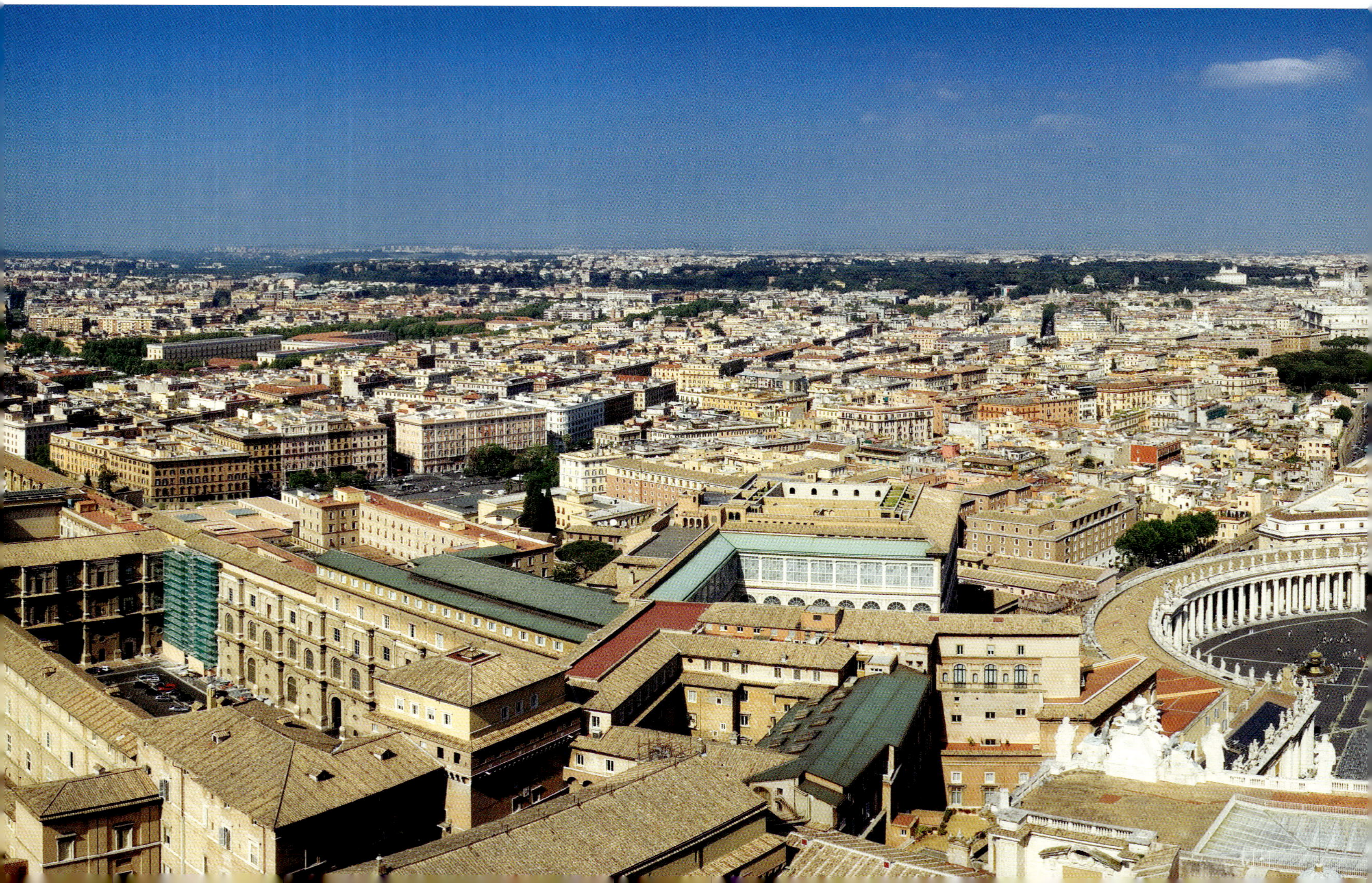

and so in that same year they founded the Roman Republic, and for the next half millennium the city and its expanding "empire" would be governed by *Senatus Populusque Romanus*—by the Senate and the People of Rome. The expulsion of King Tarquin led to war with the Etruscan people immediately to the north in 507 B.C., a conflict that gave rise to the story of Horatius defending the bridge over the Tiber against the attacking Etruscan army. Rome won the campaign, and the Republic prospered.

While much of Livy's early history is clearly little more than legend, archaeological evidence supports some of his story. For instance, there was a pastoral Iron Age settlement on the Palatine Hill, and it expanded outwards from there to encompass the other six Latin hills that surrounded the marshy low ground on the eastern bank of the River Tiber. Another settlement on the Quirinal Hill a mile north of the Palatine Hill has tentatively been identified with the Sabines (or Titientes). The remaining hills that circled the Palatine—running clockwise from the Quirinal—were the Viminal, Esqueline, Celian, Aventine, and the Capitoline. At this point the River Tiber was bridged to provided access to the western bank, where a track crossed the great trade route that ran north and south along the western side of the Italian peninsula. Rome soon became a flourishing marketplace.

REPUBLICAN ROME

So began the era of the Roman Republic, probably the most vibrant phase in Roman history. With monarchy abolished the Romans adopted a system of consular rule—two consuls were elected each year, and to rule they needed the support of the Senate and its attendant popular assemblies. The offices of state were divided between elected officials, all of which were accountable to the Senate and the people of Rome. Social upheaval was avoided by a strict division of society into patricians (the aristocrats) and plebeians (the commoners), supported by a client system where the leading patrician families all carried the support of a group of plebeian voters. This seemingly ramshackle and at times volatile system constituted the Roman Republic—a semi-democratic political framework that would remain in use in some form or other until Roman civilization collapsed in the fifth century A.D. Even the Roman Emperors had to pay lip service to the Senate, or risk the wrath of the Roman mob.

BELOW: The view looking eastward over the rooftops of Rome from the top of the dome of St Peter's Basilica in the Vatican City. Numerous well-known landmarks are visible including the Vatican museums, the Via della Conciliazione, the River Tiber, Castel Sant'Angelo and Ponte Sant'Angelo, the Palazzo di Giustizia, Parco della Villa Borghese, Villa Medici, Trinita dei Monti, Quirinale, and the Colosseum as well as the ancient ruins of the Palatino and the Parco Gianicolense.

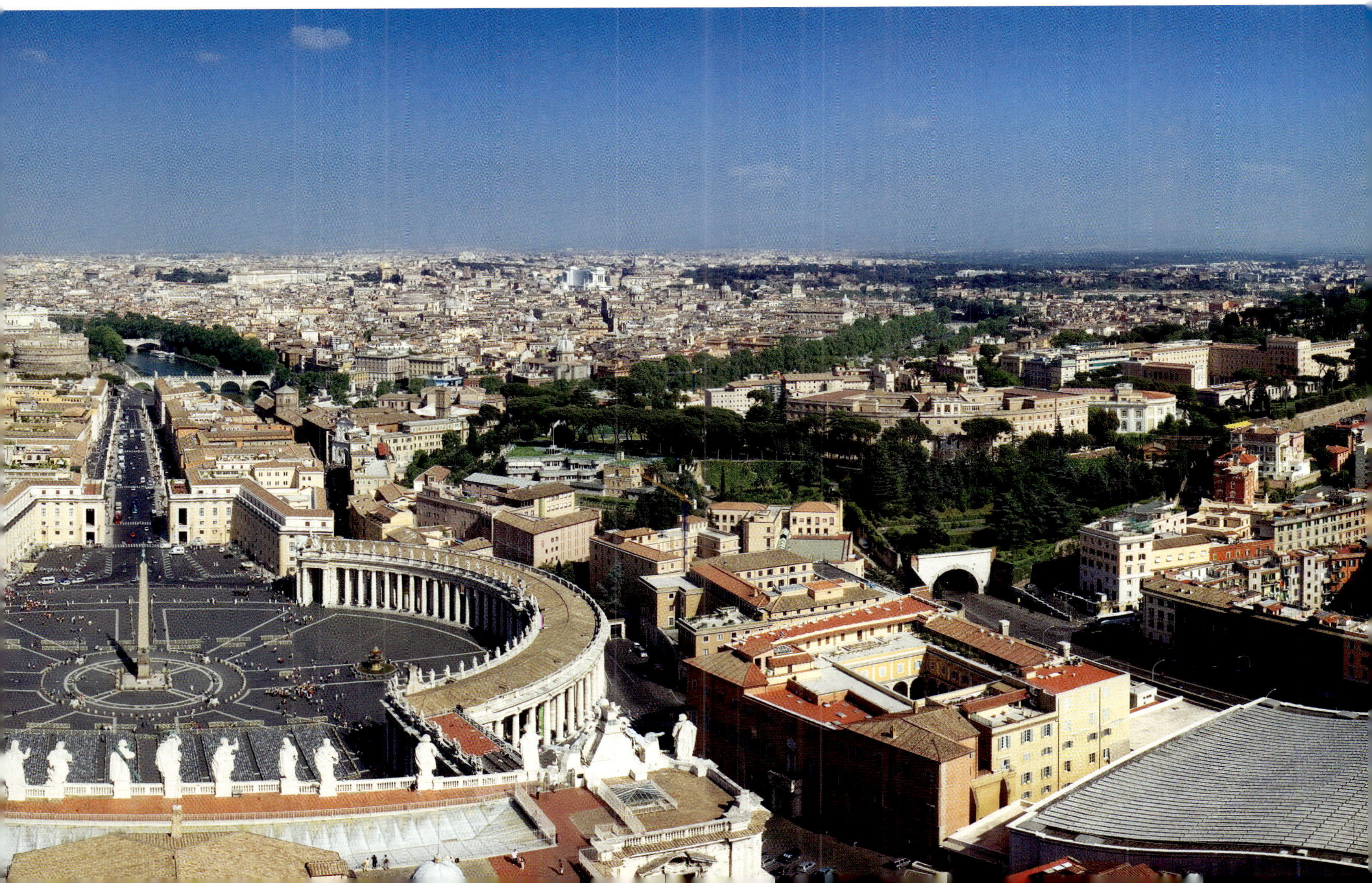

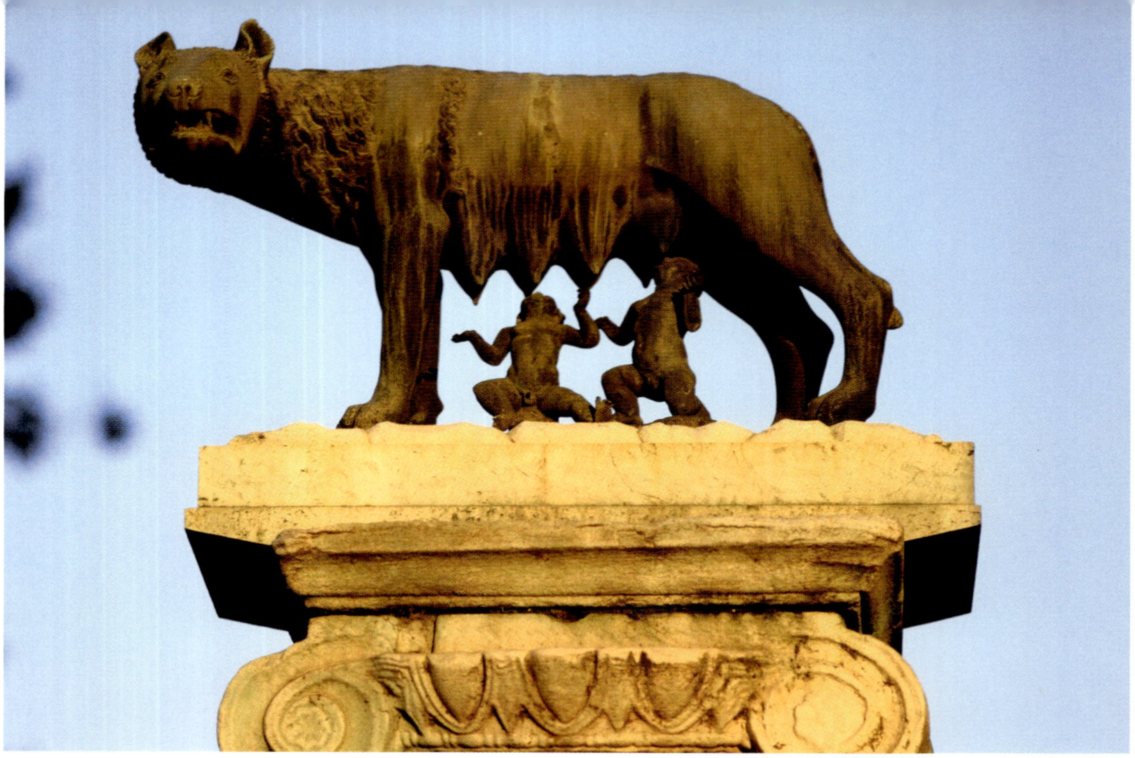

This was also a period when Rome expanded her borders by battling the neighboring Latin tribes. The Temple of Castor and Pollux was built in 499 B.C. to commemorate the first of these victories, and from then on it served as the meeting place for the Roman Senate. These wars culminated in capture of the Etruscan capital city of Veii in 396 B.C. However, this simply opened the door to invasion from the north, and in 390 B.C. the Gauls attempted to capture the city by stealth. Fortunately the geese kept on the Capitoline Hill began to cackle, the alarm was raised, and Rome was saved. In those days the defenses of the Capitoline were the only effective protection the city had, so as soon as the threat passed the rest of Rome was encircled by the Servian Wall, the first of several defensive measures that girded the city. The defenses were soon expanded to encompass all of the seven hills of Rome.

Other civic changes were also taking place. The Gauls had burned most of the city to the ground—archaeologists have discovered a deposit of ash and burnt rubble reaching to the foot of the Capitoline Hill. The city was quickly rebuilt, although the speed of reconstruction meant that any urban planning was abandoned, leading to narrow and irregular streets in some of the poorer areas such as the Subura, to the east of the Forum. As a result many sections of Rome would become intimidating and overcrowded—a far cry from the stately temples and public buildings surrounding the Forum. As Rome's conquests brought a flood of plunder into the city this program of civic and religious building work continued, adding an imposing grandeur to the heart of the Roman city.

During the years that followed the Republic continued her policy of expansion, by defeating the Samnites to the south, and she secured her conquests by establishing Roman colonies in the conquered territory. By the start of the third century B.C. the Romans effectively controlled the entire Italian peninsula south of the River Po. To maintain control of their new provinces the Romans built a network of roads that radiated out from the city. Sections of the Via Appia, which led south towards Capua, and the Via Flaminia, which led east towards the Adriatic coast, can still be seen today. Then as now, all roads still appear to lead to Rome.

Rome's hard-won peace was brought to an end by a series of three Punic Wars, fought against the Carthaginians of North Africa. These began in 264 B.C. and would continue intermittently for more than a century. During the First Punic War (264–241 B.C.), Rome gained control of Sicily—"the breadbasket" of Italy—and regular grain shipments from the island fed the rapidly growing population of the city. The Second Punic War (218–201 B.C.) was an altogether more bloody conflict, as Rome's consular armies faced Hannibal, one of the great captains of history. After the defeat of Rome's army at Cannae (216 B.C.) the Roman war cry became *Hannibal ad portas*—Hannibal is at the gates—even though the Carthaginian general was never able to seriously threaten Rome itself. The war ended with the comprehensive defeat of Rome's enemy in North Africa, outside the gates of Carthage rather than Rome. The Third Punic War (149–146 B.C.) was really about the settling of scores, and by its end Carthage had ceased to exist. Rome entered the war as a regional power

ROMULUS AND REMUS

The traditional founders of ancient Rome, Romulus and Remus were reputedly the twin sons of Mars, the Roman god of war and Rhea Silvia, the priestess niece of the King of Alba Longa. Her family claimed to be exiles from Troy who had settled in what is now Lazio during the ninth century B.C. In fact, some Roman legends claim that the Trojan hero Aeneas was the grandfather of the two boys. As a Vestal Virgin, Rhea Silvia took an oath of chastity, so when she sired two sons she was put to death by order of her wicked uncle. According to the law her babies should have been drowned in the River Tiber, but as the legend has it they were spared byTiberinus the river god, who rescued the boys, and took them to the Palatine Hill, where they were nursed by Lupa, a she-wolf. This story was recorded by the Roman historians Plutarch and Livy, who entwined legend and history to created a mythical origin for their city. They claimed that the twins were discovered by a shepherd and his wife, who raised the boys as their own. It was claimed that their noble birth became apparent as they grew into strong, handsome youths. When they learned of their family history they sought out and killed their uncle, and reinstated their grandfather as the King of Alba Longa. They then began establishing their own settlement. Remus chose the Aventine Hill, while Romulus opted for the Palantine. Remus began taunting his brother, claiming that his defensive wall was too low, and leaped over it to prove his point. Romulus slew his brother in a fit of rage. He went on to build his settlement, which he named Rome, after his own name. The twins can still be seen today, suckling their protective she-wolf, in an Etruscan bronze statue housed in the Capitoline Museum.

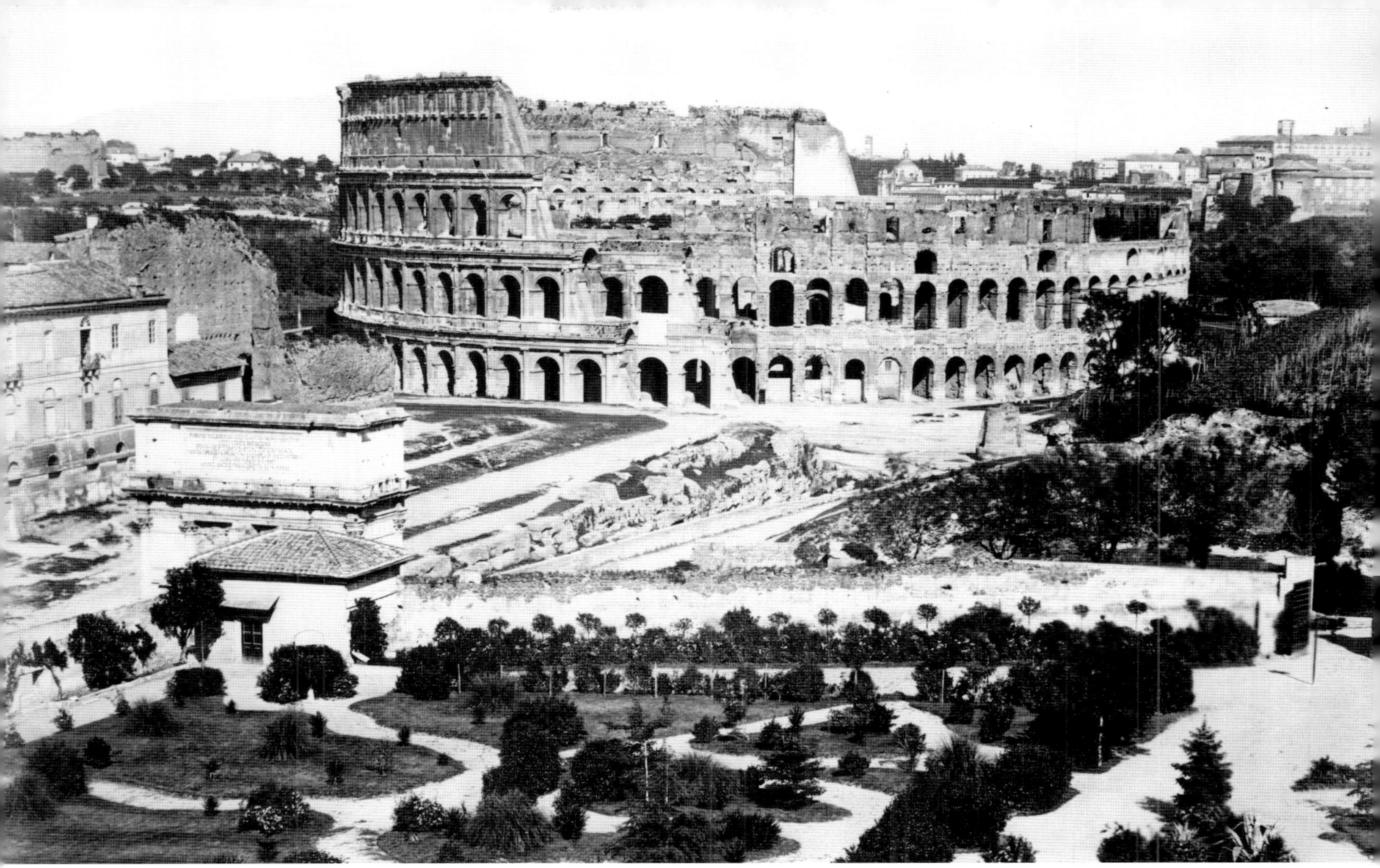

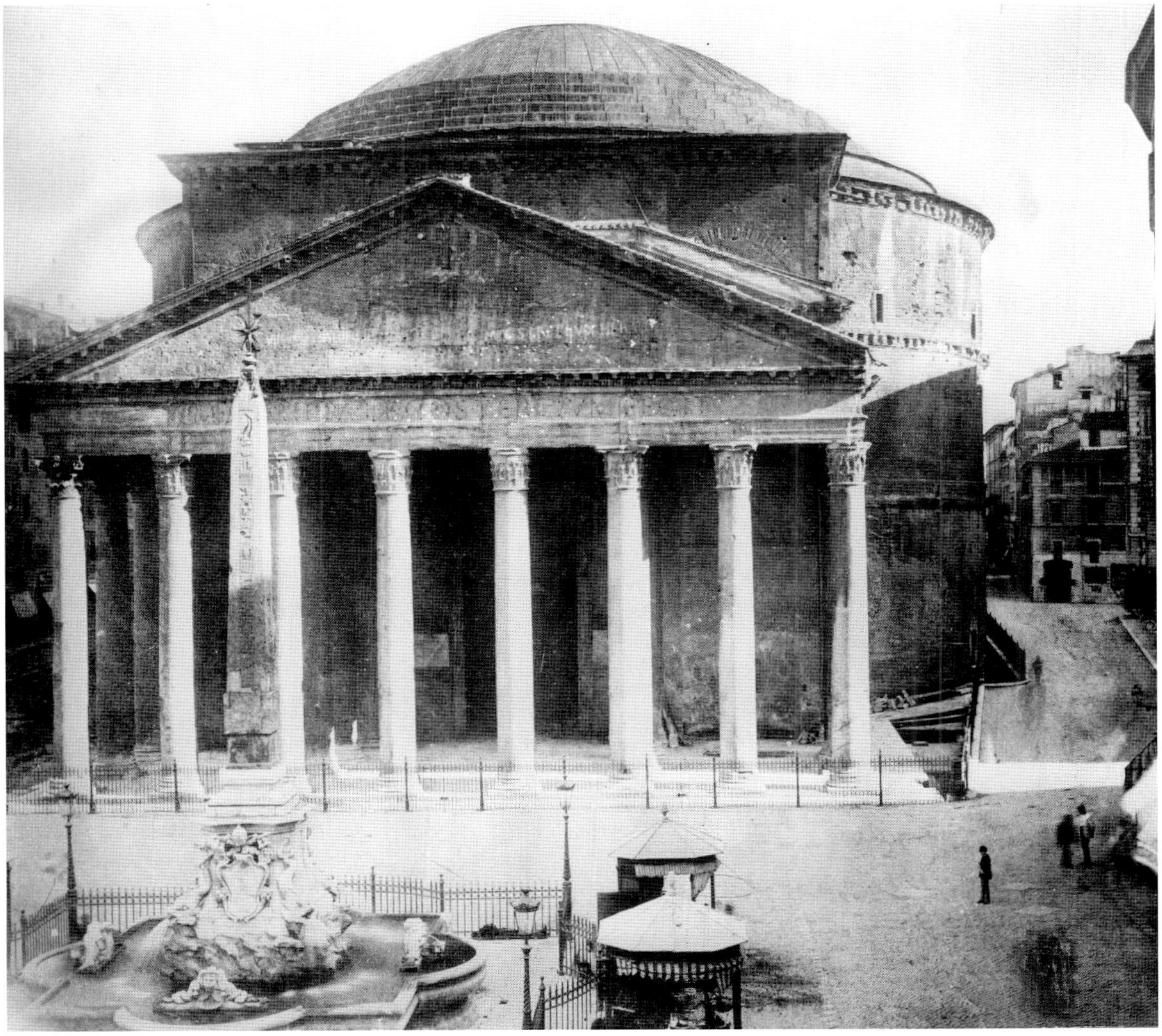

Far left: The Capitoline Wolf statue celebrates the twin brothers Romulus and Remus, legendary founders of Rome who were thrown into the River Tiber by their jealous uncle, then rescued and nurtured by a she-wolf who fed them with her milk.

Above: Rome's premier tourist sight—and much recorded in paint and photograph, the Colosseum has had a checkered history since building started between 70 and 72 A.D. under the Emperor Vespasian. In 1749, Pope Benedict XIV endorsed the view that the Colosseum was a sacred site where early Christians had been martyred and it has been protected since then.

Left: Another much-photographed location, dating from about 125 A.D. the Pantheon is the best preserved of all Roman buildings.

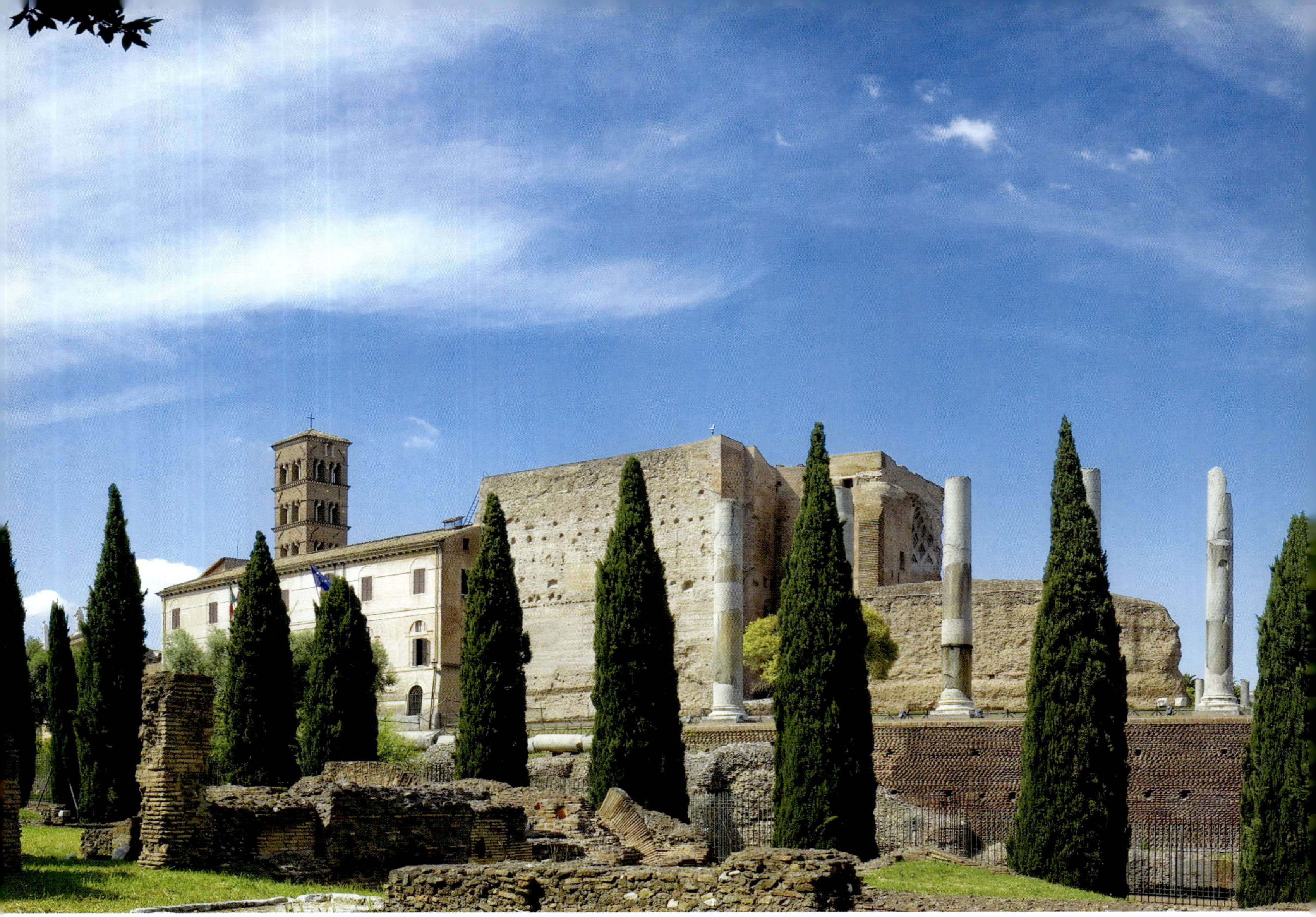

Above: Pillars from the ruined Temple of Venus and cypress trees line the route of the Via Sacra—the Sacred Road. This was the main thoroughfare through ancient Rome that led from the top of the Capitoline Hill, through the Forum, to the Colosseum.

Right: Pigeons in front of the Pantheon.

Far right: The Via della Conciliazione—the Avenue of Reconciliation—runs between St. Peter's and the Castel Sant' Angelo. It was constructed between 1936 and 1950.

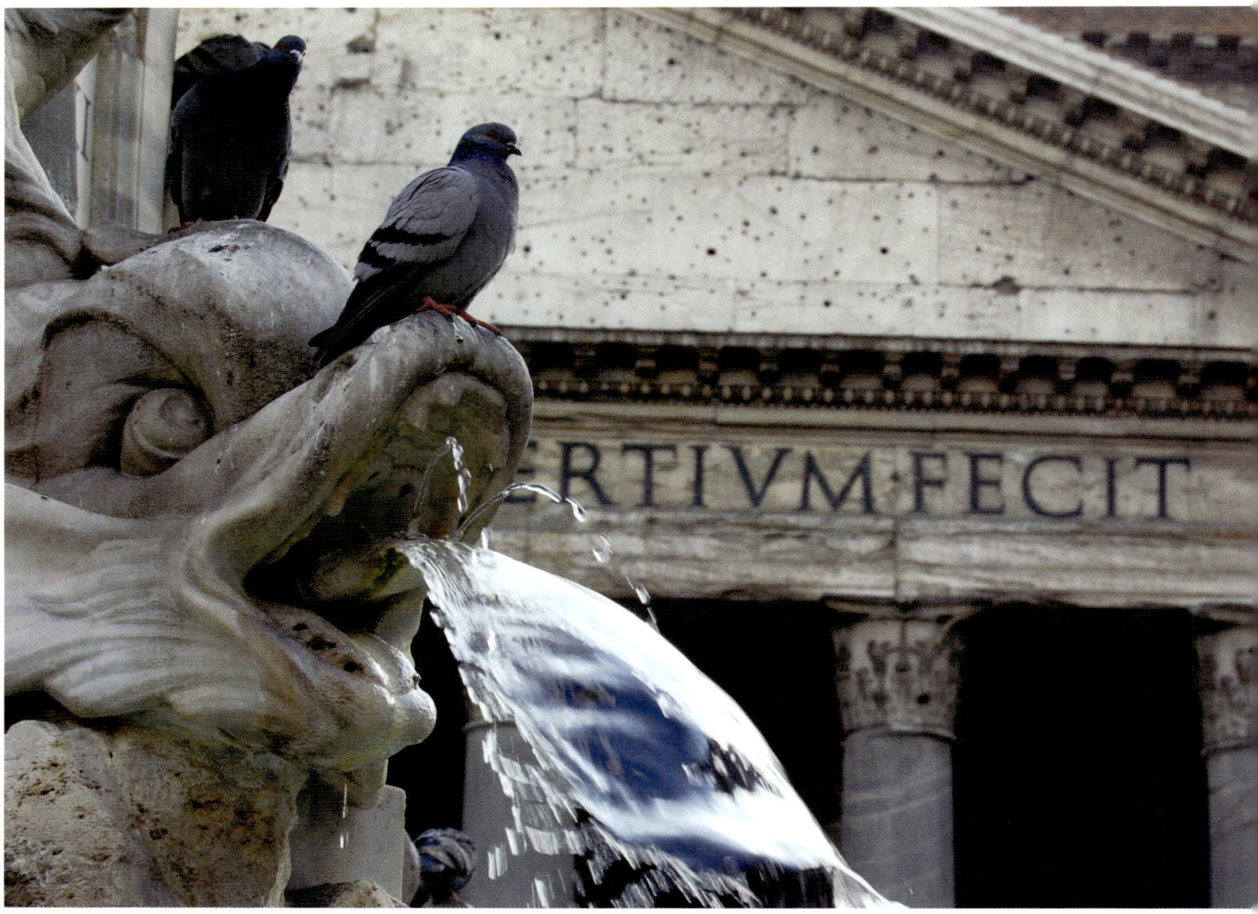

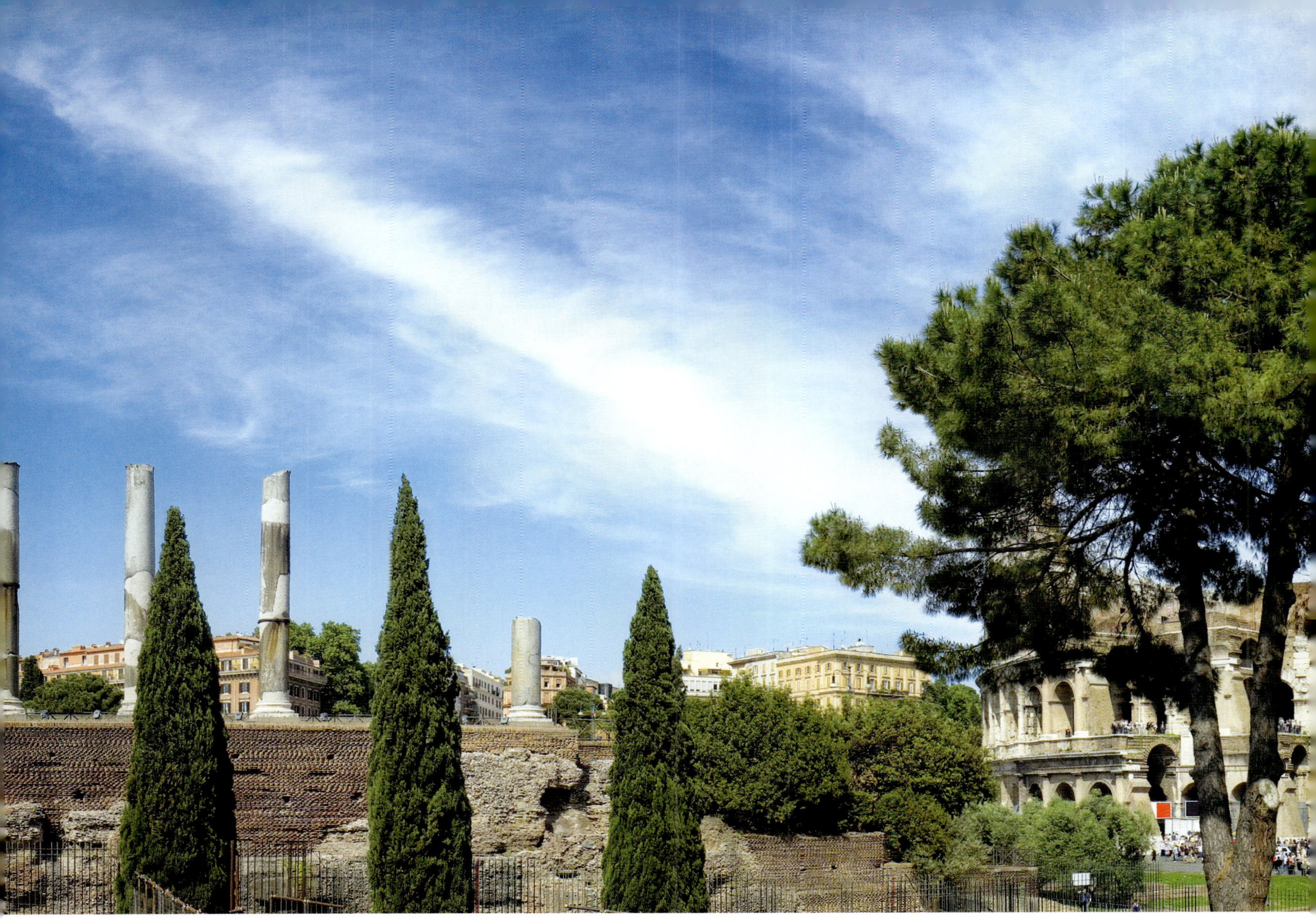

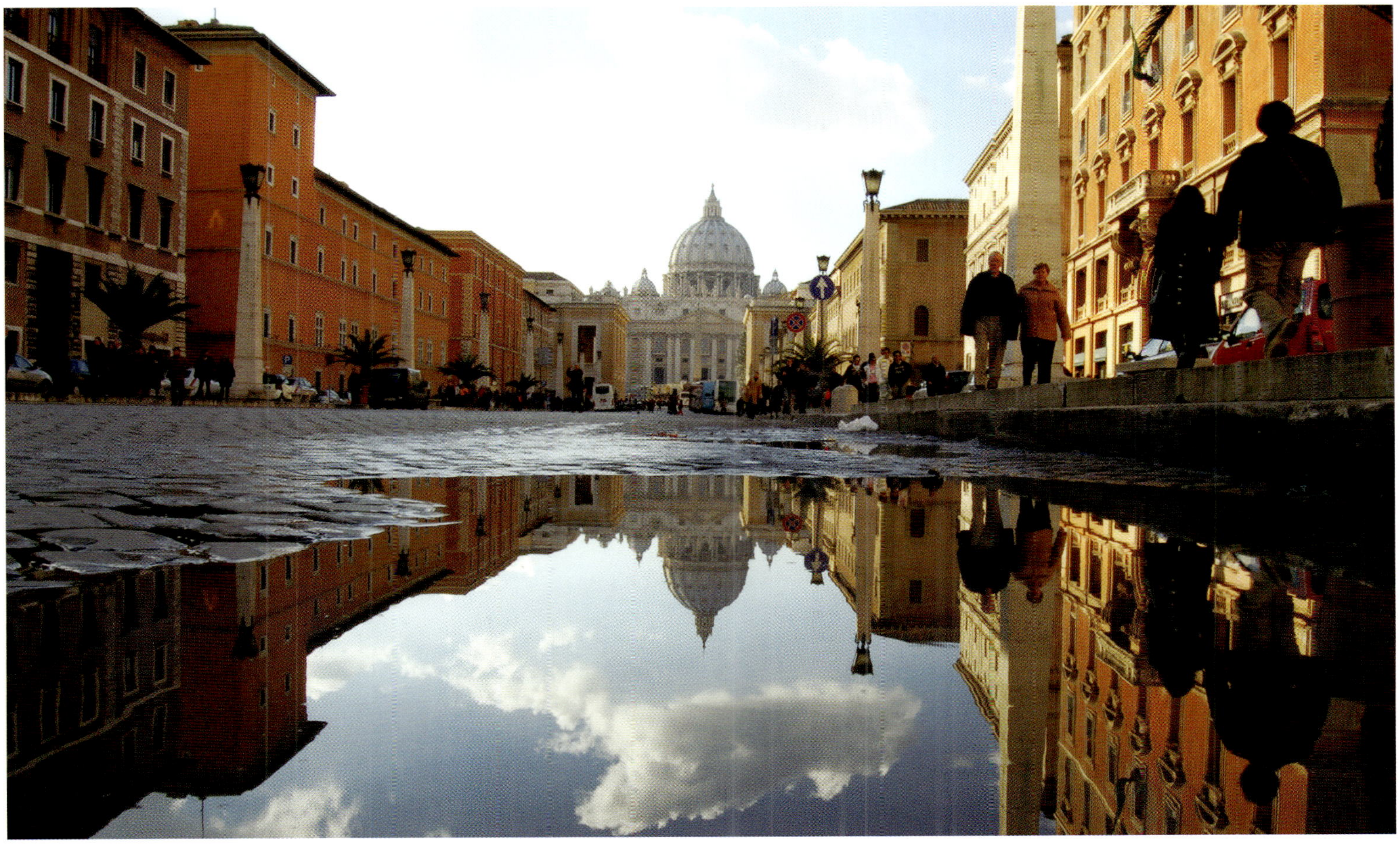

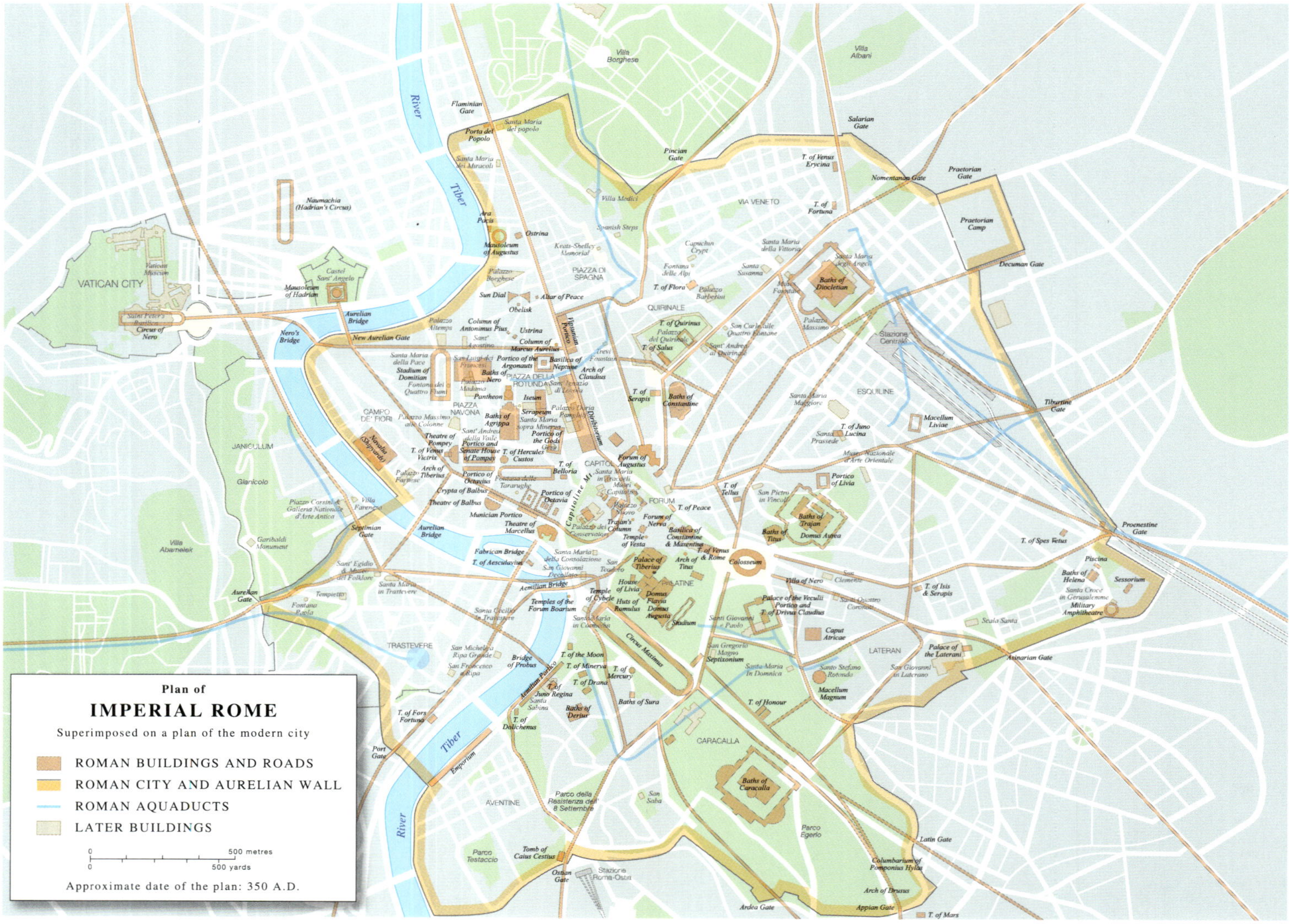
Plan of
IMPERIAL ROME
Superimposed on a plan of the modern city
ROMAN BUILDINGS AND ROADS
ROMAN CITY AND AURELIAN WALL
ROMAN AQUADUCTS
LATER BUILDINGS
0 500 metres
0 500 yards
Approximate date of the plan: 350 A.D.
Villa Borghese
Villa Albani
River Tiber
Flaminian Gate
Porta del Popolo
Salarian Gate
Pincian Gate
Praetorian Gate
Praetorian Camp
Nomentanan Gate
VIA VENETO
Decuman Gate
Naumachia (Hadrian's Circus)
VATICAN CITY
Castel Sant'Angelo
Mausoleum of Hadrian
Mausoleum of Augustus
Ara Pacis
Ustrina
Spanish Steps
PIAZZA DI SPAGNA
QUIRINALE
Baths of Diocletian
Aurelian Bridge
Nero's Bridge
New Aurelian Gate
Circus of Nero
Sun Dial
Altar of Peace
Obelisk
Column of Marcus Aurelius
Stadium of Domitian
PIAZZA NAVONA
Pantheon
Baths of Agrippa
Iseum
Serapeum
T. of Serapis
Baths of Constantine
ESQUILINE
Stazione Centrale
Tiburtine Gate
Macellum Liviae
CAMPO DE' FIORI
JANICULUM
Gianicolo
Theatre of Pompey
Porticus of Octavia
Crypta of Balbus
Theatre of Balbus
CAPITOL
Forum of Augustus
FORUM
T. of Peace
Forum of Nerva
Trajan's Column
Baths of Trajan
Domus Aurea
Baths of Titus
Colosseum
T. of Venus & Rome
Arch of Titus
Basilica of Constantine & Maxentius
Temple of Vesta
Palace of Tiberius
House of Livia
Domus Flavia
Domus Augusta
Stadium
PALATINE
Theatre of Marcellus
Fabrician Bridge
Aemilian Bridge
Aurelian Bridge
Septimian Gate
Aurelian Gate
TRASTEVERE
Circus Maximus
T. of the Moon
T. of Minerva
T. of Diana
T. of Mercury
Juno Regina
Baths of Decius
Baths of Sura
T. of Honour
Septizonium
Caput Africae
LATERAN
Palace of the Laterani
Asinarian Gate
Proenestine Gate
T. of Spes Vetus
Sessorium
Military Amphitheatre
CARACALLA
Baths of Caracalla
AVENTINE
Emporium
Port Gate
T. of Fors Fortuna
Parco della Resistenza dell 8 Settembre
Parco Testaccio
Tomb of Caius Cestius
Ostian Gate
Stazione Roma-Ostia
Parco Egerio
Latin Gate
Columbarium of Pomponius Hylas
Arch of Drusus
Appian Gate
Ardea Gate
T. of Mars

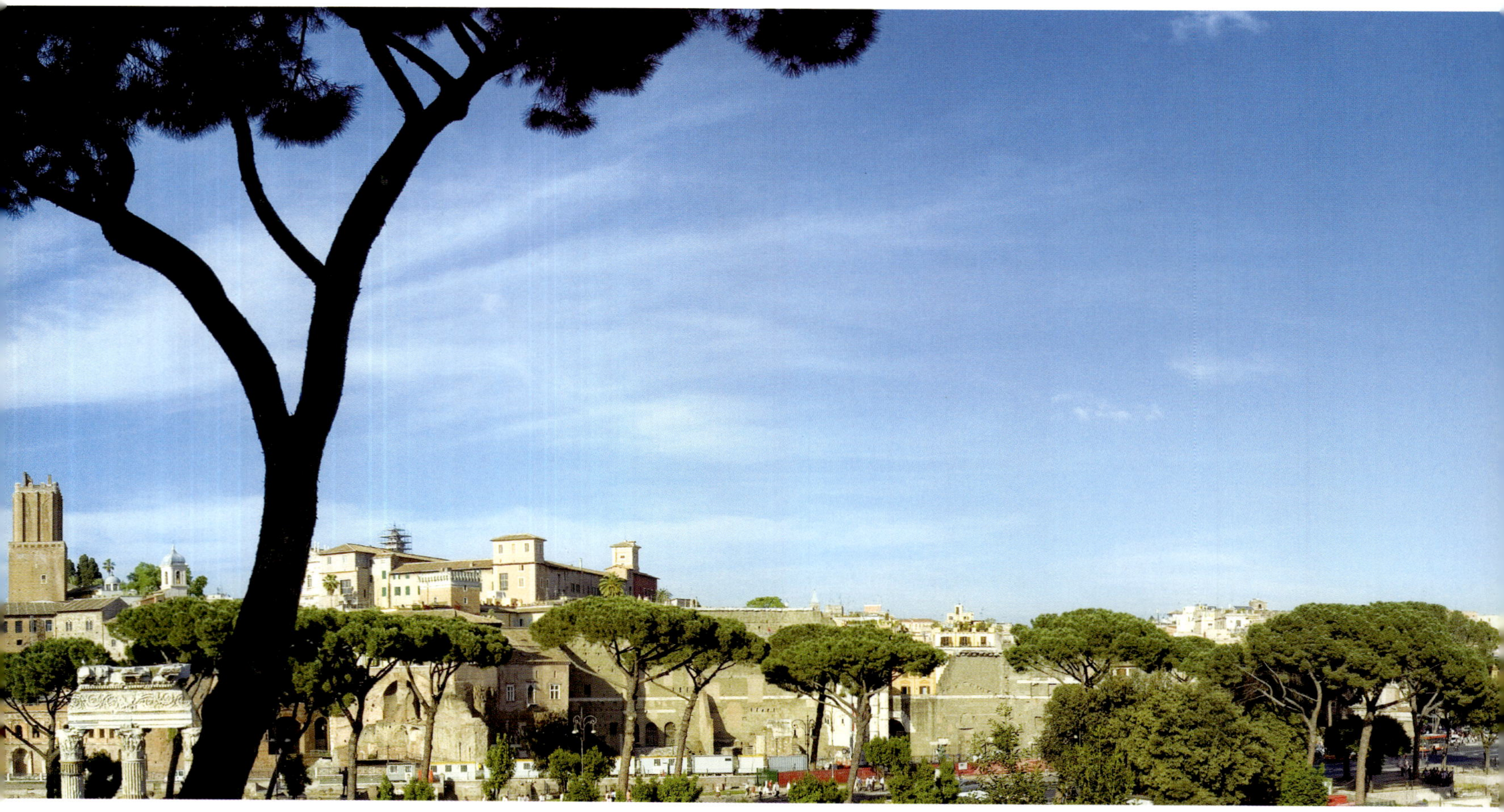

in Italy. By its end she had become a superpower.

By the middle of the second century B.C. Rome controlled most of the Mediterranean, from Spain to Asia Minor. One of the most significant of her new provinces was Greece, which was brought into the Roman sphere in 146 B.C. The Romans embraced Greek culture with a passion, linking Grecian deities with Roman ones, importing Greek statuary to decorate the houses of the wealthy, and even adopting Greek styles of architecture. One of the most imposing Grecian structures was the Theater of Pompey (55 B.C.), the largest place of entertainment in Rome until the building of the Colosseum.

This expansion continued during the last century of the Roman Republic, despite growing social and political upheavals at home. The merchants and lower social classes in Rome came to resent the consolidation of power into the hands of Rome's patrician elite. Then there was the question of Roman citizenship, which was demanded by most non-Roman Italians. The result was a series of slave revolts and provincial conflicts that led to a crisis in the Republic. As the historian Appian put it, this was an era when "violence ruled everything."

Order was restored by a series of "First Men of Rome"—military men whose authoritarian position was supported by their legionaries. Gaius Marius (157–86 B.C.) and Lucius Cornelius Sulla (138–78 B.C.) both brought their legions into the city and ruled by military might. For almost half a century the city became a pawn, fought over by those who pursued their own personal policies, and others who sought to preserve the Republic. This culminated in the conflict between Gnaeus Pompey "the Great" (106–48 B.C.) and Julius Caesar (100–44 B.C.). This power struggle reached a head after Caesar's conquest of Gaul, and Rome was plunged into Civil War that ended only when Caesar emerged victorious. However, his assassination before the Senate in the Theater of Pompey sparked a new round of fighting that only came to an end when Caesar's adopted son Octavian (63 B.C.–A.D. 14) emerged victorious in 31 B.C.

LEFT: Map showing the boundaries and major buildings of ancient Rome.

CAPITAL OF THE WORLD

Although Octavian officially handed power back to the Roman Senate, in reality he retained con-

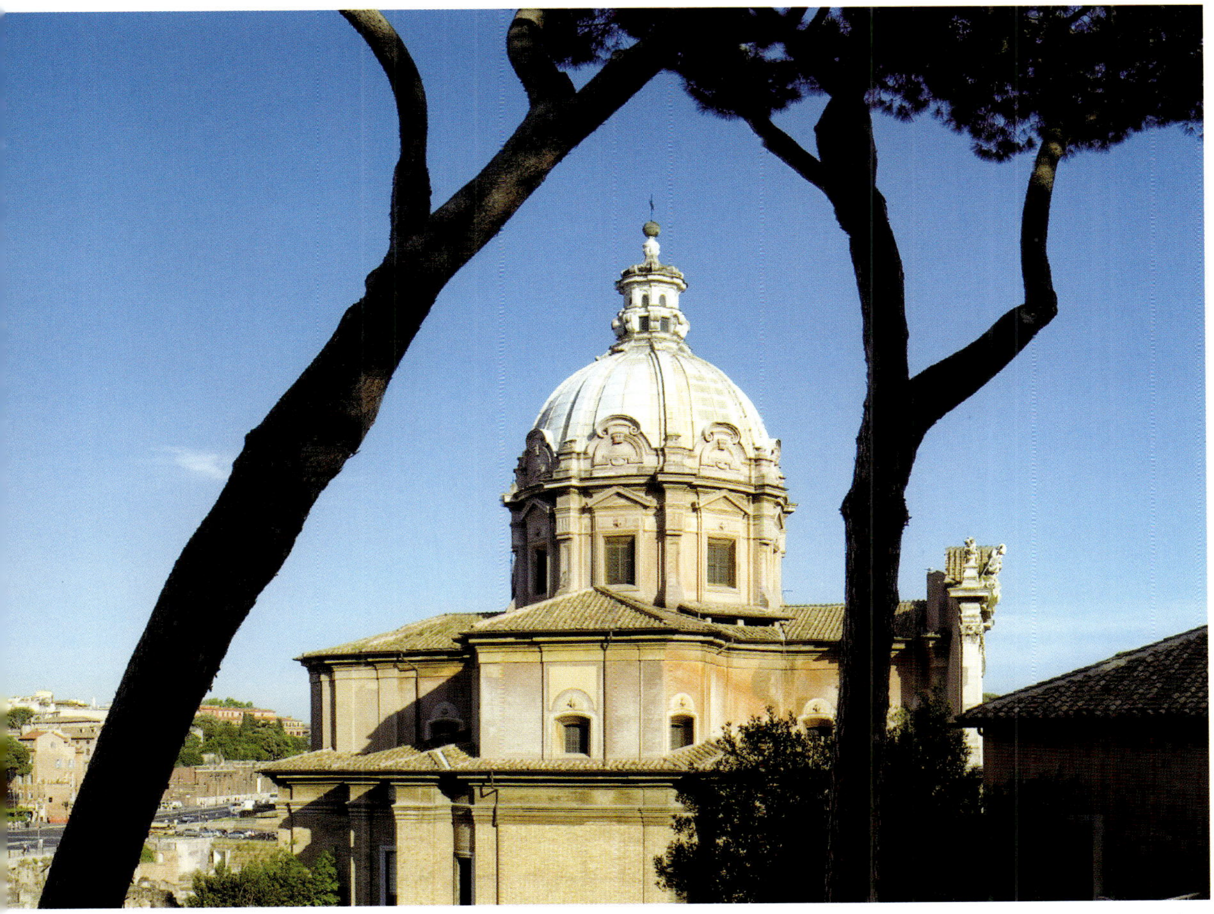

BELOW: The dome of Santi Luca e Martina on Capitol Hill looks out over the ancient columns and temples of the Forum. The center of Rome remains remarkably green thanks to the trees and gardens of the ancient villas and the distinctive pine trees that dot the hills of Rome.

SAINT PETER

Appropriately enough, St. Peter is the patron saint of Rome. According to the New Testament, Peter (originally called Simeon or Shimon) was a fisherman from Galilee and one of the original Twelve Apostles. It was claimed that after the death of Jesus he became the leader of the fledgling Christian movement, and today he is closely associated with the foundation of the church in Rome. Like other sources, the New Testament is unclear about Peter's movements during the last two decades of his life, but by all accounts he was actively involved in the Christian "underground" in Rome during the reign of the Emperor Nero (A.D. 54–68), if not before. Catholic tradition claims that he founded the first Christian church in Rome and claimed authority as its bishop. It is also claimed that Nero blamed the Christians for starting the fire that engulfed Rome in A.D. 64, and Peter was duly arrested, tried, and executed. It is traditionally believed that Peter was crucified head down, and that after his death he was buried on the west bank of the River Tiber, on the spot where St. Peter's Basilica now stands. In Christian art he is often depicted holding the keys of heaven, symbolizing both his role as heavenly gatekeeper and his primacy over the church. Following the recognition of Christianity by the Emperor Constantine, the Bishop of Rome gained primacy over other Christian prelates, largely due to its association with Peter. By the late fifth century A.D. the Roman prelate was being described as both the "pope," and the "rector of the whole church." Traditionally the pope still holds the title of Bishop of Rome, and is seen as the successor of St. Peter. It is no coincidence that the main papal symbol is a crossed set of keys—a direct link to the original primacy of St. Peter.

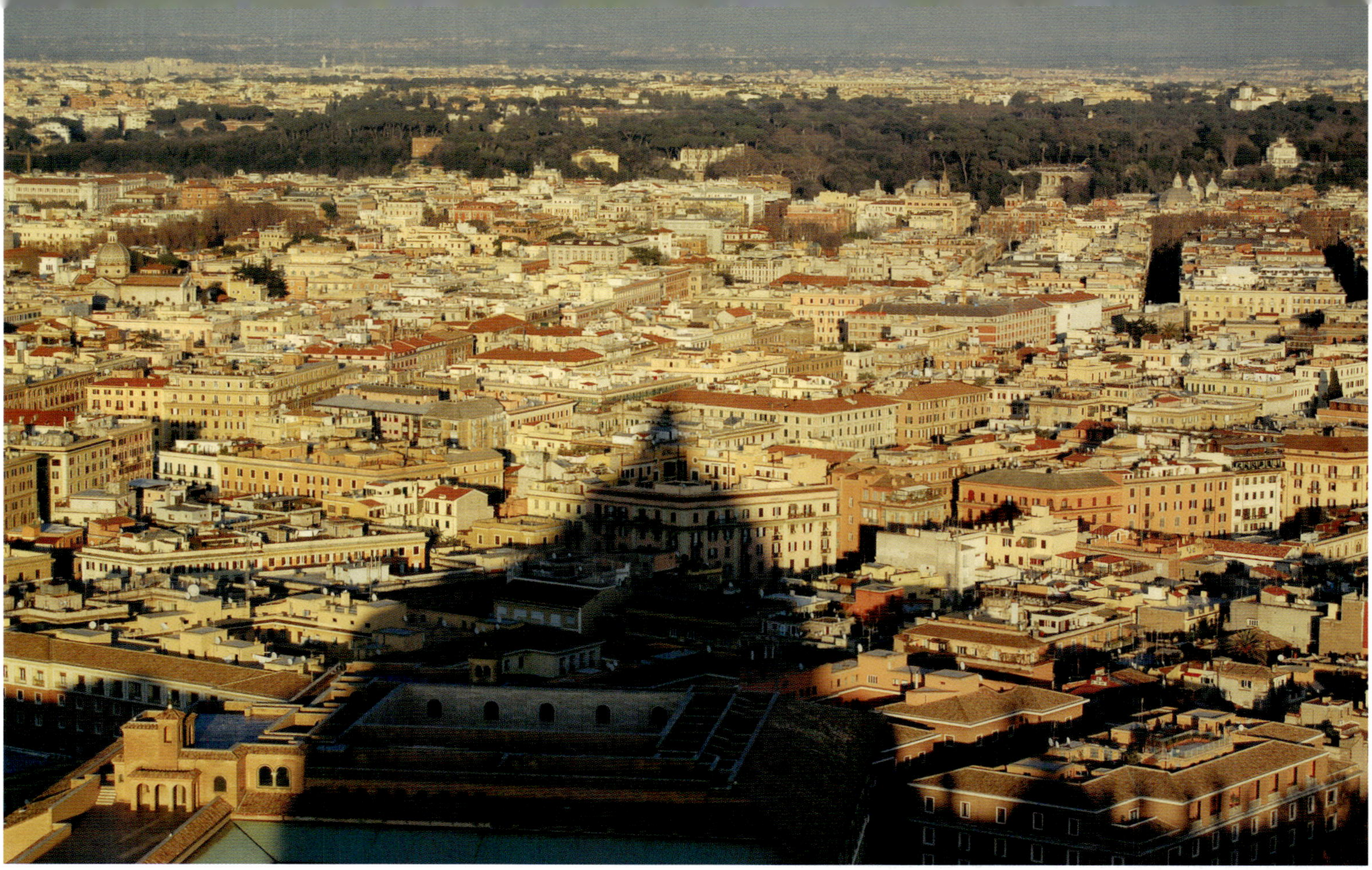

ABOVE: The dome of St. Peter's casts a long shadow over the city.

RIGHT: The front of St. Peter's Square in the Vatican City is commanded by a statue of St. Peter, the principal patron saint of Rome. It is the work of Giuseppe de Fabris and completed in 1840.

FAR RIGHT: In the Vatican City statues line the top of the colonnade around Piazza San Pietro—St. Peter's Square—in front of St. Peter's Basilica.

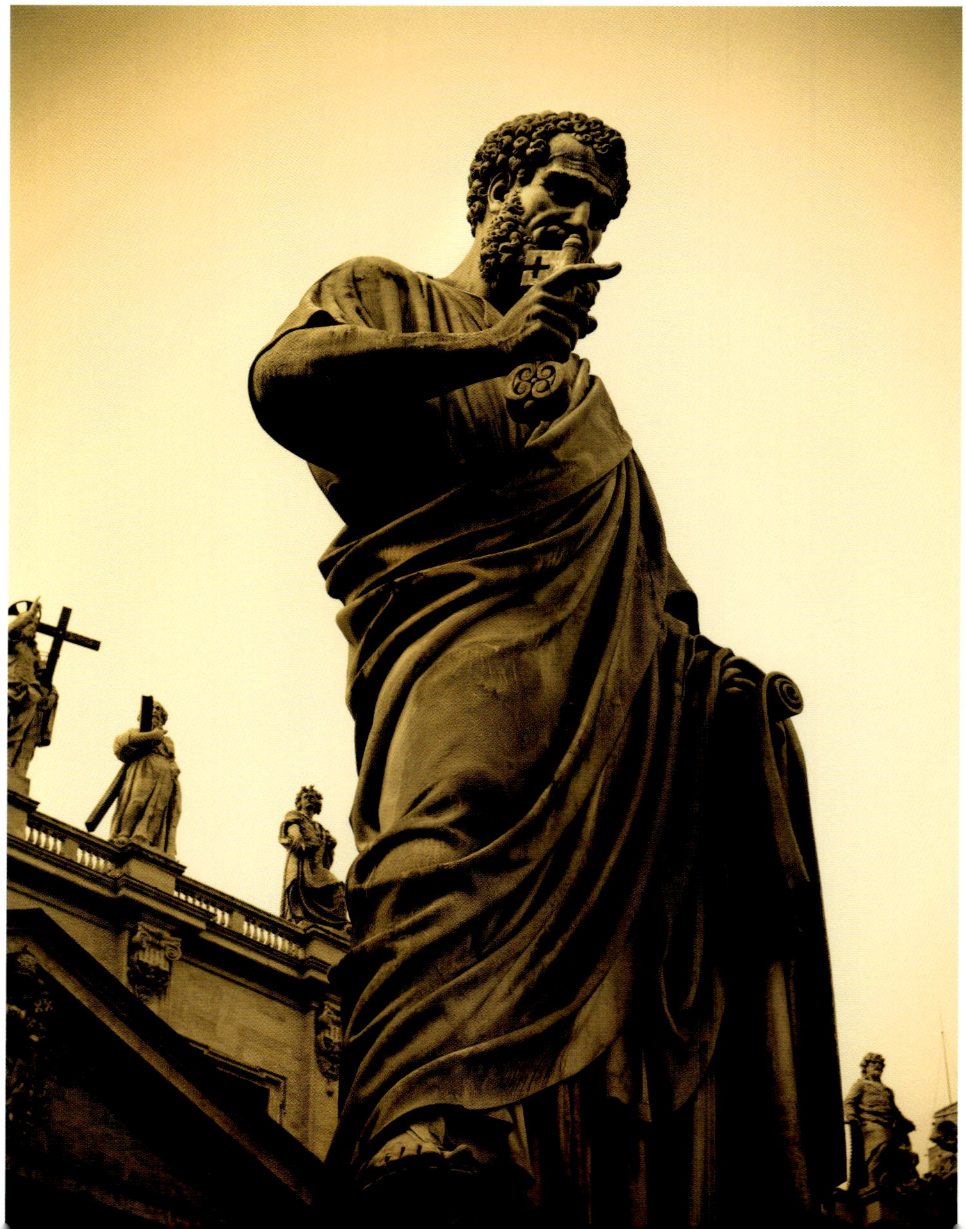

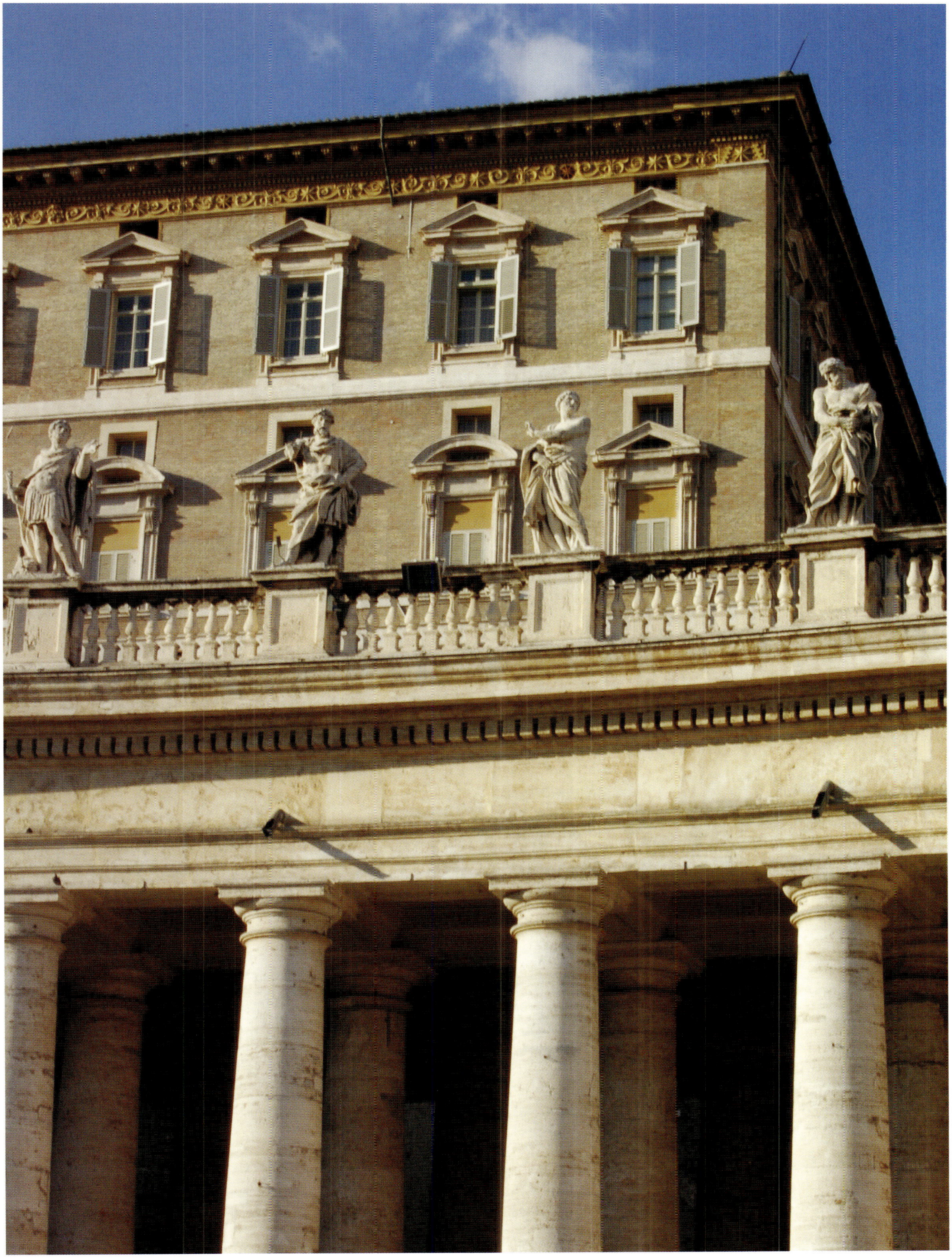

JU;IUS CAESAR

The one ancient Roman that everyone has heard of is Julius Caesar, and modern Rome is littered with places bearing his name, along with souvenir shops touting busts of the great man. You could be forgiven for thinking that he was a great Roman emperor, rather than a mere general, politician, and author. Gaius Julius Caesar (ca. 100-44 B.C.) was a patrician of the Julia family—"Caesar" was added (according to the historian Pliny) because he was delivered by what is now termed caesarean section. Brought up amid the political turmoil of the late Republic, at one stage he was sentenced to death by the tyrant Sulla, and had to go into hiding, so he spent several years in the East, where he earned his military spurs. After Sulla's departure he returned to Rome to pursue a political career and quickly made a name. He was elected as Consul in 59 B.C., and then secured his political position by forming a triumvirate with rivals Pompey and Crassus. In effect the three men ruled Rome together. This allowed Caesar to continue his military career without looking over his shoulder. He spent the next decade conquering Gaul, a feat that ensured his place among the great military captains of history. However, all was not well in Rome. Crassus was killed in 53 B.C., while Pompey began plotting against his remaining rival. Caesar's solution was to lead his troops across the Rubicon River and invade Rome, an act that led to a brutal civil war (49–45 B.C.) between the two factions. In 48 B.C. Caesar emerged victorious and returned to Rome in triumph; he went on to rule the city as a benign dictator. Then, in 44 B.C. he was murdered in the Senate, provoking another civil war. Eventually Caesar's adopted son Octavian triumphed, Caesar was pronounced a god, and the Republic died with hardly a whimper as Octavian became Augustus, the first Emperor.

trol of the Roman state. In 23 B.C. he became known as Augustus, and was granted the *Imperium*—the power to rule. In the process he became the first Roman Emperor. So began the period of peace and prosperity that became known as the *Pax Romana*—the Roman peace. The era of Imperial greatness that followed saw the consolidation of Rome's provinces into a mighty Empire that encompassed the known world, from the mountains of Scotland to the deserts of Arabia. Rome now lay at the hub of all this, and while the city itself spilled beyond its old walls its center was transformed into the administrative heart of the Roman Empire. At the same time a succession of Emperors built a series of grand palaces—the word itself derived from the Palatine—where the greatest of these imperial residences were sited. The political cut-and-thrust of the Senate had been replaced by the intrigues of the imperial court.

The biggest disaster to overtake Rome in almost four centuries occurred during the reign of the Emperor Nero (37–68 B.C.). In A.D. 64 a fire spread through the city, leaving more than half of it in ashes. There is no evidence that Nero "fiddled while Rome burned." In all probability that was a myth propagated by later Christian historians who resented his intolerance of the new religion. What is recorded is the extensive program of restoration he initiated, although the bulk of this work was actually carried out during the reign of his successor Vespasian.

The greatest architectural achievement of his reign was the construction of the Colosseum, the giant amphitheater built immediately to the east of the Forum. Work began on the project around A.D. 70, and the 50,000-seat arena took a decade to complete. The Colosseum remained in use for more than five centuries—until well after the fall of the Roman Empire, by which time it was used both as a religious shrine and as a source of stone for the rest of the city. In its heyday it was the premier gladiatorial arena in the Roman Empire, as well as the vast theater where staged battles, mock sea fights, the feeding of Christians to wild animals, and other similar bloodthirsty spectator sports were held. Today the Colosseum remains the premier symbol of the grandeur that was once Ancient Rome.

Historians generally agree that the Roman Empire reached its zenith during the reign of the Emperor Trajan (A.D. 98–117), one of the "five good Emperors" of the Antonine dynasty. The Antonine emperors helped safeguard the borders of the Empire, which brought substantial financial benefits to both Rome and its provinces.

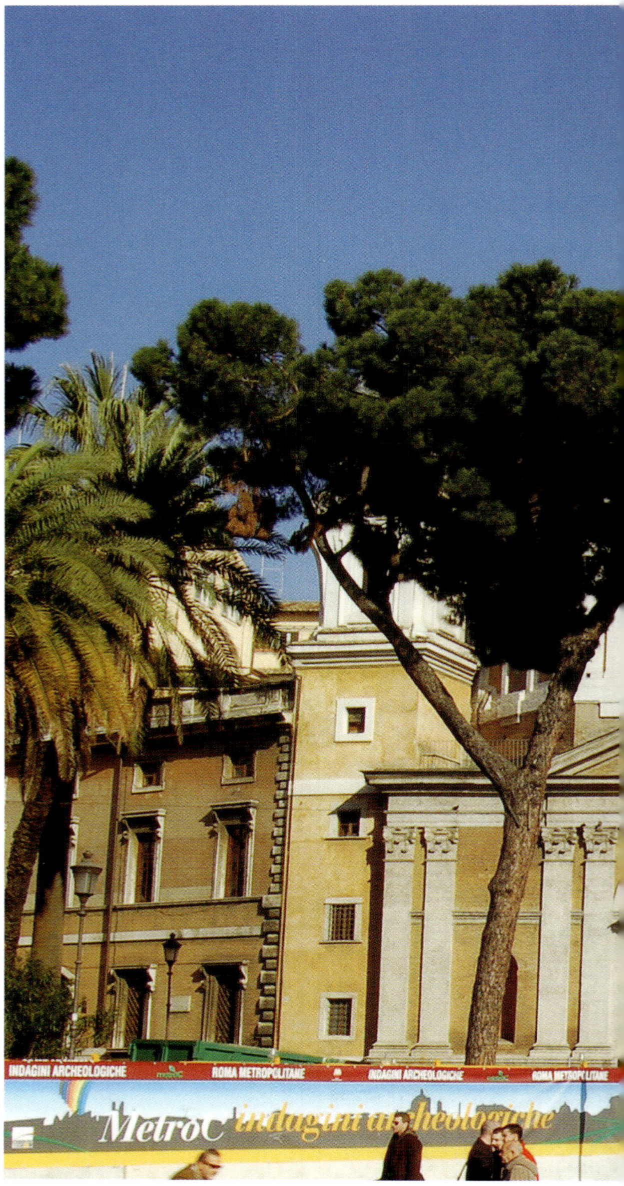

Meanwhile the rule of Roman law was extended throughout the Empire, which encouraged sound government. In Rome itself the Antonines rebuilt their capital and added public monuments to celebrate their triumphs. The most notable of these was Trajan's Column, erected to the north of the Forum in A.D. 113 to celebrate Rome's victory over the Dacians. Trajan also rebuilt the Forum and commissioned the market area that still bears his name—a structure that was essentially the world's first shopping mall. His successor Hadrian also commissioned great public and private buildings, most notably the Pantheon (a temple to all the gods), which had been destroyed by fire in A.D. 80.

Marcus Aurelius (A.D. 161–180) was another great builder. He rebuilt much of Rome, clearing slums, laying good roads and sewers, and reconfiguring the civic heart of the city. His equestrian statue now dominates the Capitoline Hill. Rome's population also reached a peak during his reign, with the number estimated at around

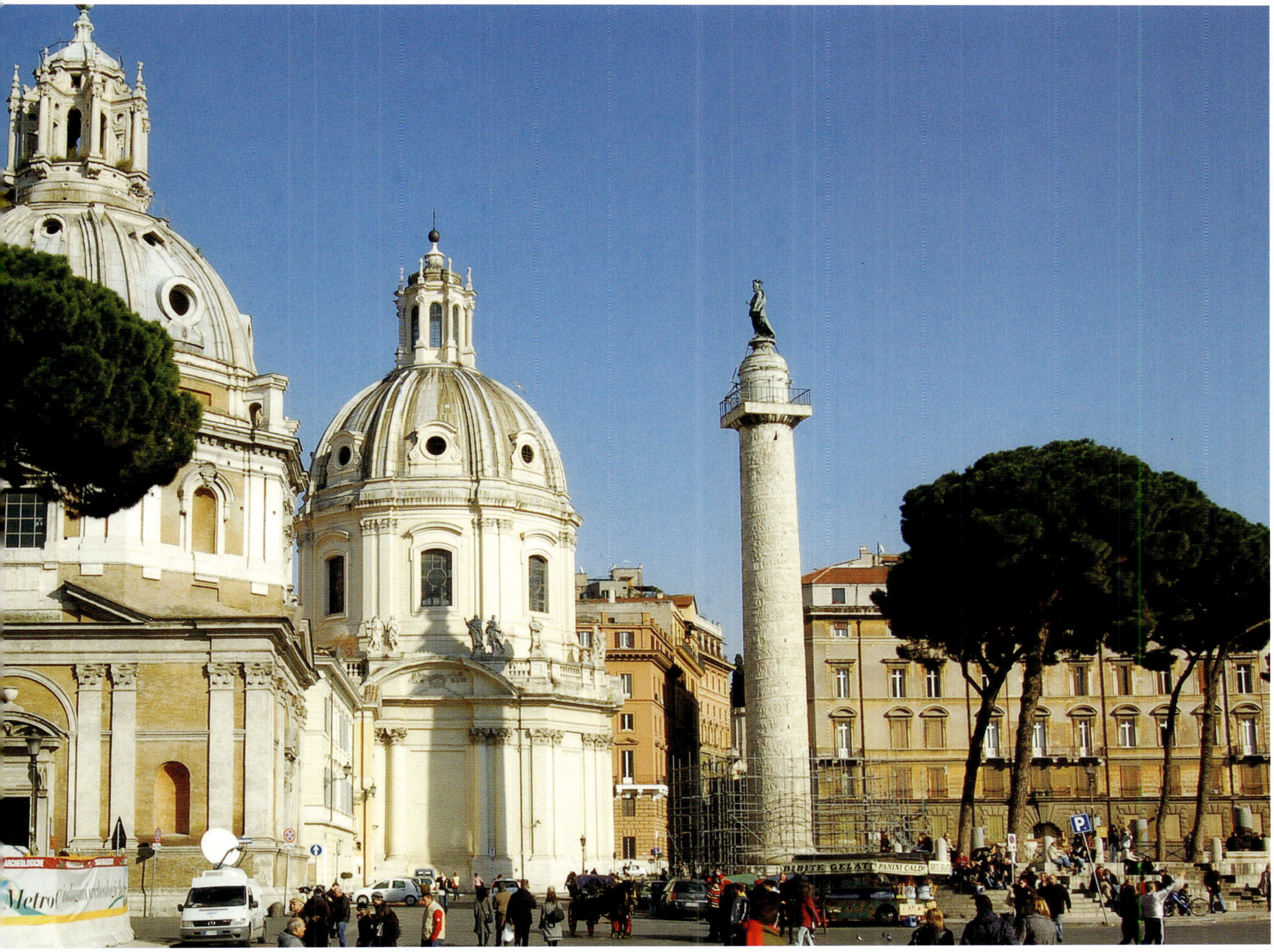

2 million. The Severan Dynasty (A.D. 193–235AD) that followed marked a troubled period in Roman history, an era of rebellion in the provinces and political strife in the capital. However, the Emperor Septimus Severus (A.D. 193–211) managed to complete his predecessor's reconstruction of the city, and his son Caracalla continued this initiative by ordering the construction of the Roman public thermae, now know as the Baths of Caracalla (A.D. 216).

A political and military crisis in the mid-third century A.D. plunged the Empire into a series of civil wars, coups, and provincial rebellions that would last half a century. The economy suffered, and so little was spent on public works or on the improvement of the city. The exception was the building of the Aurelian Wall, which was completed in A.D. 273. This was the first new wall to encircle the city since the construction of the old Servian Wall over five centuries before. Impressive though this wall was, its very construction underlined the decline of the Roman Empire. For the first time since Hannibal threatened to besiege the city it was considered necessary to defend the city itself, rather than to protect Rome by guarding the borders of the empire.

The Emperor Diocletian (A.D. 245–312) split the Roman Empire to ease its administrative problems, and for a time the great imperial decline was held at bay. The Emperor Constantine (A.D. 280–337) granted freedom of worship to the Christians in A.D. 313 after he converted to the new religion. Christian worshippers emerged from the catacombs where they had secretly practiced their religion, and soon Christian places of worship began to spring up across the city. Constantine went on to found a Christian shrine on the site of St. Peter's Tomb (A.D. 320)—now the site of St. Peter's Basilica. Rome has remained a center for the Christian faith ever since. Six decades later the Emperor Theodosius made Christianity the official religion of the empire, and in A.D 384 Siricius (now St. Siri-

ABOVE: Trajan's Column is next to the early sixteenth century church of Santa Maria di Loreto. The church's principal architect was Antonio da Sangallo the Younger, but the dome and lantern were completed 75 years later to a design by Jacopo del Duca. The interior contains important frescoes and statues.

cius), the Bishop of Rome, first adopted the title of pope, claiming his authority from his Roman predecessor St. Peter.

This newfound religious fervor did little to save the empire from collapse in the face of barbarian invasion. In A.D. 410 the Goths led by Alaric breached the Aurelian Wall at the Porta Salaria and sacked the city. On that occasion the city was spared from wanton destruction, but 35 years later the Romans were less fortunate. In A.D. 455 the Vandals led by Geiseric sacked the city again, this time making off with much of its wealth. Two decades later the city was sacked again, this time by an army of barbarians in Roman pay. It is this point that historians have chosen to mark the fall of the Western Roman Empire. Although Rome would rise from the ashes, it would never retain its former glory, and only the ruins would serve as a reminder of the past glories of Ancient Rome.

The Holy City

For the Romans, the centuries following the fall of the Western Roman Empire really were the Dark Ages. Italy was controlled by the Ostrogoths, who established their capital in Ravenna. Although the Eastern Roman Empire (the Byzantines) recaptured Rome in 536, this was only the start of a bitterly fought campaign. Rome would change hands four times before the Byzantines were finally able to gain control of the city. By that stage Rome was a shadow of her former self. Many of her once great buildings were in ruins, her aqueducts had dried up and weeds grew in the Forum. The population was now reduced to less than 50,000.

A new wave of Germanic barbarians—the Lombards—drove the Ostrogoths out of Italy during the second quarter of the sixth century A.D. These invaders forced the Byzantines to withdraw from most of Italy, leaving the "Duchy of Rome" to defend itself. However, Pope Gregory I (590–604) brokered a deal with the Lombards, and the city was left in peace. The Franks finally drove the Lombards from Italy during the second half of the eighth century A.D., a campaign that was begun at the behest of the pope. The Frankish King Pepin III "the Short" (714–768) then donated a swath of captured territory stretching from Rome to Ravenna to the pope. This territorial belt spanning the Italian peninsula became officially known as The Patrimony of St. Peter—although most historians simply call it The Papal State.

On Christmas Day 800, in a ceremony held

Below and Below right: Two more late nineteenth century views of the city showing what the city looked like before road vehicles, pollution, and tourists altered the face of Rome forever. The Pyramid of Caius Cestius near St. Paul's Gate (**Below**) was built in masonry covered with marble tiles and was known in the Middle Ages as the Tomb of Remus. Vesta's Temple (**Below right**) housed the city's sacred fire and stands in front of the house of the Vestals who tended it.

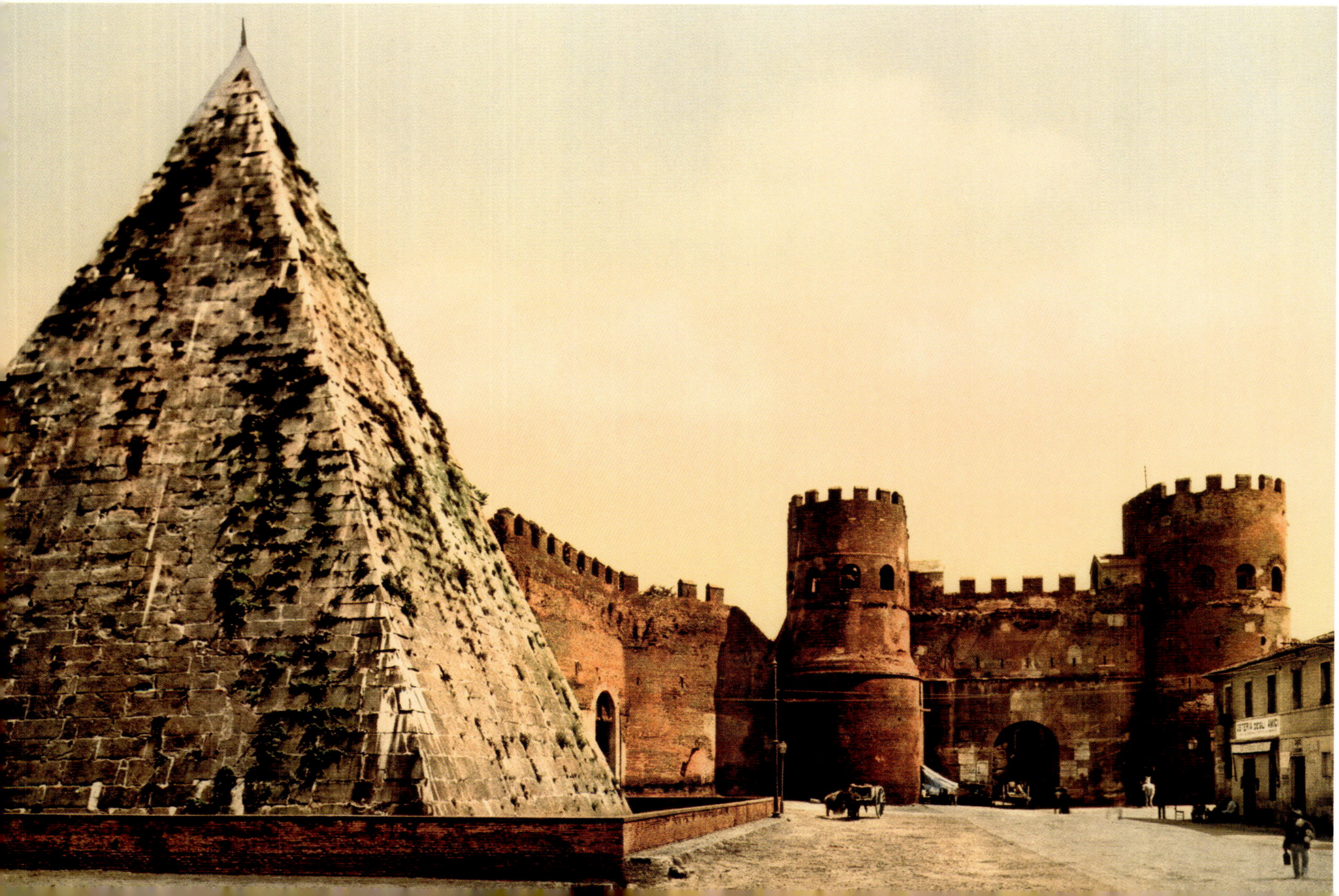

in St. Peter's Basilica, Pope Leo III crowned Pepin's successor—the Frankish monarch Charlemagne—as the Holy Roman emperor, the secular protector of the Roman church. For a while it seemed as if a new Western Roman Empire would emerge, but following Charlemagne's death in 814 the whole imperial edifice crumbled to dust. His empire was divided between his sons, and once again Rome was left without a secular protector. The extent of the city's helplessness was demonstrated in 846 when Arabic pirates sacked St. Peter's. Consequently Pope Leo IV ordered the construction of a wall to protect the papal enclave around the Lateran Palace and St. Peter's Basilica on the western bank of the Tiber.

By the mid-eleventh century Rome had become a place of pilgrimage, a holy city that was effectively ruled by the pope. Then a new political and religious crisis emerged, as a reconstituted Germanic Holy Roman Empire began a long-running feud with the papacy over political authority and territory. A byproduct of this conflict between pope and emperor was the creation of rival political parties in Rome and the rest of Italy. These rivals adopted the factional names of Guelph (for the church) and Ghibelline (for the emperor), and used the conflict to pursue their own partisan agendas. In Rome the leading aristocratic families—the Orsinis, Colonnas, and Savellis—all participated in this struggle. In 1277 the violence in the streets became so bad that Pope Nicholas III (an Orsini) moved his palace from the Lateran to the Vatican, and then improved the defenses of the papal enclave by anchoring its walls on the Castel San Angelo, a papal fortress built on top of Hadrian's mausoleum.

By the end of the thirteenth century the papacy had largely emerged victorious from its clashes with the Holy Roman Emperor, but a chain of circumstances would conspire to humiliate the church. Pope Clement V (1304–14) elected to avoid the violence of the Roman political scene and so he was consecrated in the neutral French town of Avignon. The papacy remained there until 1377, leaving the Romans to their feuding. When the papacy returned the Roman nobility resumed their intimidation of the pontiff, prompting the College of Cardinals to escape from the city and declared a recent papal election illegal because of Roman coercion. They elected their own pope—a Frenchman. This schism split the church for 40 years, and the rift was only healed in 1414, when a single pontiff was elected in Rome—Pope Martin

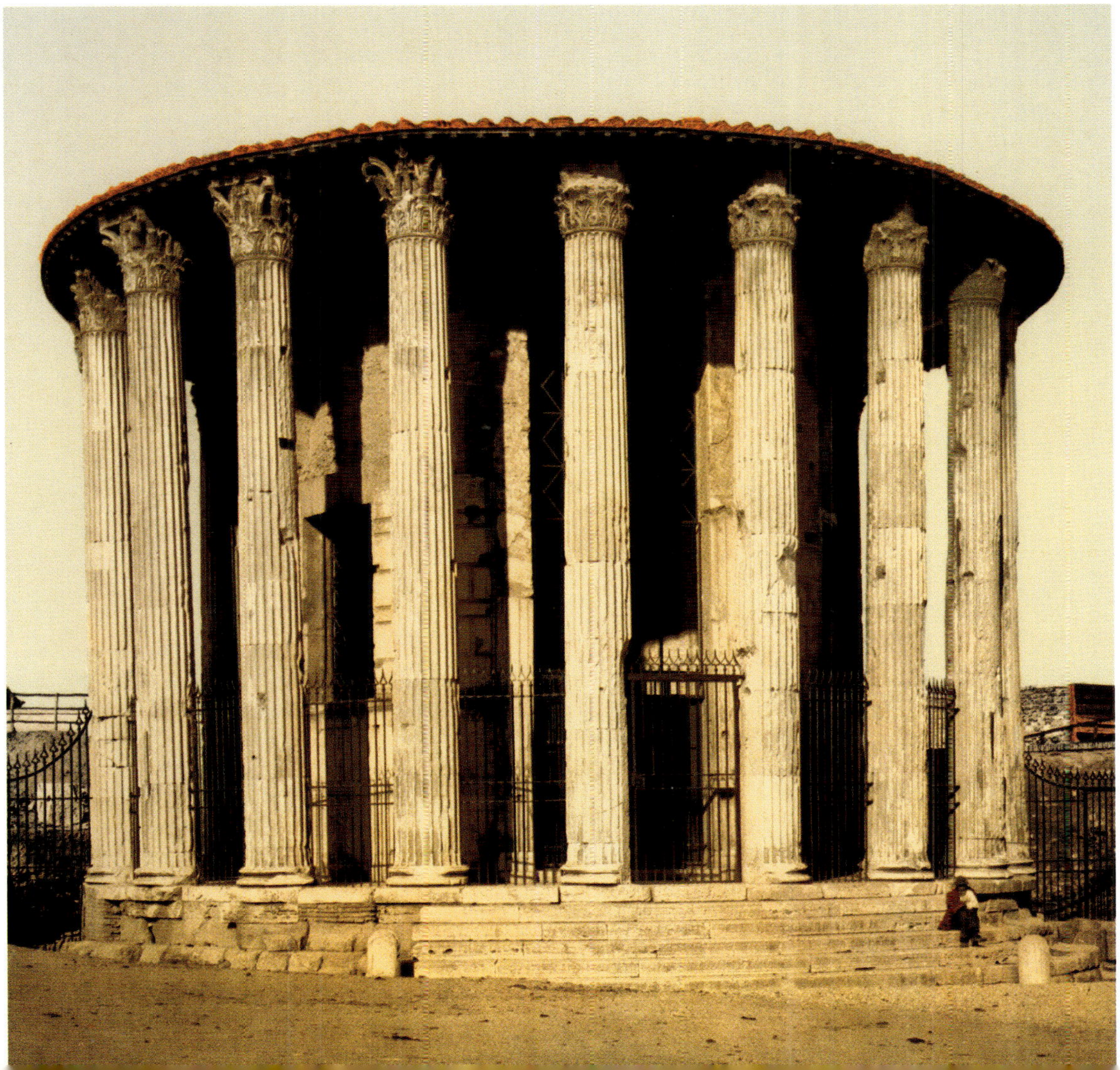

VICTOR EMMANUEL II

Rome might once have been the center of an empire, but it has been a capital city for less than 150 years. Rome defiantly maintained its independence during the nineteenth century, when the rest of Italy was moving toward a political union—an initiative spearheaded by King Victor Emmanuel II, the King of Sardinia-Piedmont, a small monarchy in Italy's northwest corner with its capital in Turin. In 1858 he suceeded in driving the Austrians from northern Italy after soliciting French help, and added Lombardy to his possessions. He also supported Garibaldi's expedition to capture Sicily in the name of a united Italy in 1861. Garibaldi went on to capture Naples, the capital of the Kingdom of the Two Sicilies, which added southern Italy to the king's domains. After winning the Battle of Castelfidardo (1860), Garibaldi and Victor Emmanuel occupied the eastern side of the Papal State—a move that led to the king's excommunication. However, because French troops were stationed in and around Rome, the Italian nationalists were unable to capture the city. In March 1861 a plebiscite resulted in the establishment of a united Italy, and Victor Emmanuel was named as its first king. Only Venice (under Austrian control) and Rome remained separate from the new Italian state. Venice was ceded to Italy following the Austrian defeat by the Prussians in 1866. When Prussia defeated France in the war of 1870–71, Rome was left undefended after French troops withdrew. In 1871 Victor Emmanuel declared war on the Papal State, and his troops entered Rome; in 1872 the city became the official capital of the new Kingdom of Italy. Victor Emmanuel established his court in the Quirinal Palace. He died in 1878 and is celebrated by *Il Vittoriano*, the monument that dominates the Piazza Venezia.

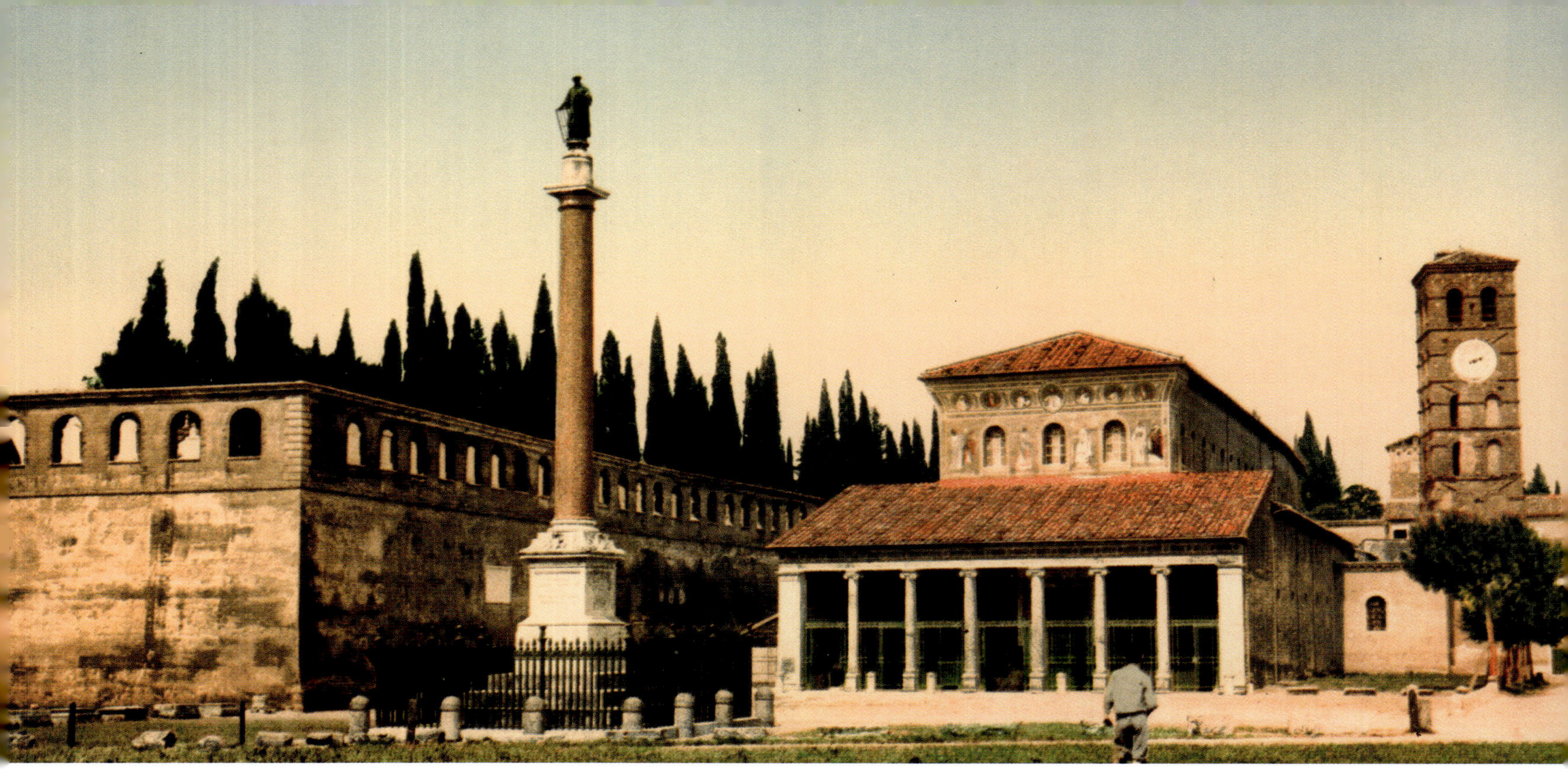

Above: The Basilica di San Lorenzo fuori le Mura (Saint Lawrence Outside the Walls) is one of the five patriarchal basilicas of Rome. As its name suggests, it is dedicated to St. Lawrence and is located outside the old walls of Rome.

Below: Mosaics were used on floors, walls, and ceilings by the Romans, and the preserved examples in Ostia—Rome's port at the mouth of the Tiber—are notable.

Right: Green ivy growing on a typical stucco apartment building with stone arch and heavy wooden door in the Centro Storico district of Rome.

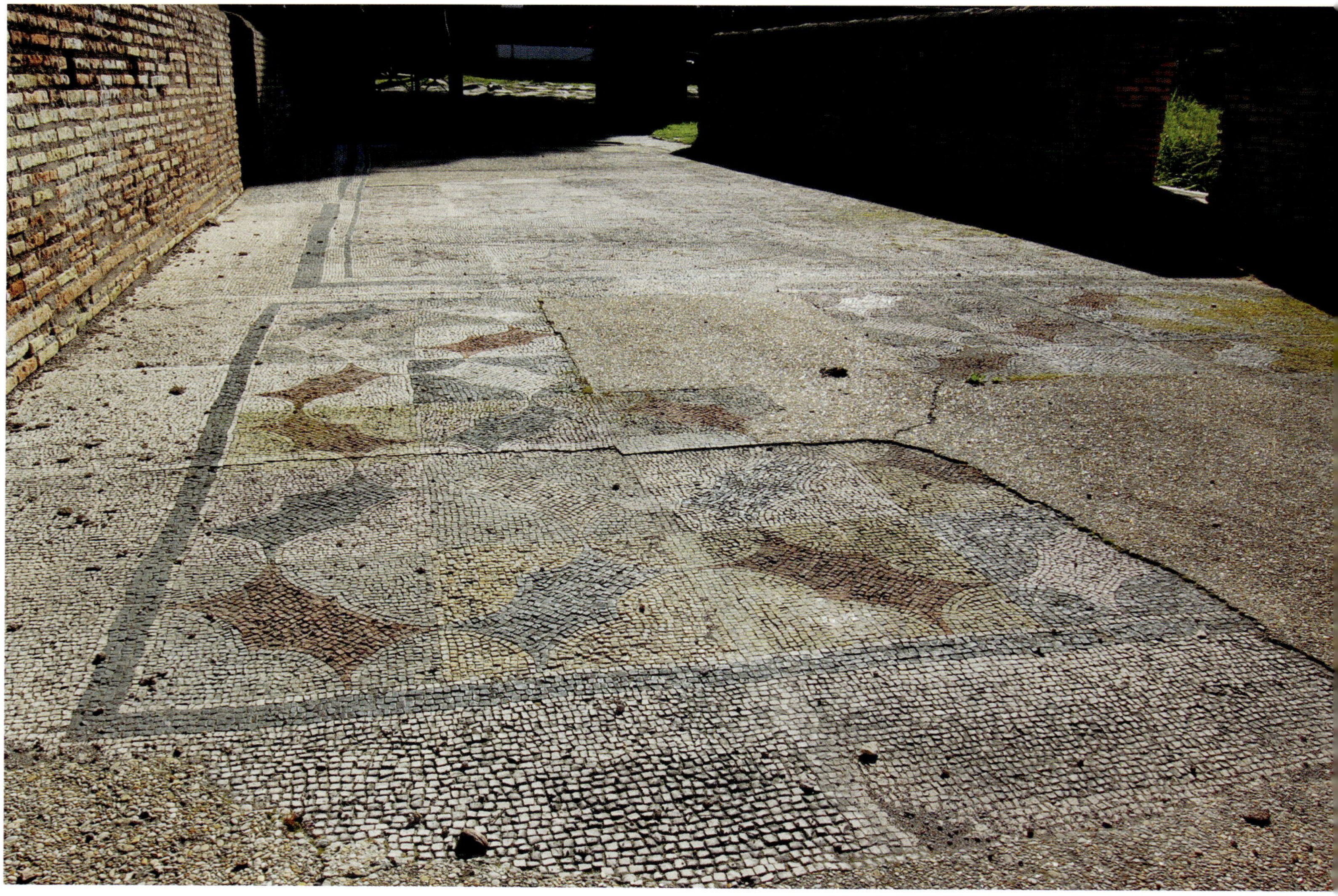

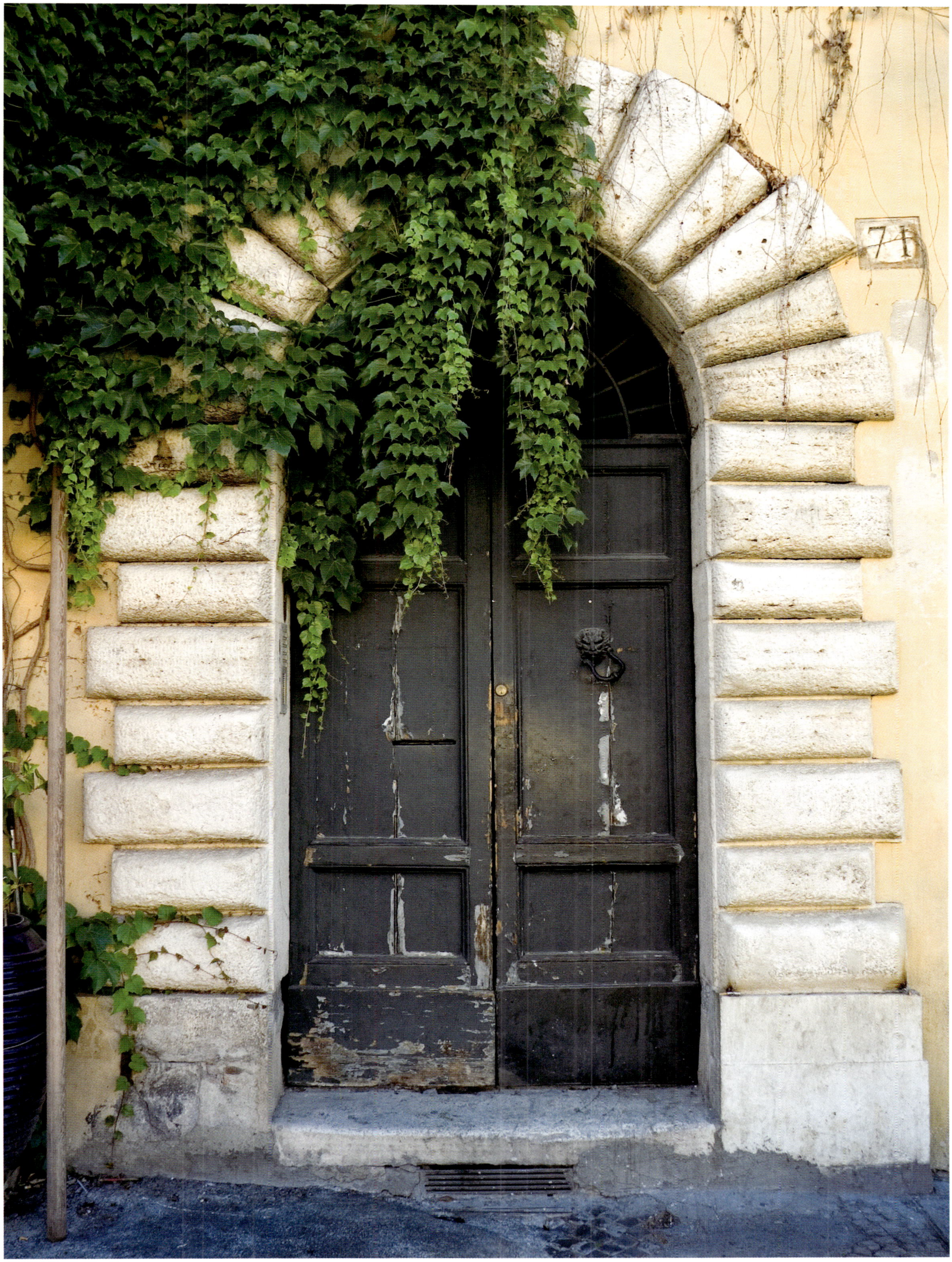
71

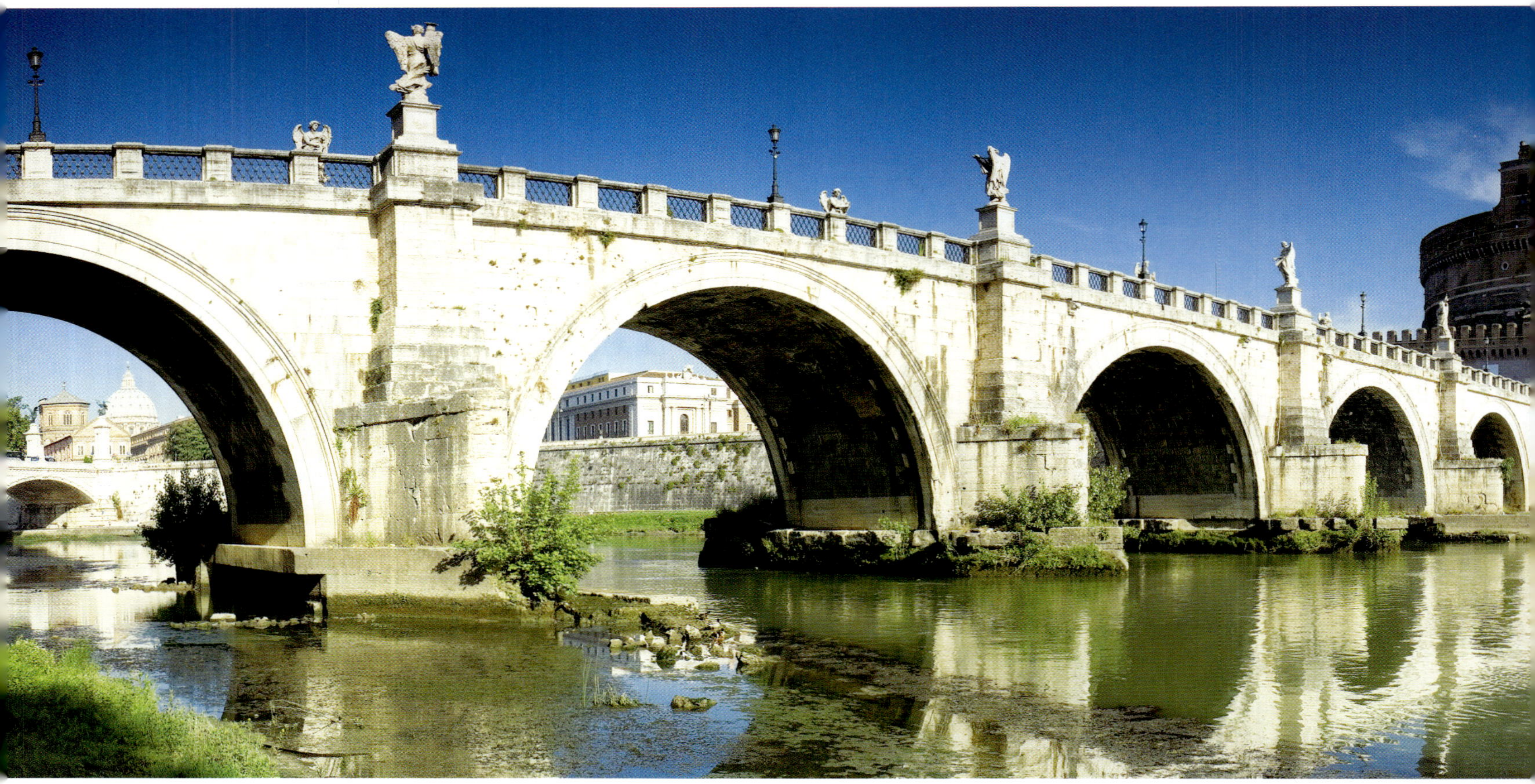

Above: Ponte Sant' Angelo joins the Castel Sant' Angelo to the ancient Campus Martius (the Plain of Mars) district of Rome. It was originally built in the second century A.D. as the processional way over the river to Hadrian's mausoleum. Ten angel statues were added in the mid-seventeenth century. These were made by Bernini's apprentices to the master's drawings.

V. Ironically, this new pope was a Colonna—a member of the Roman family who had caused the move to Avignon in the first place.

The Eternal City

The fifteenth century was the era of the Italian Renaissance, the revival of learning based on humanism and the study of classical sources, the rise of cultural patronage, the development of art, architecture, and science. At first the papacy was wary of these developments and viewed the growth of humanist Roman academies with suspicion. However, they later came to see the movement as a tool that could help them improve their image and authority. Of course the pope was a secular as well as a spiritual leader. His control of the Papal States guaranteed papal involvement in Italian secular affairs. In fact some popes embraced their secular role—most notably Alexander VI (1492–1503), who established his ruthless son Cesare Borgia as the head of the papal army, and allowed him to launch an aggressive campaign to extend the boundaries of the Papal States. Pope Alexander tried to strengthen his position by targeting the Orsinis, but without much success, as the roman family assassinated Juan Borgia, the pope's political henchman. Pope Alexander died in 1503, probably after being poisoned.

This was a unique period in Roman history, when the cultural achievements of the Renaissance became intertwined in the Machiavellian intrigues of politics. After 1503 no Pope would wield quite so much secular power, or stray so far from his spiritual path. By that time Rome had replaced Florence as the creative powerhouse of the Italian Renaissance. The patronage of popes such as Innocent VIII, Alexander VI, Julius II, and Leo X did much to encourage a revision of religious art and architecture that transformed the image of Rome and the papacy. In 1475 the Vatican Library was founded, and in 1506 work began on a new St. Peter's Basilica—a project that would continue for more than a century. Artists like Bramante, Raphael, Cellini and Michelangelo were hired to great buildings, statues and works of art that would transform Rome into the glittering centerpiece of the Western world.

Encouraged by this papal patronage, Michelangelo (1477–1564) created the stunning Pietà for St. Peter's Basilica, the statue of Moses for the Church of San Pietro ad Vincoli, and his painting of the roof of the Sistine Chapel. He also worked on the redesign of St. Peter's itself. Inspired by these papal initiatives, Rome's leading families and secular leaders commissioned their own splendid villas and palazzi, ordered the construction of churches, grand squares and thoroughfares, and filled their dwellings with magnificent works of art. Bramante's Palazzo Caprini was seen as a model for palazzi design,

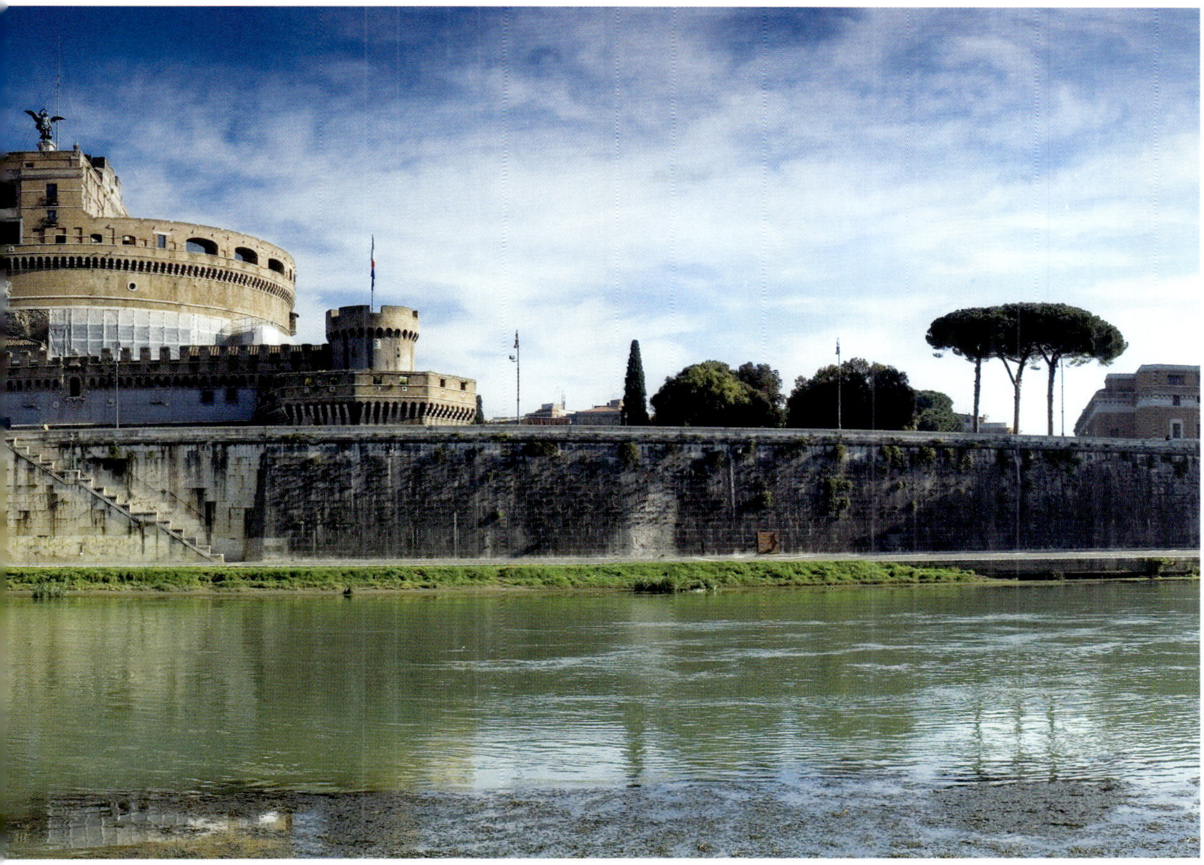

and buildings like the Villa Giulia or the majestic Palazzo Faranese designed by Sangallo and finished by Michelangelo are some of the most magnificent High Renaissance buildings to be found in Italy. One other important initiative of Raphael was his encouragement of protection for Rome's ancient ruins. Without him much of the ancient landscape would have been built over.

Rome's flirtation with the Renaissance came to a temporary halt in 1527 when the city was sacked by an imperialist army—almost a last hurrah in the old conflict between pope and emperor. Although countless statues and works of art were destroyed, the city recovered, and work was eventually resumed on St. Peter's, this time with Michelangelo named as the architect. By the mid-sixteenth century the Counter Reformation movement had begun, and under Sixtus V (1585–90) the church was thoroughly reformed, and the Holy City "cleaned" of the unworthy. This culminated in the burning at the stake of the Roman philosopher Gierdano Bruno in 1600. The pope also initiated a major building program in the city, particularly in the Esquiline, Viminal, and Quirinal areas. His aim was to make Rome a better place for pilgrims to visit. By this time the city's population had climbed to 90,000.

Another legacy of the Counter-reformation was the development of the Baroque style, which was introduced to Rome by the Jesuits when they commissioned the building of the church of Gesù in 1568. Bernini and Borromini transformed the city, building churches that made novel use of geometric forms to create a space of wonder and grandeur. One of his most impressive architectural masterpieces was the Church of San Carlo alle Quattro Fontane on the Quirinal. Under the patronage of Pope Urban VIII (1623–44) Bernini built palaces, fountains, and monuments throughout the city including his monument to Pope Alexander VII in St. Peter's, an ornate and dramatic work designed to highlight the supremacy of the pontiff.

Rome's love affair with the Baroque continued after the deaths of its two main architects. For instance, Nicolas Salvi's magnificently theatrical design for the Trevi Fountain was drawn up in the 1730s, a half century after Bernini's death. The project was only completed in 1762. Although by that stage Rome had become a political backwater, it still played a minor role on the world stage. It was here that James Stuart ("The Old Pretender"), exiled son of the deposed British monarch James II (James VII of Scotland), lived until his death in 1766. Pope Clement XI presented the Palazzo Balestra in the Quirinal to the exiled claimant, and the area became a haven for exiled Jacobites throughout the eighteenth century. His son Charles Edward Stuart ("Bonnie Prince Charlie") was born in Rome in 1721, and died there in 1788. Both

THE VATICAN

After the collapse of the Roman Empire, the city and its environs remained a political anomaly, ruled as a secular province by the pope himself. In its heyday the Papal State stretched across the Italian peninsula, encompassing Ravenna and Ancona on the Adriatic coast. Following the unification of Italy in 1861 this papal territory was reduced to a small enclave around Rome itself, and a decade later, in 1871, even this secular fiefdom was stripped from the church. Today only the Vatican City remains, the smallest independent nation on earth, encompassing a mere 108 acres. Crammed into this small space are some of the most magnificent buildings and works of art in the world.

Named after Vatican Hill on which it sits, the Vatican City sits on the western bank of the River Tiber. Its territory includes St. Peter's Basilica, the Apostolic Palace (the residency of the pope), and the adjacent Sistine Chapel, as well as museum, administration, and archive buildings. Its centerpiece is St. Peter's Square, where thousands come to hear the pope. The pope remains the sovereign head of state as well as being both the Bishop of Rome and the head of the Roman Catholic Church. This means that the Vatican is a form of elective monarchy, with its head selected by the College of Cardinals. His state is protected by the Vatican's own small police force and by the Swiss Guard, that has protected the security of the pontiff since the fifteenth century.

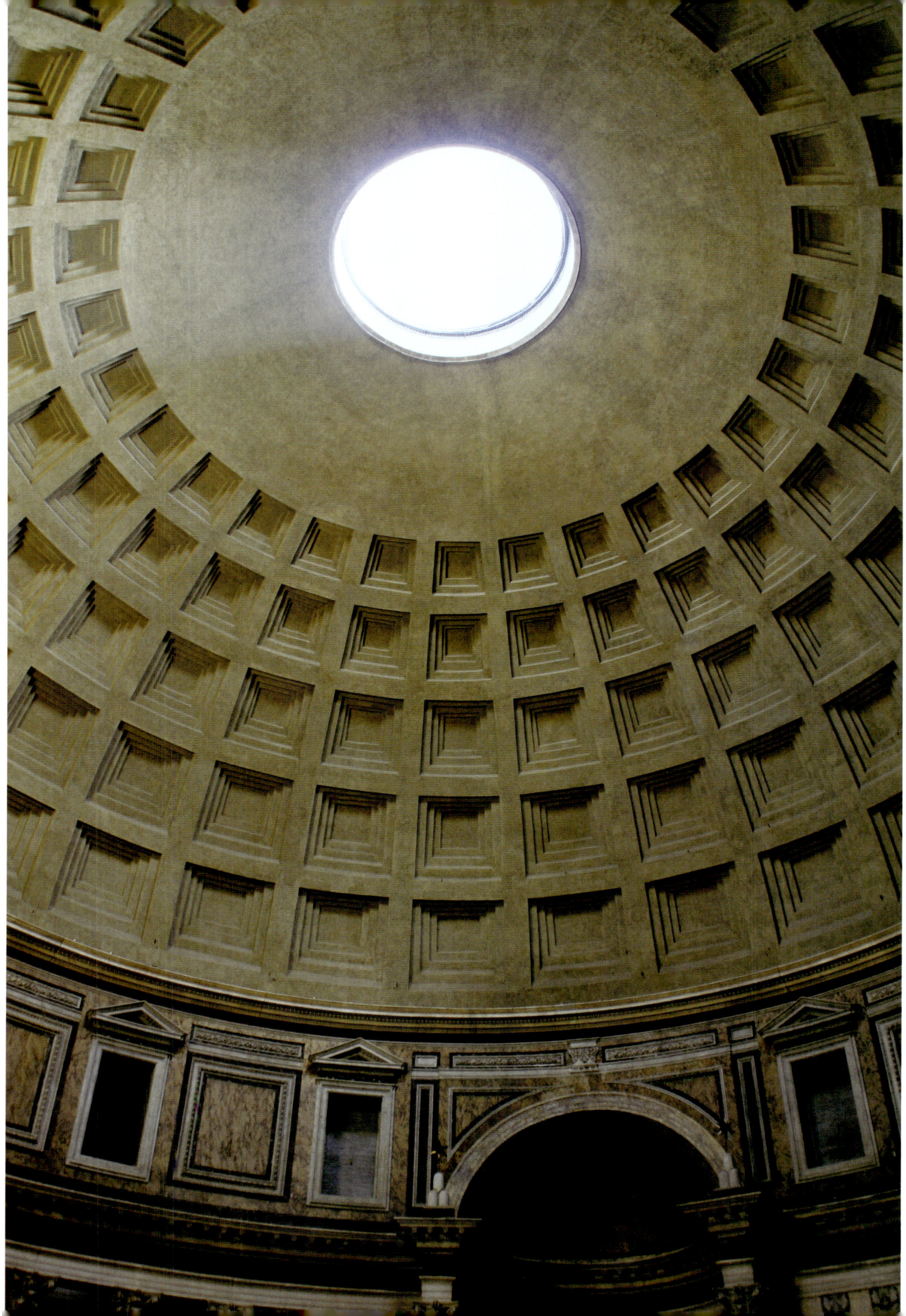

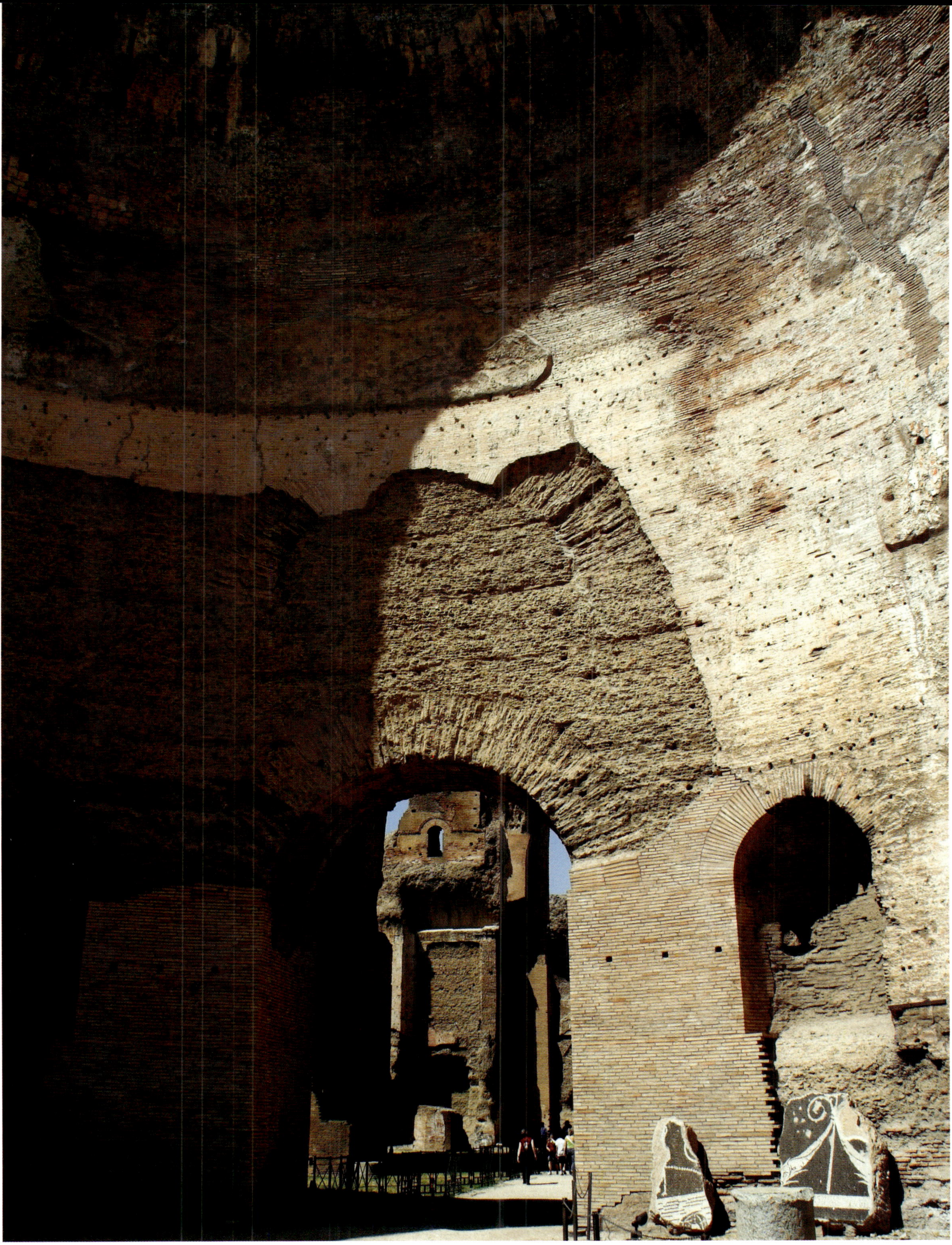

LEFT: The Pantheon's dome. *Bojan Vogrin/Fotolibra.*

ABOVE: The Baths of Caracalla. *Bojan Vogrin/Fotolibra.*

Stuart exiles are buried in St. Peter's.

By this stage Rome had become an important stopping point on "the Grand tour," and the area around the Piazza di Spagna became a center for British travelers, including Lord Byron, whose viewing of the Colosseum by moonlight inspired him to write part of *Childe Harold's Pilgrimage*. These tourists loved the ruined romantic grandeur of the city. In 1819 Romantic poet Percy Shelley even wrote *Prometheus Unbound* amid the ruins of the Baths of Caracalla.

The French Revolutionary and Napoleonic wars were a strange time for the Romans, as the French dismantled the Papal State (replacing it with the short-lived Roman Republic in 1798), and requisitioned thousands of pieces of art and sculpture, which ended up in Paris. In 1814 the papal territories were returned, and Rome became the conservative backwater it had been before the coming of Napoleon. However, new political forces were stirring, and in November 1848 a Roman mob overthrew the papal government and founded a new republic. Pope Pius IX fled the city, and remained in exile until the following summer, when the city was recaptured on his behalf by a French army. One of the defenders of the Republic was Giuseppe Garibaldi, whose goal of Italian unification was dealt a major blow by the re-establishment of papal rule.

Garibaldi returned to Italy after spending a decade in exile, and in 1860 his volunteer army conquered Sicily in the name of King Victor Emmanuel II of Piedmont-Sardinia, then continued on to occupy Naples. During the months that followed, the rule of Piedmont-Sardinia was extended throughout Italy—including much of the Papal State, which had been occupied by Garibaldi's troops. By the time the Kingdom of Italy was established in February 1861 only Rome and its environs remained under papal control, despite being named as the future capital of a united Italy.

The final showdown was inevitable, and Victor Emmanuel was victorious when the French Army withdrew from Rome to defend its own borders against the Prussians. In September 1870 his government declared war on the Papal State. Nine days after the war began General Cardorna's Italian army reached the city, and prepared to launch an assault. The pope reviewed his troops, then sent them to line the old Aurelian Walls. The following morning the Italian guns opened up, and troops stormed the Porta Pia. Within an hour a white flag was flown from the cupola of St. Peter's. The Kingdom of Italy had finally conquered its own capital.

Below and Right: Tourists have always loved the melancholy grandeur of the Roman remains. At right a French railway poster showing the Roman Forum at dawn.

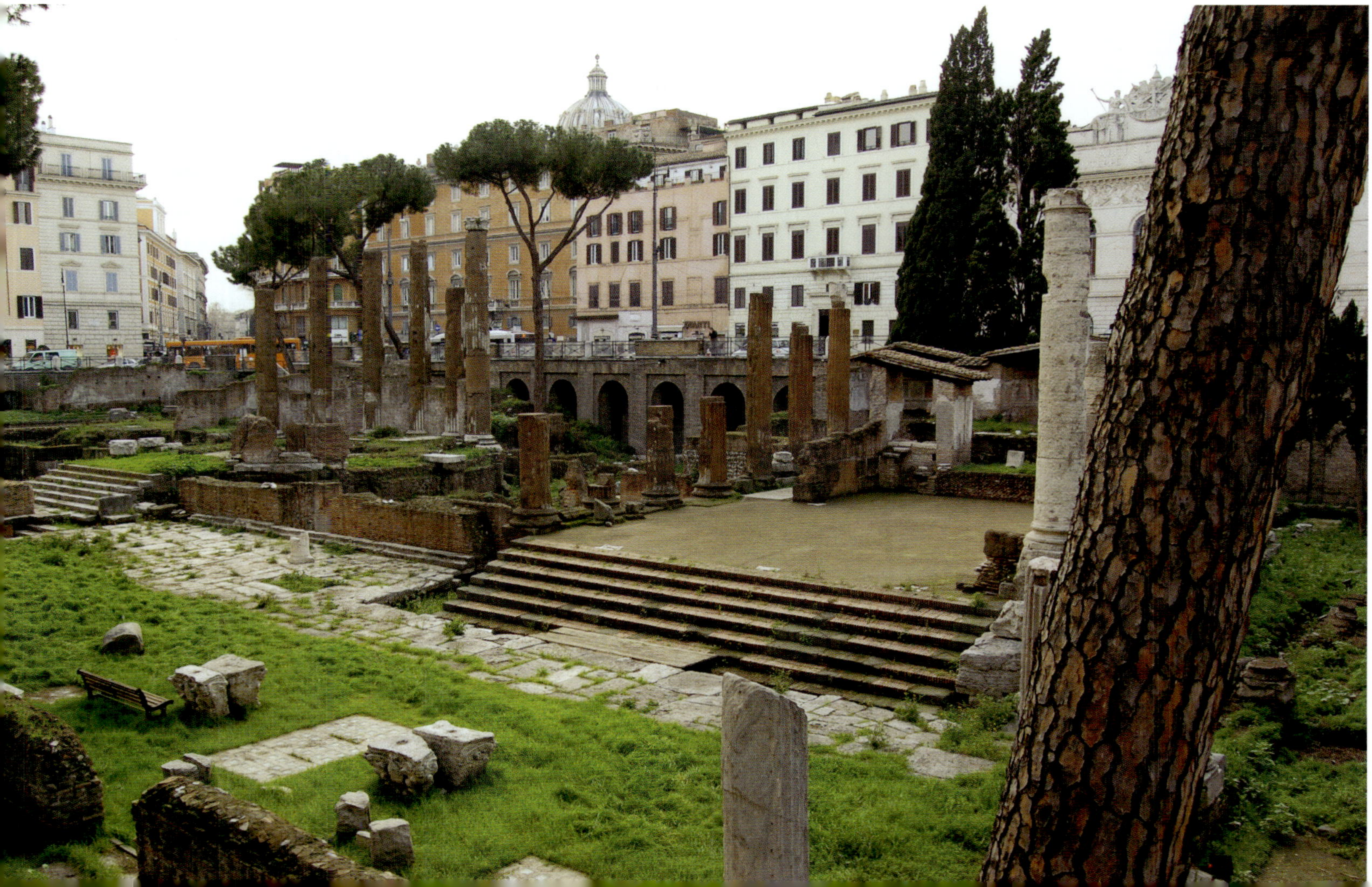

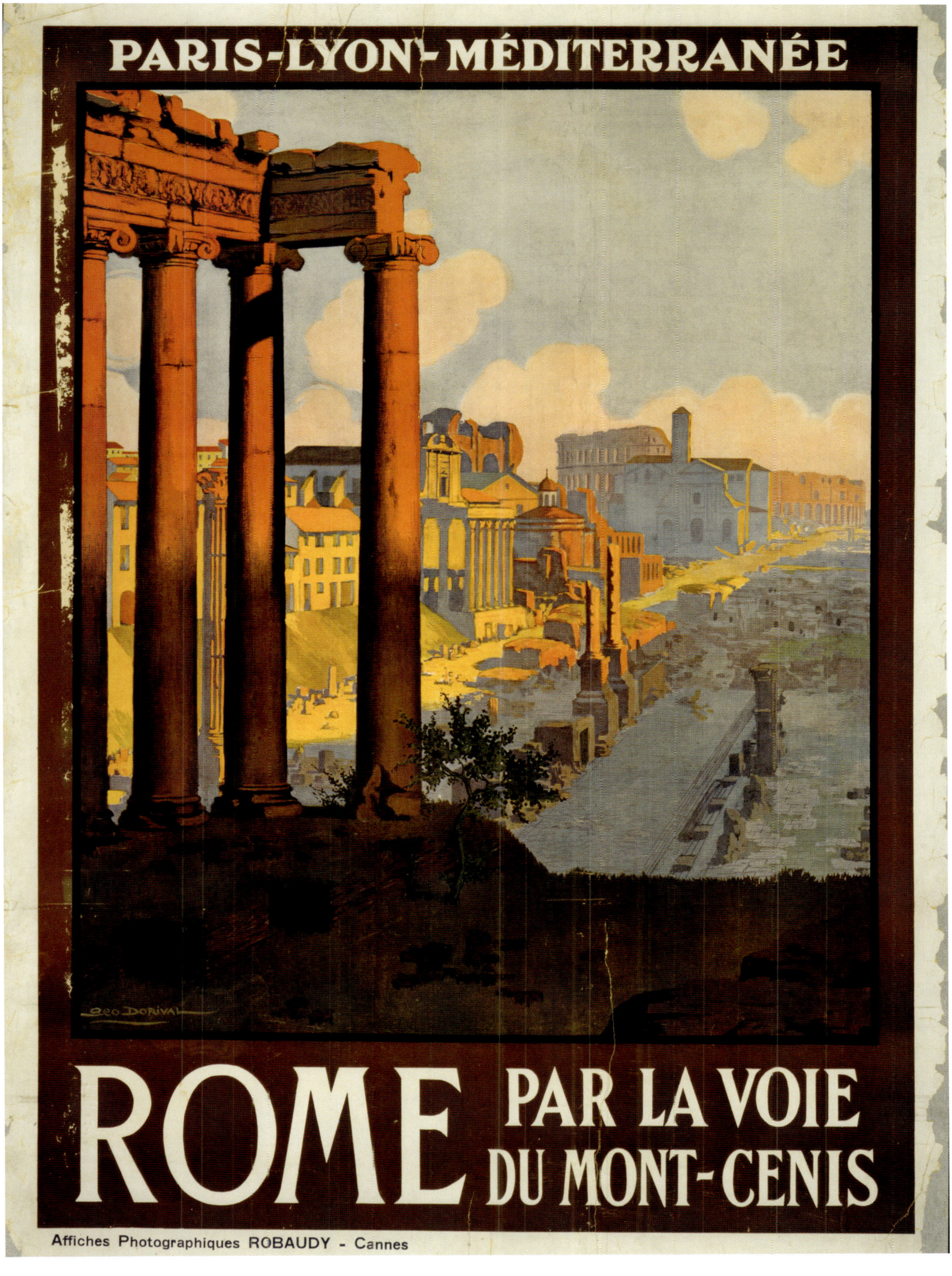
PARIS-LYON-MÉDITERRANÉE
GEO DORIVAL
ROME PAR LA VOIE DU MONT-CENIS
Affiches Photographiques ROBAUDY - Cannes

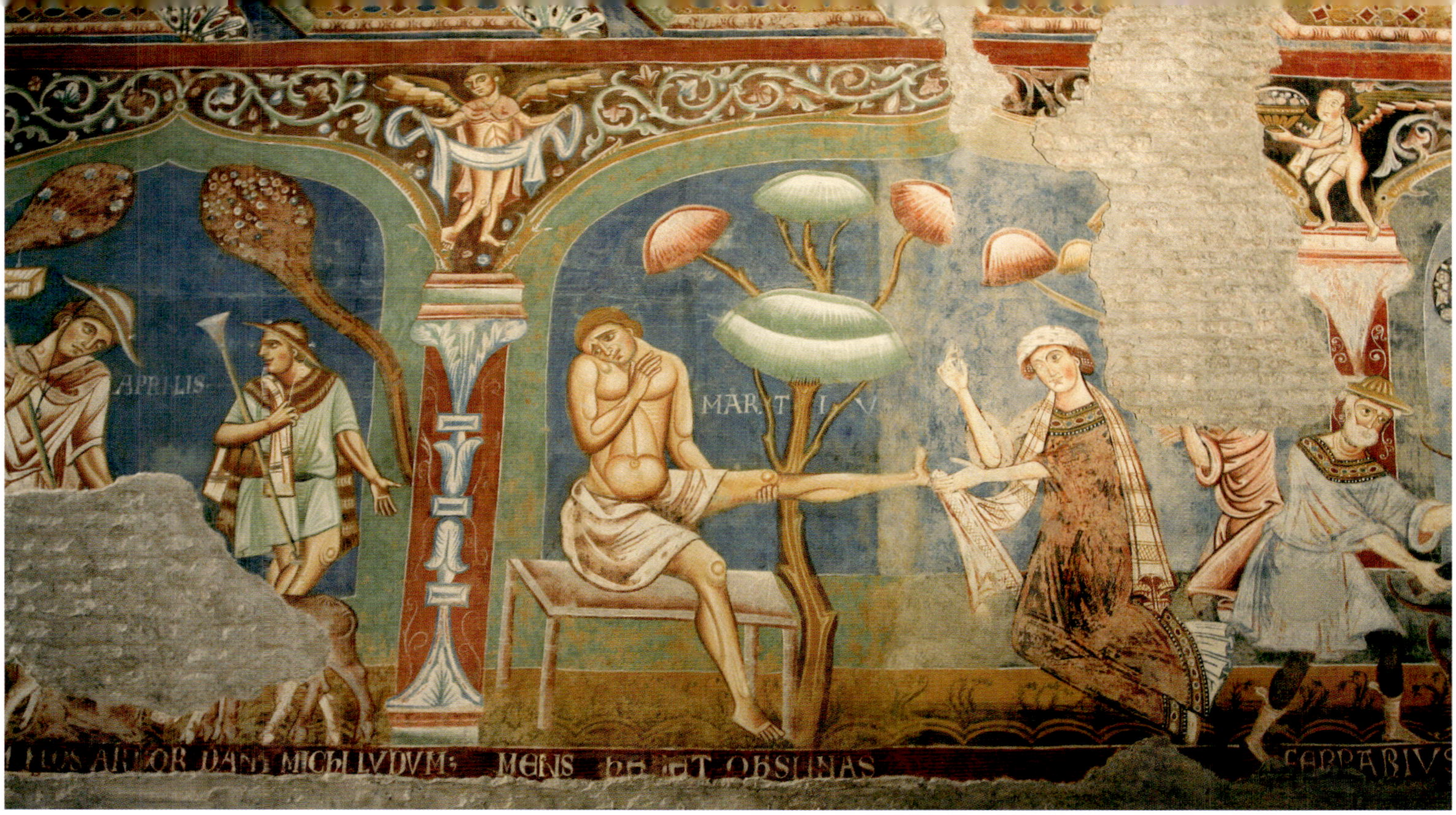
APRILIS

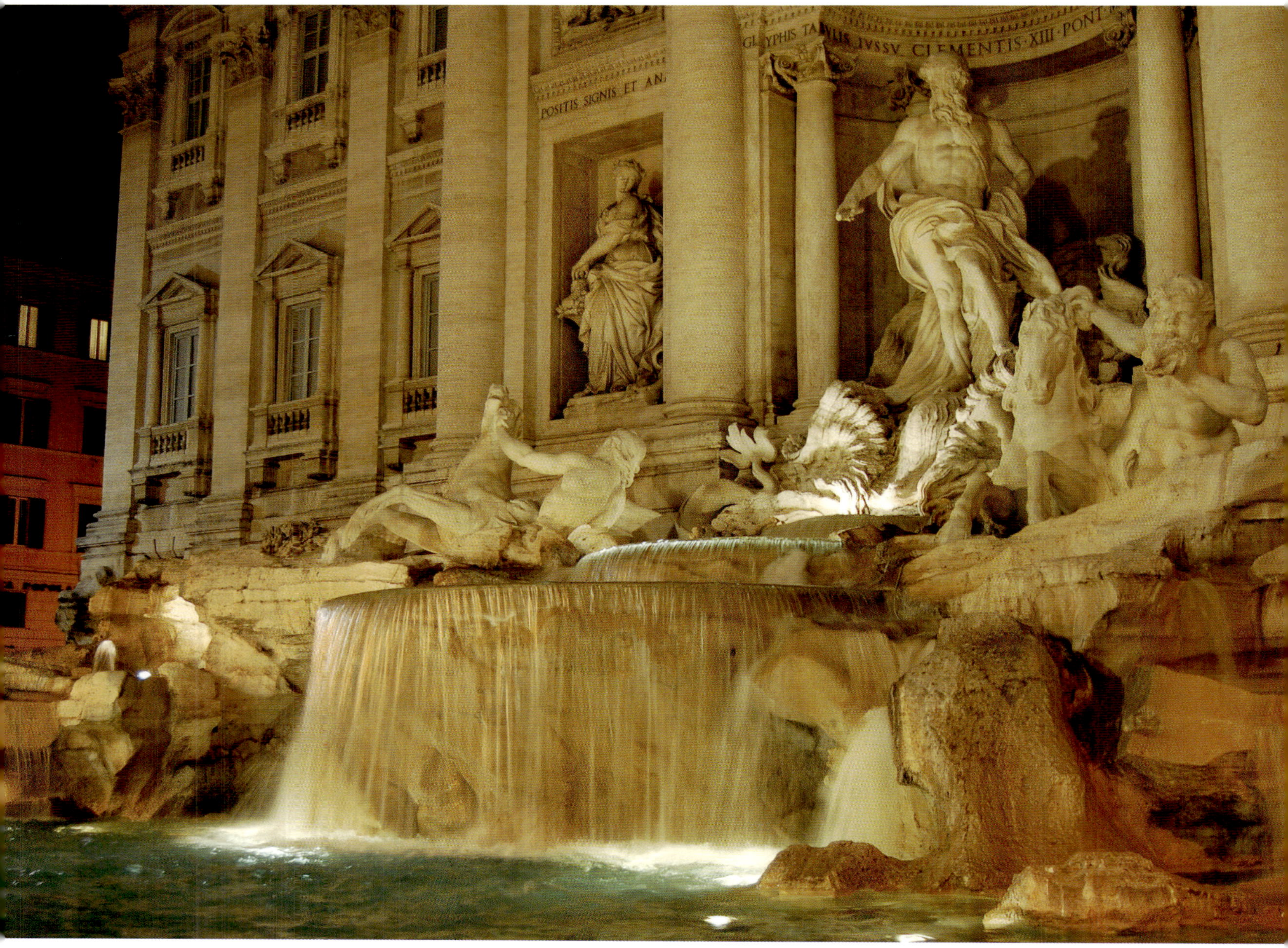
POSITIS SIGNIS ET
IVSSV CLEMENTIS·XIII·PONT

LEFT: Santi Quattro Coronati is an ancient basilica in Rome dating back to the fourth century A.D. It is known for its frescoes—those in the apse of the four patron martyr saints, Severo, Severiano, Carpoforo e Vittorino,dating to the seventeenth century. These older, medieval, frescoes were restored and unveiled in the cloister of Santi Quattro Coronati monastery on December 5, 2006. *Patrick Hertzo/AFP/Getty Images*

BELOW LEFT: The Fontana di Trevi—Trevi Fountain—is one of the greatest of the many highlights of Rome because popular superstition says that anyone who throws a coin over their shoulder into the fountain while wishing to return to Rome is guaranteed to do so. The fountain was originally commissioned by Pope Urban VIII and designed by Bernini, but the project was abandoned when the pope died and was only revived a century later. The main figure is Ocean, surrounded by seahorses and Tritons.

RIGHT: Another of Rome's famous fountains—Bernini's Fountain of the Four Rivers, can be found in the Piazza Navona. commissioned by Pope Innocent X as a centerpiece for Piazza Navona and completed in 1651. It celebrates the major rivers of the four continents—the River Danube for Europe, the River Ganges for Asia, the River Nile for Africa, and the River Plate for the Americas. Additionally, an obelisk from the circus of Maxentius stands over a rocky grotto from where a sea monster and lion are emerging.

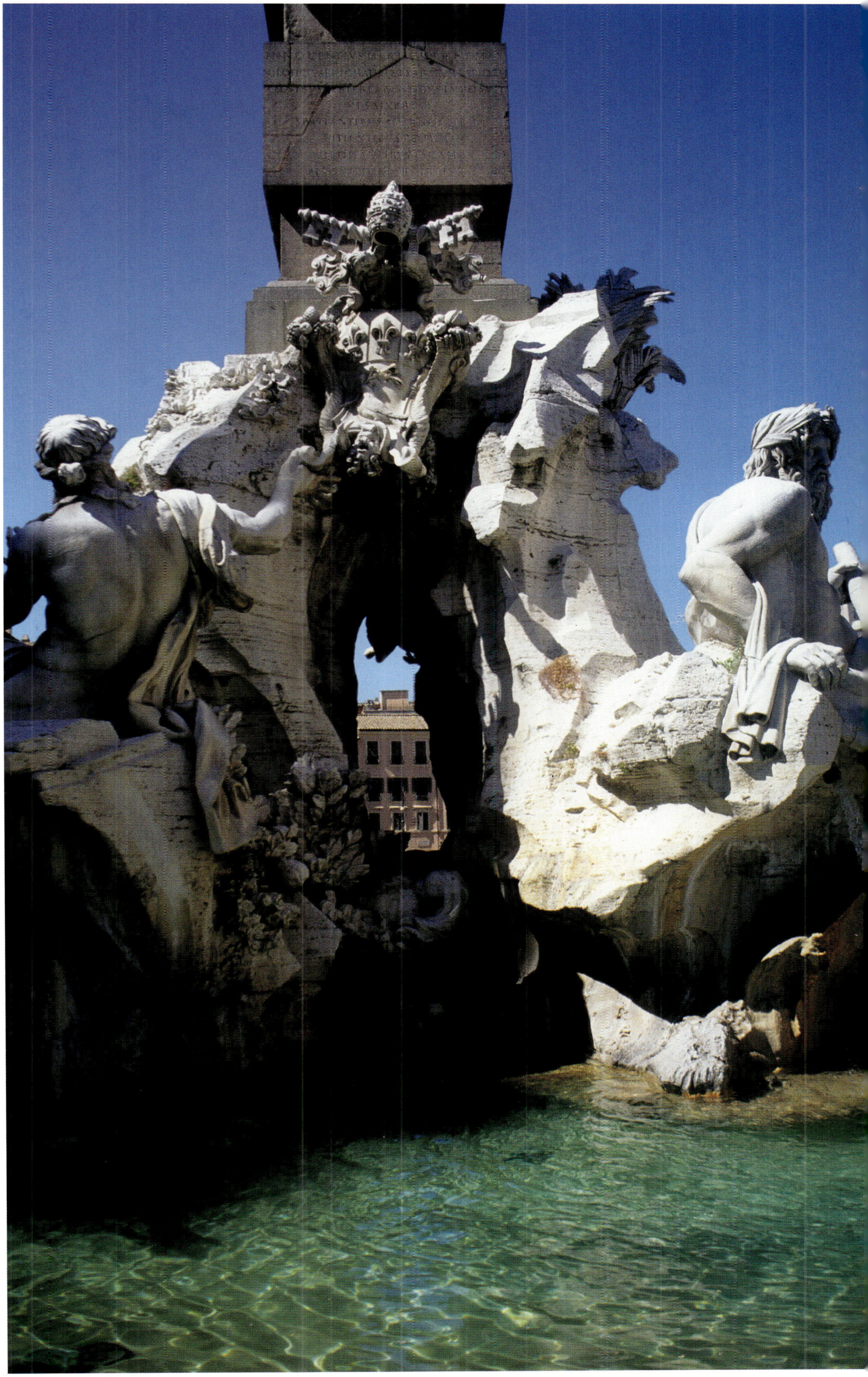

The following year Victor Emmanuel II established his court in the Quirinal Palace, while the Pope withdrew to the Vatican, which was all that remained of Pope's secular fiefdom. Relations remained strained between the crown and the papacy long after the death of both Victor Emmanuel and Pope Pius in 1878. Rome remained the seat of the Italian royal family until the abolition of the monarchy in 1946. Today the most notable reminder of these heady days of national unification is the vast white marble monument—known as *Il Vittoriano*—erected to Victor Emmanuel, which looms over the Piazza Venezia like an oversized wedding cake.

The King's son Umberto succeeded his father, and following his death in 1900 his own son became Victor Emmanuel III. This young monarch's reign would embrace two world wars, and witness the rise and fall of Italian fascism. In 1915 Italy entered World War I on the Allied side, and despite a stunning loss of life the country benefited little from siding with the winners in the conflict. In fact the war all but bankrupted Italy, leading the country into a severe economic depression, which only served to encourage political extremism. Still, Rome continued to expand, spurred on by the migration of people from all over Italy into the capital in search of work. In 1850 the population of Rome stood at around 150,000. By 1900 it had reached 600,000, and in 1931 it passed 1 million. During the 1880s the city witnessed a great expansion in housing, where aesthetics were overruled by commercial necessity. In 1883 the writer Augustus Hare declared that, "Twelve years of Sardinian rule have done more for the destruction of Rome, with its beauty and interest, than the invasions of the Goths and Vandals."

The political upheaval caused by Italy's economic degeneration after World War I led directly to the seizure of power by the fascists. In 1922 Benito Mussolini and his supporters staged their "March on Rome", and victor Emmanuel III invited the fascist leader to form

BELOW: An unusual view of St Peter's under the wing of the Blériot monoplane in which André Beaumont won the Paris–Rome air race in 1911. On May 31, 1911, he completed the 910-mile course in 28 hours, 5 minutes.

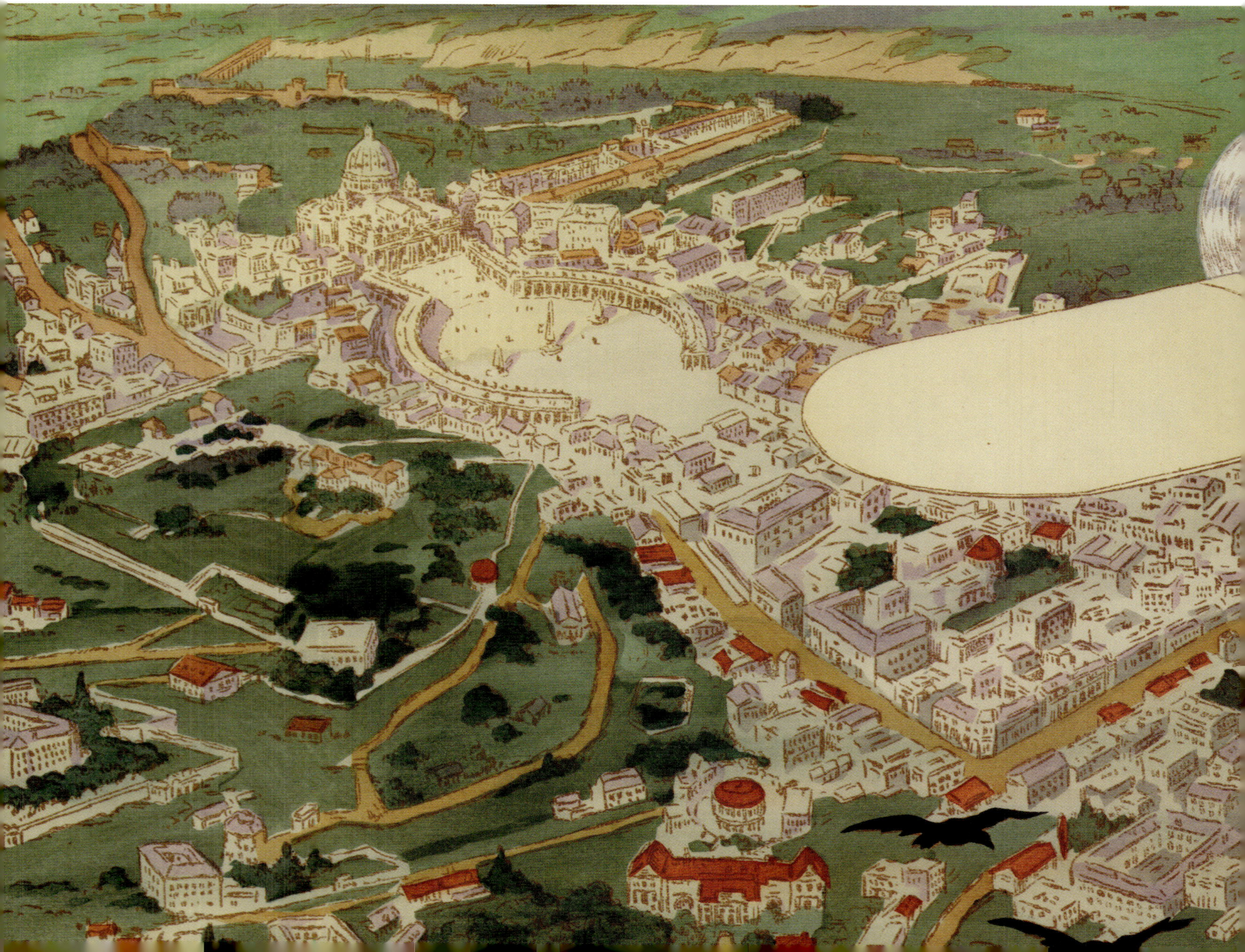

a new government. Within four years all opposition parties had been banned, and Mussolini proclaimed himself *Il Duce* (supreme leader). He embarked on an ultimately disastrous foreign policy, involving Italy in the Spanish Civil War, the invasion of Abyssinia and then a "Pact of Steel" with Nazi Germany. In June 1940 Italy entered the war on the Axis side, but within a year it was clear that her military forces could only survive with the support of the Germans. As the war spread to involve Russia and the United States the outlook for Italy became increasingly bleak. By July 1943 the Italians had enough, and Mussolini was removed from power by his own government. Two months later Italy surrendered to the Allies, although the Germans continued to occupy much of the country, and maintained a tenacious defense of the Italian peninsula. Rome was only liberated in early June 1944—just a day before the D-Day landings in Normandy.

In Rome the legacy of the Mussolini years can be seen in grandiose public building projects such as the Via dei Fori Imperiali which stretches from the Piazza Venezia to the Colosseum, and the Esposizione Universale di Roma (EUR) suburb to the south of the city, which integrated housing areas with modernistic civic buildings. After the war Rome became the capital of the new Italian Republic, and the city continued to expand to meet the needs of business, industry and government. By the time the city hosted the Olympic Games in 1960 it was regarded as one of the most fashionable cities in Europe—the home *of la dolce vita* (the sweet life). Her population now stands at just over 3 million. Rome also played host to the World Cup in 1990, and a decade later her civic buildings were restored as part of the millennium "Jubilee." Today Rome is a thriving place, where millions of tourists come to see her historical and cultural treasures, and despite the congestion and pollution she remains one of the great cities of the world.

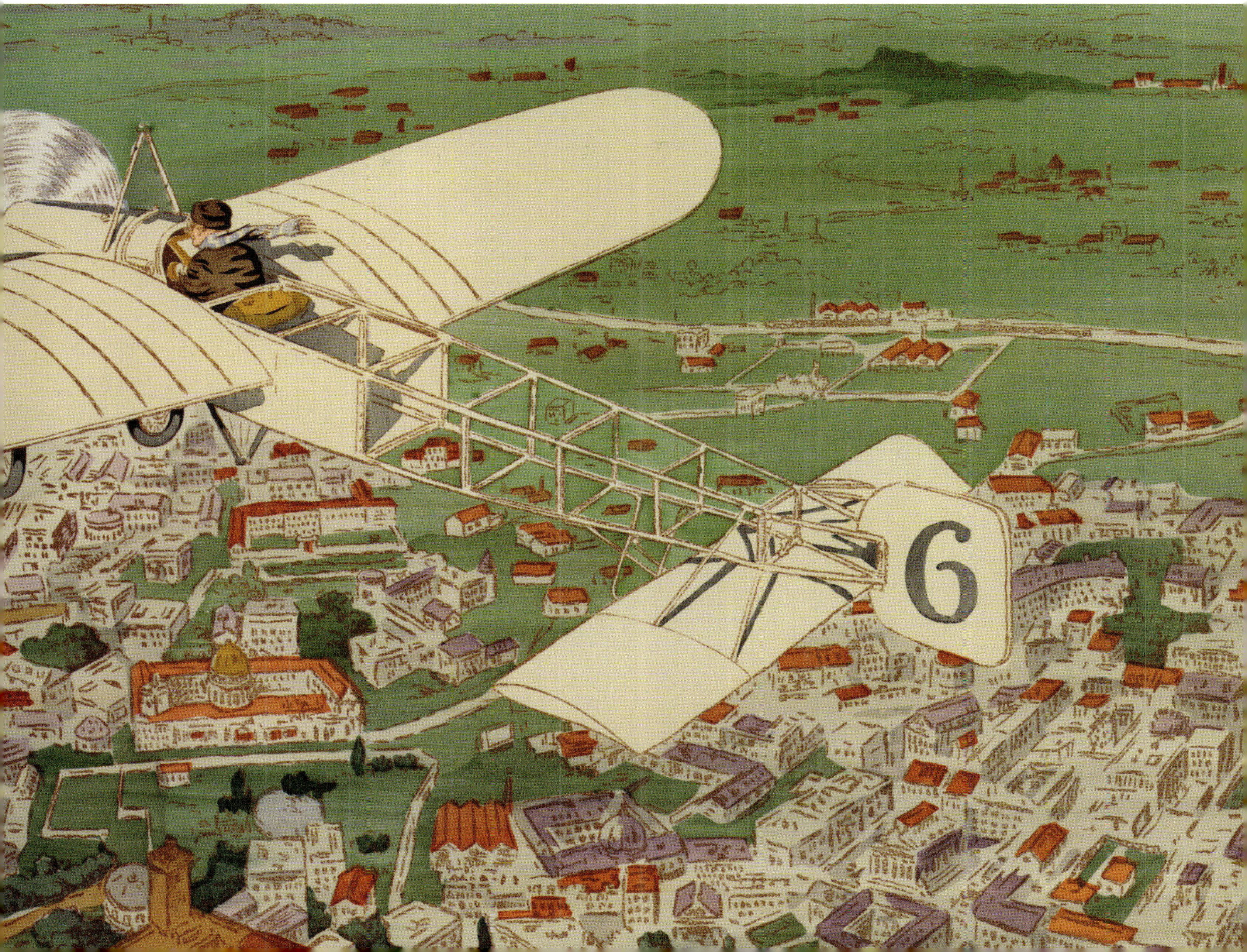

Lazio

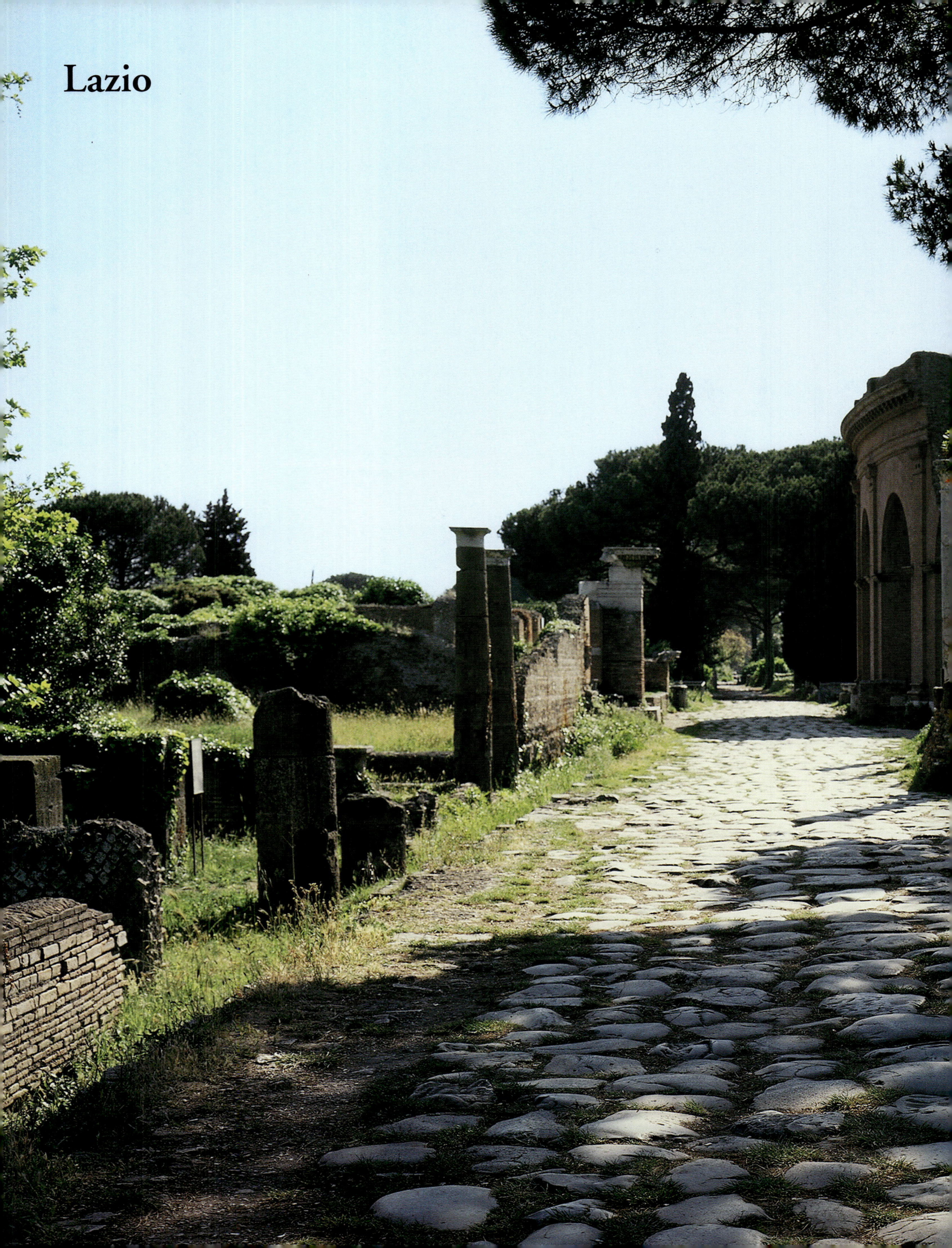

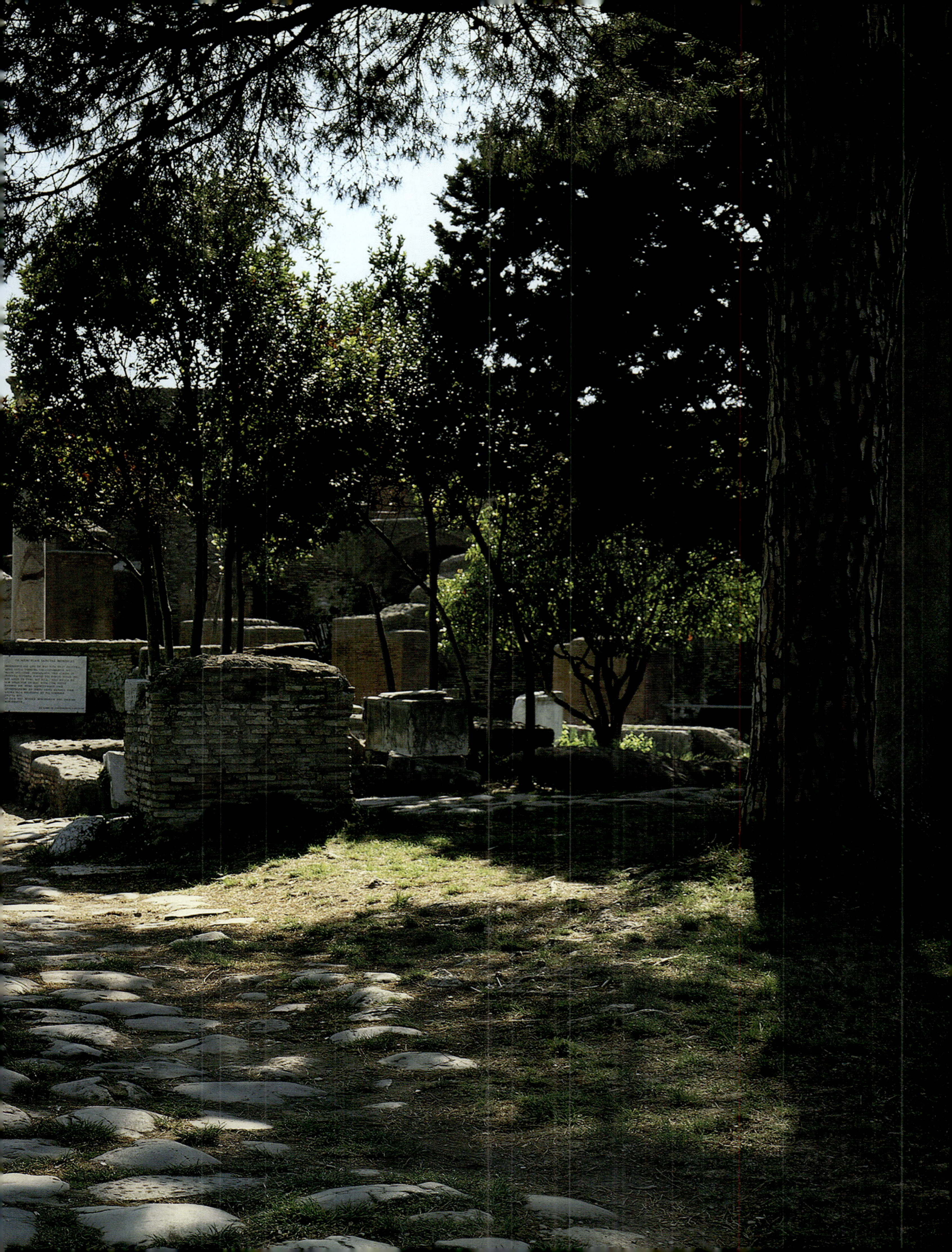

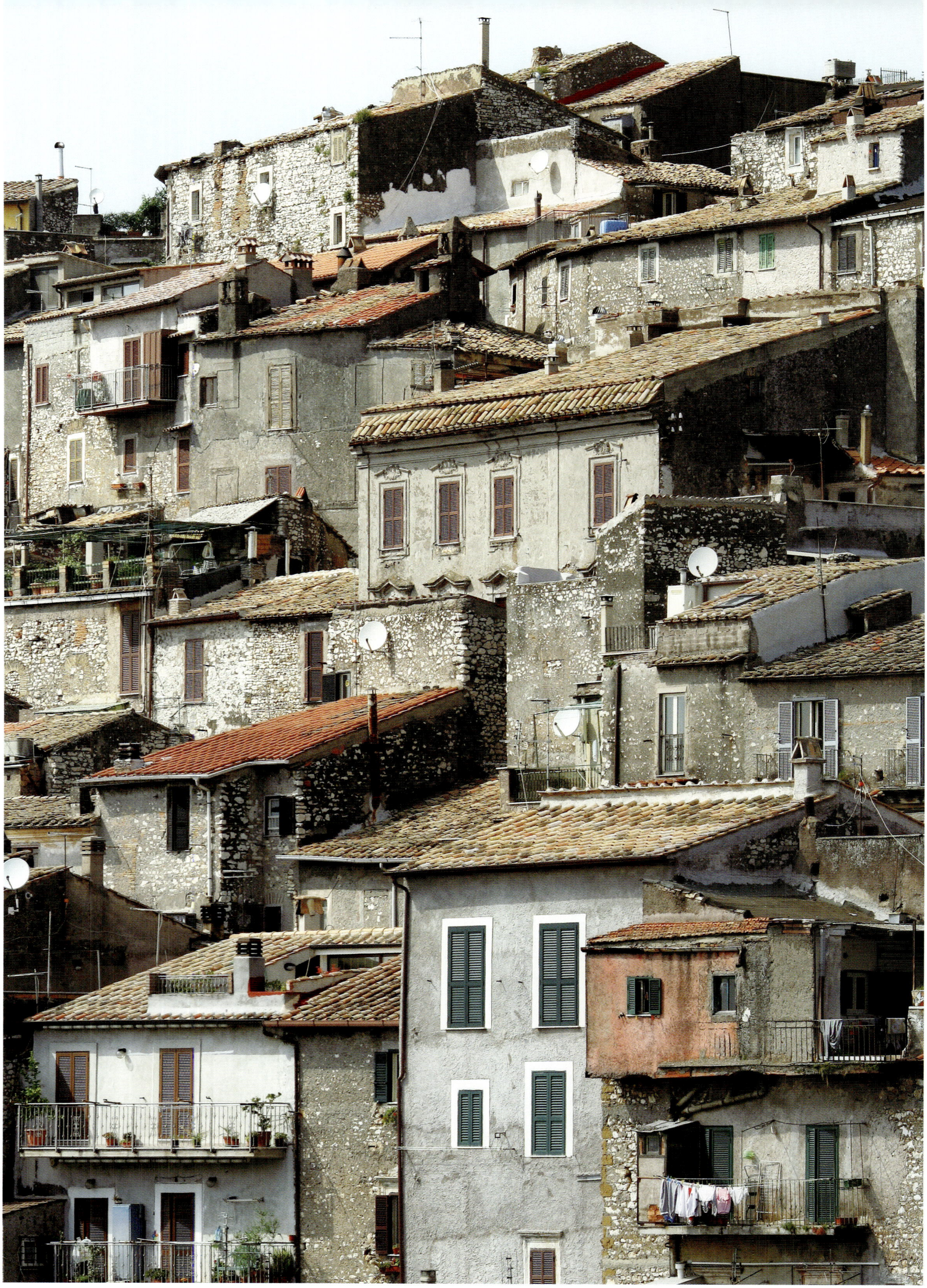

The region surrounding Rome derives its name from *Latinus*, the name for the pre-Roman people who first settled in the area. The same source produced the term for the Latin tongue, and of course is now used when referring to those who speak the modern "Romantic languages" of Spanish or Italian. The Romans themselves were proud of their Latin roots, and according to their mythology they owed their origins to King Latinus of the Latins, who played host to Aeneas and his Trojan exiles. The descendants of Aeneas founded the neighboring Kingdom of Alba Longa, and in turn produced Romulus and Remus, the mythological founders of Rome. However, modern scholars have suggested that the term Latin originally applied to the flat lands surrounding Rome, in contrast with the higher land nearby, which was associated with the term Sabine—which became another local tribal name. Today the name Lazio refers to a clearly defined province, and one of Italy's premier soccer teams.

After the establishment of the first settlement of Rome in the eighth century B.C the Romans (or Latins) extended their borders as they conquered or assimilated their neighboring tribes. This process continued during the era of the Roman Republic following Roman victories over (among others) the Samnites, the Marsians, the Campanains and the Volscians. When these territories came to be administered by Rome they were deemed to be Latium Novi (New Latin), as opposed to Latium Veteres (Ancient Latin), which consisted of the boundaries of the original Roman kingdom. Toward the end of the Republican period all inhabitants of Latium were granted Roman citizenship, and the area developed into a rich farming region, supplying the needs of the urban population. After the collapse of the Roman Empire, Latium became the Duchy of Rome, and although it was technically part of the Byzantine Empire it effectively ruled itself until it was incorporated into the Papal State in the Middle Ages.

The pope sometimes had difficulty controlling the region because of the semi-feudal enclaves of Rome's leading families that were scattered throughout Latium. Consequently the papacy devoted a lot of its energy to the establishment of political control over the province during the late Middle Ages and the Renaissance. The region continued to be administered by the church until 1870, when the Papal State was abandoned and Latium became a province of the Kingdom of Italy. It was subsequently renamed Littoric, then in 1926 it became known as Lazio. Today Lazio boasts a population of around 5.5 million people, the majority of whom live in Rome, which is the regional as well as the national capital.

Lazio is divided into five provinces: Viterbo in the north, Rieti in the east, Frosinoni in the southeast, Latina on the southern coast, and the province of Rome itself. Latina is the most modern of these provinces, as much if it was reclaimed from the Agro Pontino (Pontine Marshes) during the early twentieth century. Cassino and Anzio in the southern part of Lazio saw some of the worst of the fighting during the Italian Campaign of World War II in 1943–44, but after the war the region returned to its traditional role as the agricultural region that supports the needs of Rome.

PAGE 32–33: Ostiense Road in Ostia. Shops, taverns and laundries line the street all accompanied by the characteristic umbrella pines that grow so well throughout the region. *De Agostini/Getty Images*

LEFT: Close-up of a hillside village in Lazio. Originally termed Latium, ownership of the region was continually contested by the Romans, numerous popes, foreigners—particularly the French—and ambitious aristocrats. It officially became part of the Kingdom of Italy in 1870.

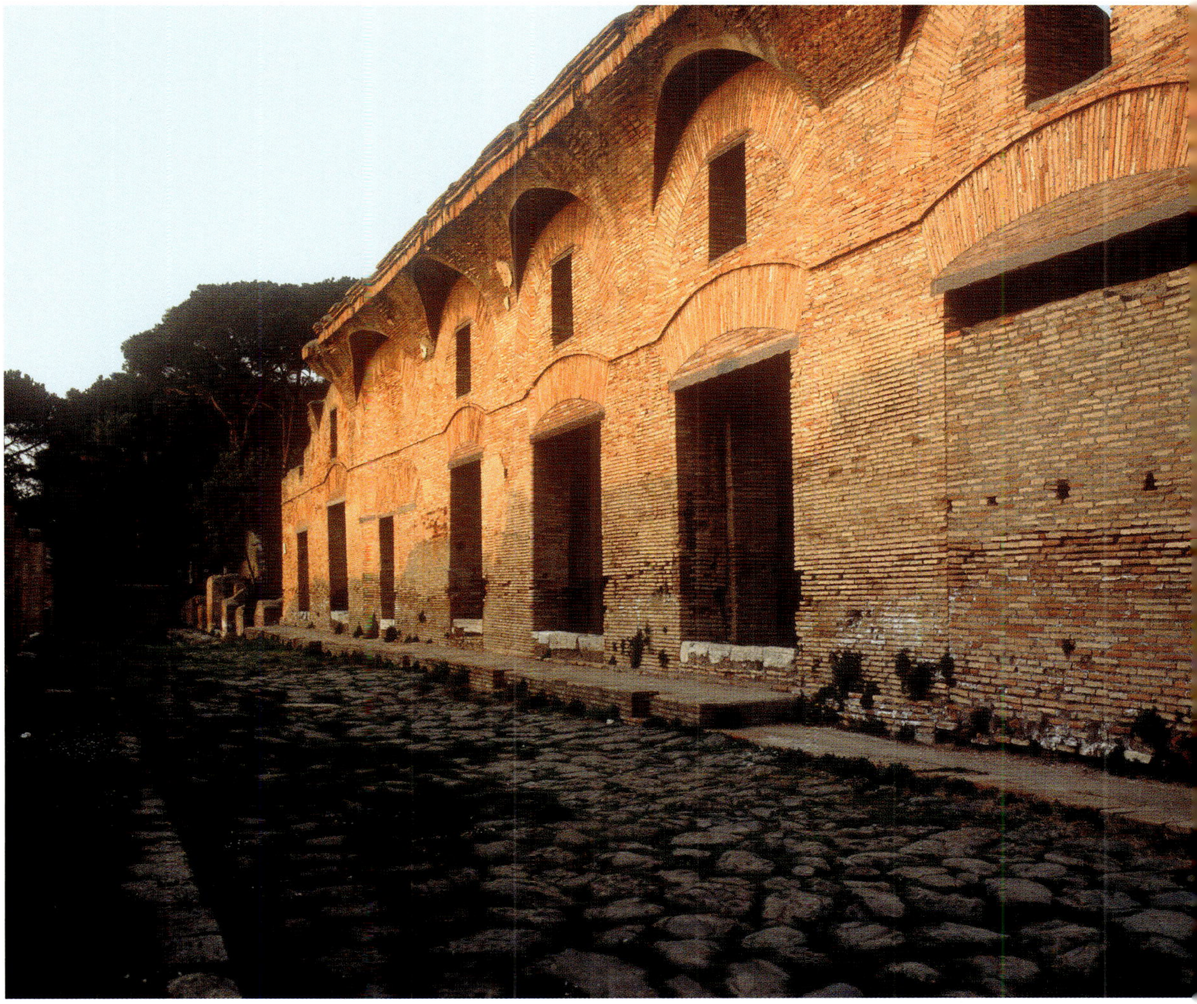

RIGHT: Most of the ruins in Ostia date from Emperor Hadrian's time and give a glimpse of everyday life in ancient Rome. Seen here is the House of Diana on the Via dei Balconi, one of the residential areas away from the main streets. It served as an *insula* or rented apartment block, with a second-floor balcony walkway around a central courtyard that contained a cistern from which tenants collected their water. The ground floor rooms contained shops and bars selling snacks and drinks. *The Bridgeman Art Library/Getty Images*

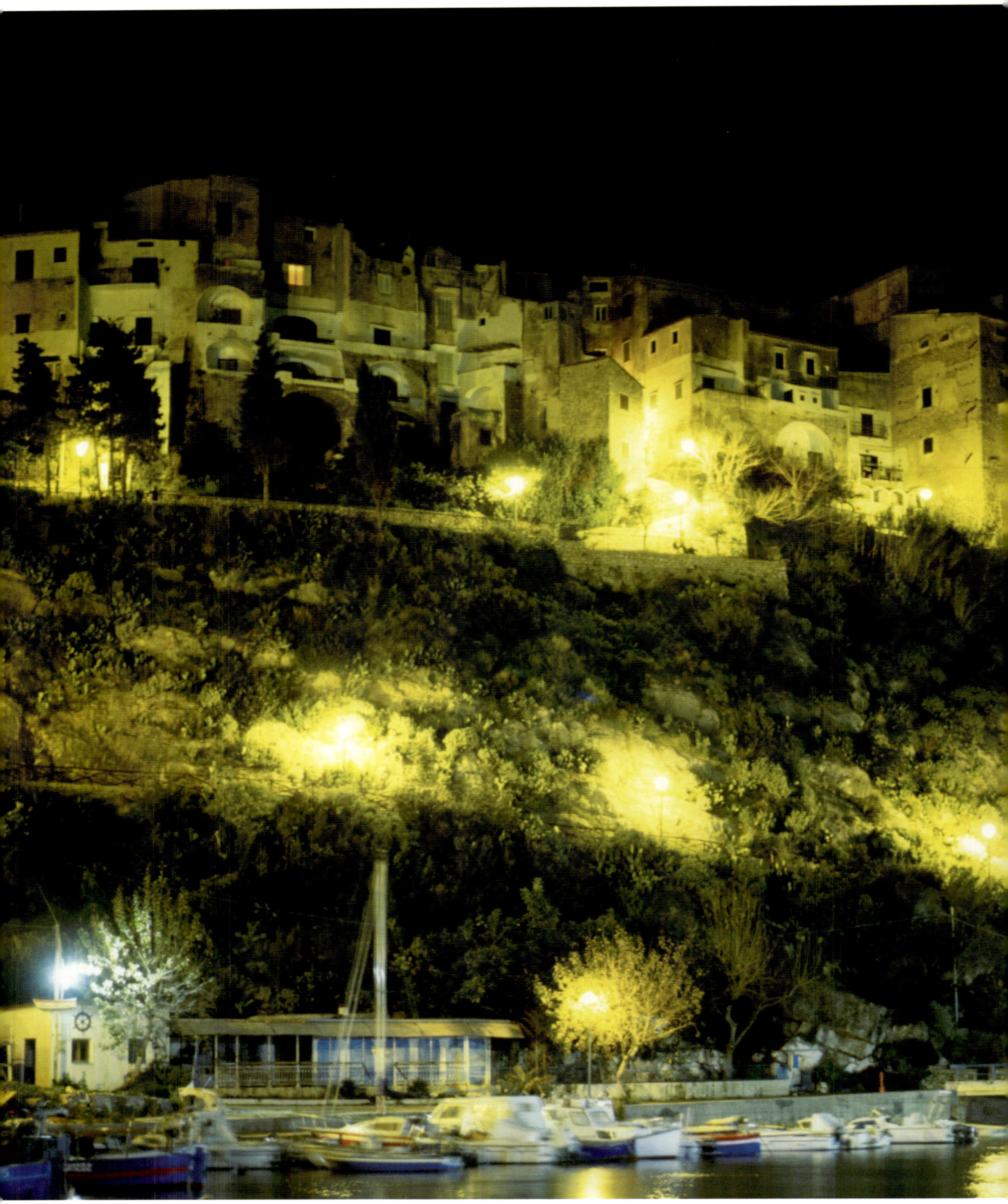

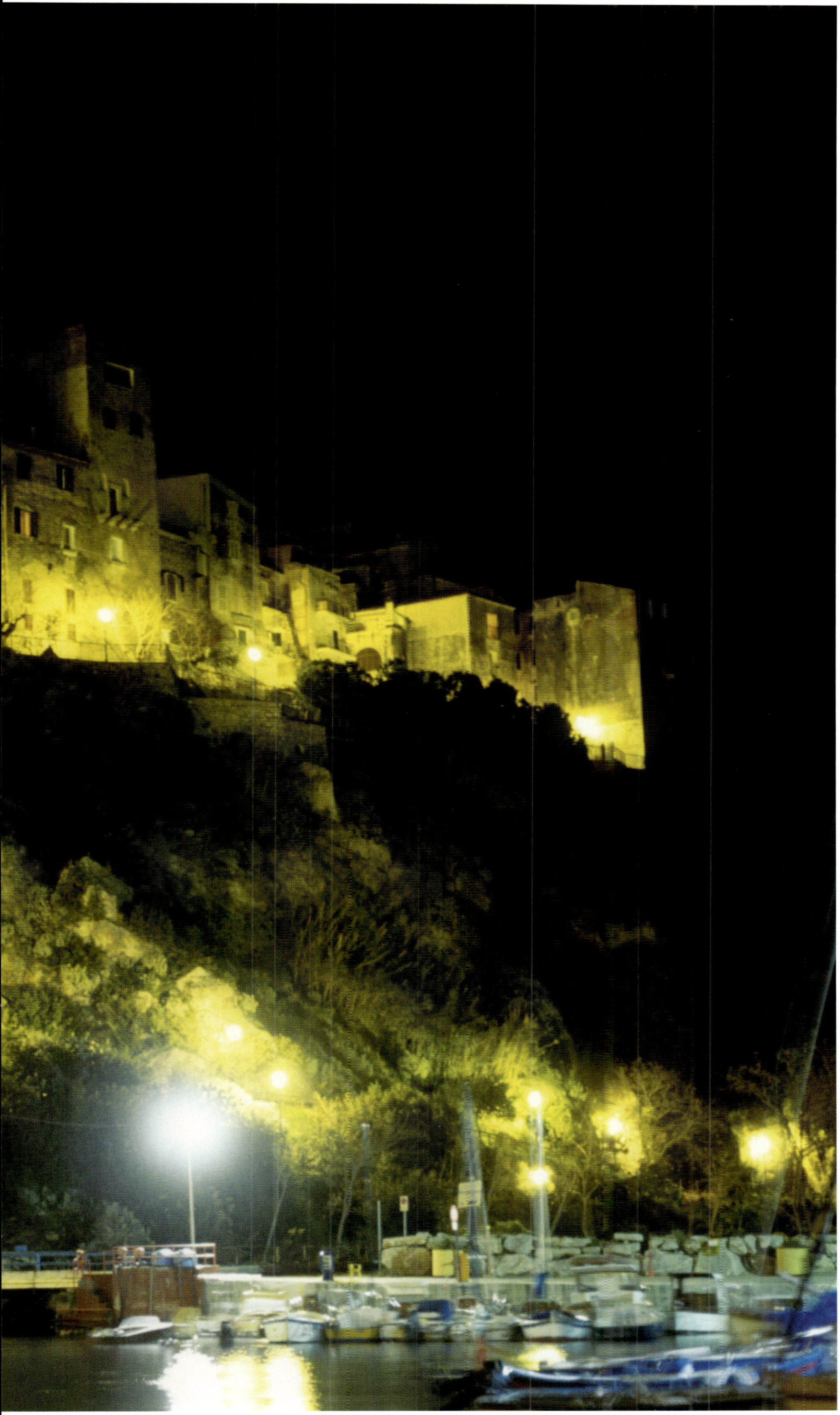

Left: Sperlonga port by night. Sperlonga is an ancient Roman resort where the Emperor Tiberius built a villa. *Anna Grossman/Photonica/Getty Images*

Pages 38–39: It is obvious why the Romans were attracted to Sperlonga—it makes a refreshing change to the heat and noise of the city. Today, this is just as true. *Getty Images/Panoramic Images*

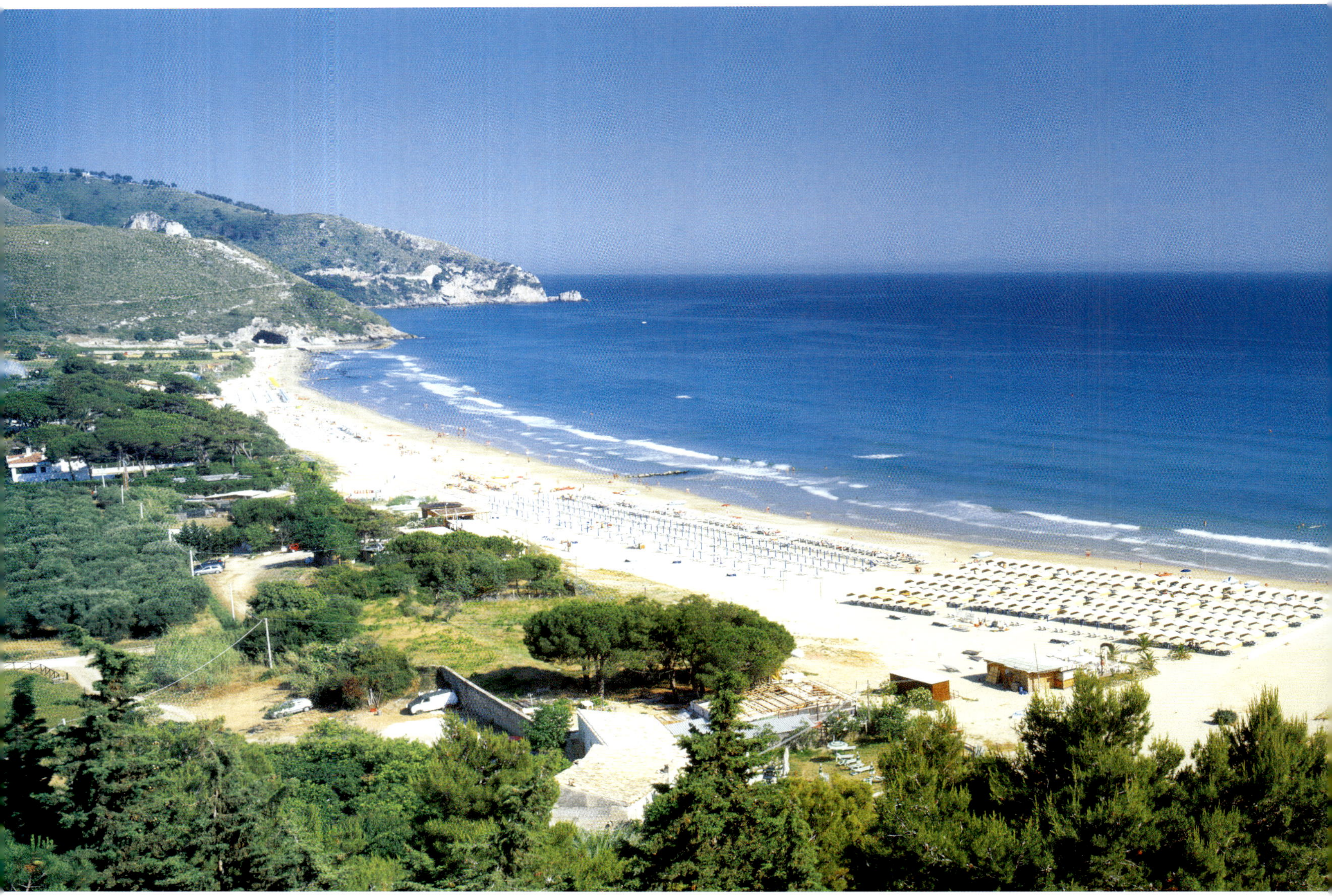

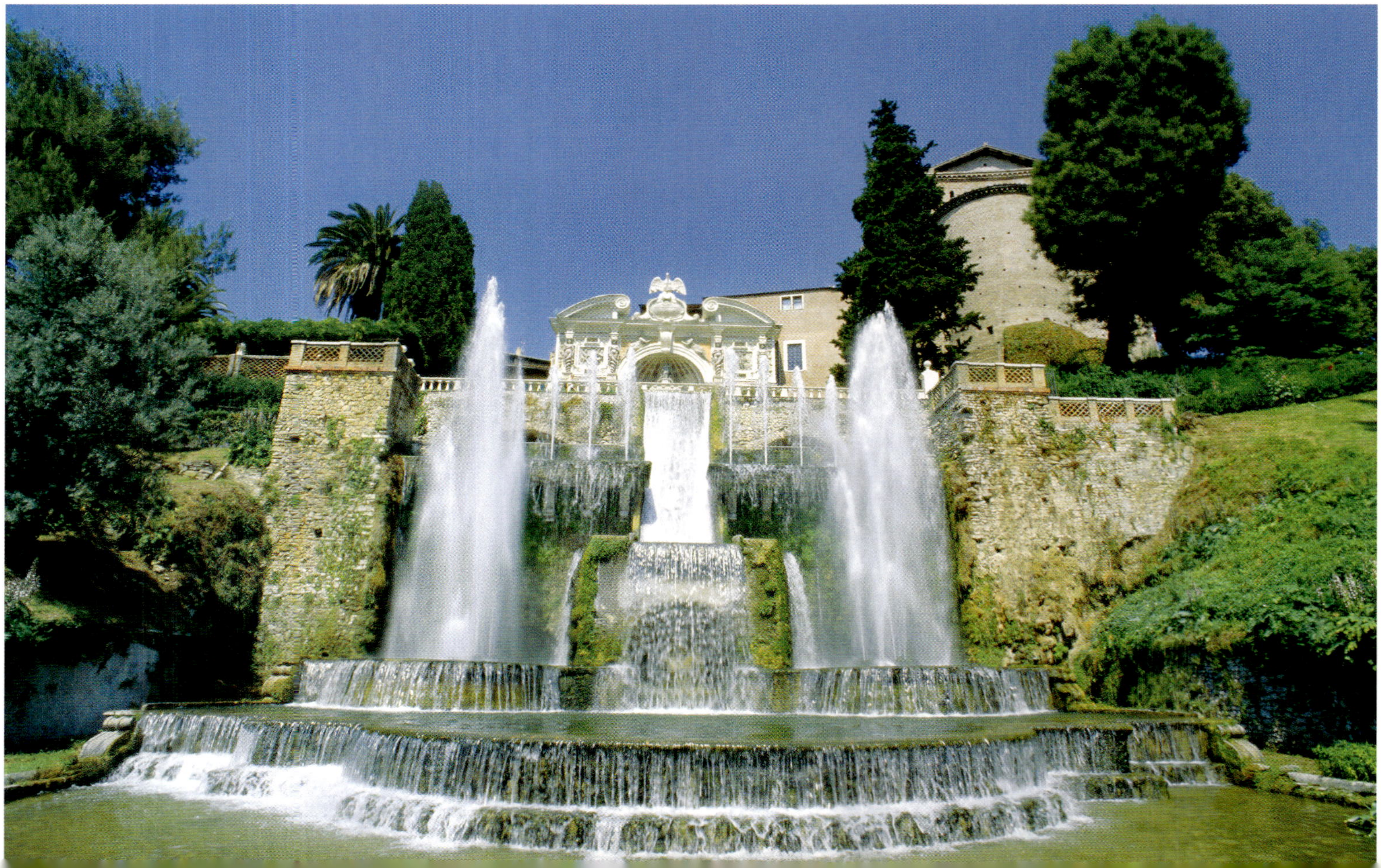

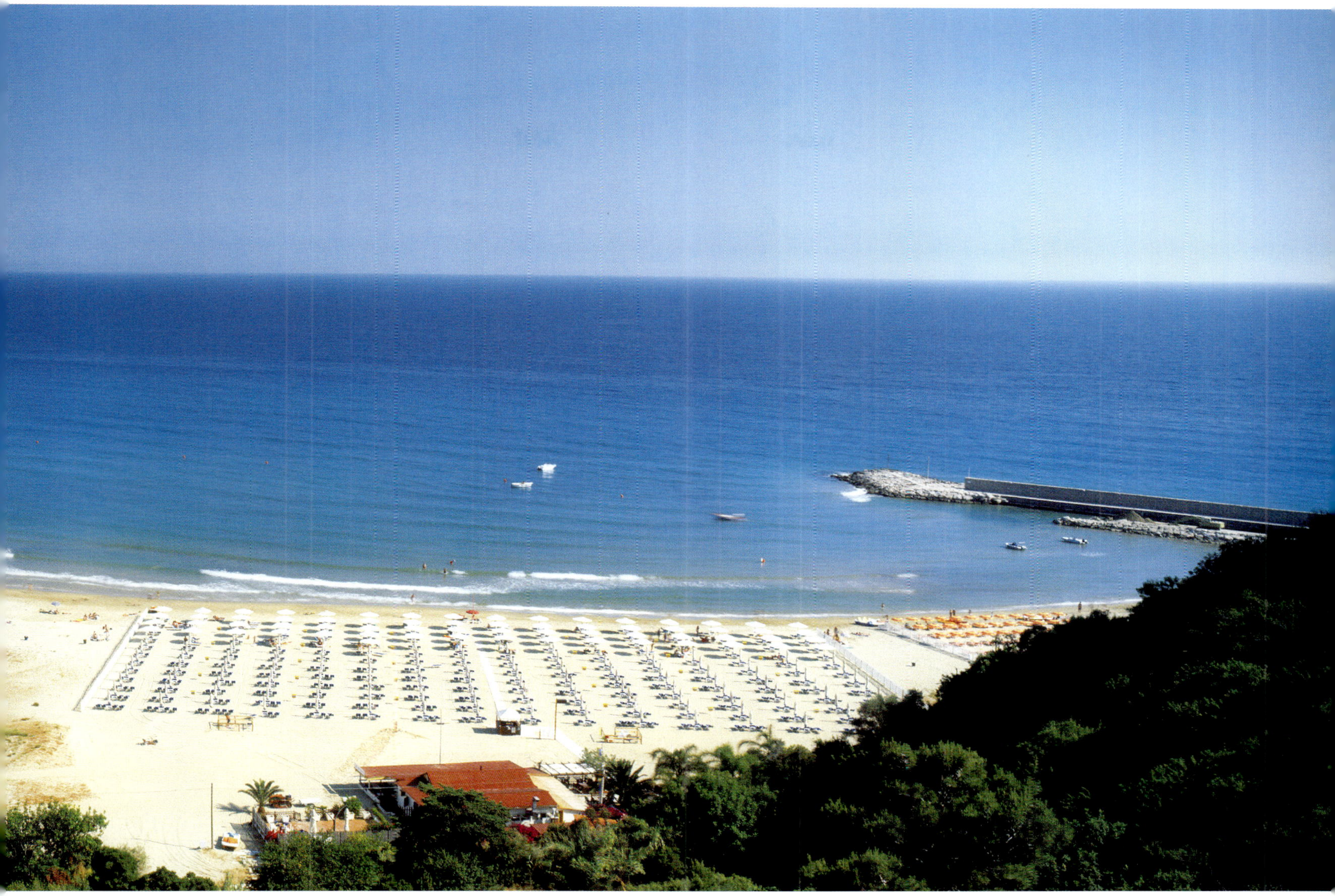

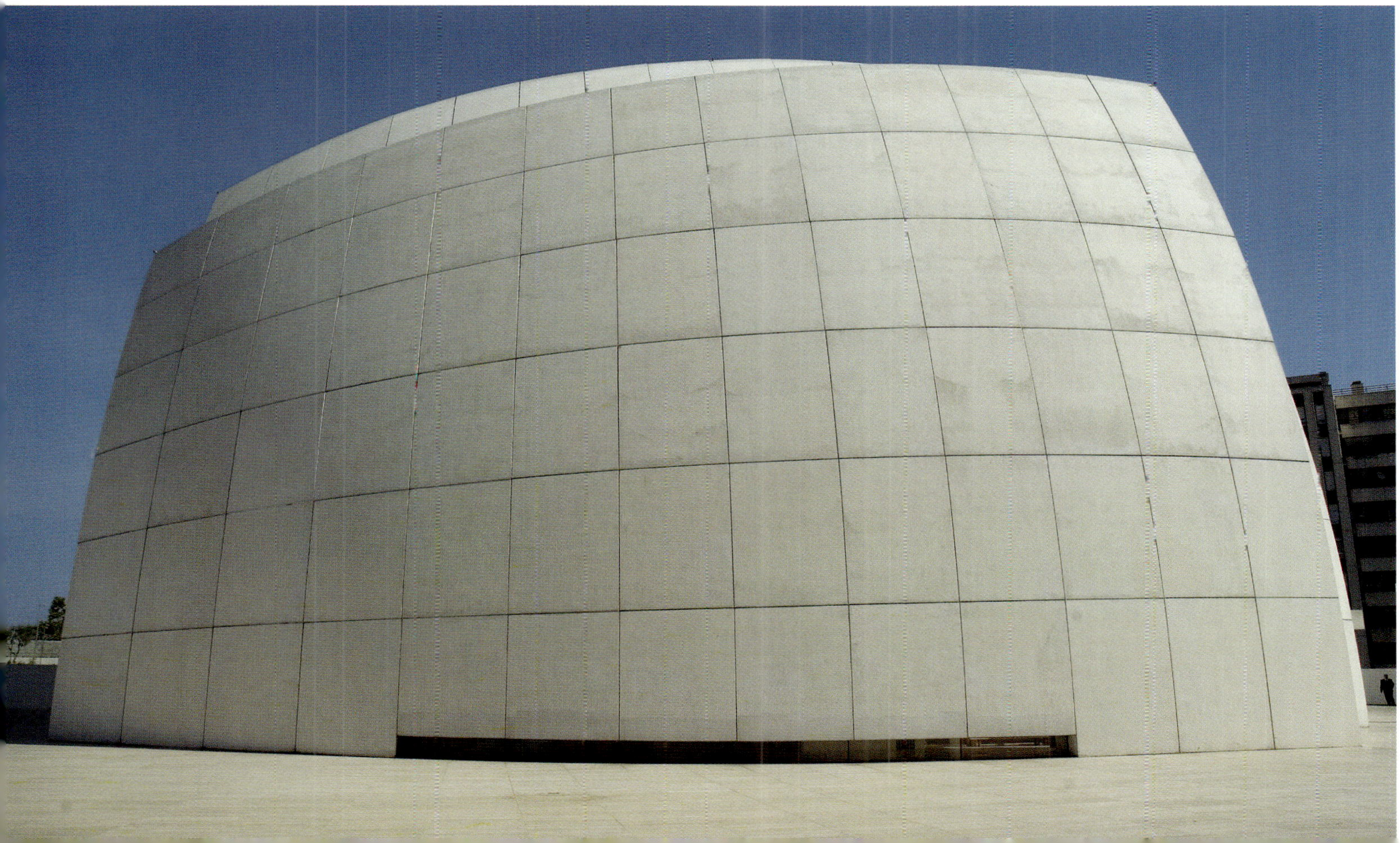

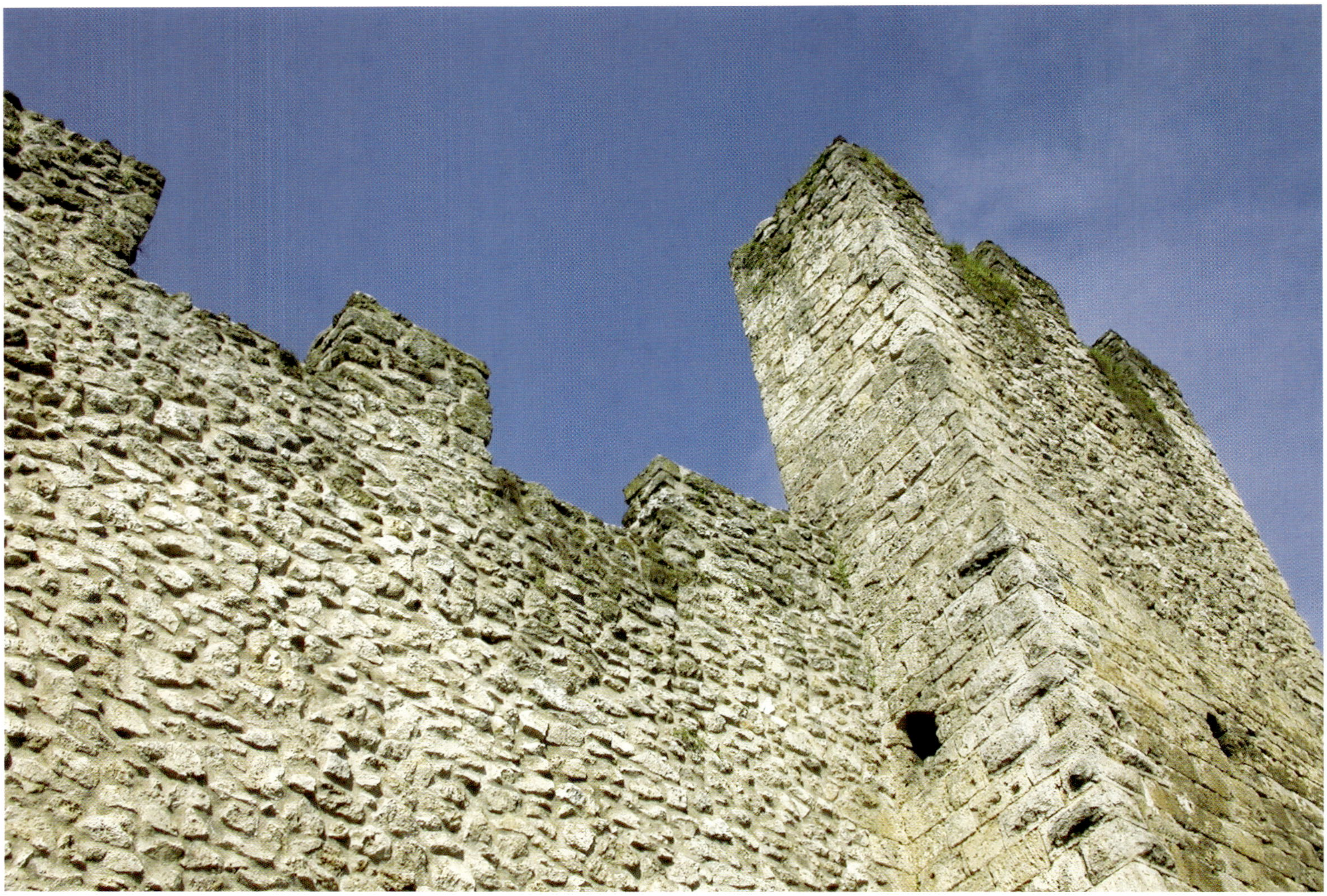

Above: The medieval city walls of Rieti, Lazio, date from the first half of the 13th century.

Right: Thirty or so miles from Rome the port of Anzio seems far removed from warfare and death—yet on January 22, 1944, as part of Operation Shingle, the ports of Anzio and Nettuno were attacked by Allied forces. There was little opposition, but the German response led to a bloody five-month battle.

Opposite, above: The American Military Cemetery at Nettuno holds the graves of more than 7,000 servicemen.

Opposite, below: The beach at Anzio.

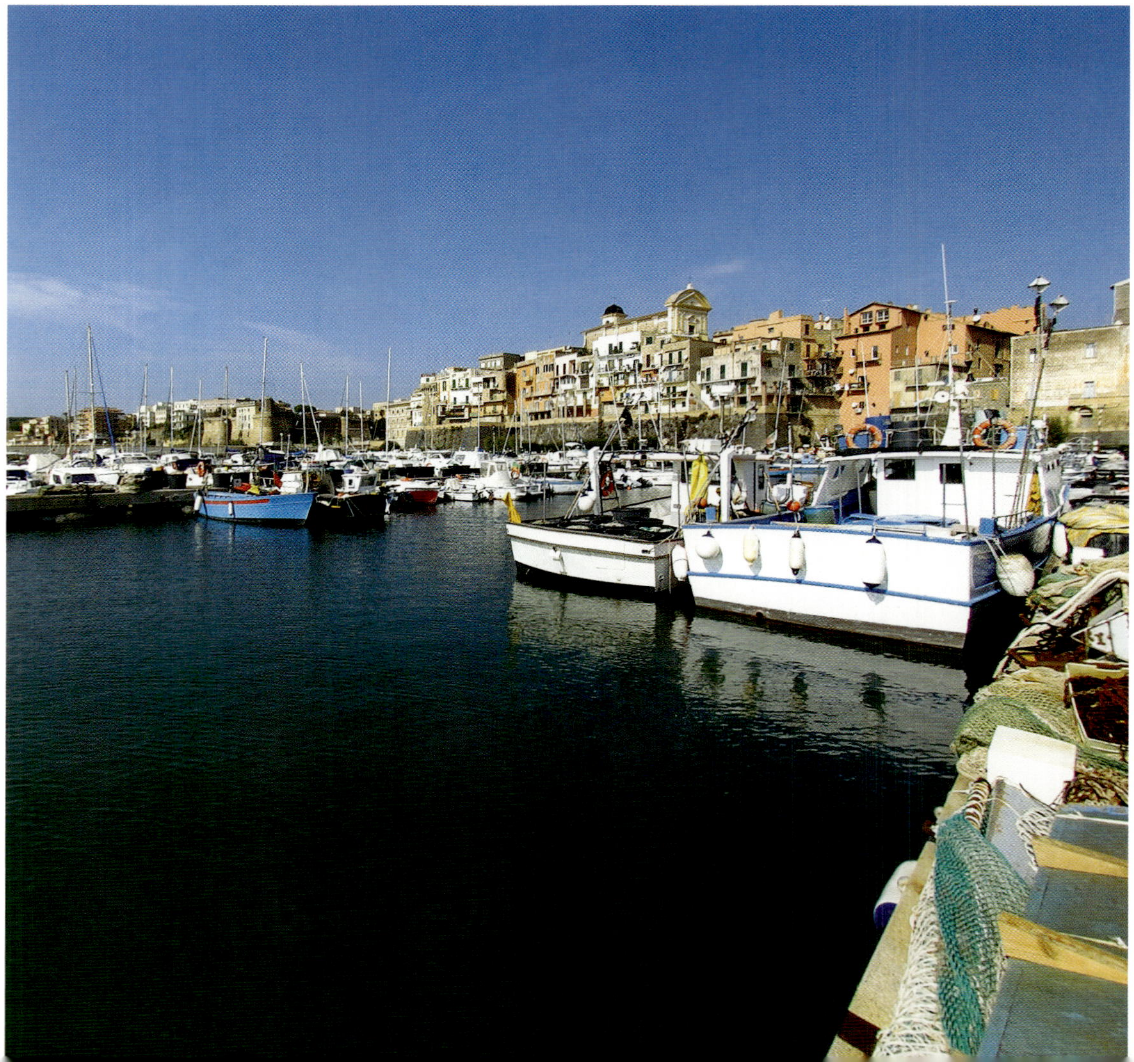

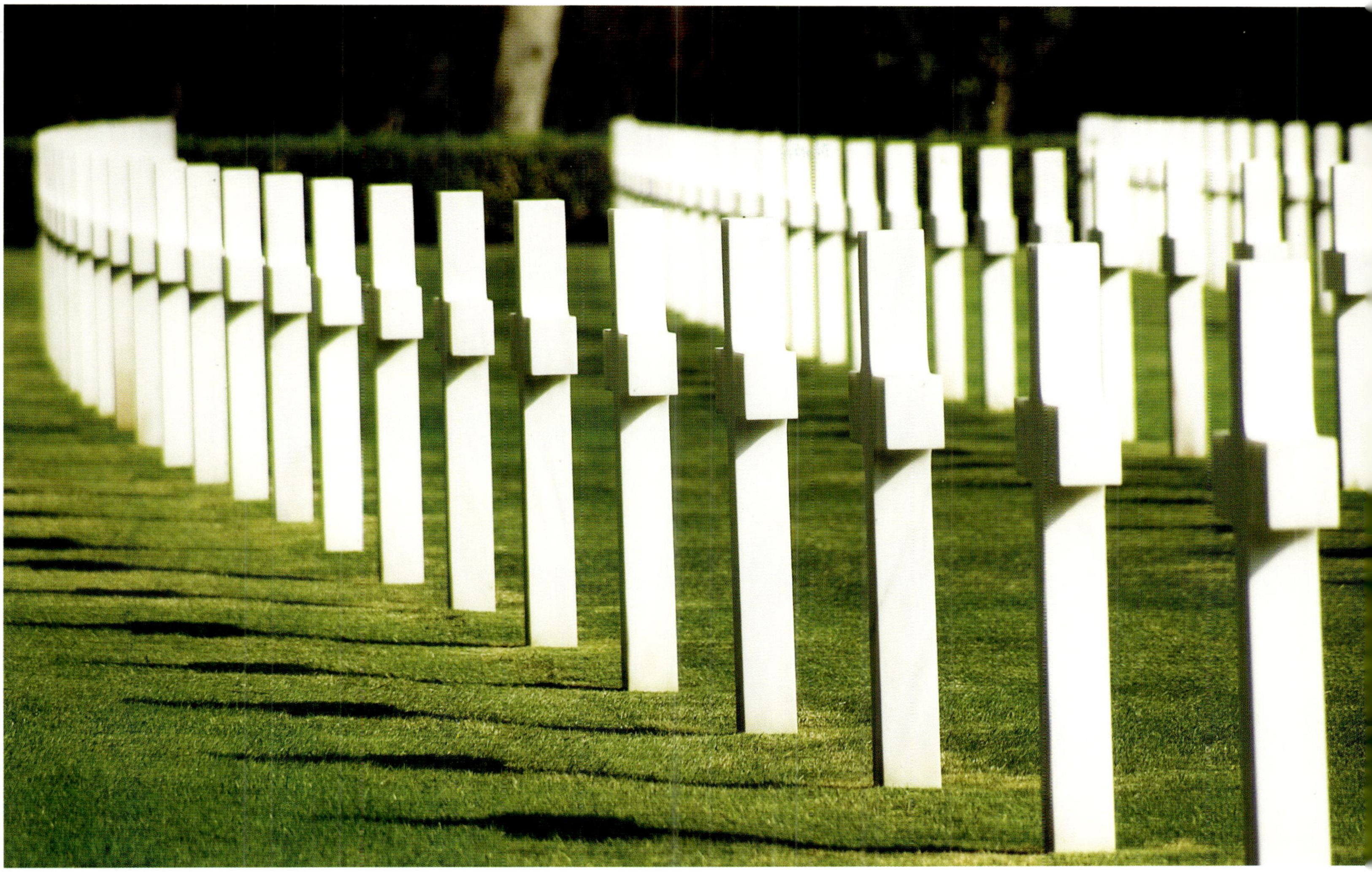

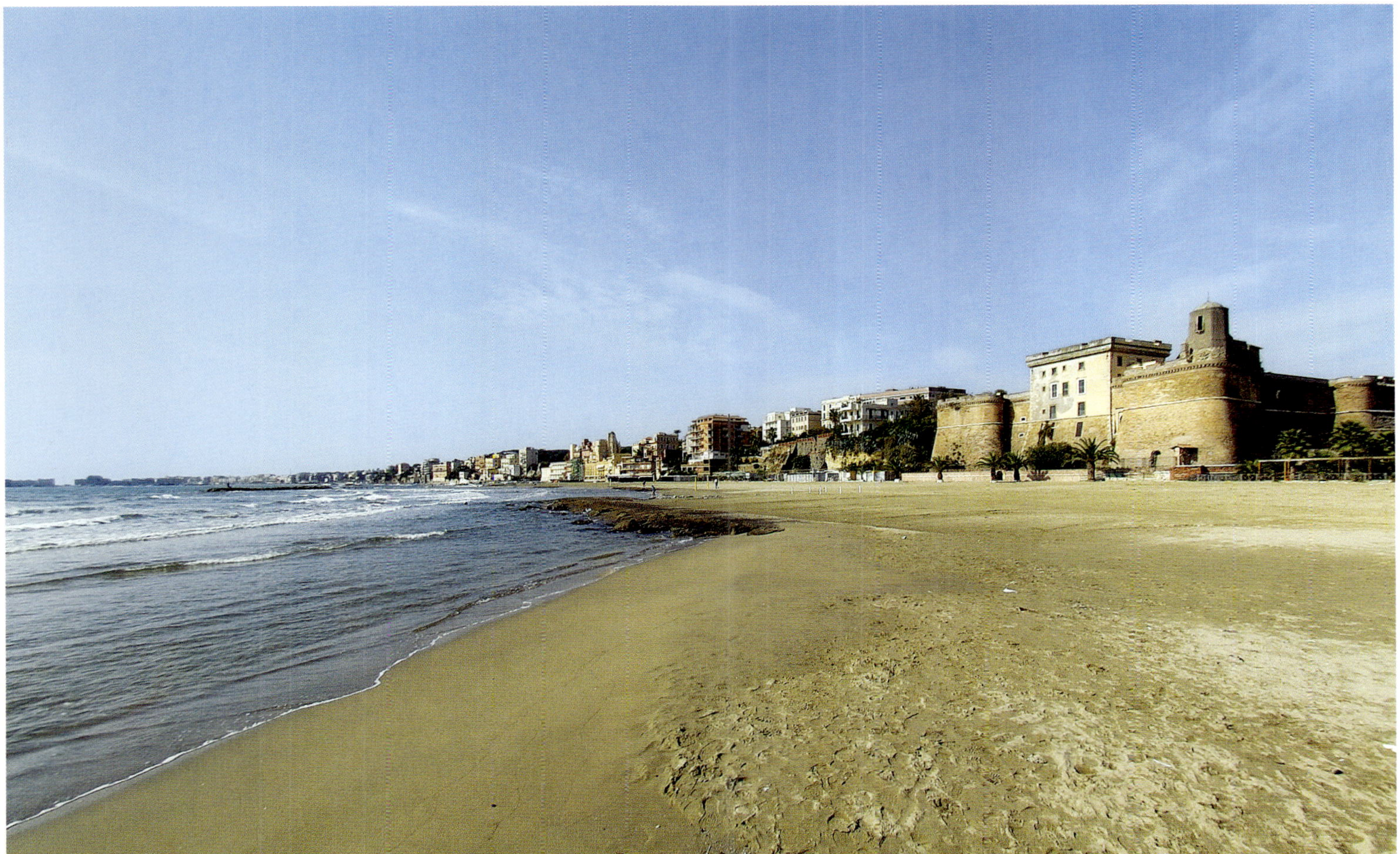

Right: The magnificent gardens of the Villa d'Este are world famous, in particular for their stunningly huge and extravagant water features. *Robert Harding World Imagery/Getty Images.*

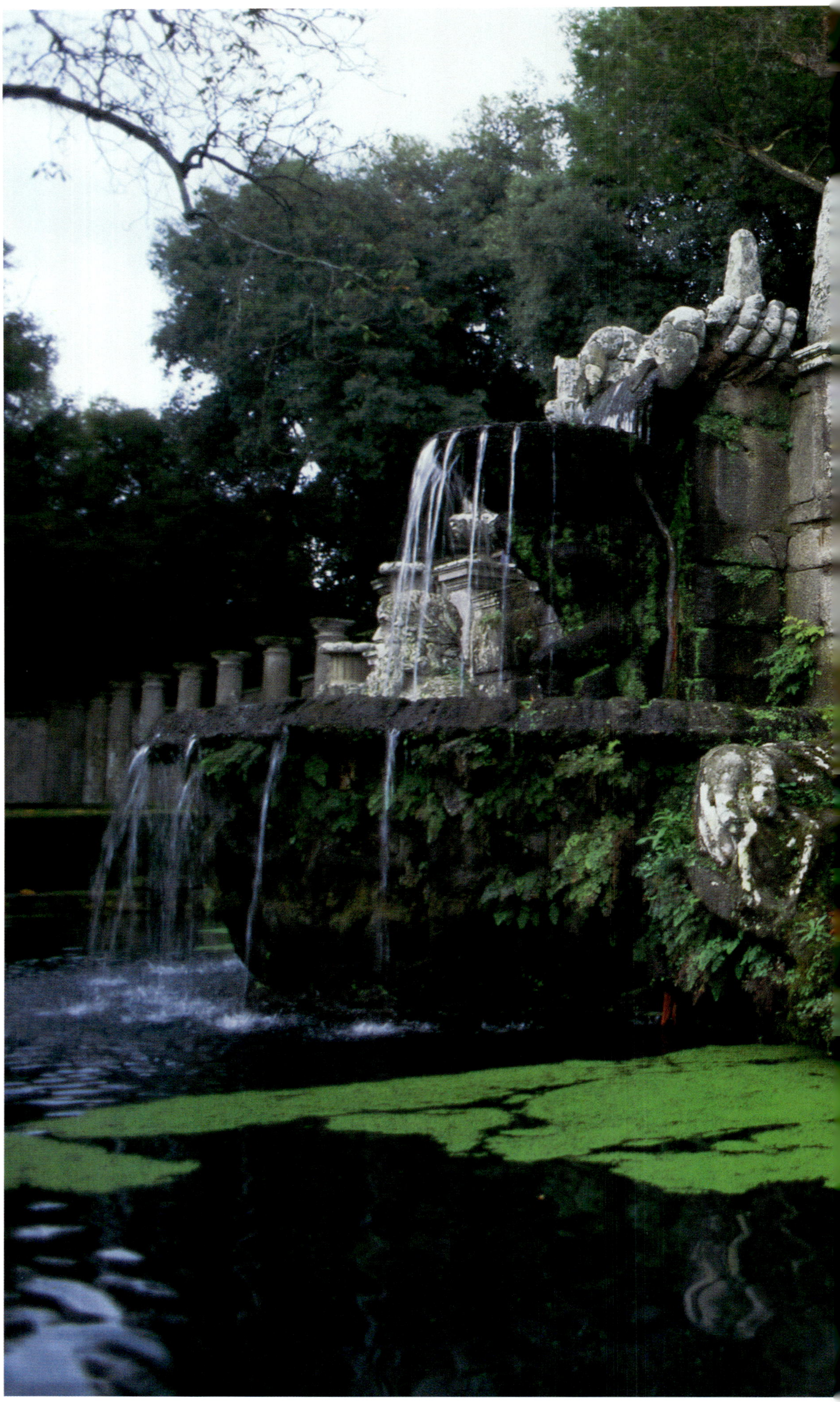

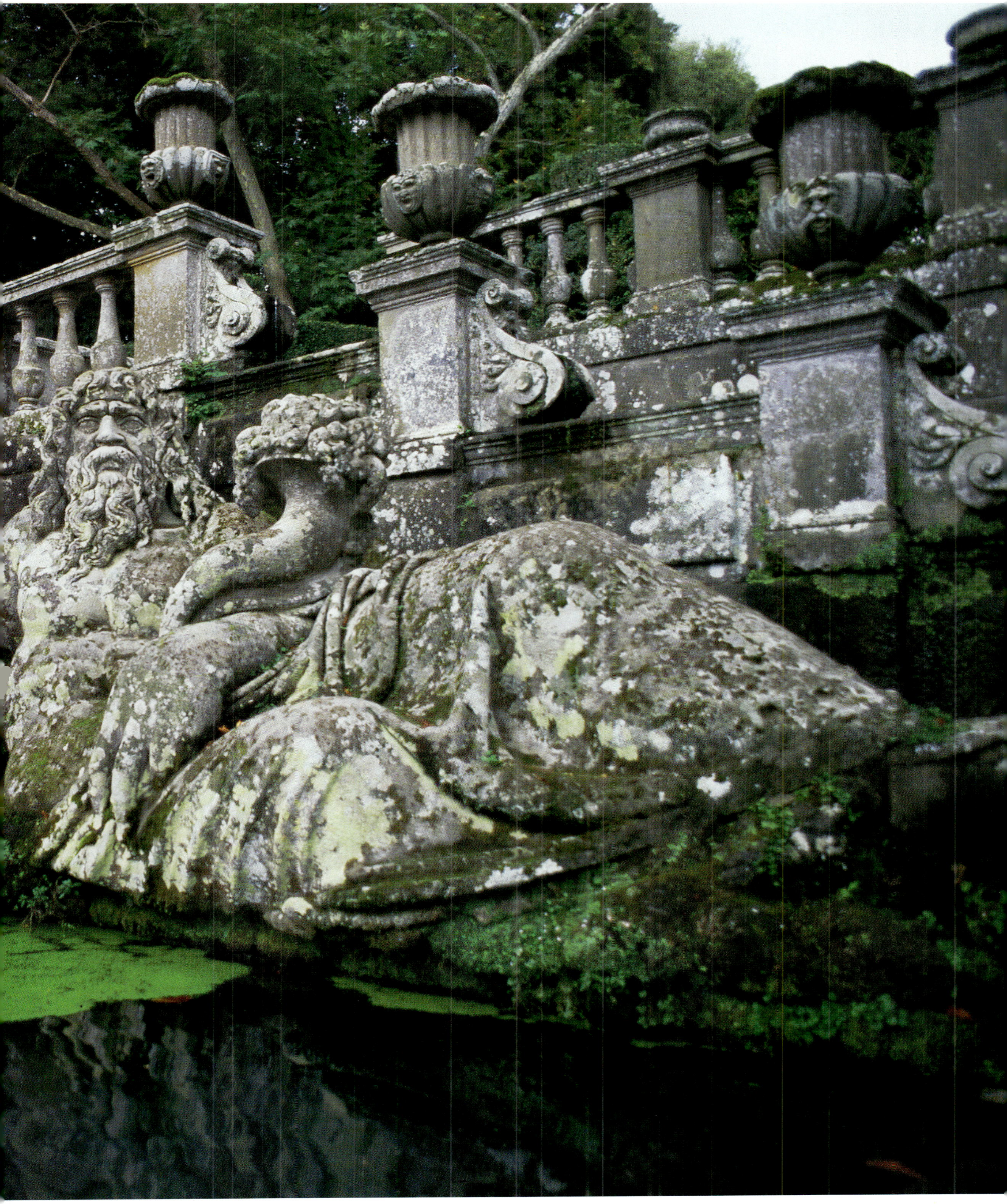

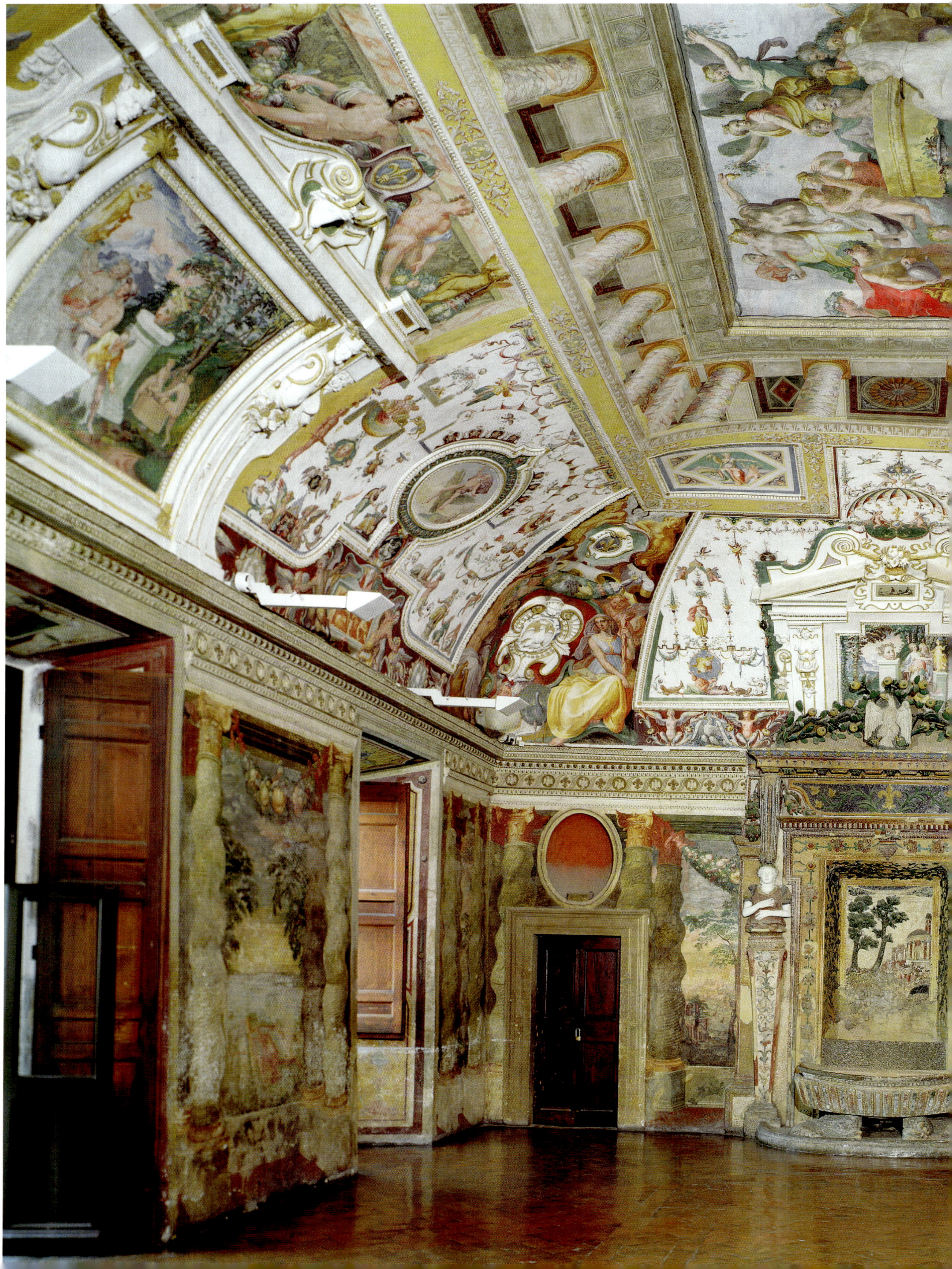

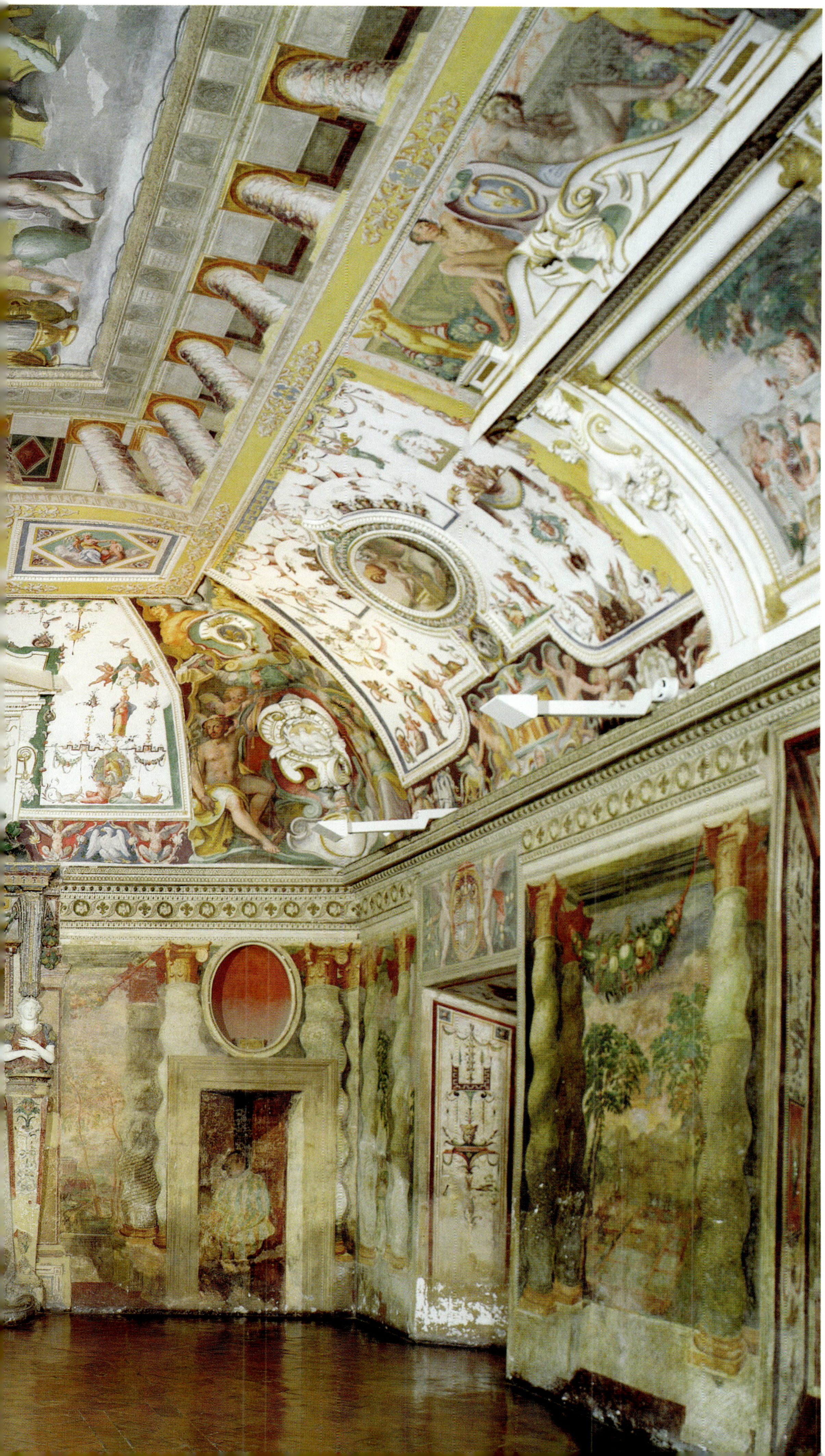

LEFT: The main salon of the Villa d'Este was designed by Pirro Ligorio (c.1500-83) for Cardinal Ippolito II d'Este (1509-72) and decorated with frescos by Livio Agresti (c.1508-1580). *The Bridgeman Art Library/Getty Images*

Right: Caryatids line Canal of Canopue, Hadrian's Villa, Tivoli. Villa Adriana or Hadrian's Villa is a UNESCO World Heritage Site. It was built in the second century for Emperor Hadrian as a retreat from the heat and intrigue of Rome. The 250 acre complex is still largely unexcavated but is known to contain over 30 buildings carefully arranged as a sacred landscape. One of the best preserved parts is the pool, called Canopus,lined on the western side by impressive marble caryatids.
Nedra Westwater/Robert Harding World Imagery/Getty Images

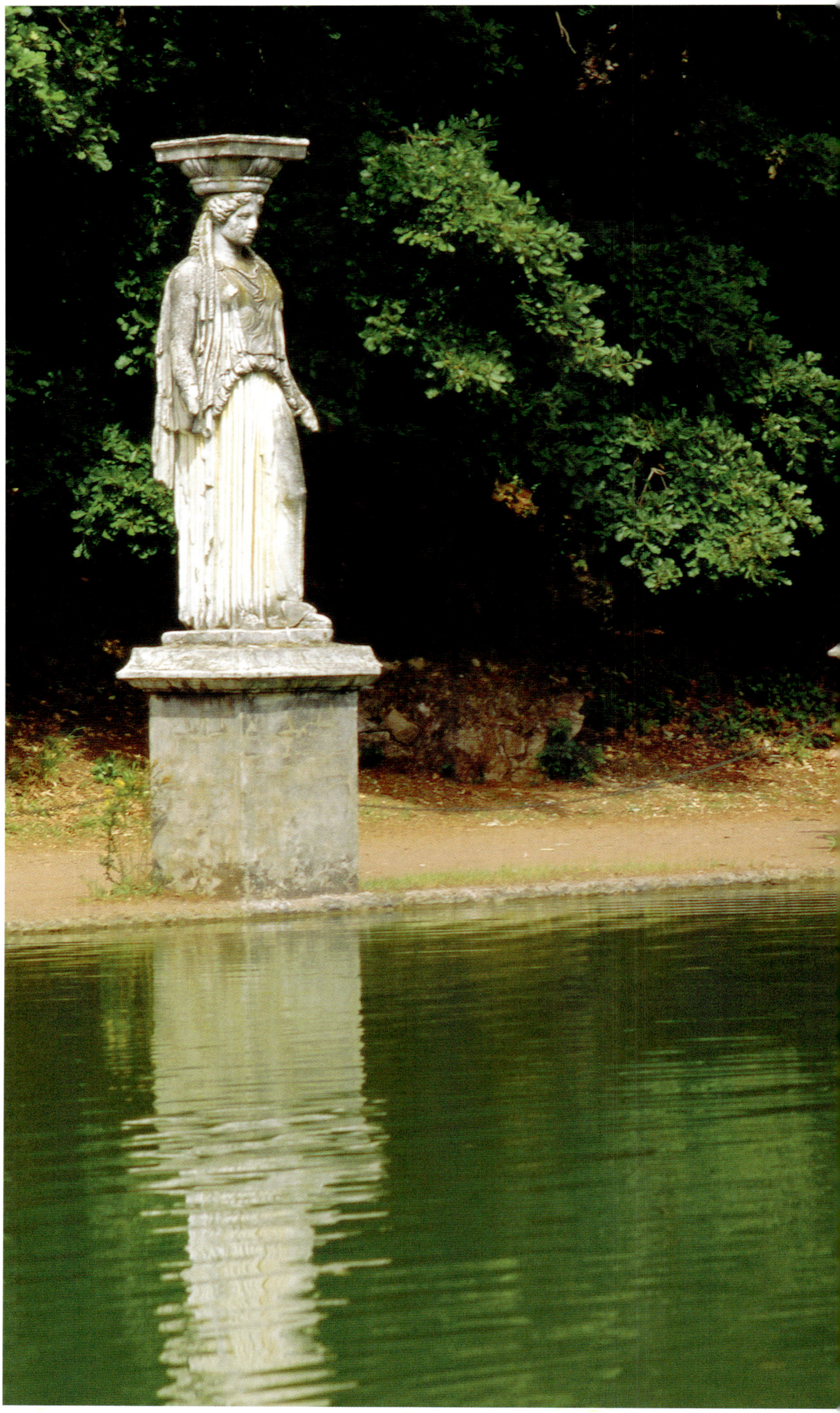

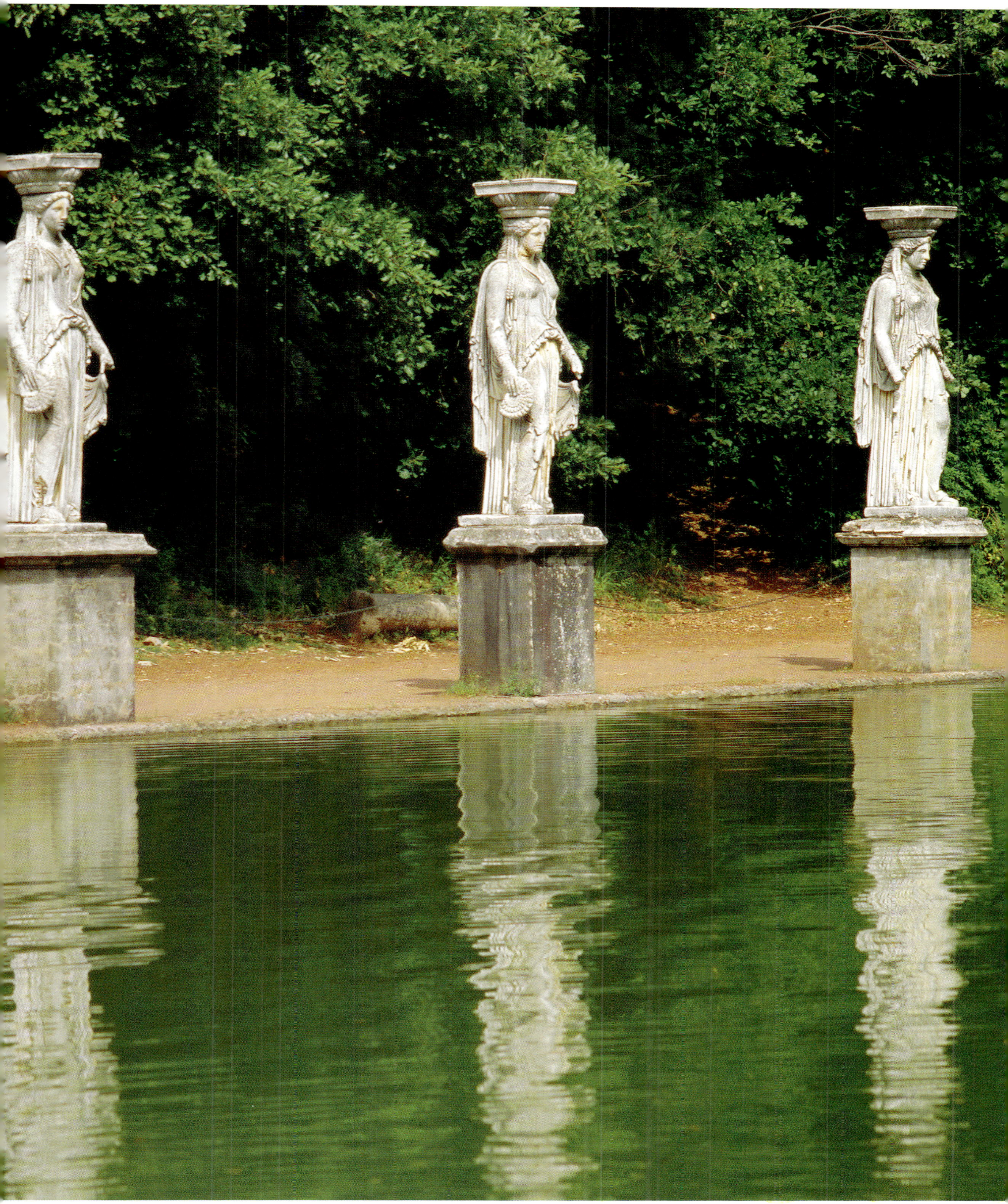

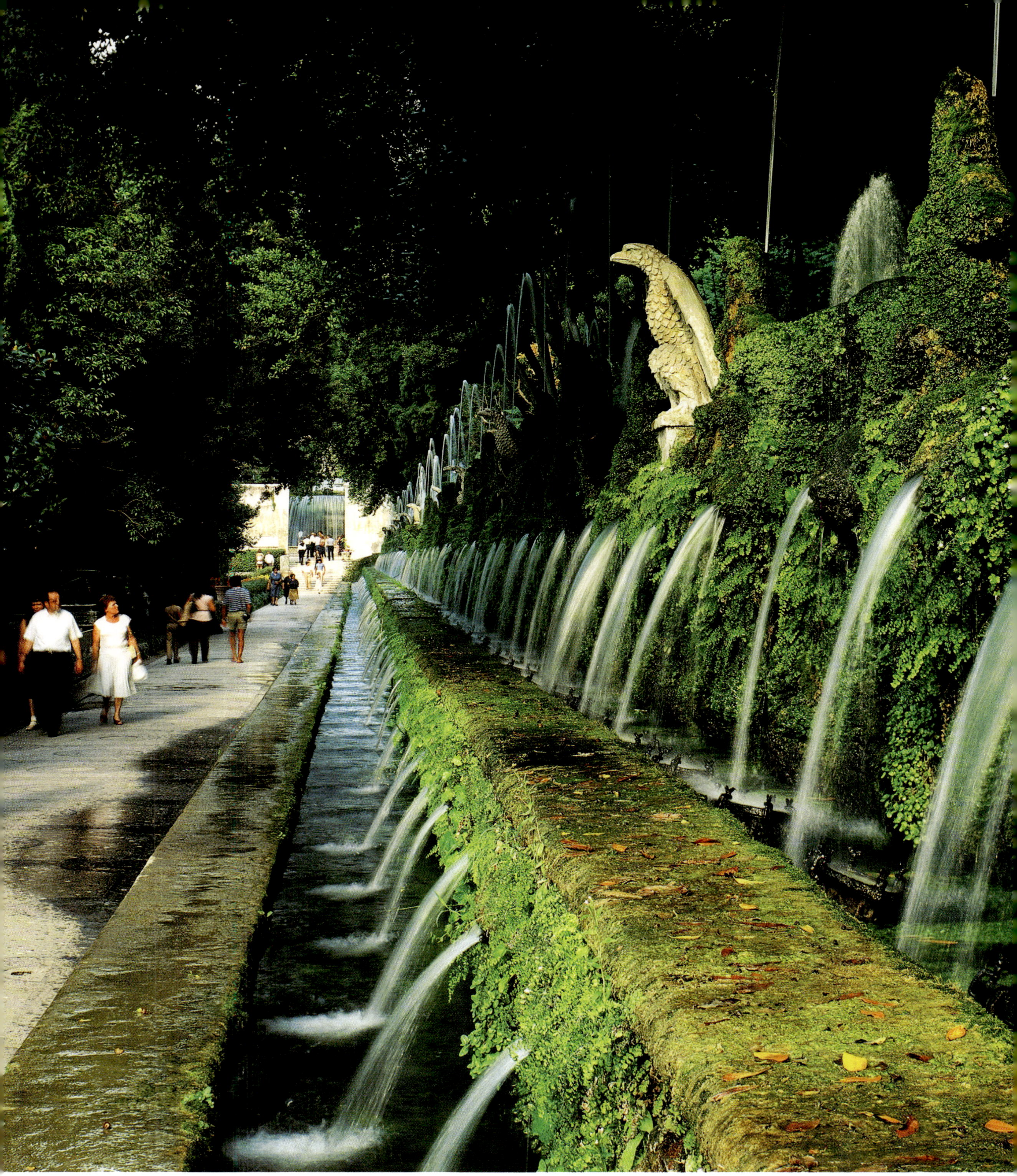

Above: Avenue Of One Hundred Fountains, Hadrian's Villa, Tivoli, Lazio. *De Agostini/Getty Images*

Right: Tivoli, Lazio. *Robert Harding/Digital Vision/Getty Images*

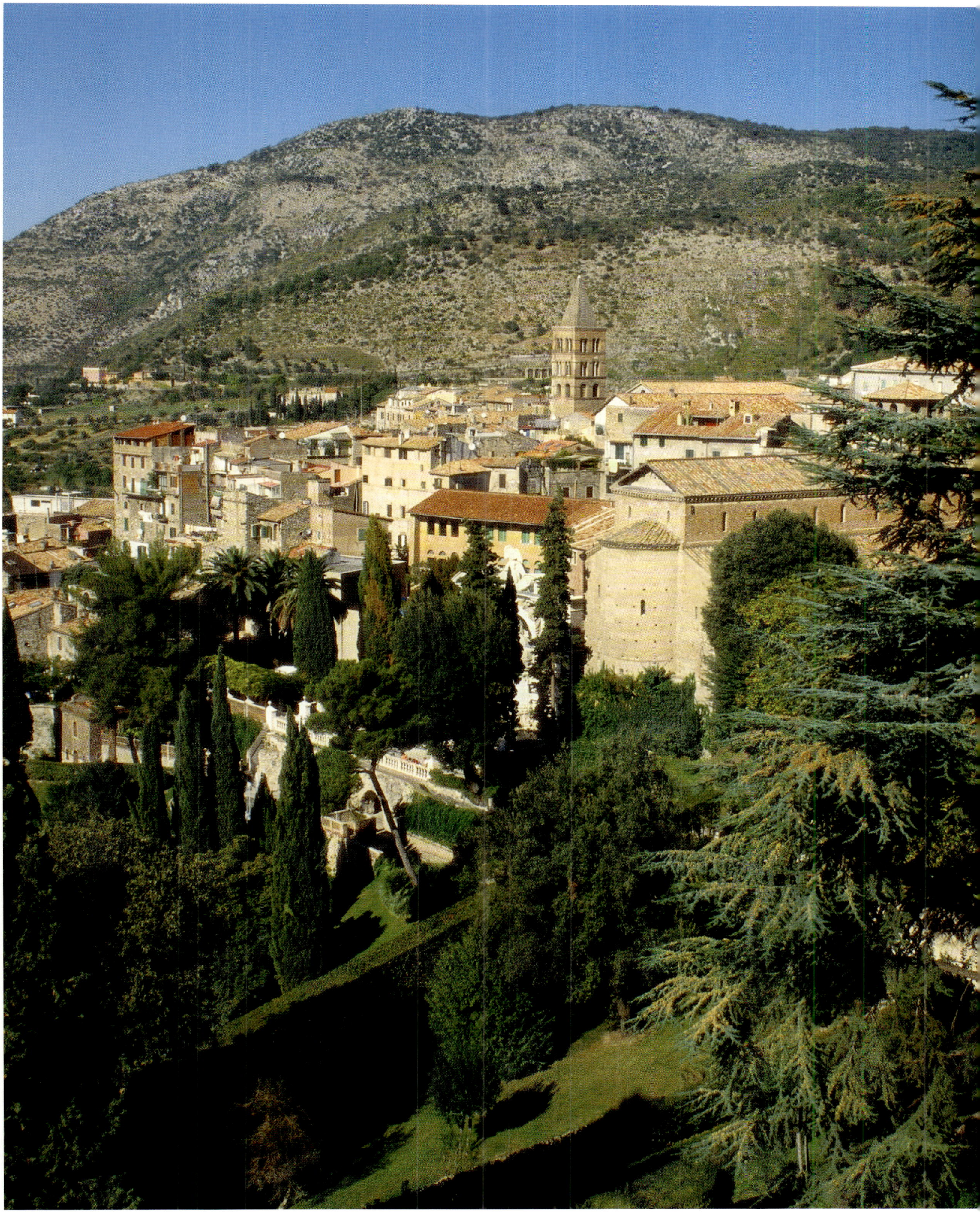

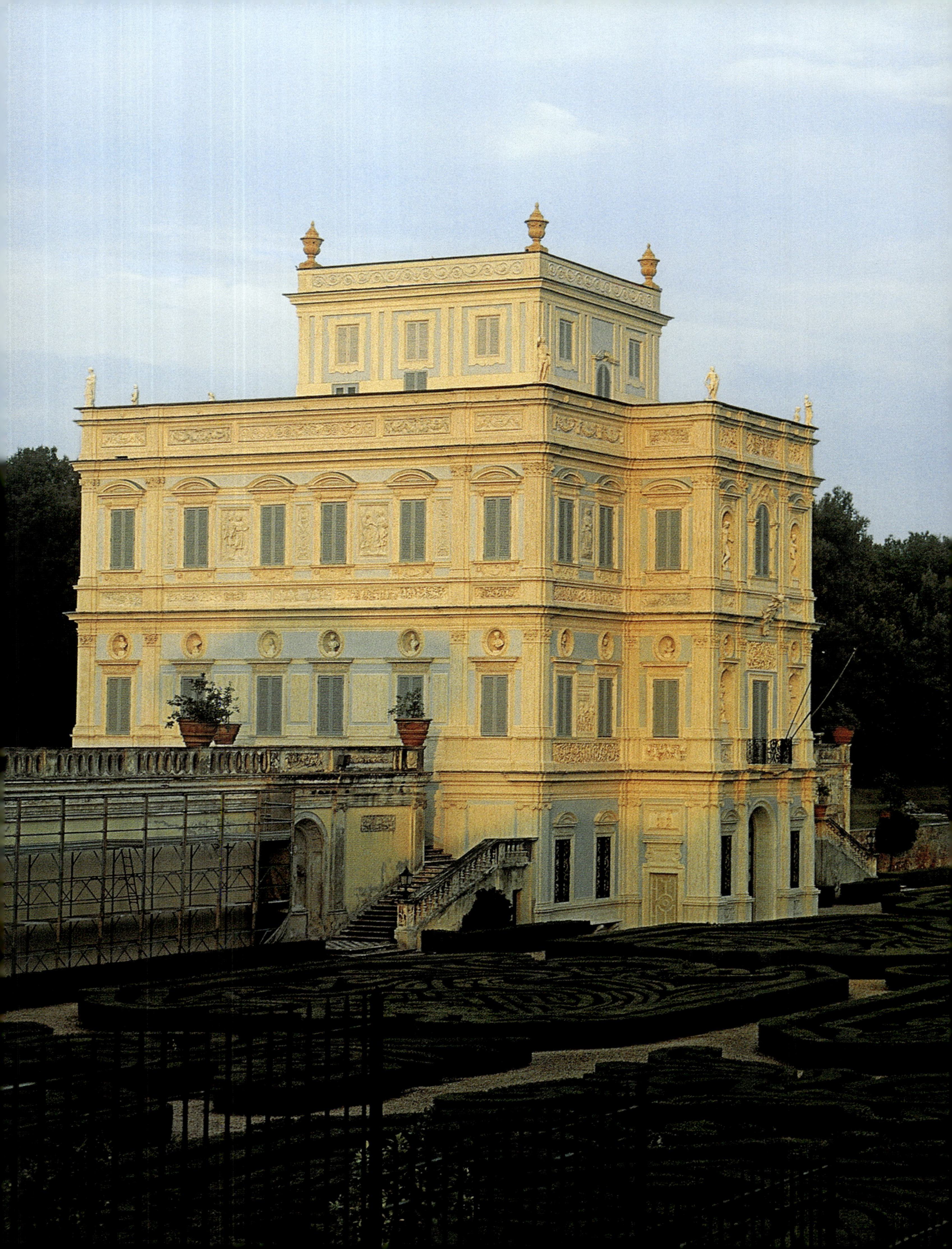

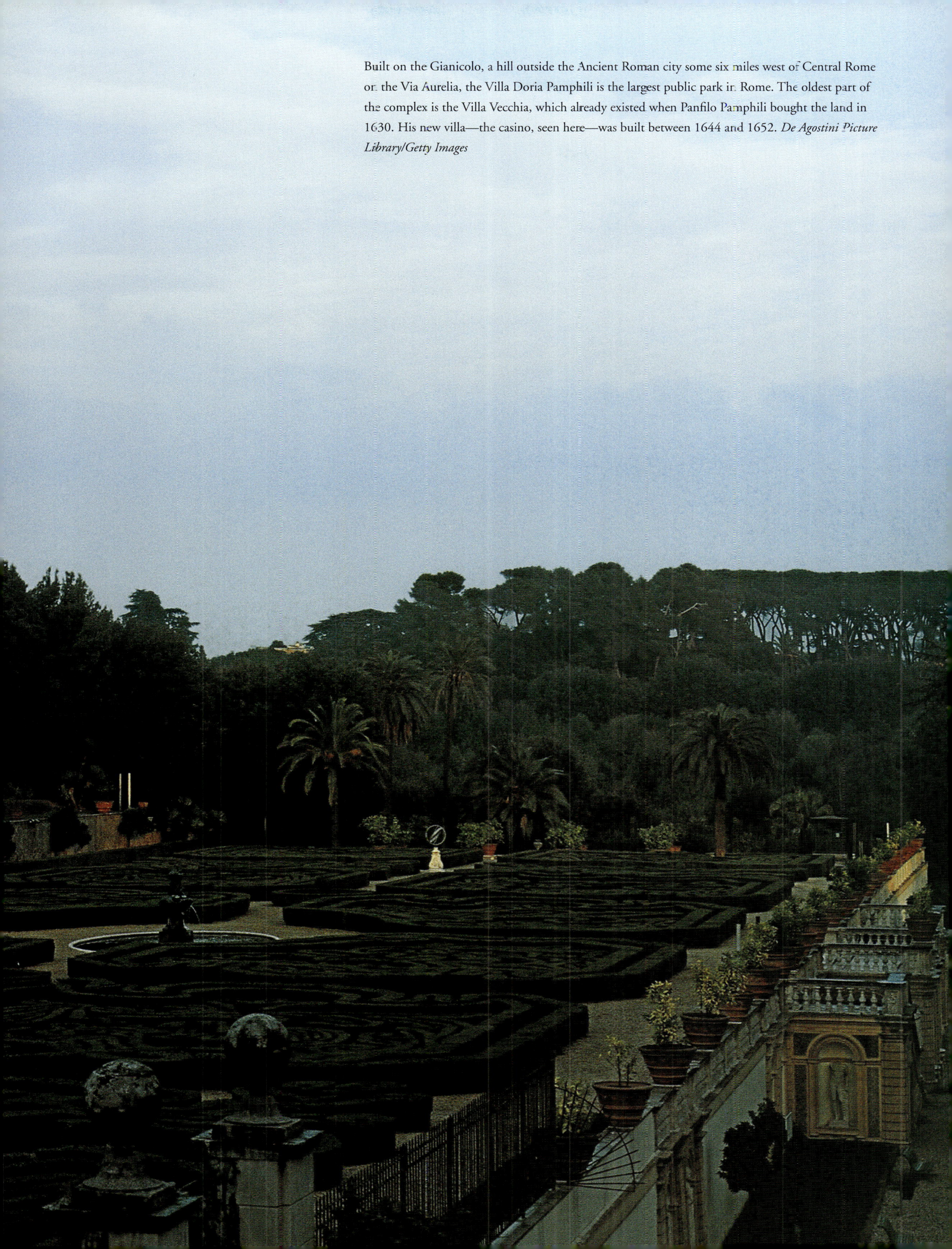

Built on the Gianicolo, a hill outside the Ancient Roman city some six miles west of Central Rome on the Via Aurelia, the Villa Doria Pamphili is the largest public park in Rome. The oldest part of the complex is the Villa Vecchia, which already existed when Panfilo Pamphili bought the land in 1630. His new villa—the casino, seen here—was built between 1644 and 1652. *De Agostini Picture Library/Getty Images*

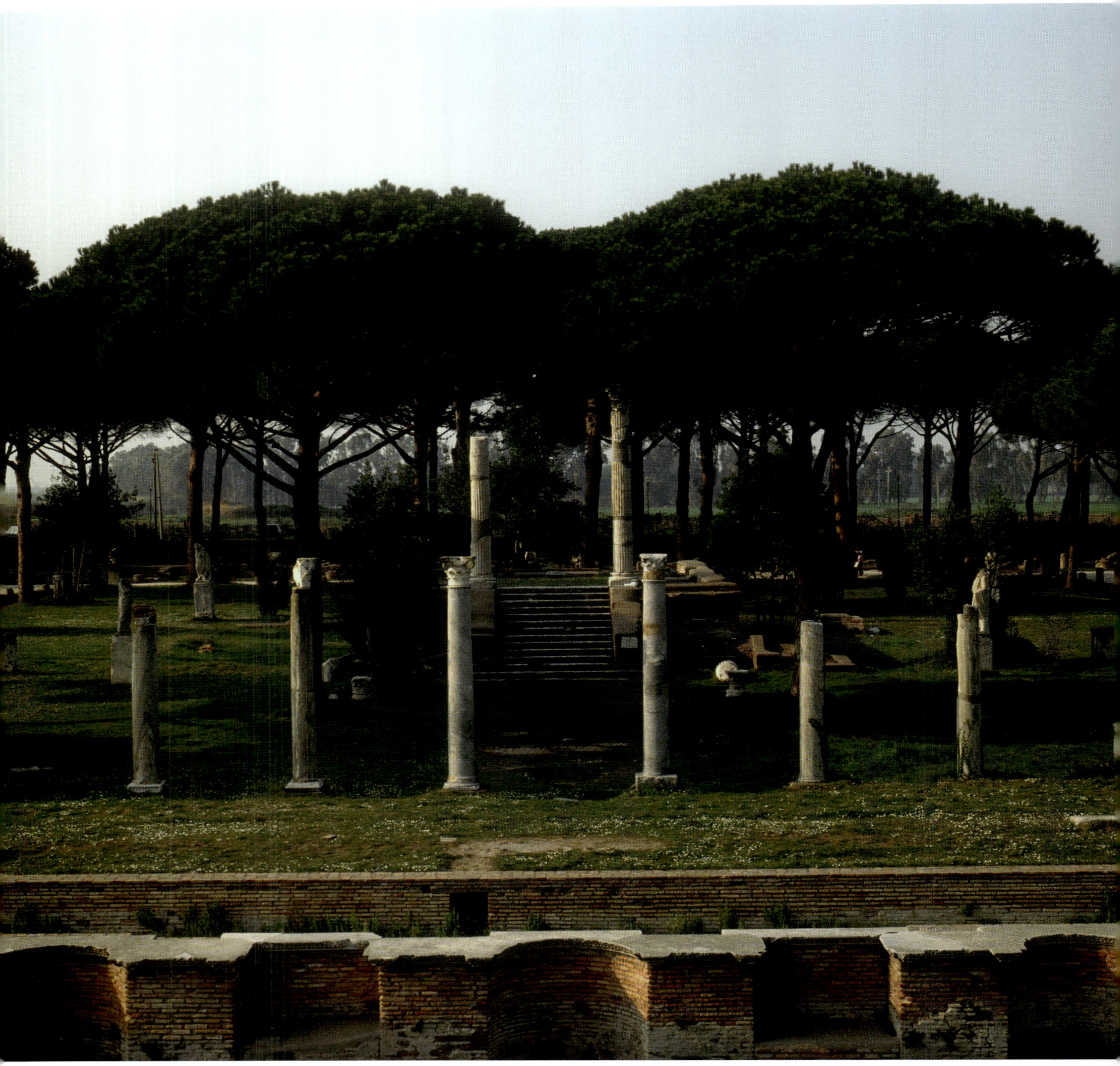

Above: View over Ostia's Square of the Guilds or the Corporations' Forum, about 350 feet long and 250 feet wide, that housed the offices of ship owners, guilds, and traders where day-to-day business was conducted. Floor mosaics, depicting the area occupied by each of the various businesses, remain. *The Bridgeman Art Library/Getty Images*

Above right: Roman inscriptions often start with the words "Senatus Populusque" ("the Senate and People") and its most famous use is in SPQR—Senatus Populusque Roma. This is the inscription that stood at the entrance to Ostia Antica.

Right: Located at the mouth of the River Tiber, Ostia was one of the ports of Rome. At one stage in the second/third century A.D. it was home to as many as 75,000, although it fell into ruin as its harbor silted up. Its houses and palaces provided building materials for many projects in Rome and Lazio—and even as far afield as Pisa, whose Leaning Tower is said to have been built from Ostian stone.

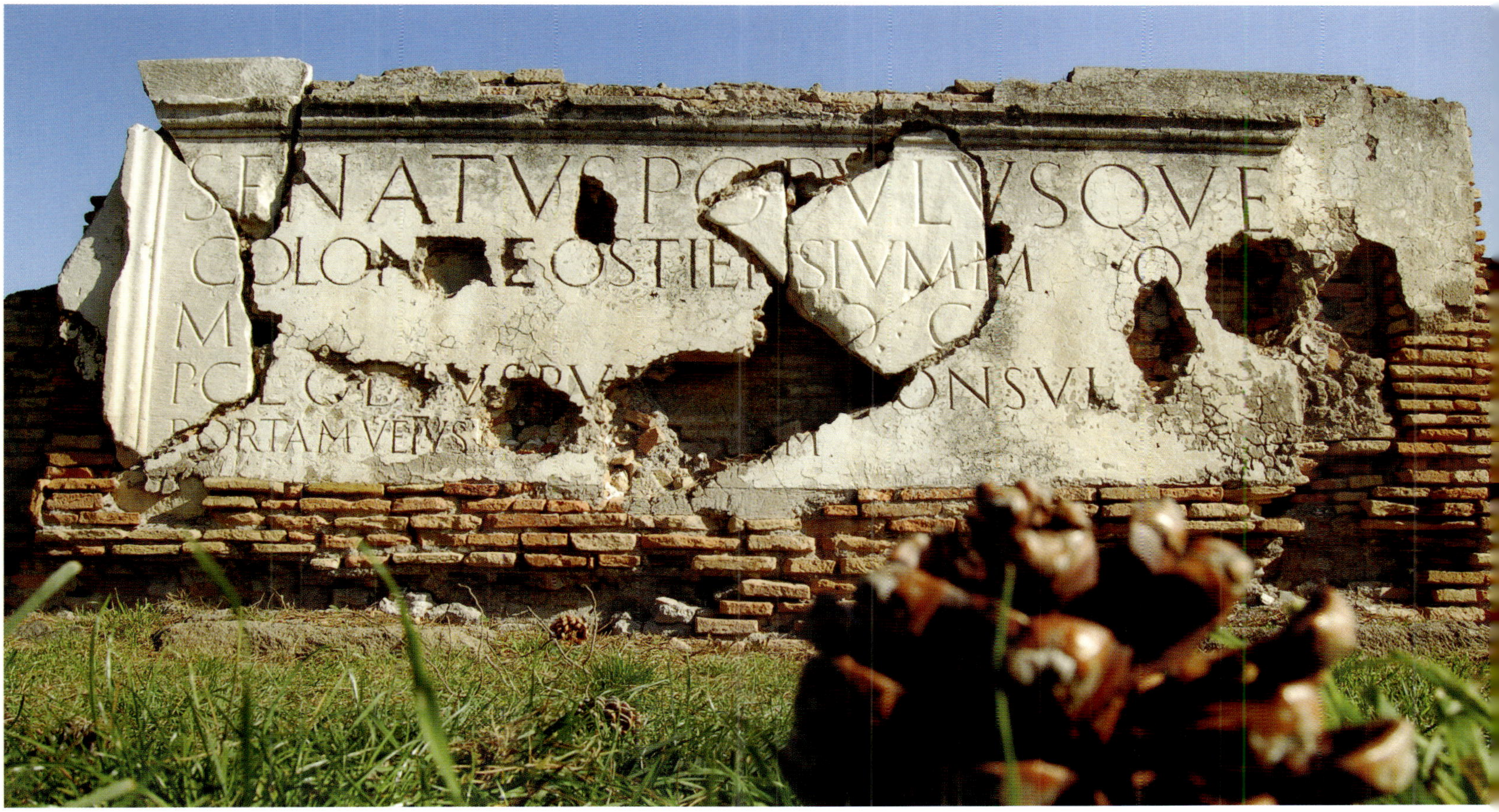

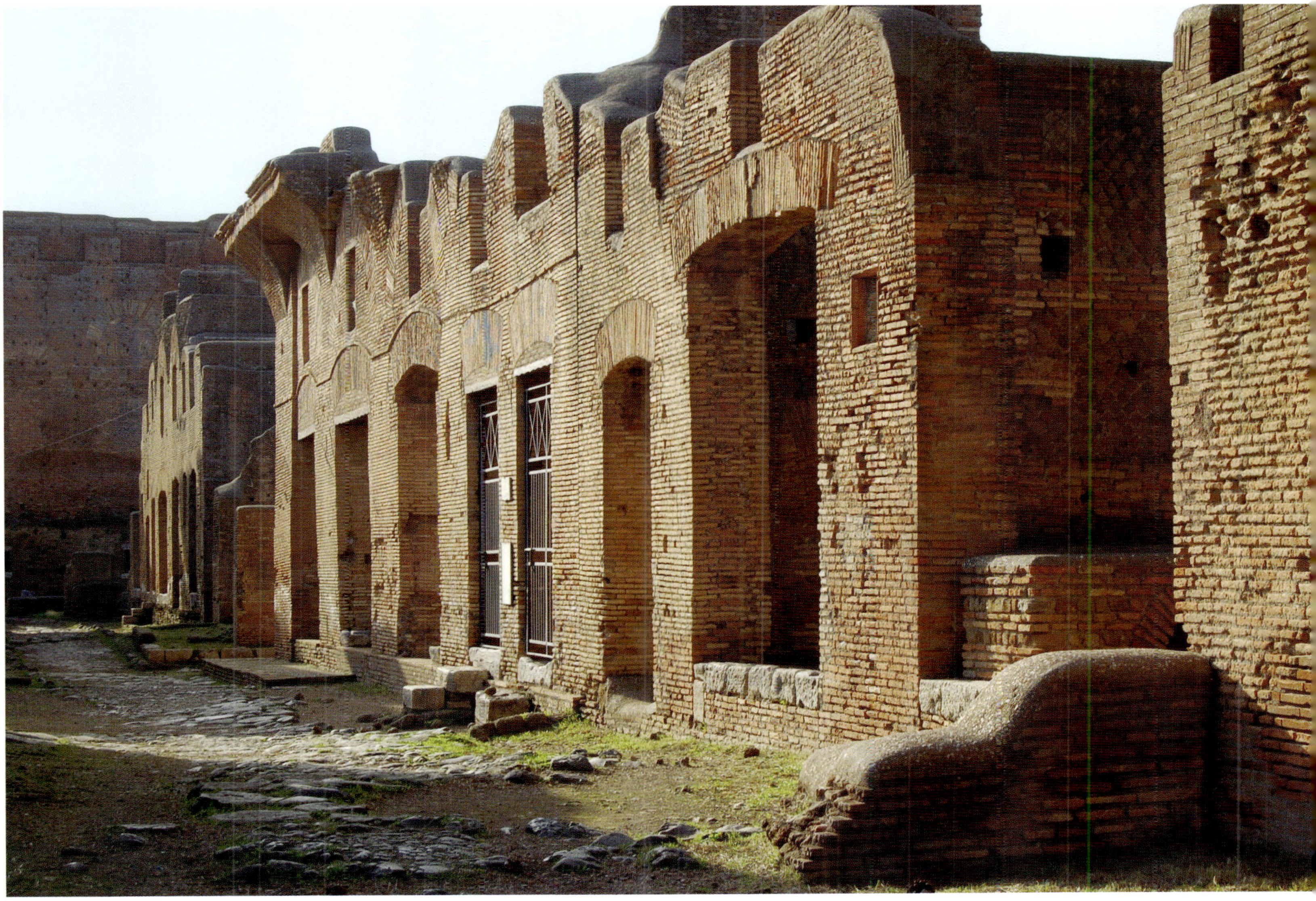

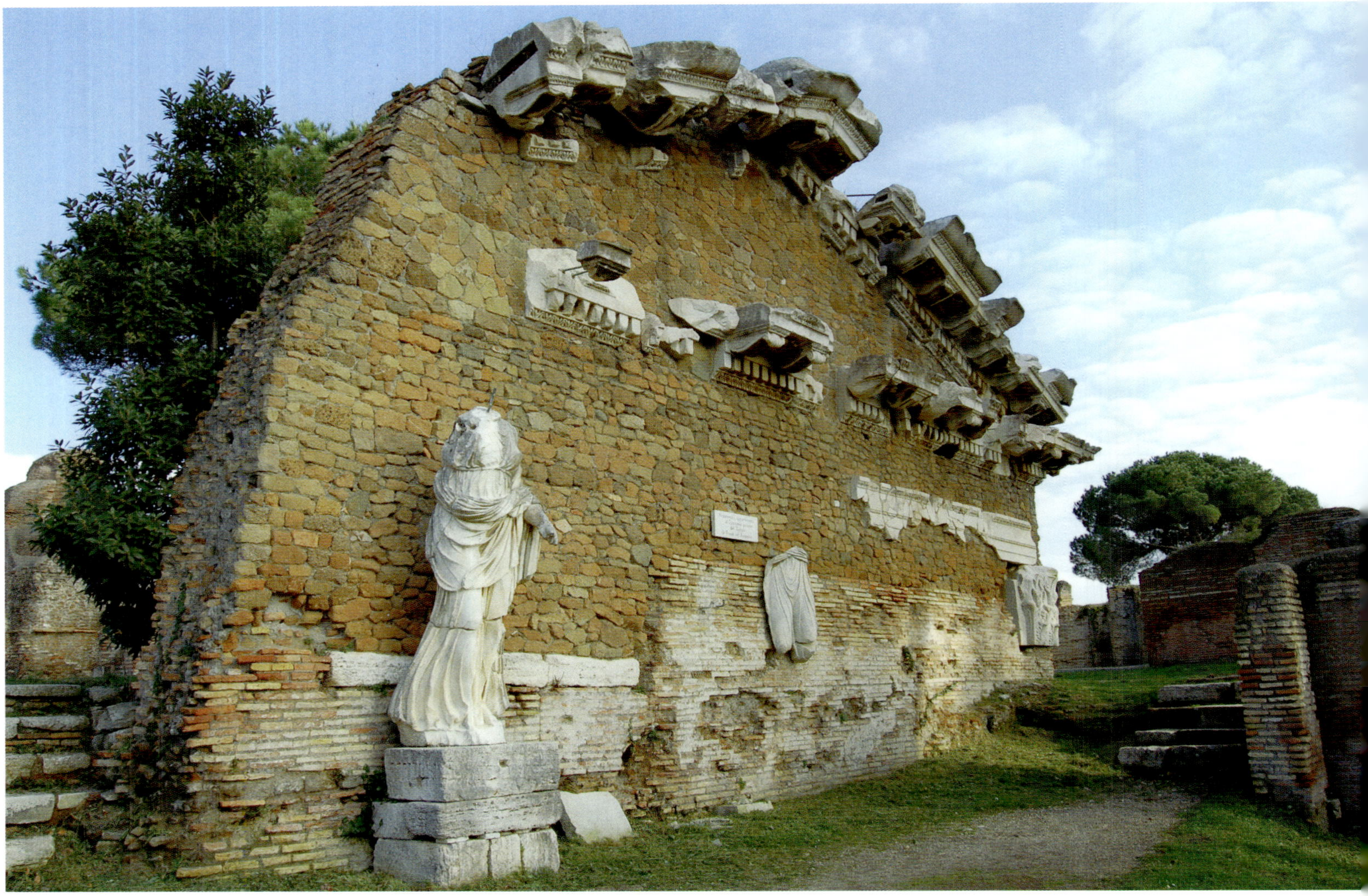

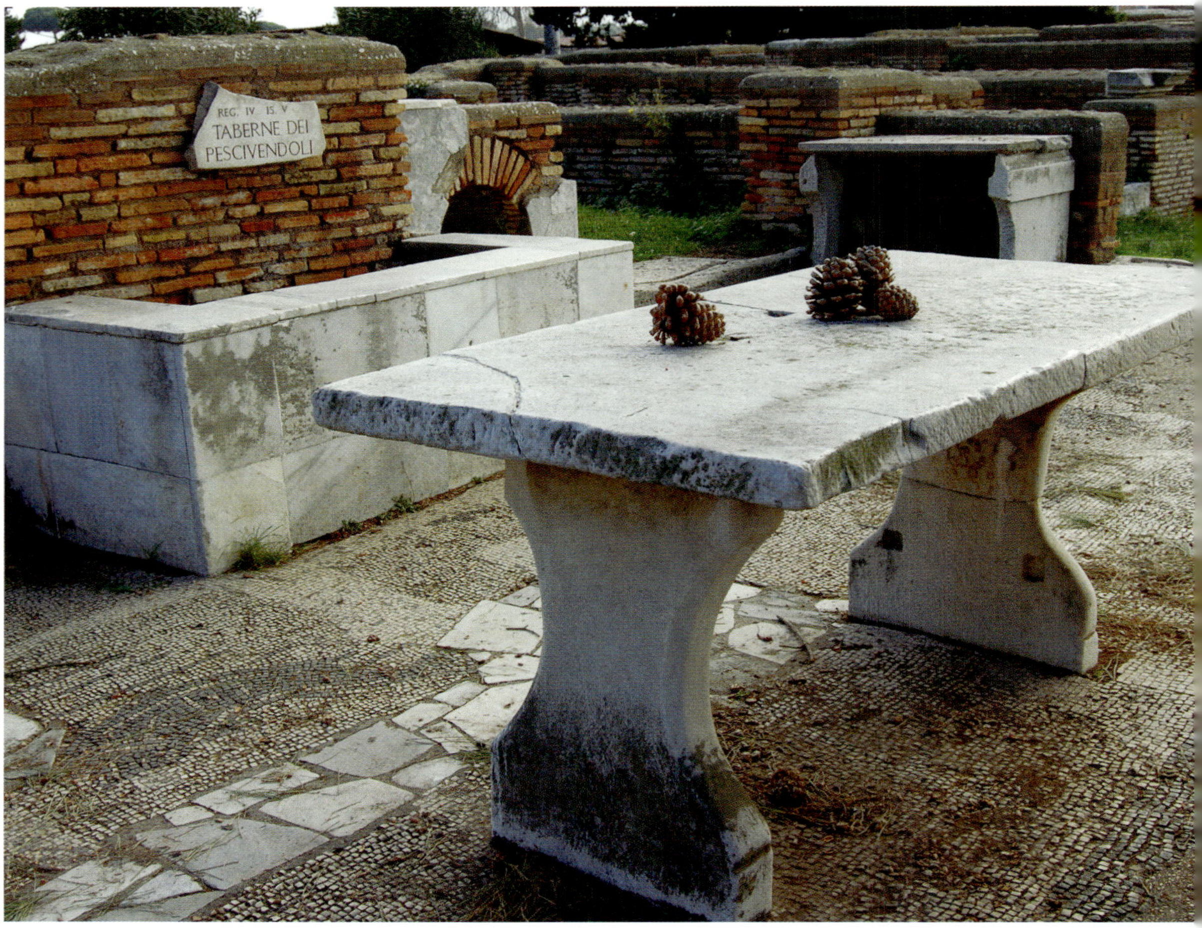

Above and Pages 56 and 57: Roman sculpture is often seen as being derivative of Greek work. It is true that Romans commissioned copies of Greek statues, but whereas the Greeks strove to reproduce perfection, the Romans wanted realism and produced lifelike statues, warts and all. Many of the Roman statues have suffered from attrition over the years. The barbarian invasions, wars over the centuries, religious concerns following the arrival of Christianity, and—probably the most destructive—burning marble to produce lime, all these factors have conspired to reduce the number of complete statues visible in Rome. These examples are from Ostia.

Right: A fishmonger's store in Ostia.

Far right: High angle view of the amphitheatre, Ostia. *De Agostini Picture Library/Getty Images*

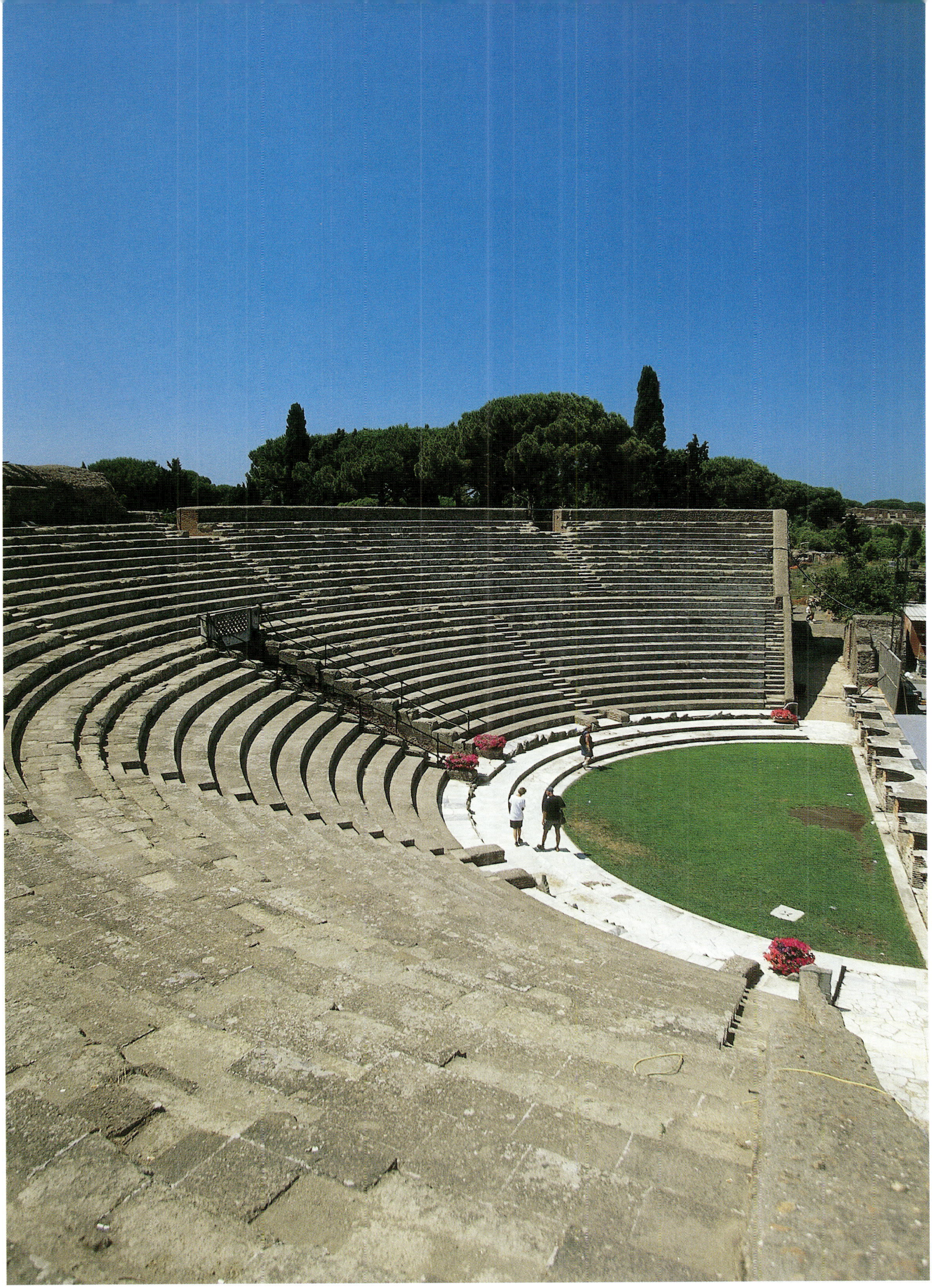

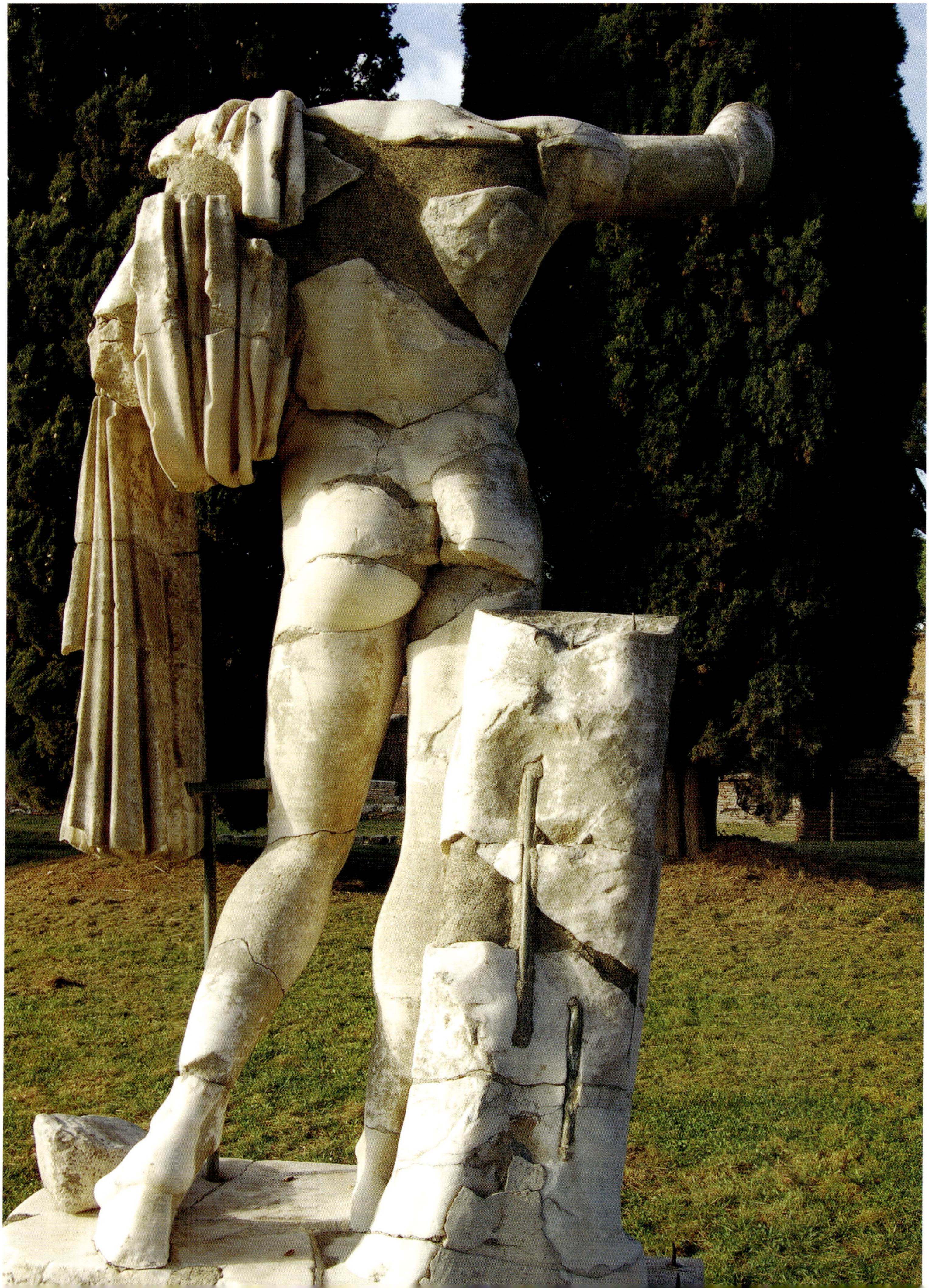

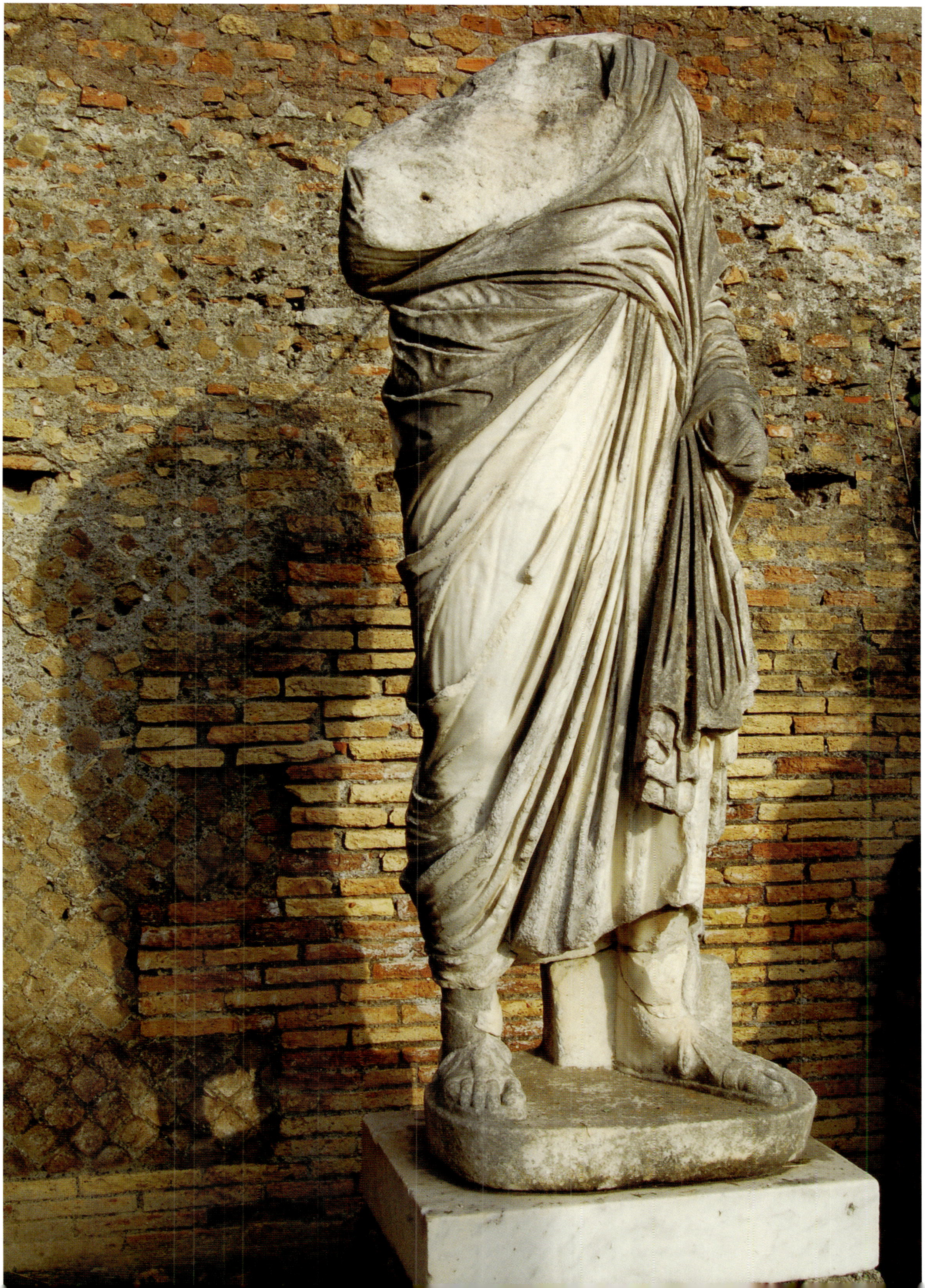

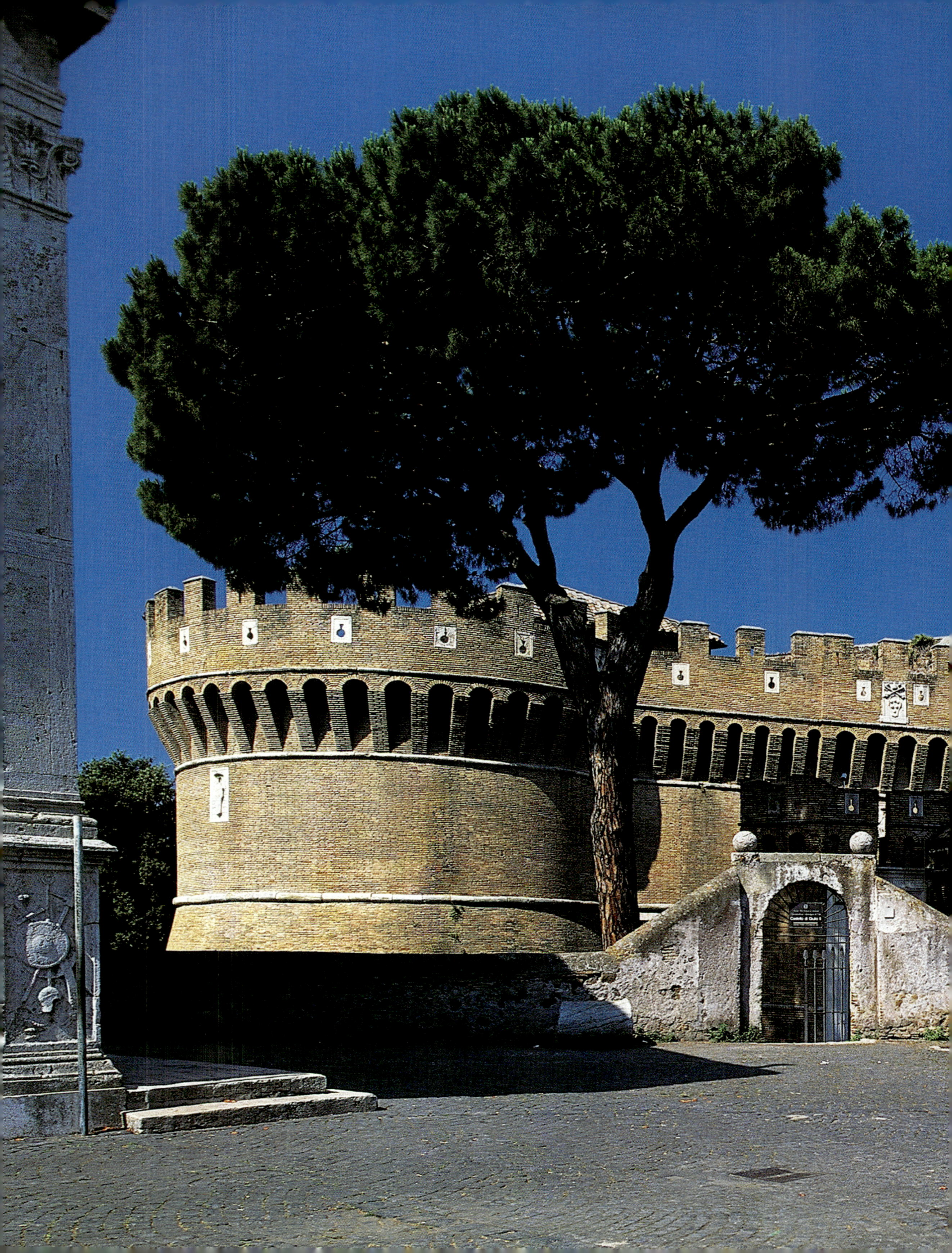

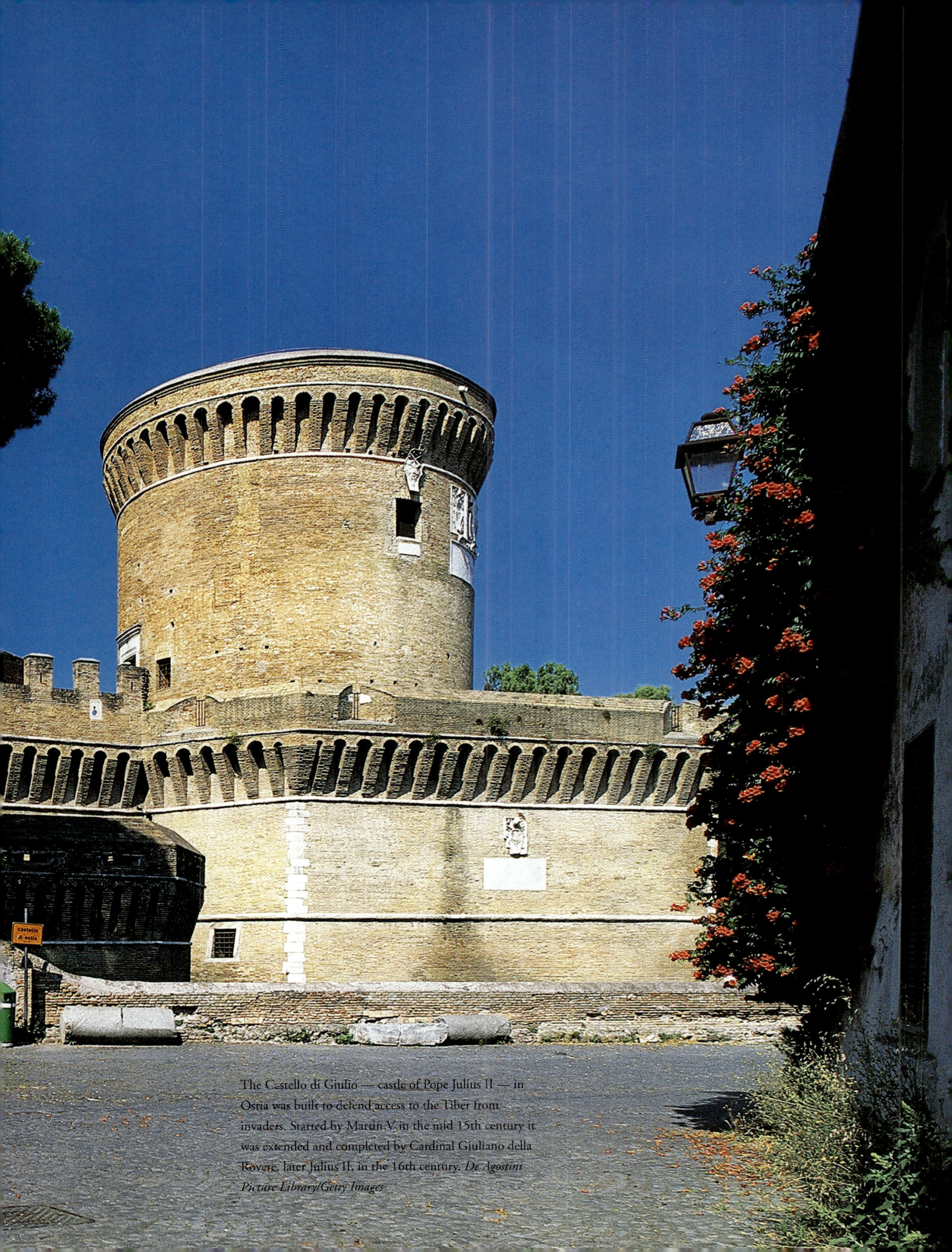

The Castello di Giulio — castle of Pope Julius II — in Ostia was built to defend access to the Tiber from invaders. Started by Martin V in the mid 15th century it was extended and completed by Cardinal Giuliano della Rovere, later Julius II, in the 16th century. *De Agostini Picture Library/Getty Images*

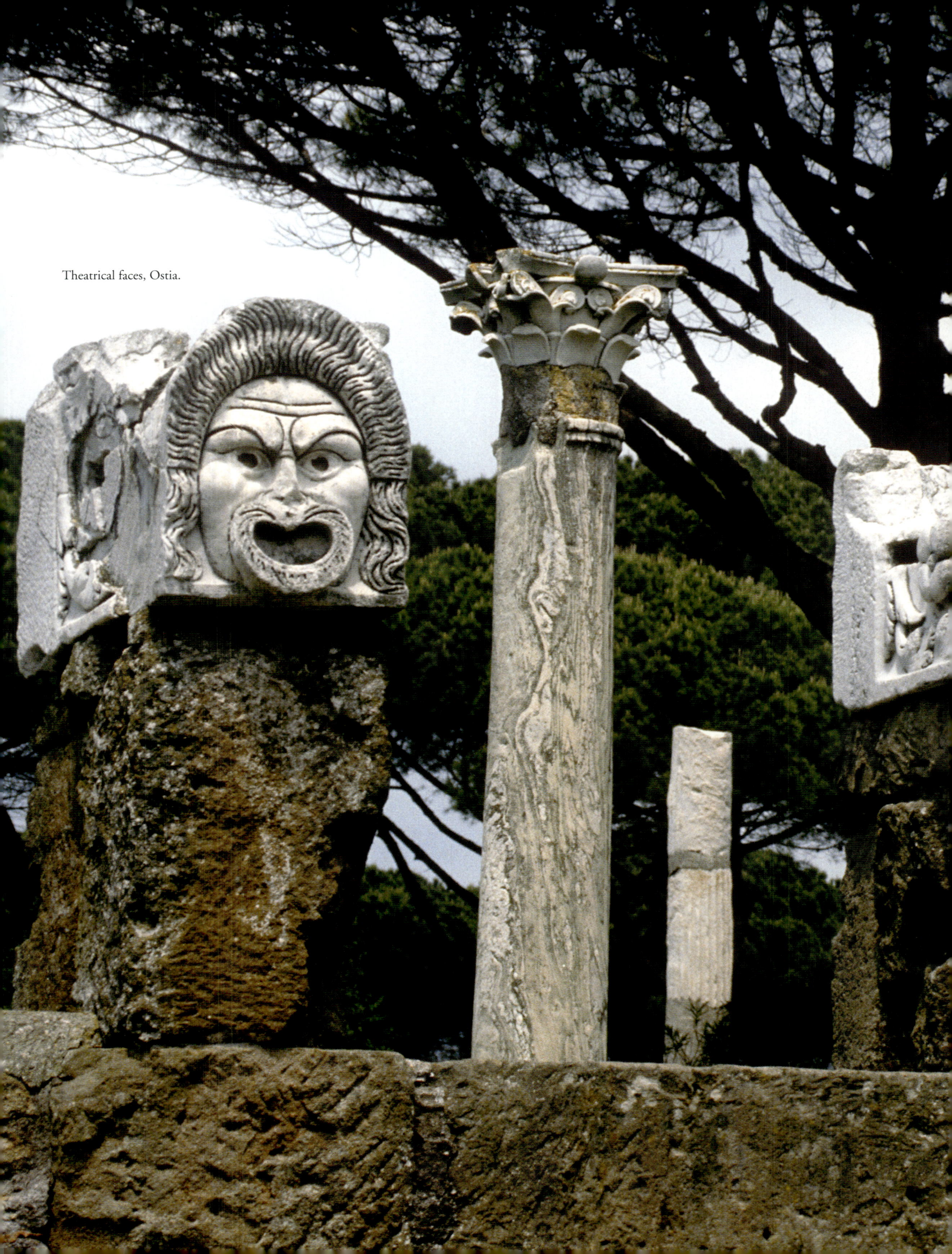

Theatrical faces, Ostia.

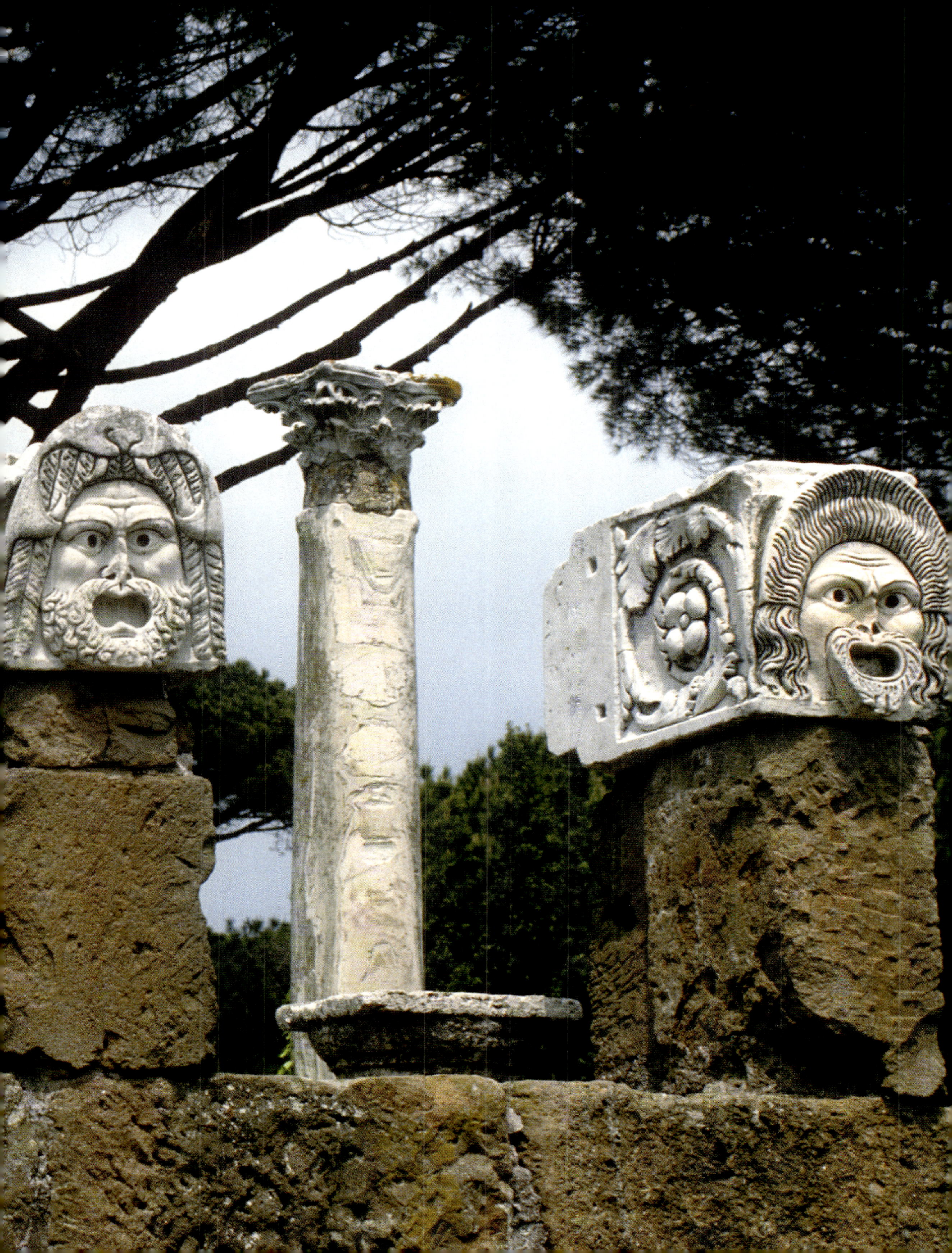

Imperial Rome

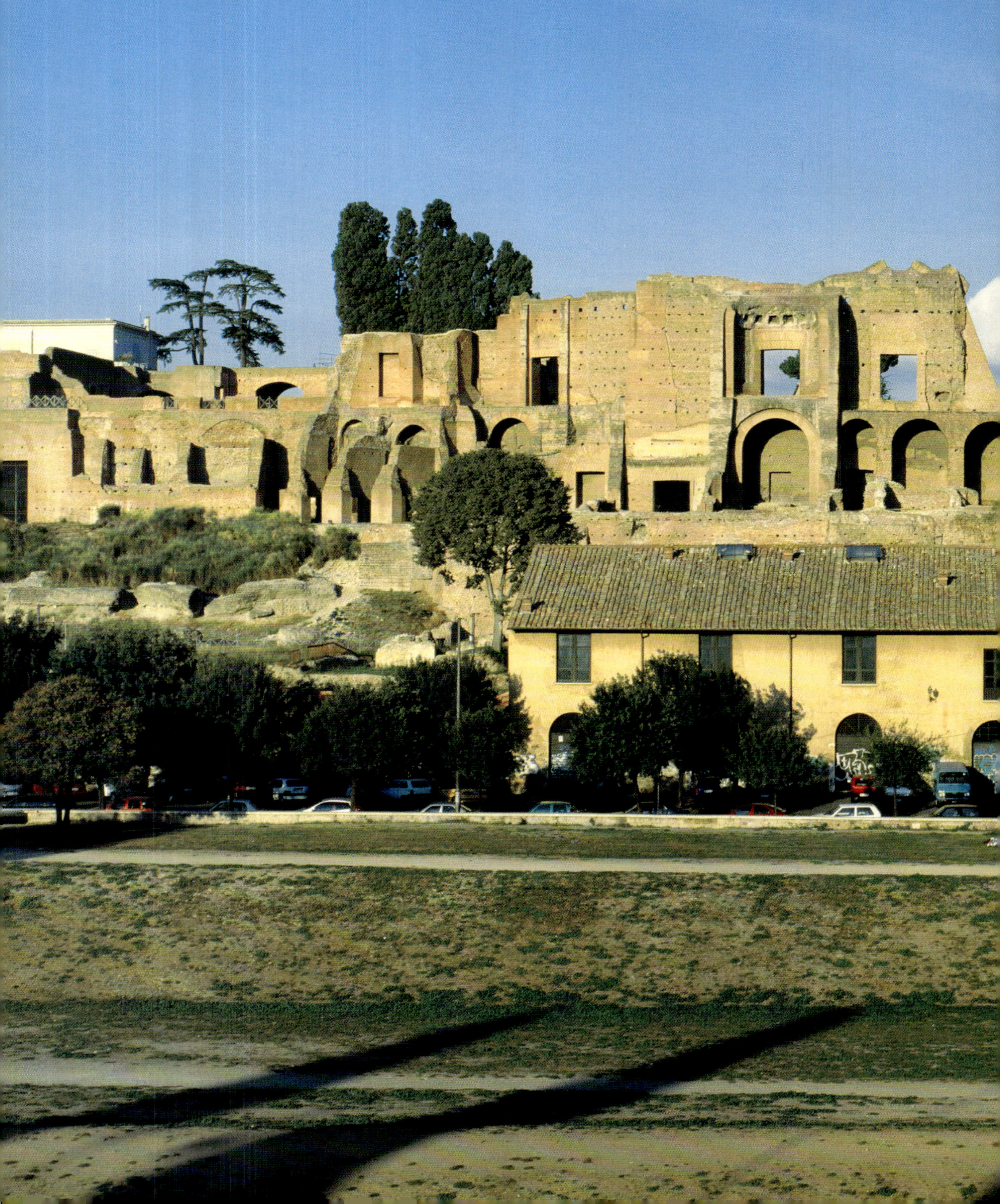

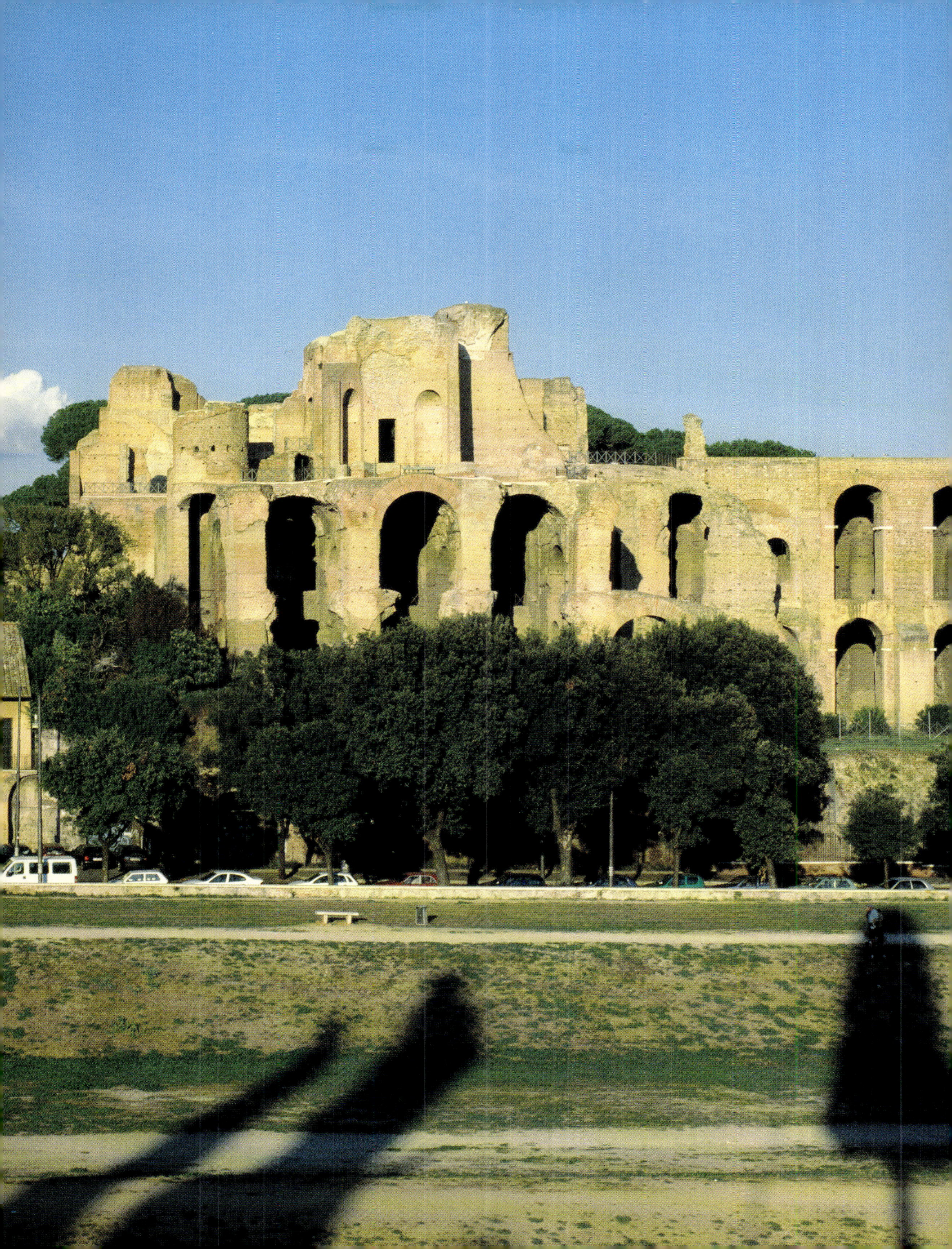

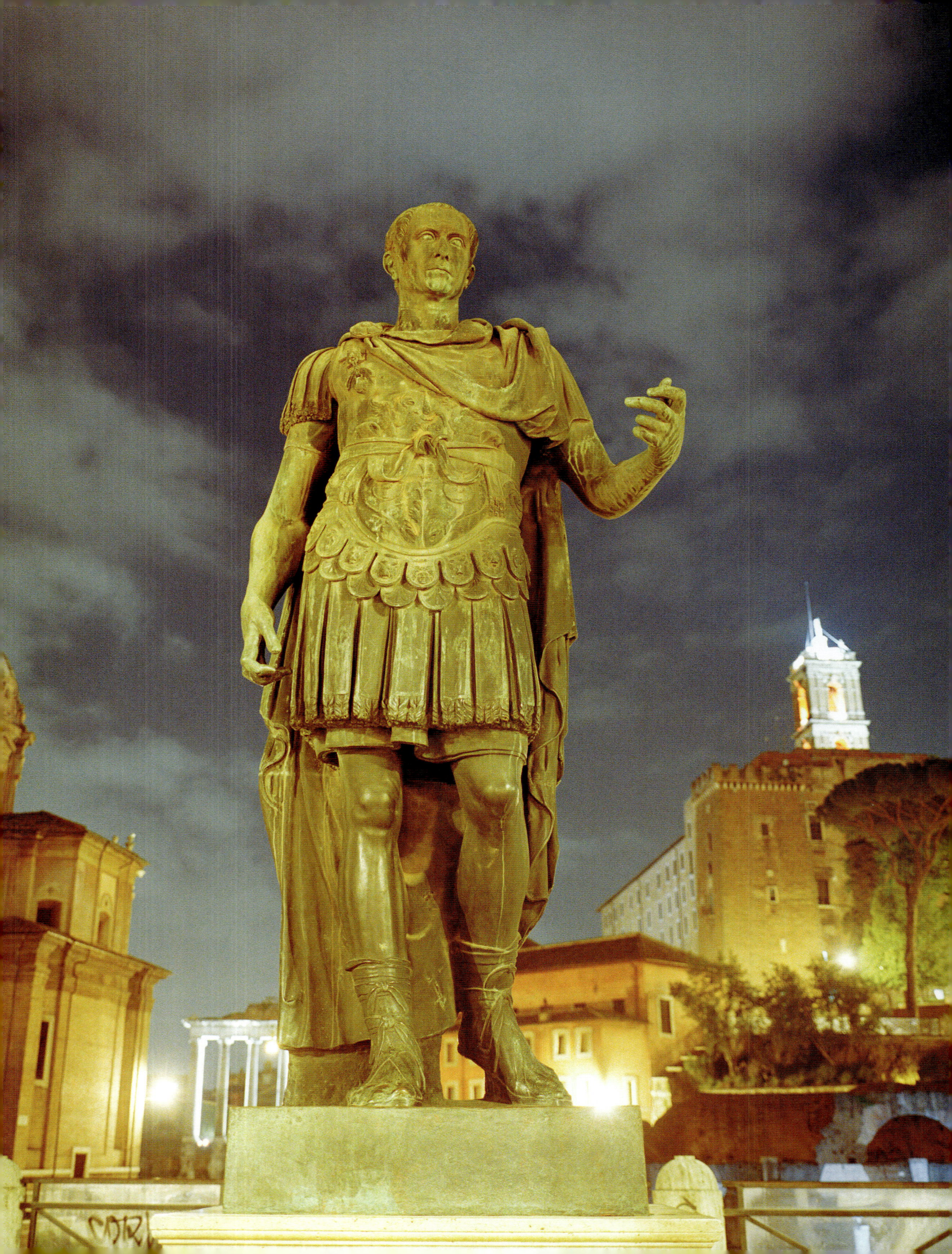

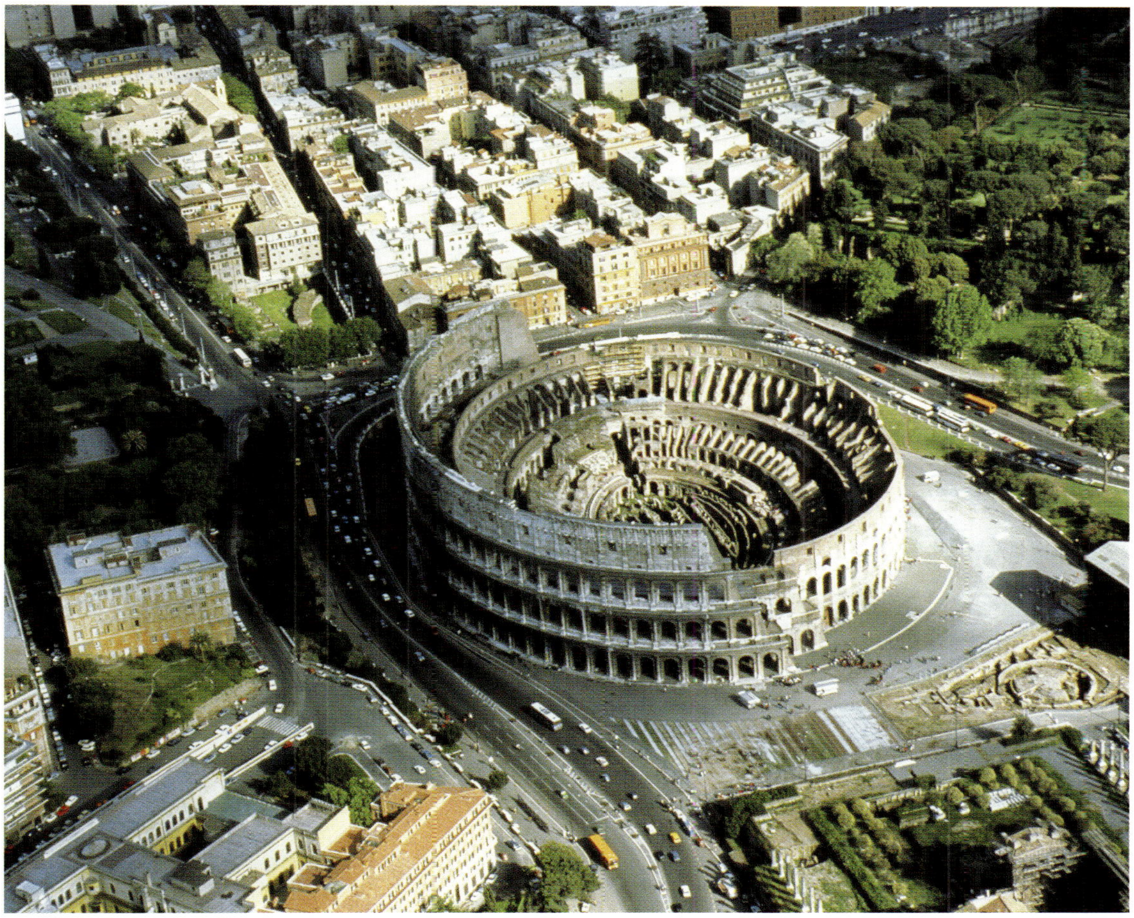

PAGES 62–63: Little was built on the scale of Imperial Rome until the Renaissance. *Getty Images/Panoramic Images*

FAR LEFT: Statue of Julius Caesar in front of the Roman Forum. *Silvia Otte/Photonica/Getty Images*

LEFT AND BELOW: The Colosseum is one of the largest surviving ancient Roman buildings. Construction started in 72 A.D. during the reign of Emperor Vespasian. It was completed by Vespasian's son, Titus, in 80 A.D. and was used until around 523 A.D. when earthquakes severely damaged the structure. Each spectator had a ticket with a specified entrance number corresponding to their individual status; the seating was divided into five areas with places allocated according to social class. The poorest people sat at the very top and the aristocrats alongside the emperor. *Jean Pragen/Stone/Getty Images*

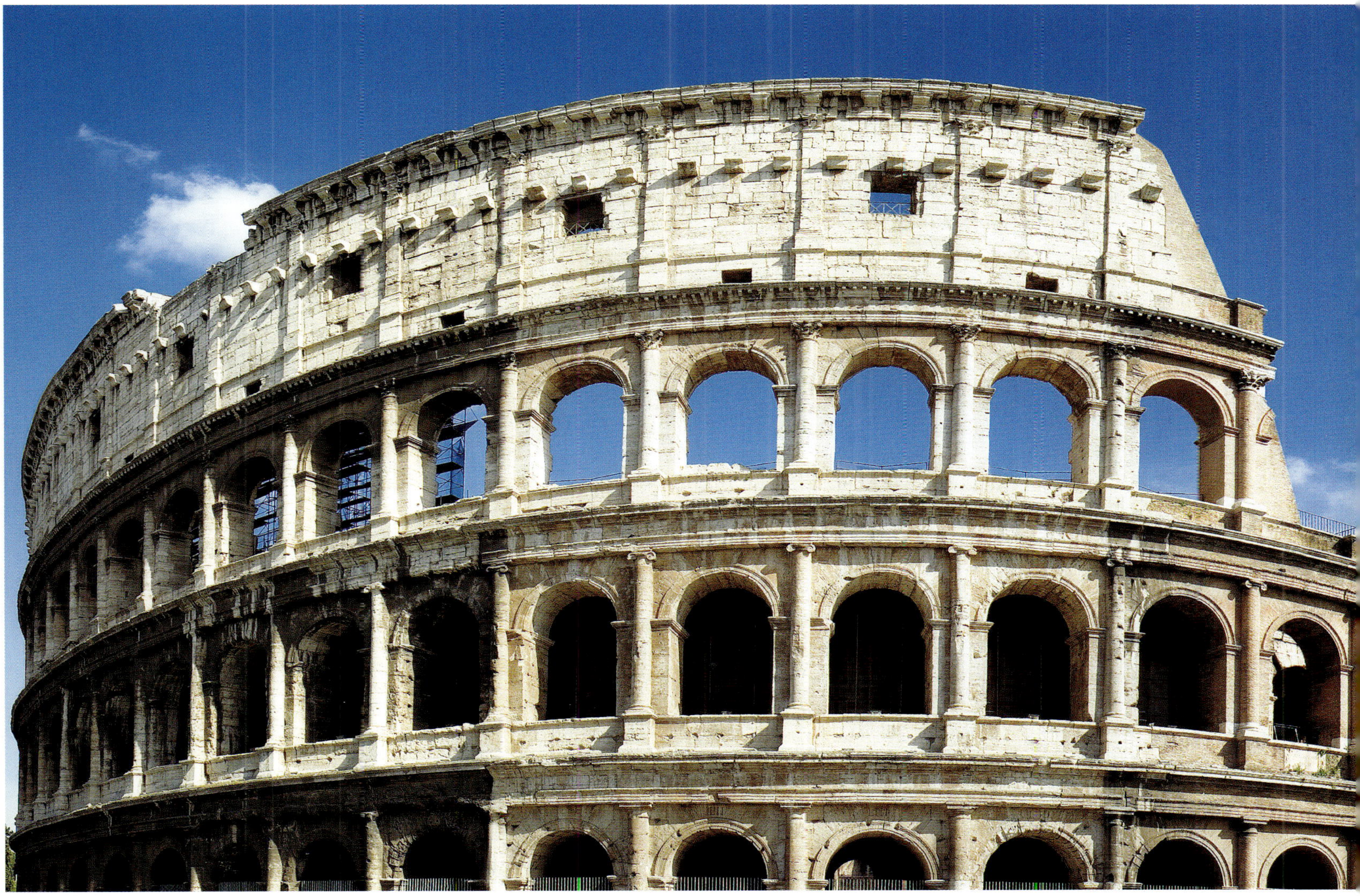

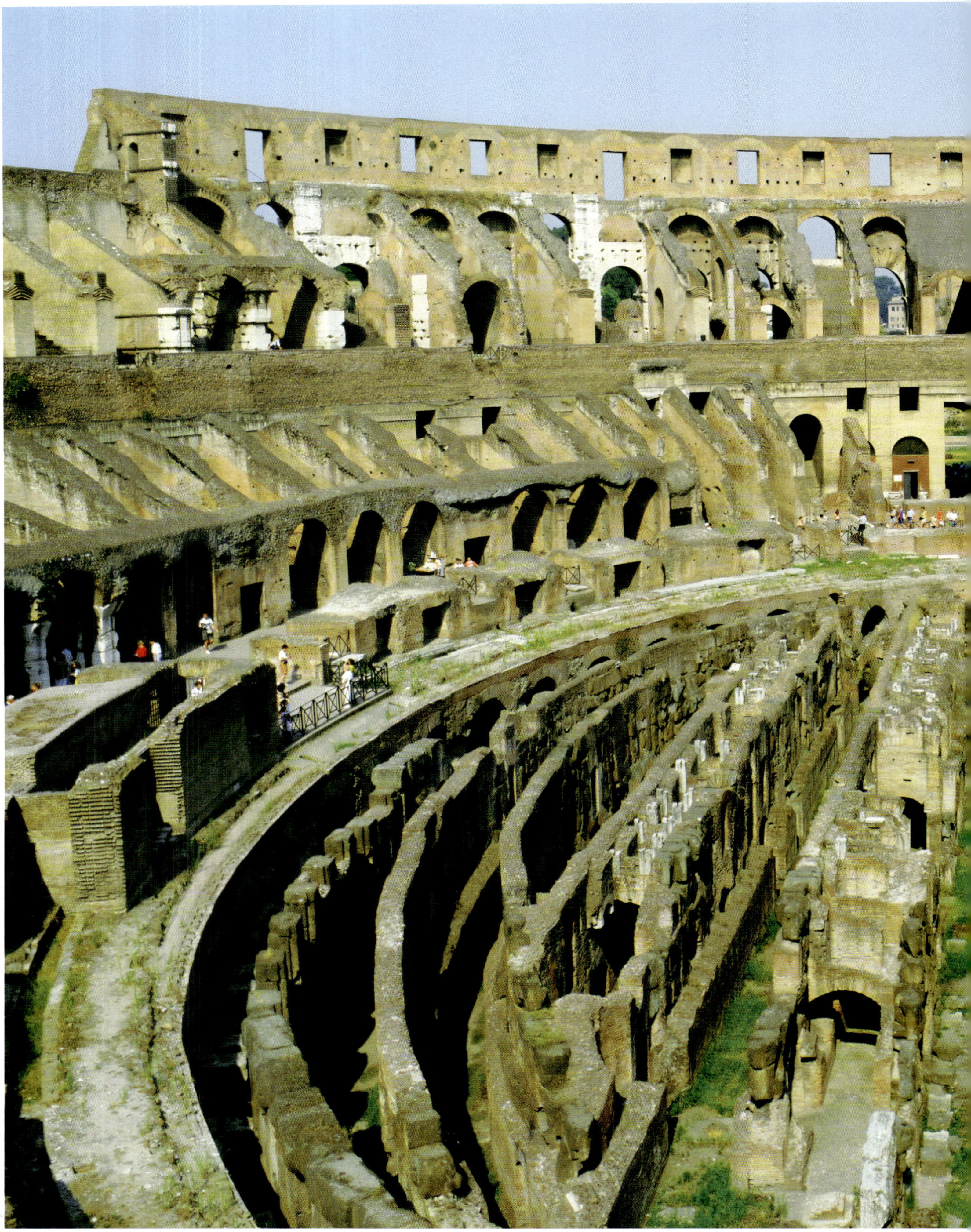

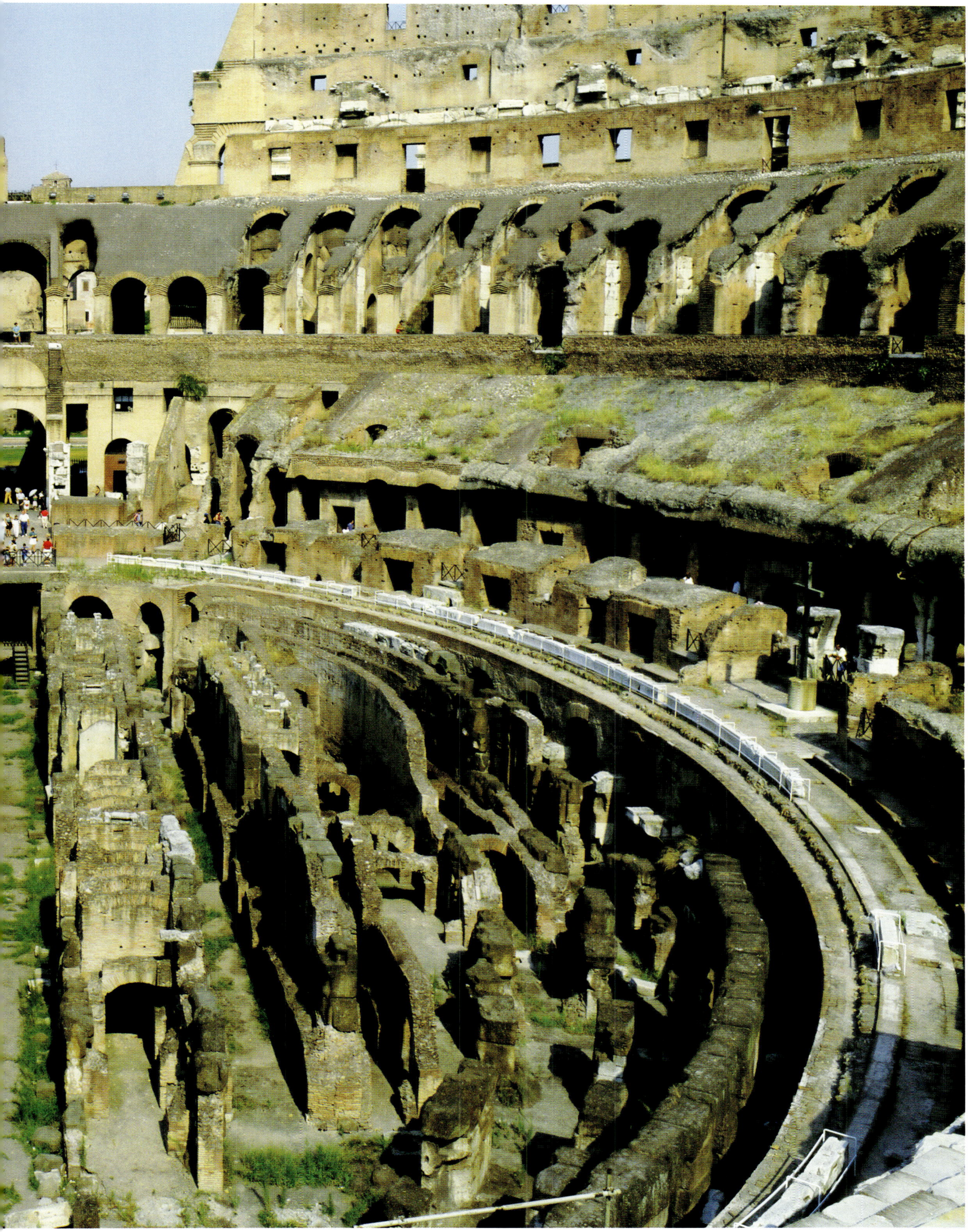

PAGES 66 AND 67, RIGHT, AND PAGES 70–71: The Colosseum was originally known as the Flavian Amphitheater and was used for gladiatorial combat until Christianity made this type of entertainment unacceptable. The interior of the Colosseum collapsed in antiquity and the structures we see today are the remains of a series of underground passages and holding cells, machinery areas, and wild animal cages. The original floor was made of wood, filled with trapdoors, and could be raised or lowered depending on the entertainment required. The arena could also be flooded for maritime spectaculars. *Jeff Hunter/The Image Bank/Getty Images; Julia Thorne/Robert Harding World Imagery/Getty Images*

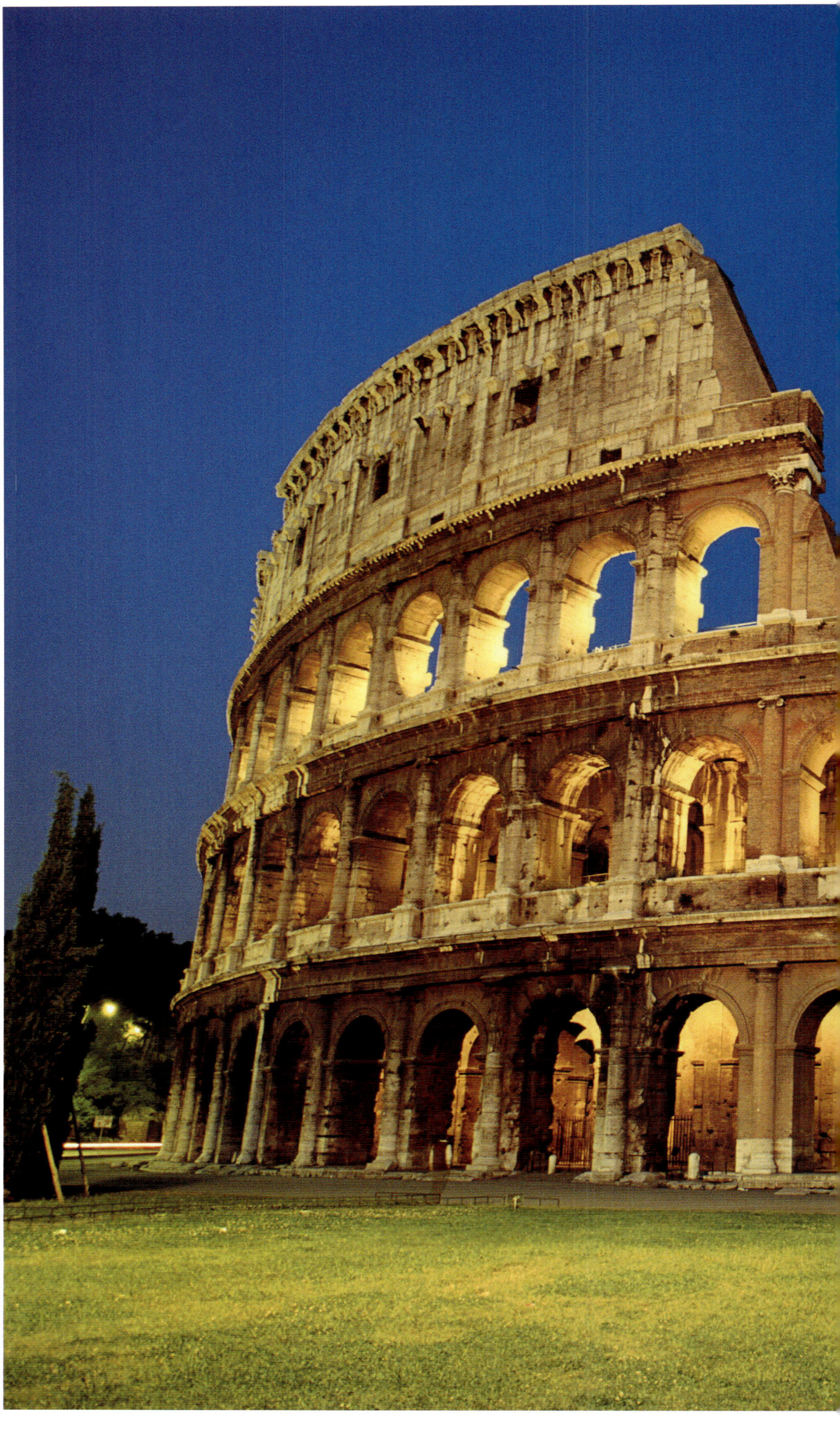

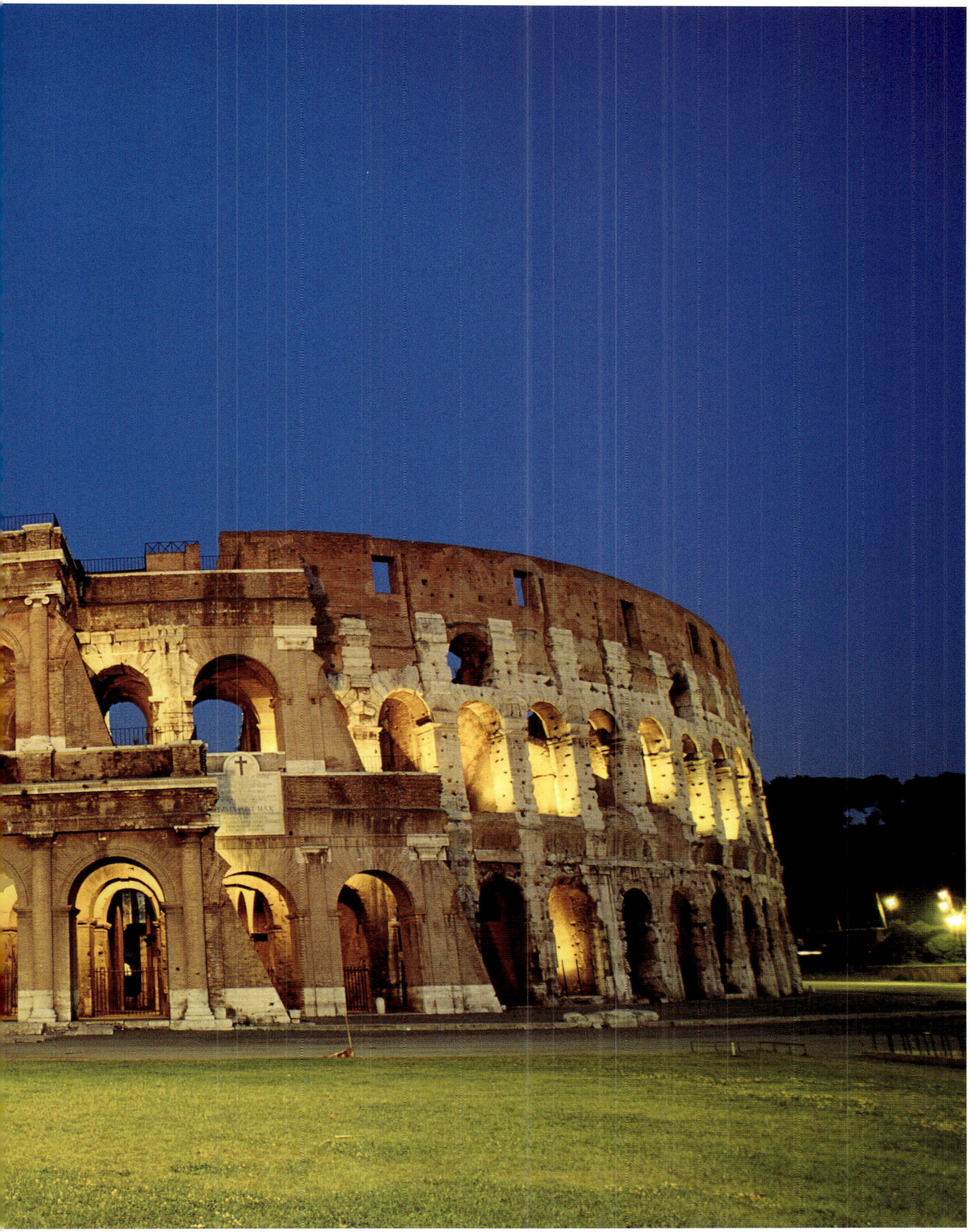

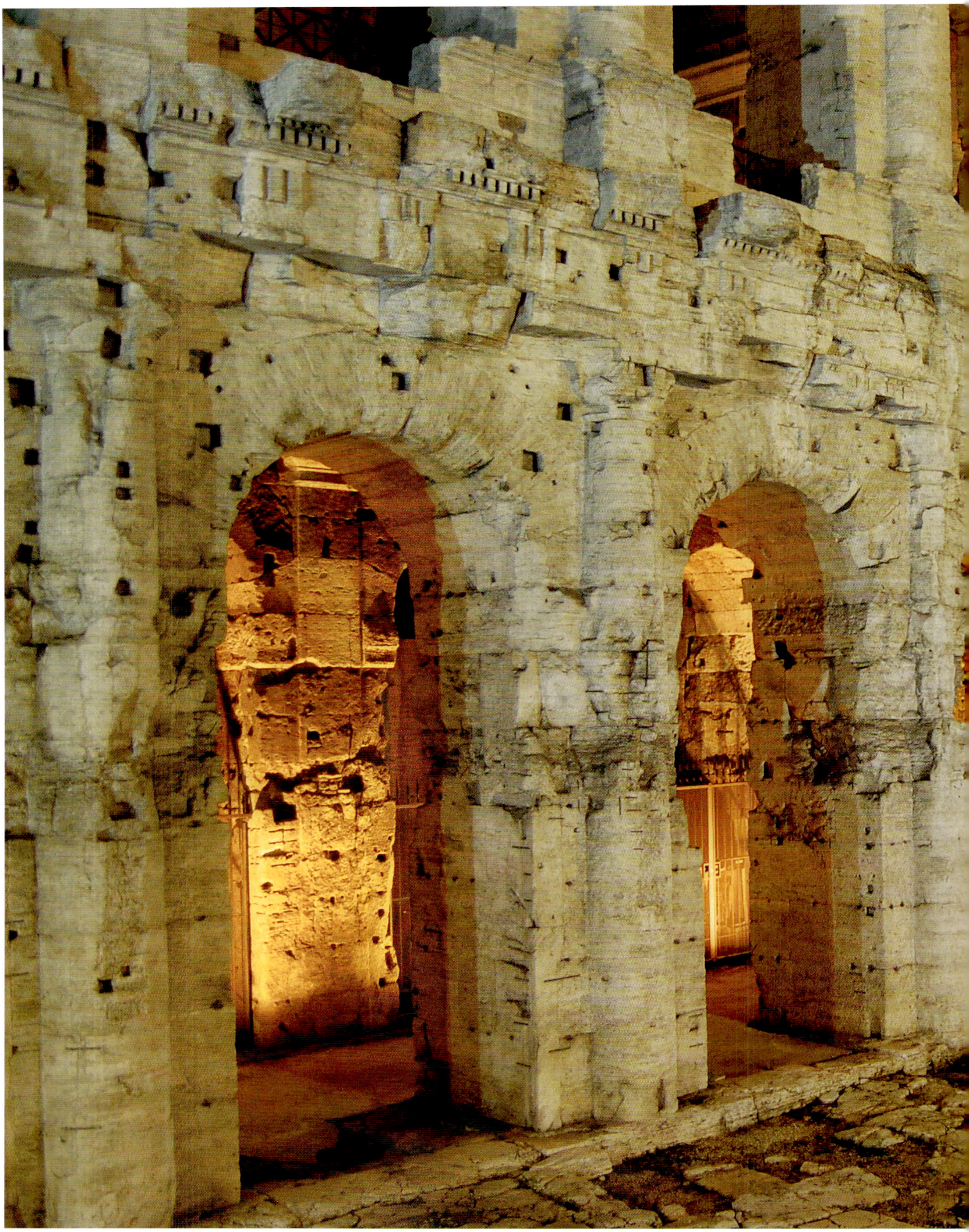

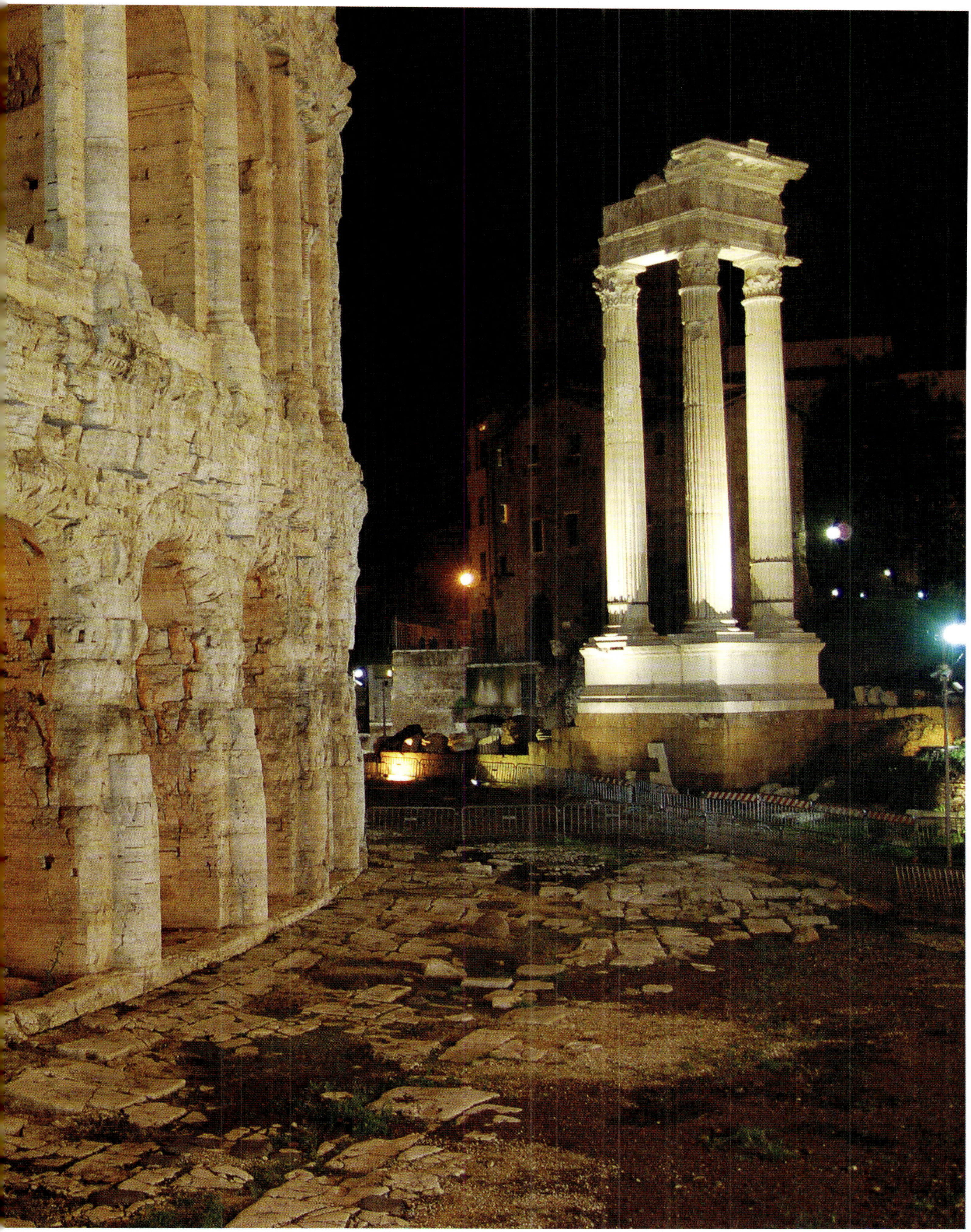

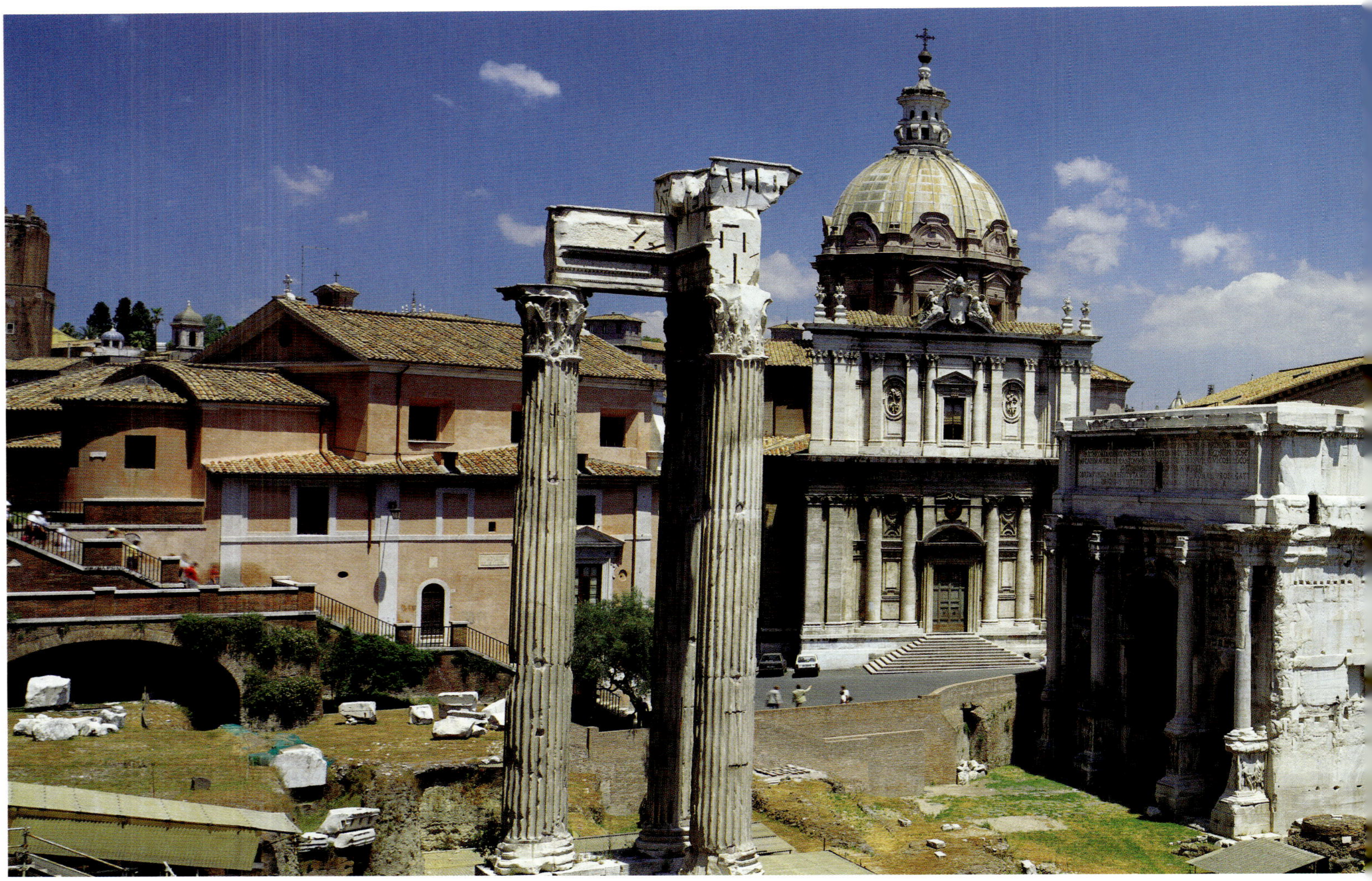

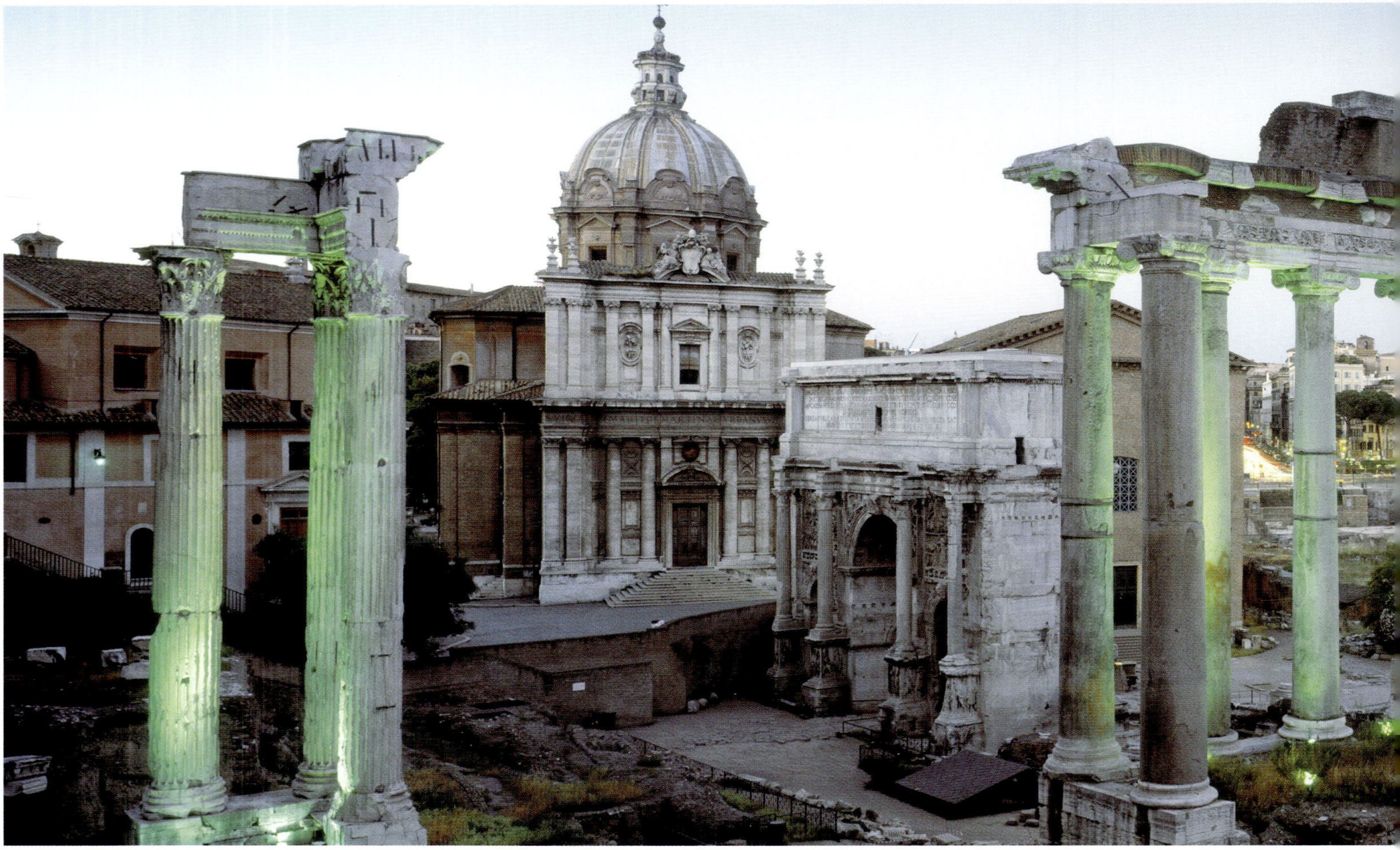

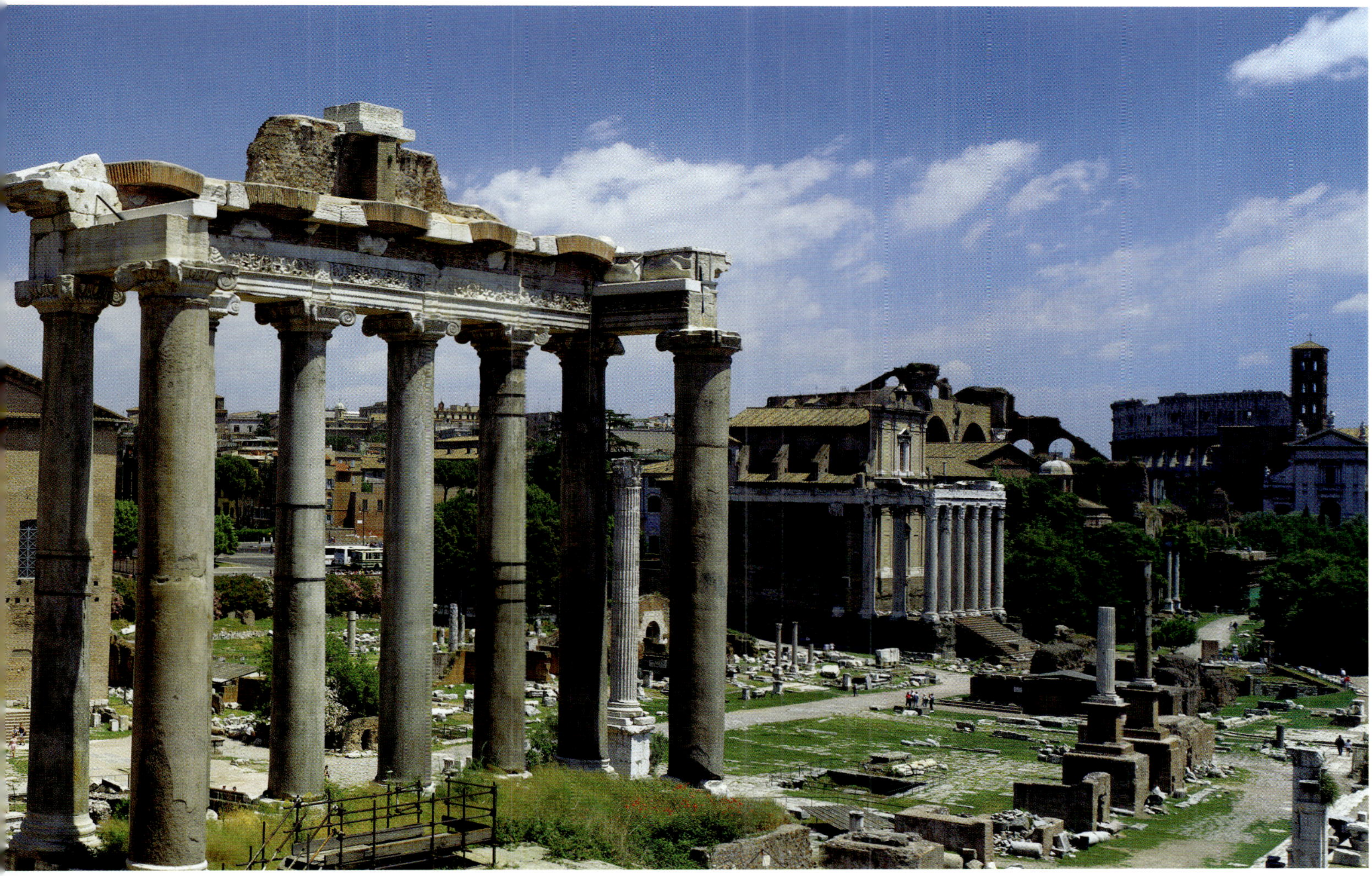

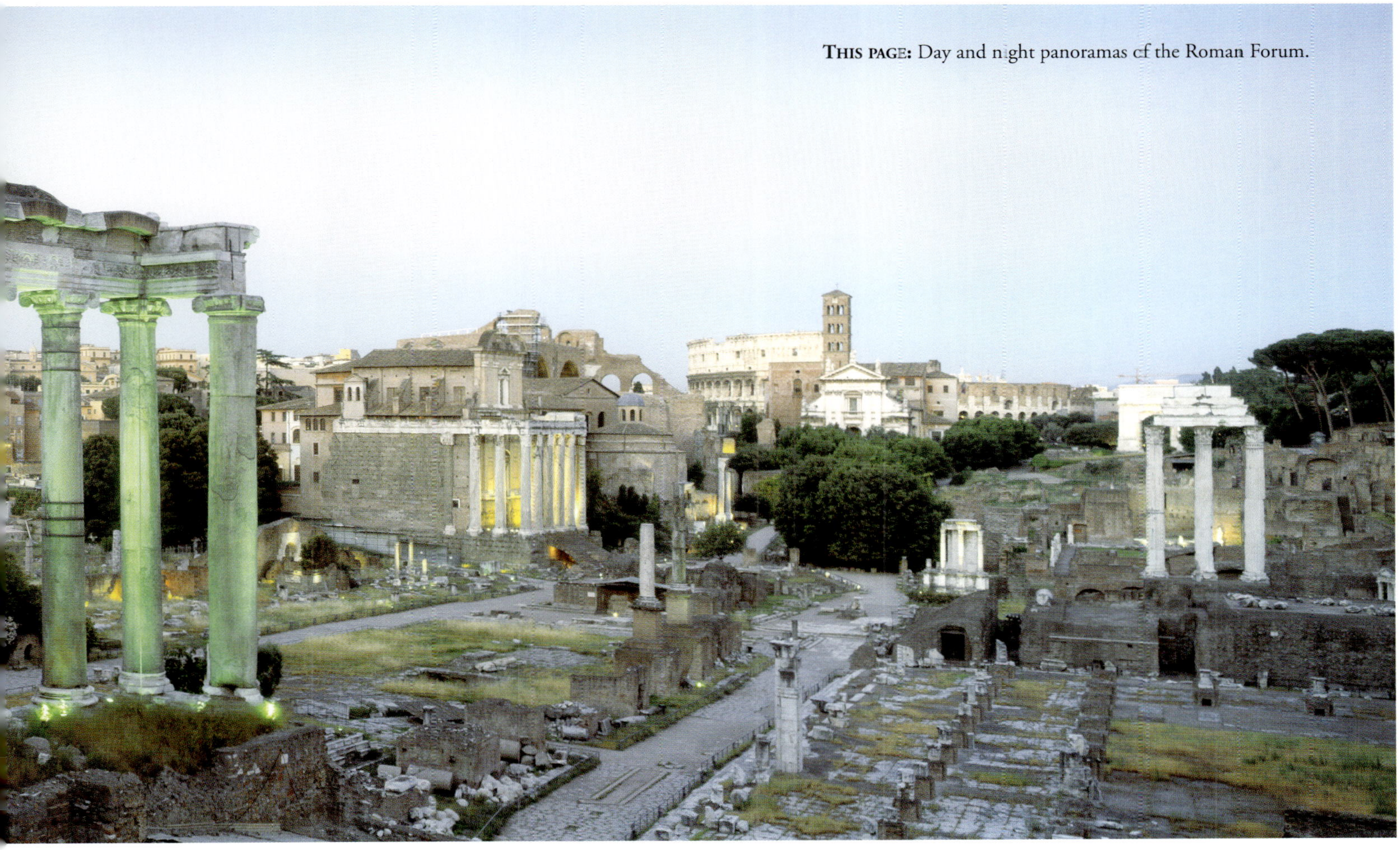

THIS PAGE: Day and night panoramas of the Roman Forum.

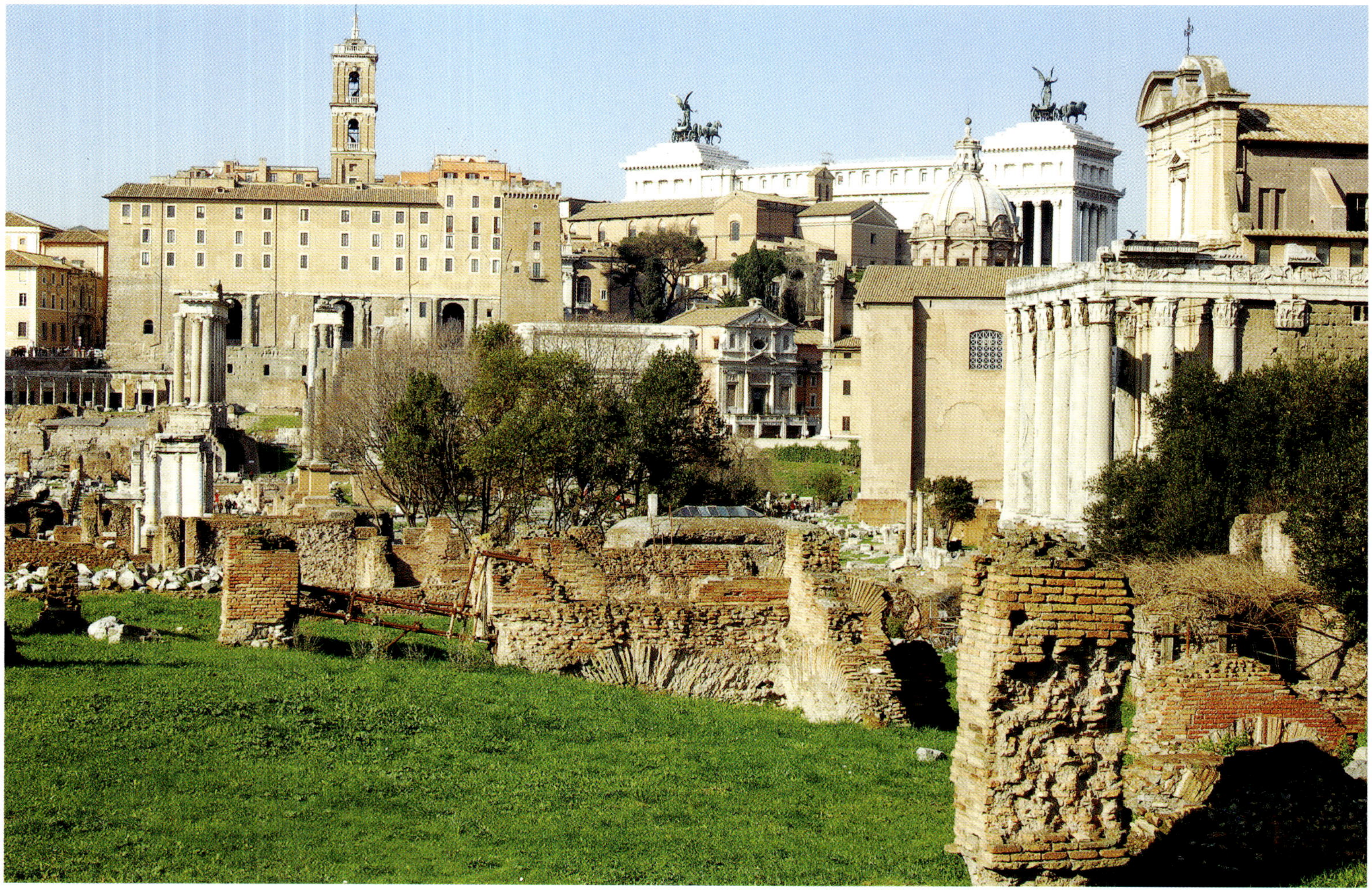

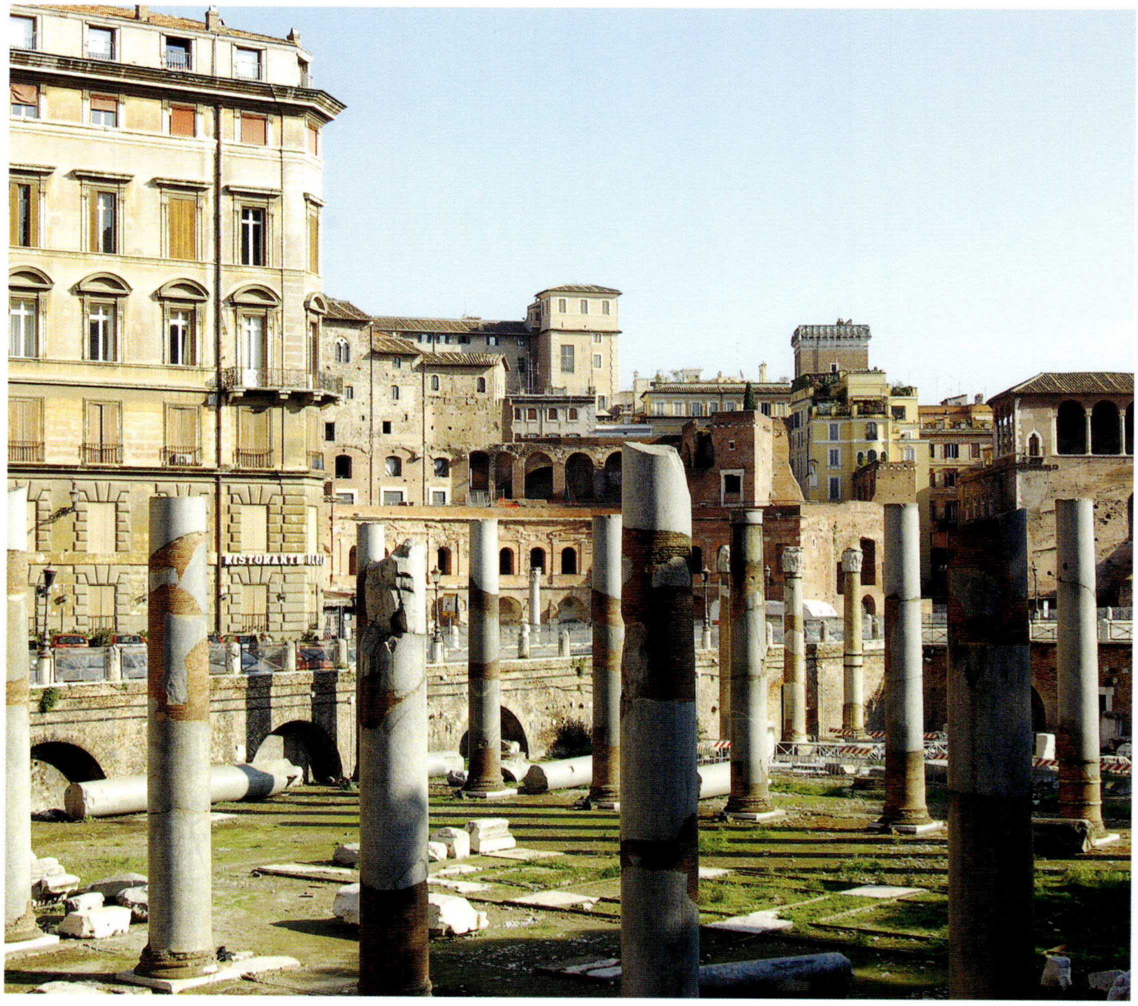

Above, Right, Opposite, and Pages 76–77: The political, administrative, and religious center of ancient Rome was the Forum. The earliest was the Roman Forum (see pages 72–73). After the decline of the Roman Empire the area was used to graze cattle, at which time it was called Campo Vaccino—the cattle field—and many of the buildings were canabalized for their stone. The forum did not reappear until archaeological excavations started in the 19th century by which time many of the remains were completely buried under many feet of soil. There were many other fora, including Trajan's forum (**Right and Pages 76–77**). This was probably built on Trajan's orders and financed by the spoils of war from the conquest of Dacia, which ended in 106 A.D.
Altrendo Travel/Getty Images (right); *The Bridgeman Art Library/Getty Images* (both page 76); *Joel Sartore/National Geographic/Getty Images* (page 77)

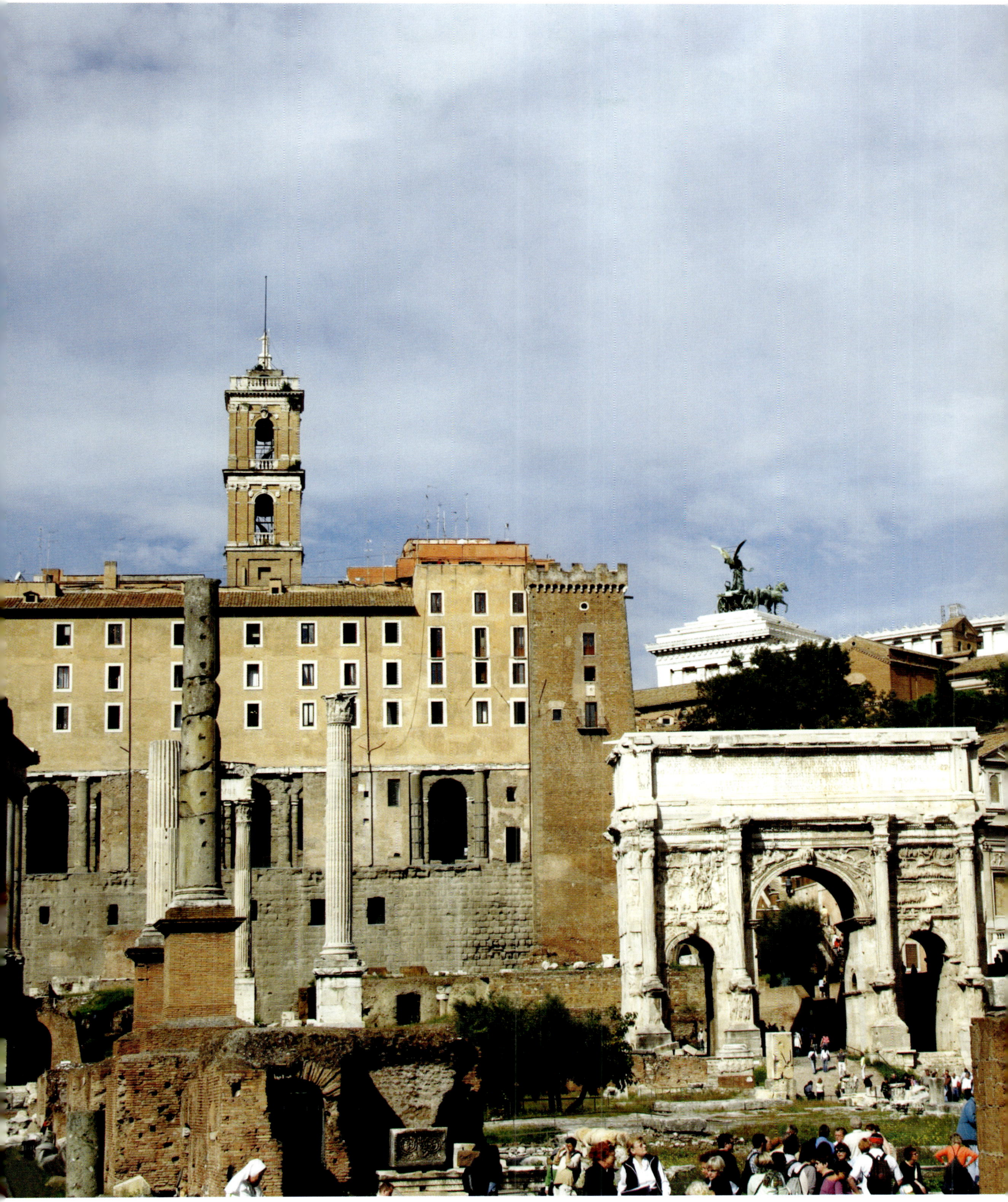

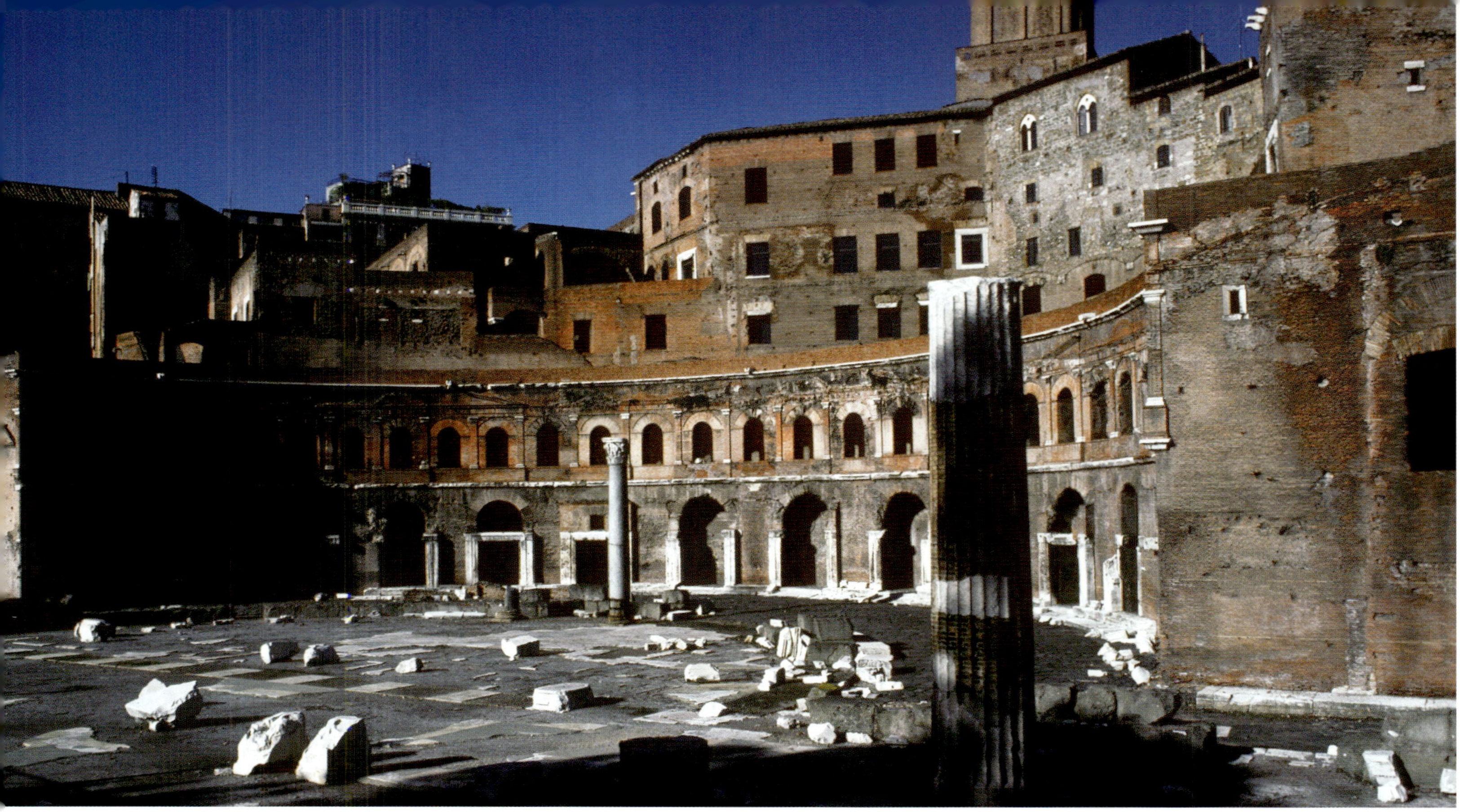

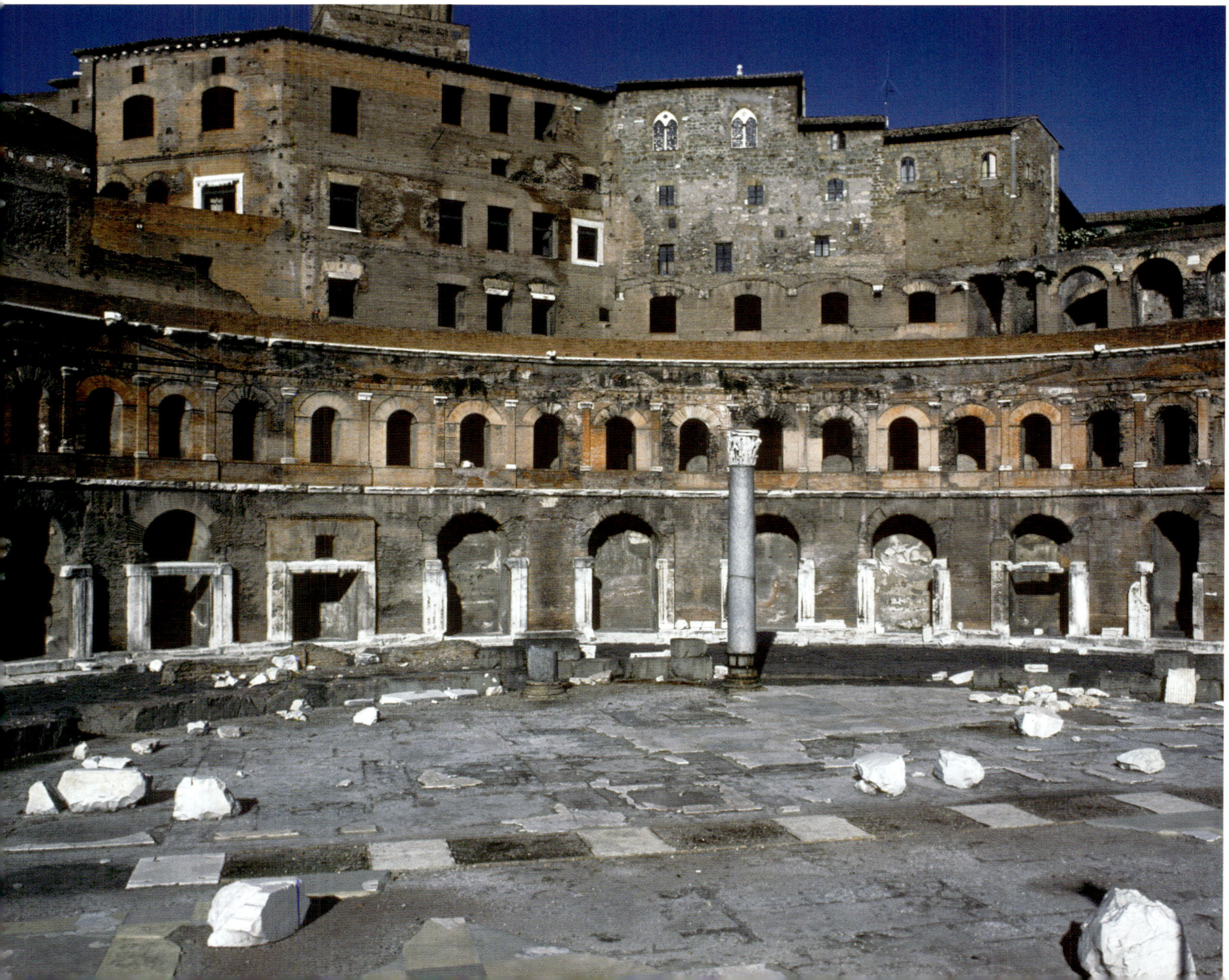

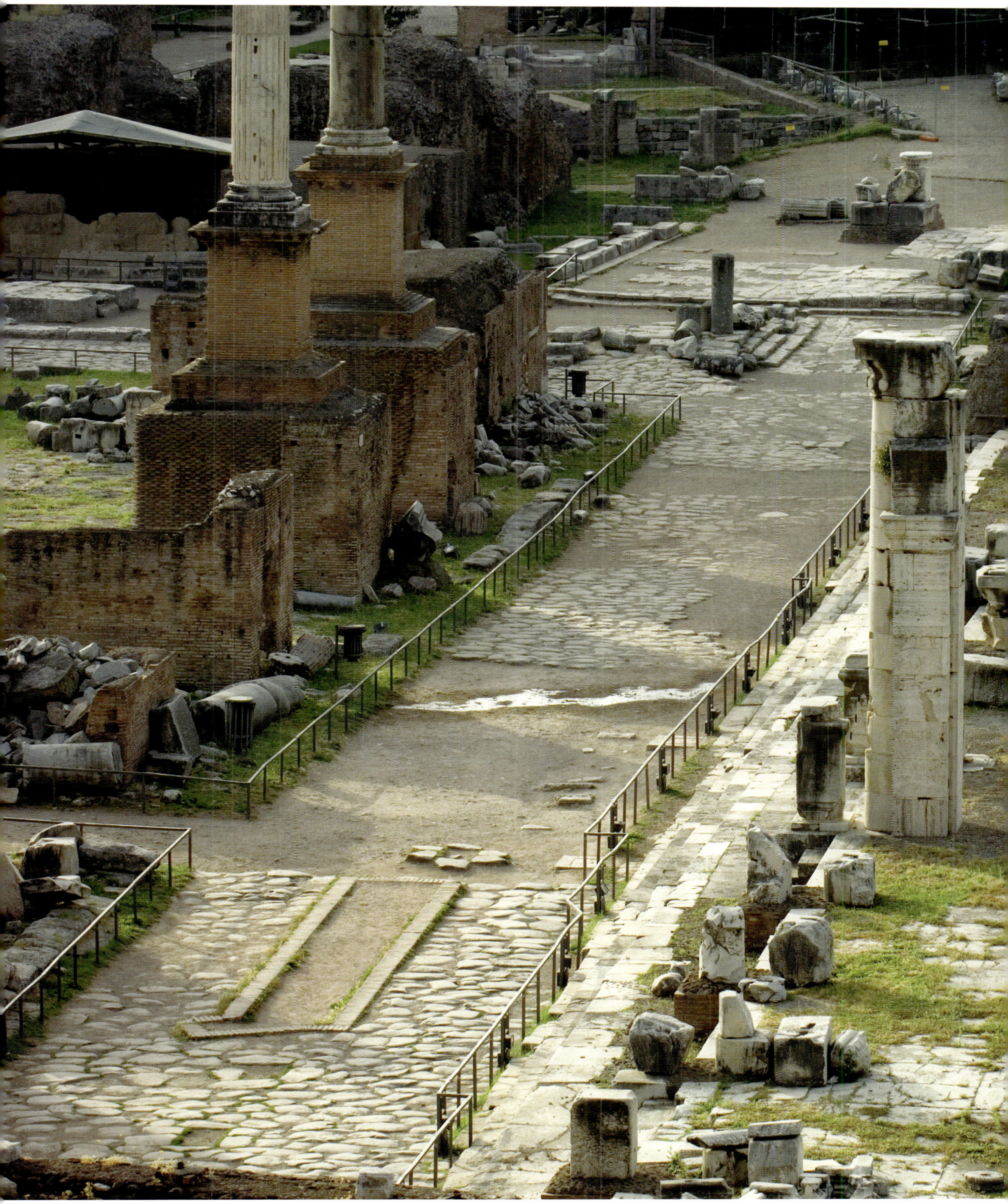

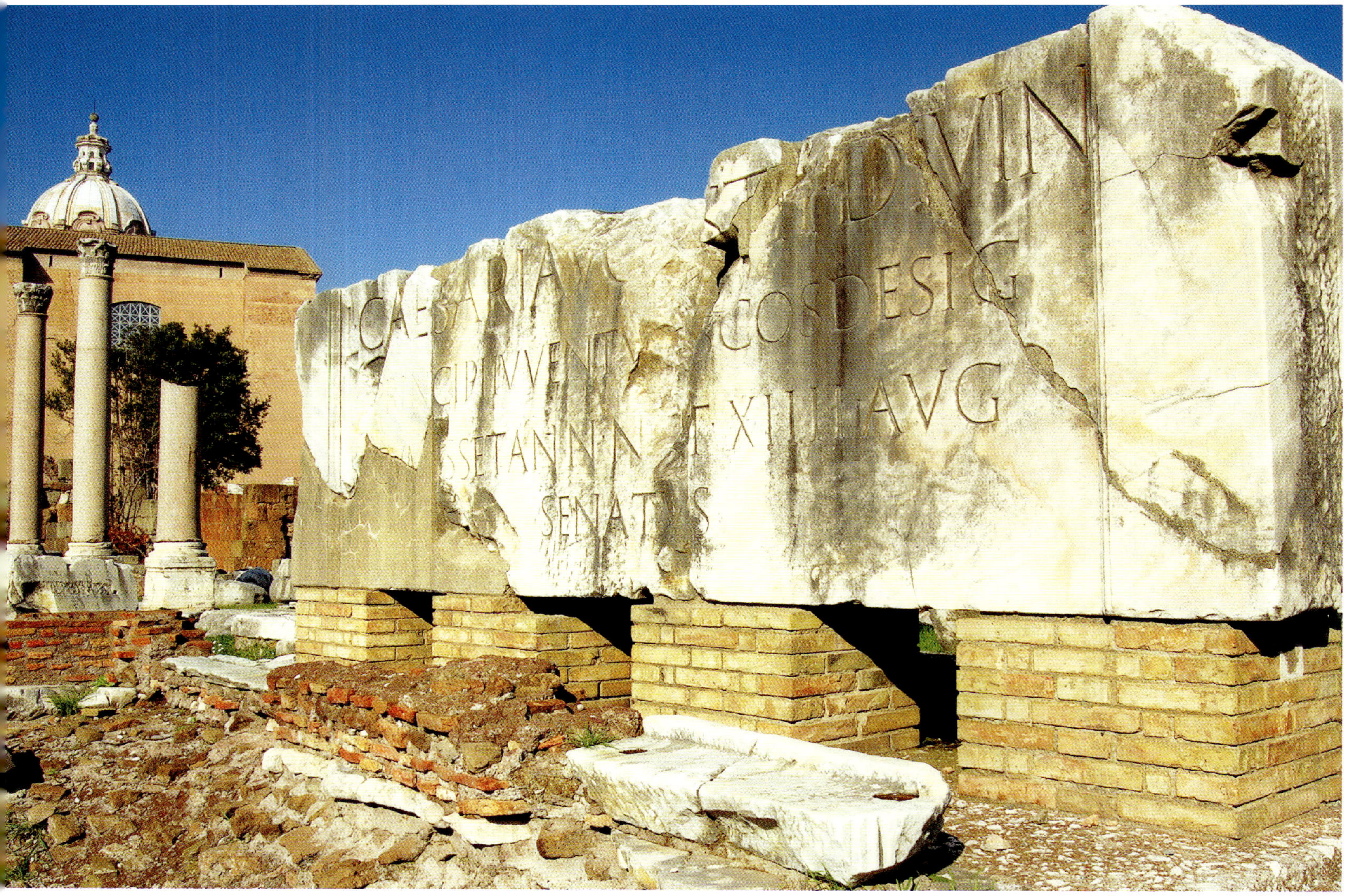
COS DESIG
XIIII AVG
SENATVS

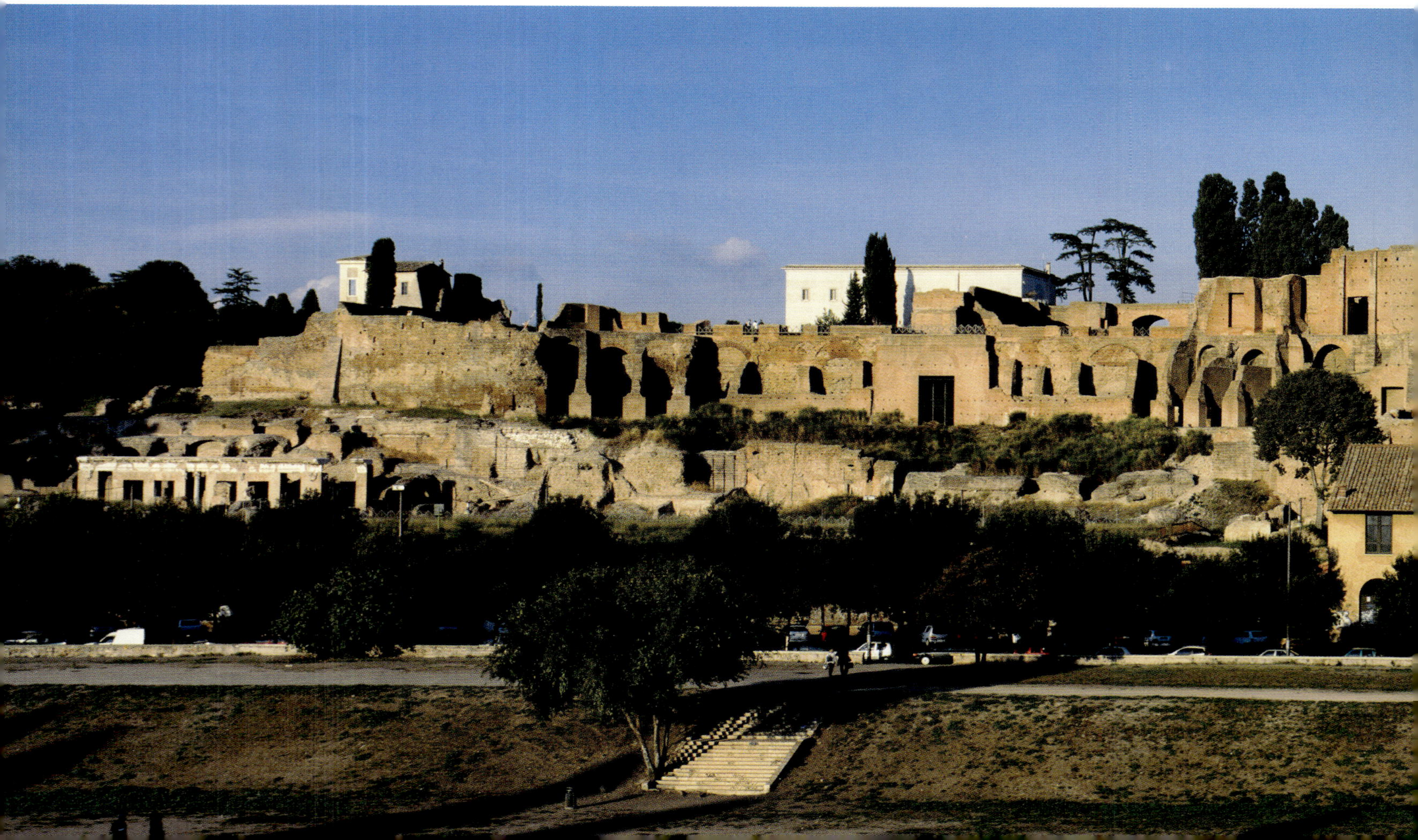

Left: This inscription stands on the Via Sacra alongside the Basilica Emilia in the Roman Forum looking toward the curia—the *Curia Hostilia* (Hostilian Court) was the favorite meeting place of the Roman Senate in the Forum Romanum at the foot of the Capitoline Hill, near the well of the Comitia. Throughout antiquity there were two main buildings that served as the official meeting-place of the Roman Senate, the Curia Hostilia and the Curia Julia.

Right: Weathered columns in the forum. Much of the stone was used for later projects by Renaissance architects.

Below: The size of the ancient remains is remarkable and would dwarf most other buildings erected in the thousand years that followed the fall of the empire. *Getty Images/ Panoramic Images*

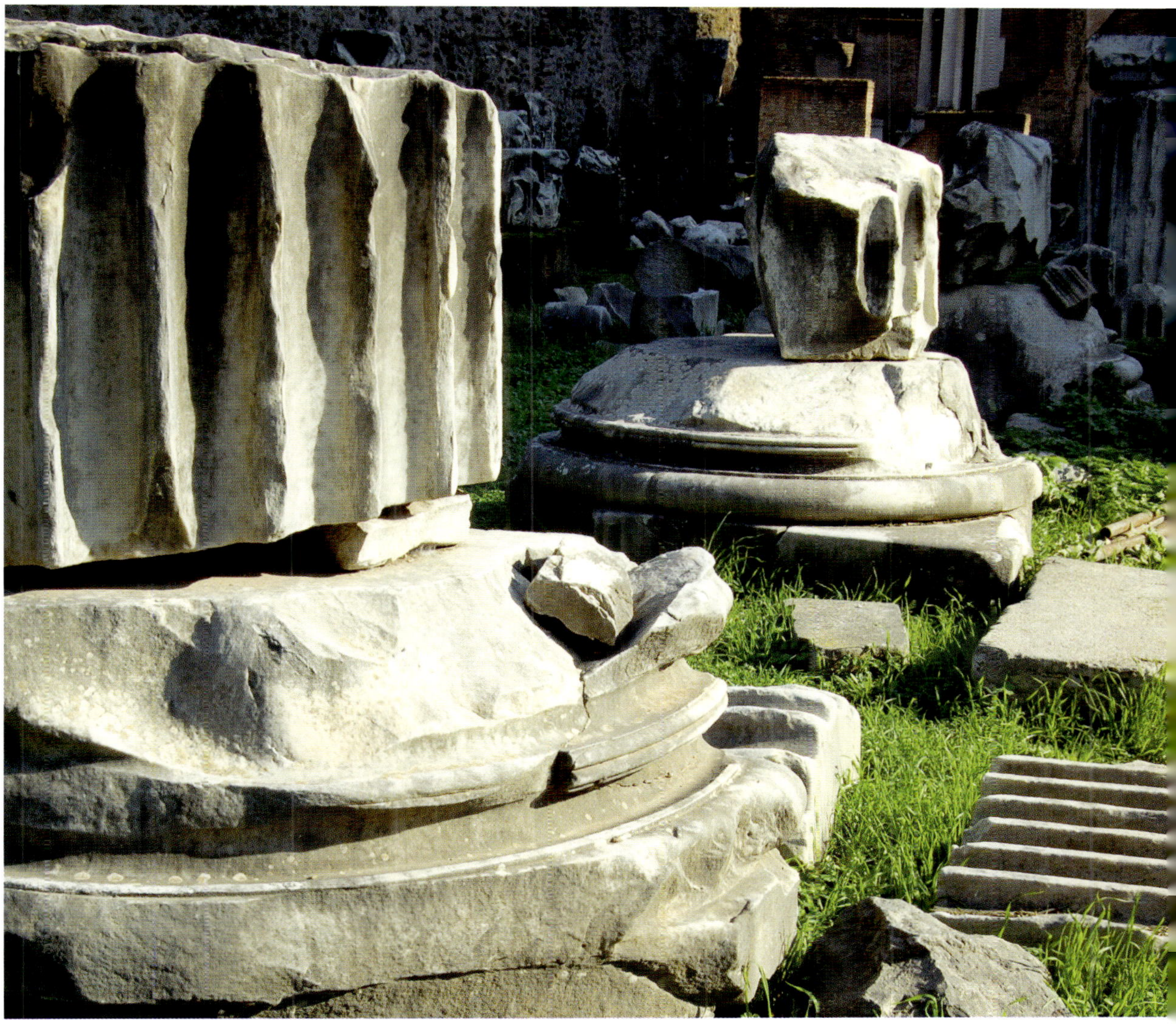

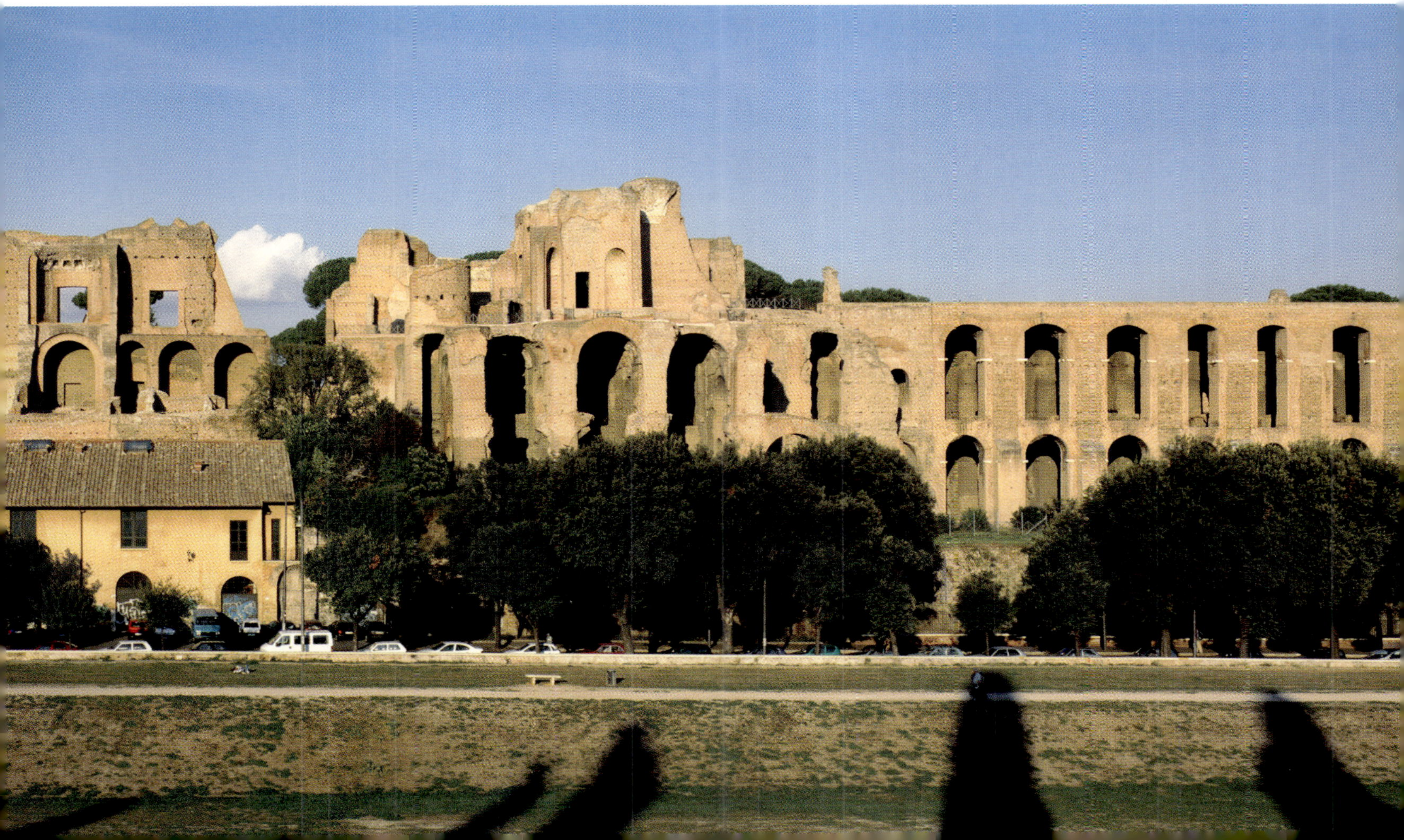

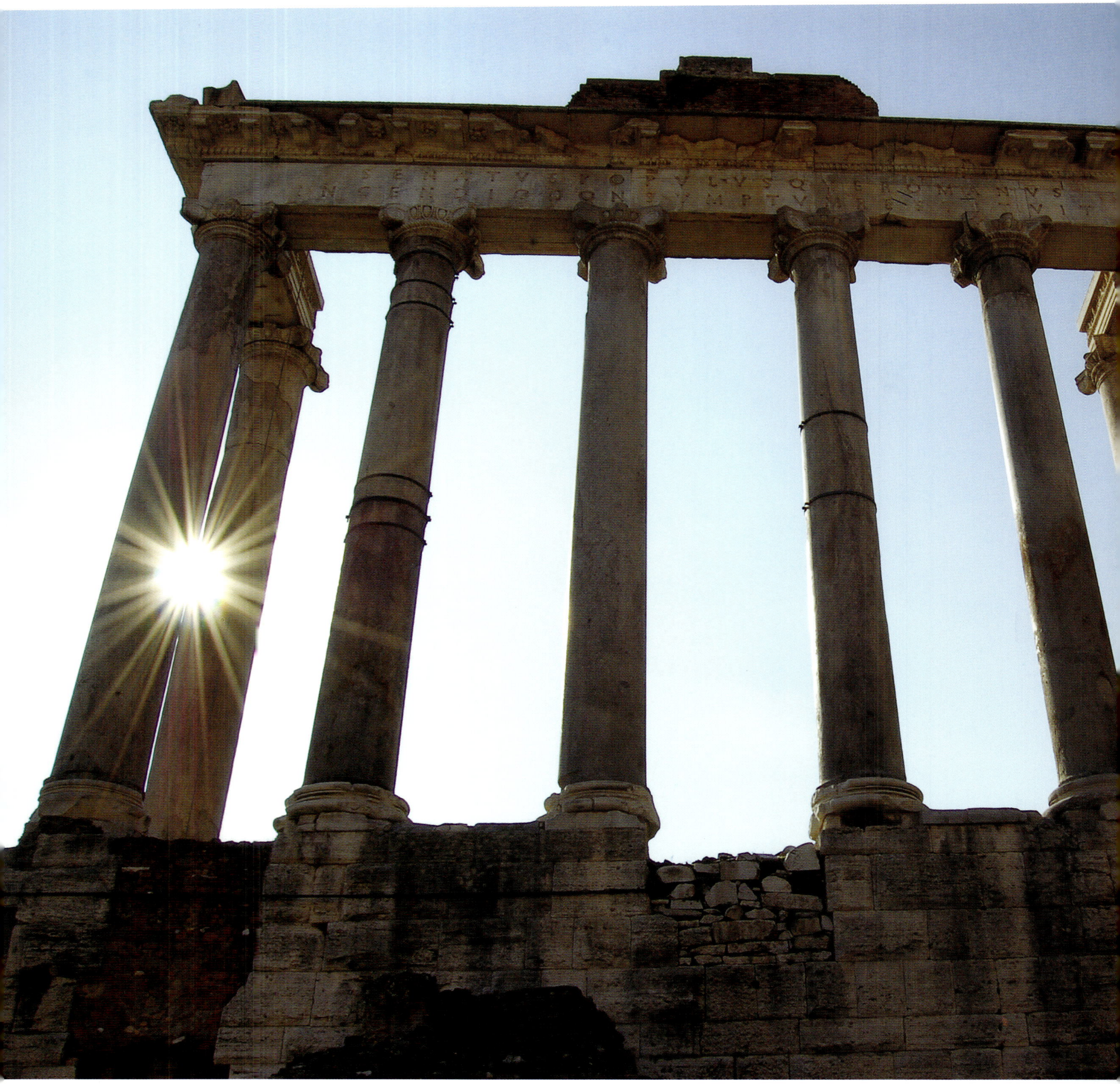

Above: The Roman Forum has many temples, showing just how important religion was to the citizens of Rome. This is the Temple of Saturn (*Templum Saturni* or *Aedes Saturnus*), a monument to the agricultural deity Saturn. It stands at the western end of the Roman Forum and represents the oldest surviving foundation in that area, having been established between 501 and 498 B.C. Some sources attribute it to the King Tarquinius Superbus.

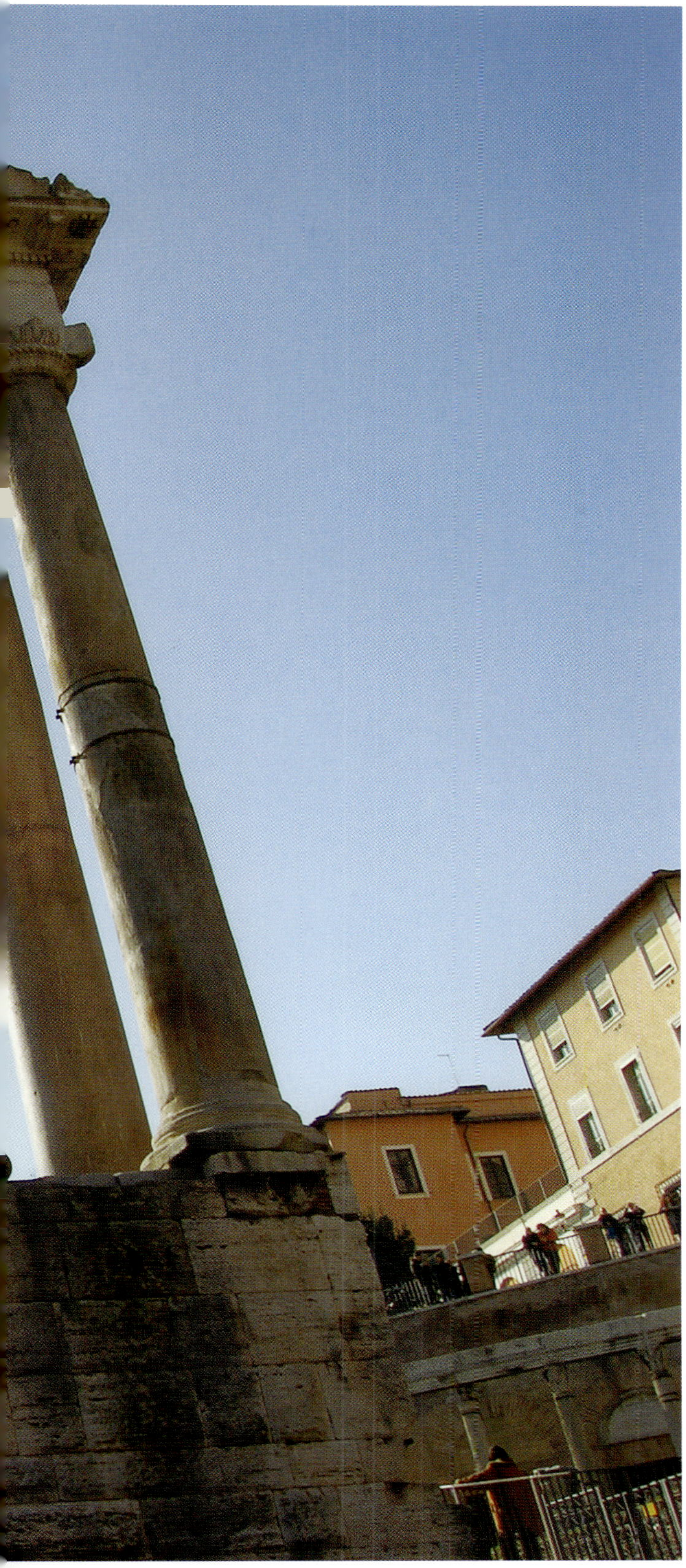

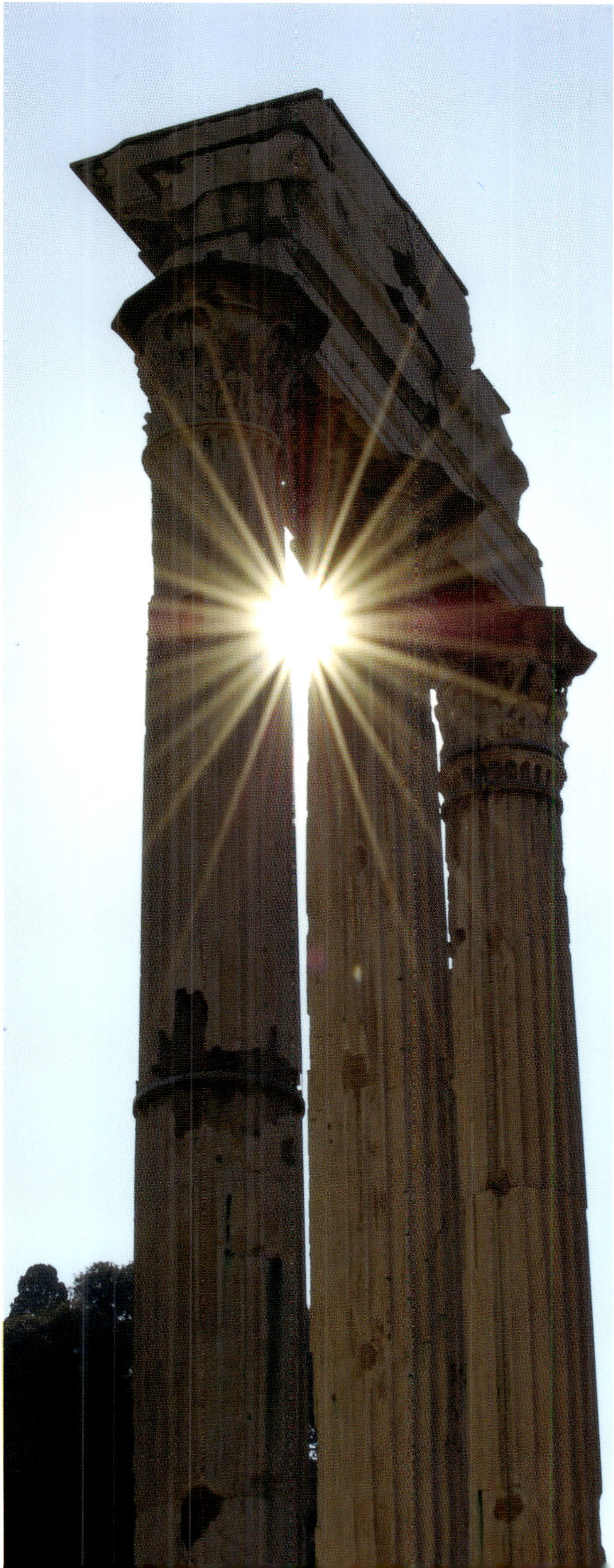

RIGHT: The temple of Castor and Pollux in the Roman Forum was originally built by Aulus Postumius in gratitude for victory against the Latins and Tarquinius Superbus, the former Etruscan king of Rome, at the legendary battle of Lake Regillus (around 495 B.C.). Castor and Pollux, the twin sons of Zeus (Jupiter) and Leda, were said to have helped the Roman victory appearing on the battlefield as horsemen.

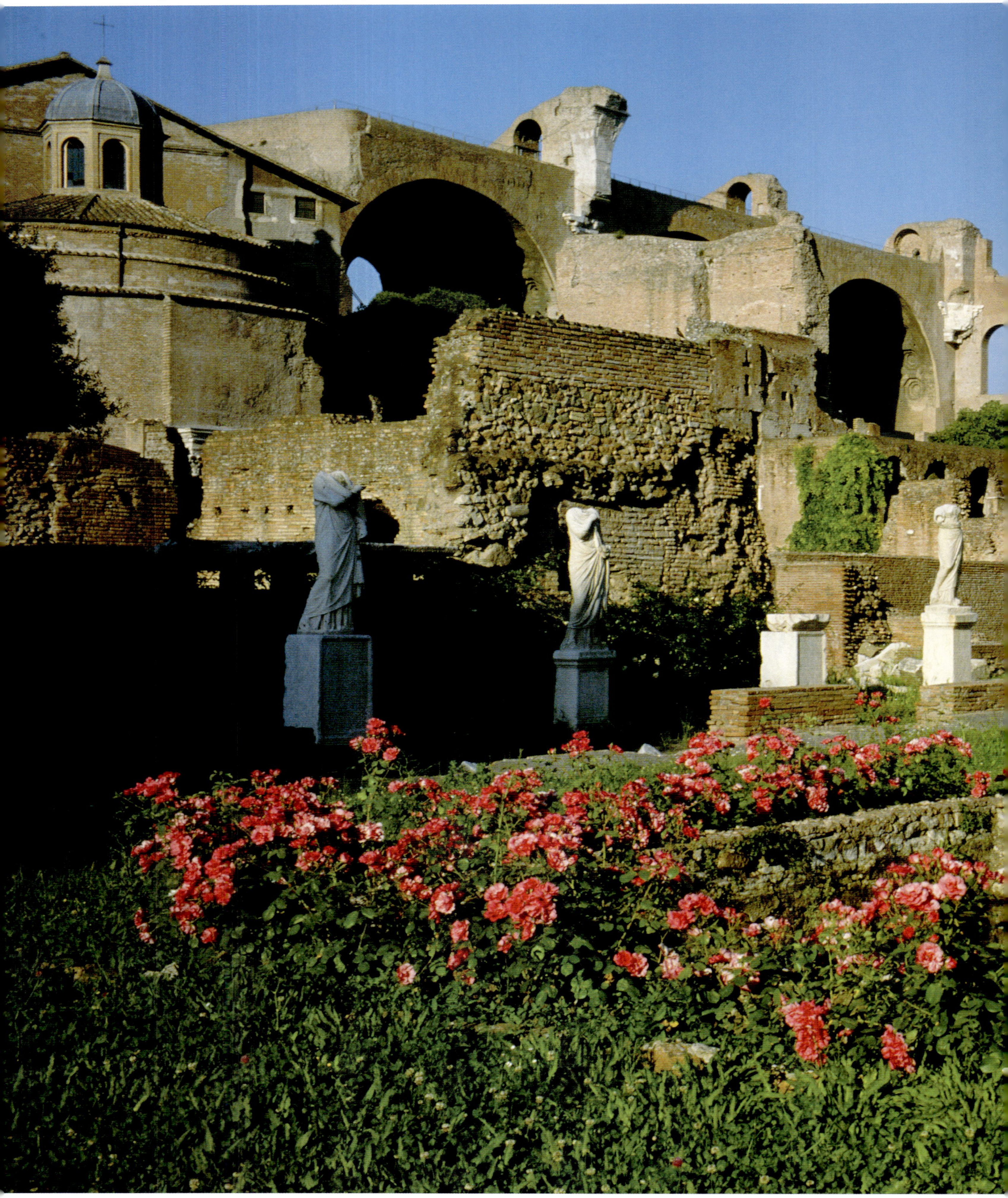

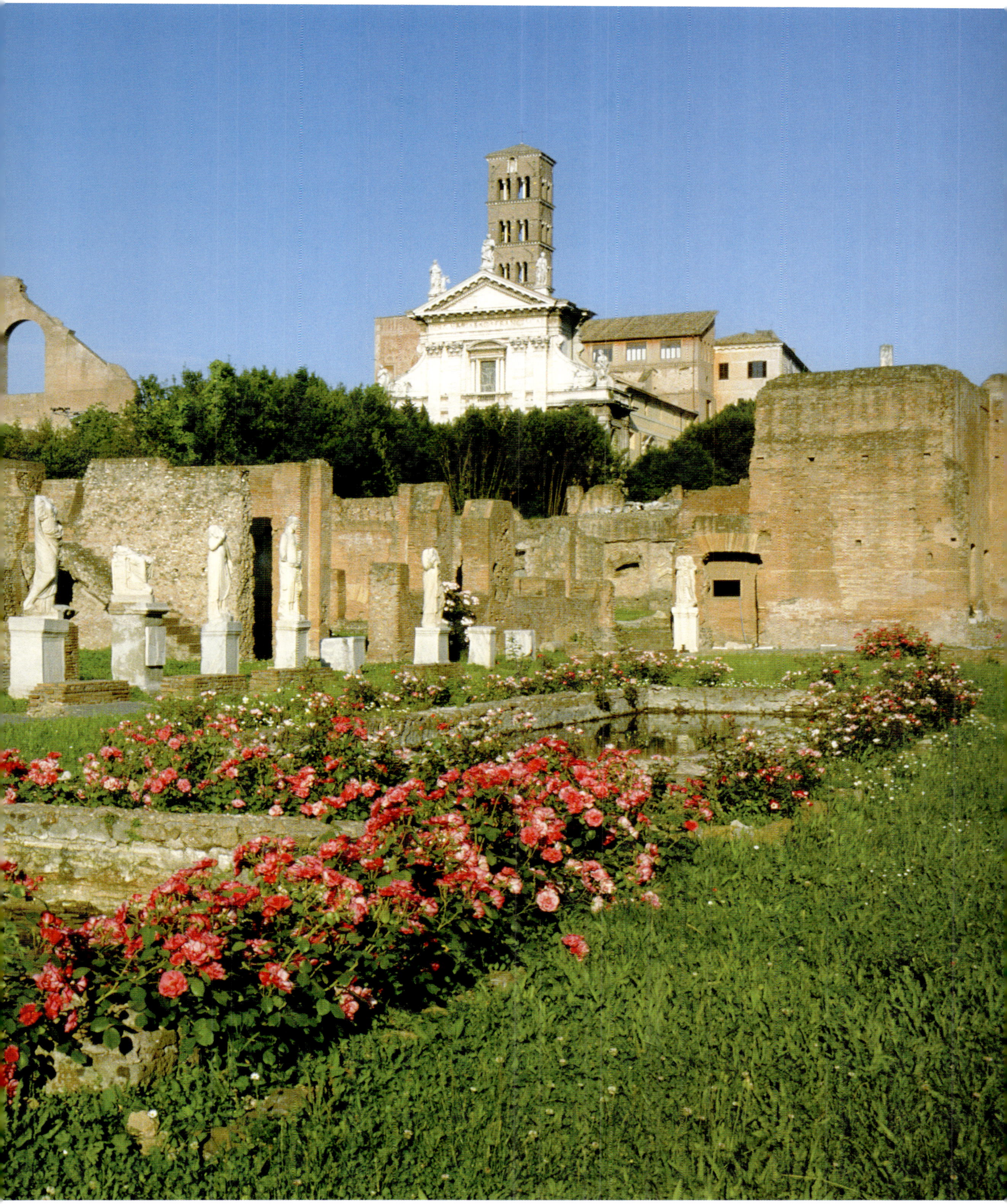

PAGES 82–83: The Garden of the Vestel Virgins in the Roman Forum. Six priestesses known as the Vestals guarded the city's sacred fire that burned in the Temple of Vesta. The priestesses were chosen at the age of six from among a select group of patrician families. Their duty lasted for thirty years during which time they had to remain virgins. If they broke their vows their punishment was to be buried alive in the Campus Sceleratus on the Quirinal Hill. *Taylor S. Kennedy/National Geographic/Getty Images*

BELOW: Copy of the Marcus Aurelius sculpture on Capitol Hill. Marcus Aurelius Antoninus Augustus (April 26, 121–March 17, 180 A.D.) was Roman Emperor from 161 to his death in 180. He is considered one of the most important stoic philosophers.

RIGHT: Bronze doors that belonged to the ancient Roman temple in the Forum have long since become part of the church of Santi Cosma e Damiano. This church was built in 526–30 on the site of the Temple of Romulus and part of the library belonging to the Forum of Peace. The church is particularly famous for its 6th and 7th century mosaics. *Getty Images/Altrendo*

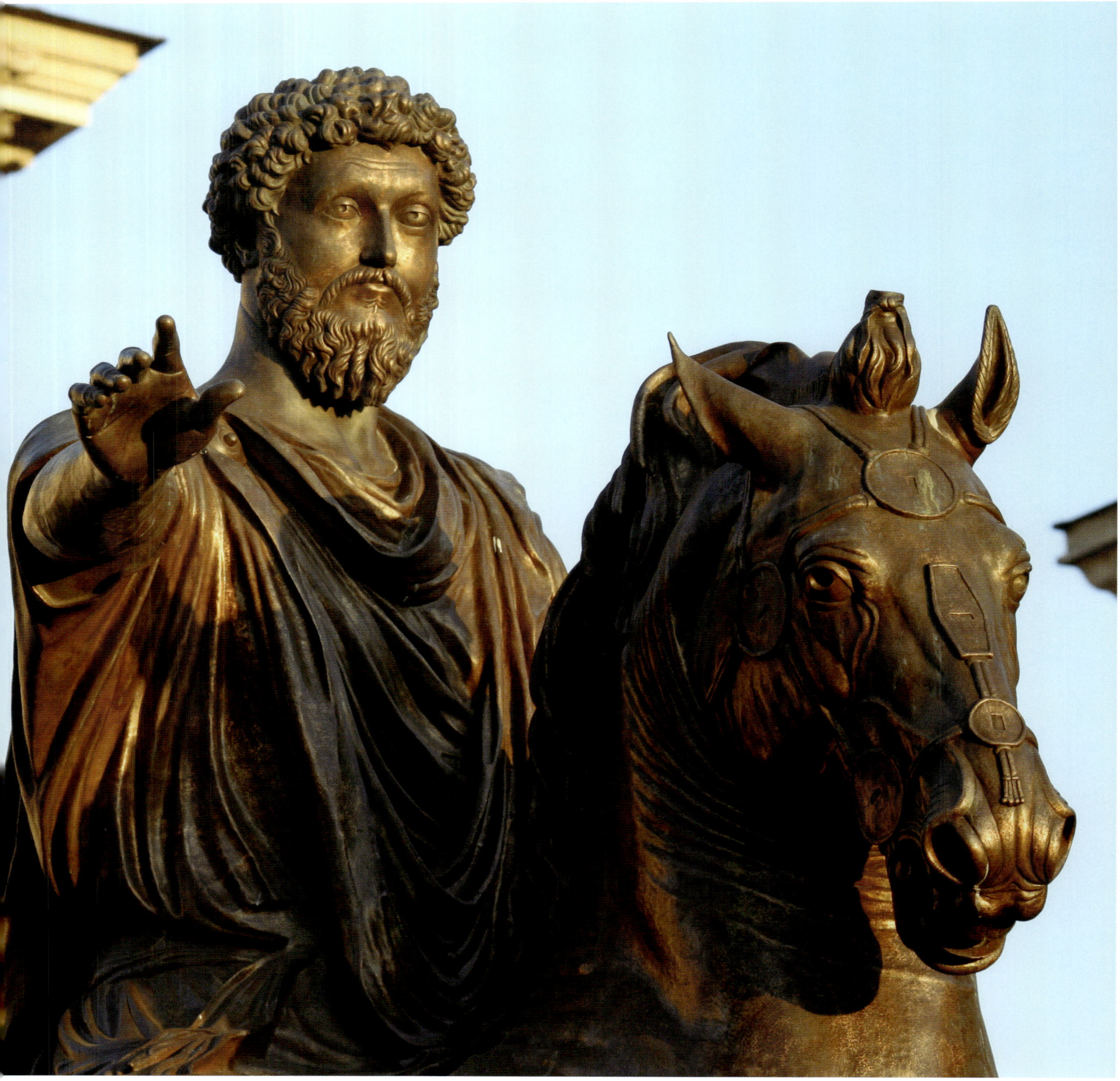

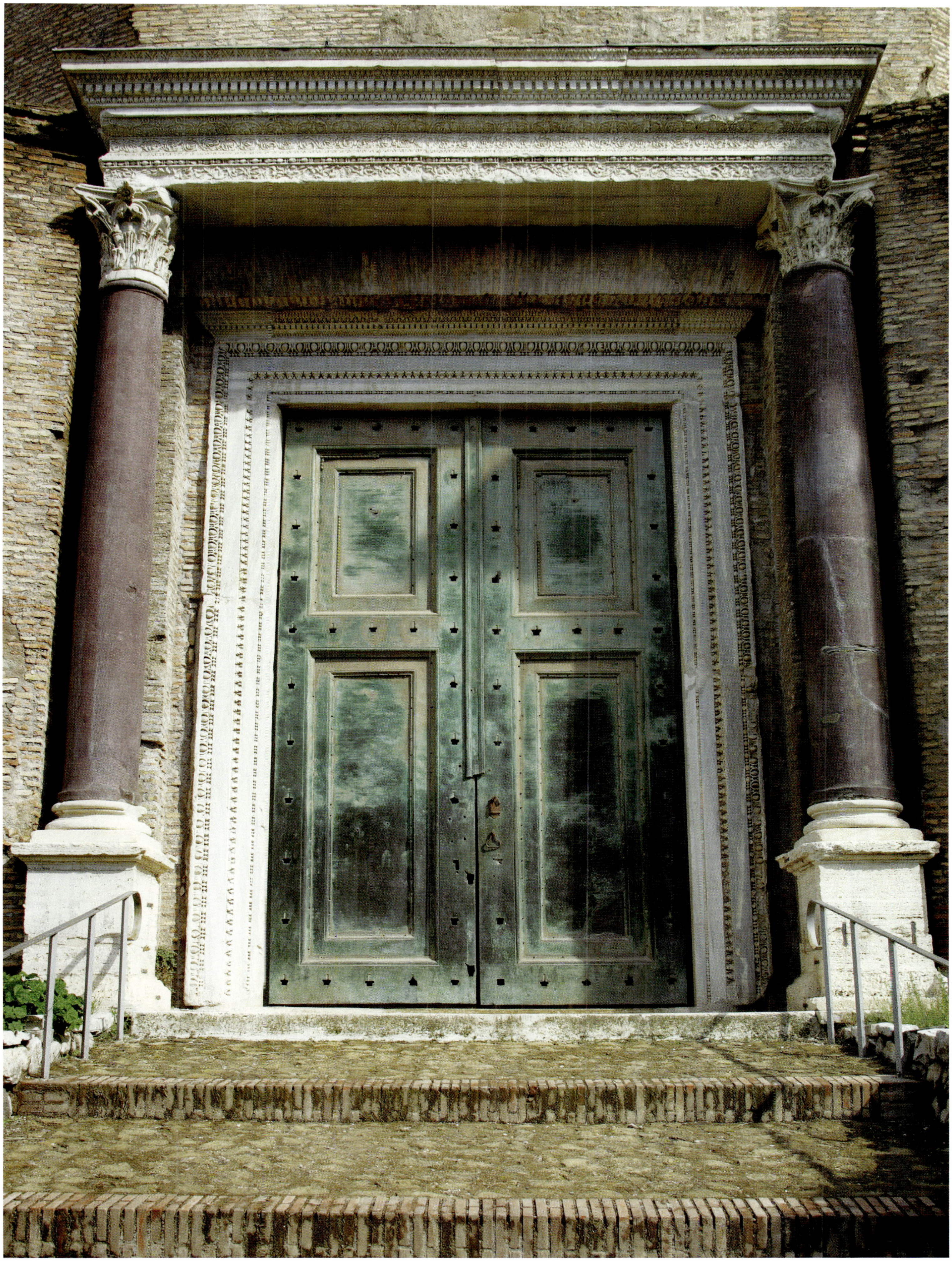

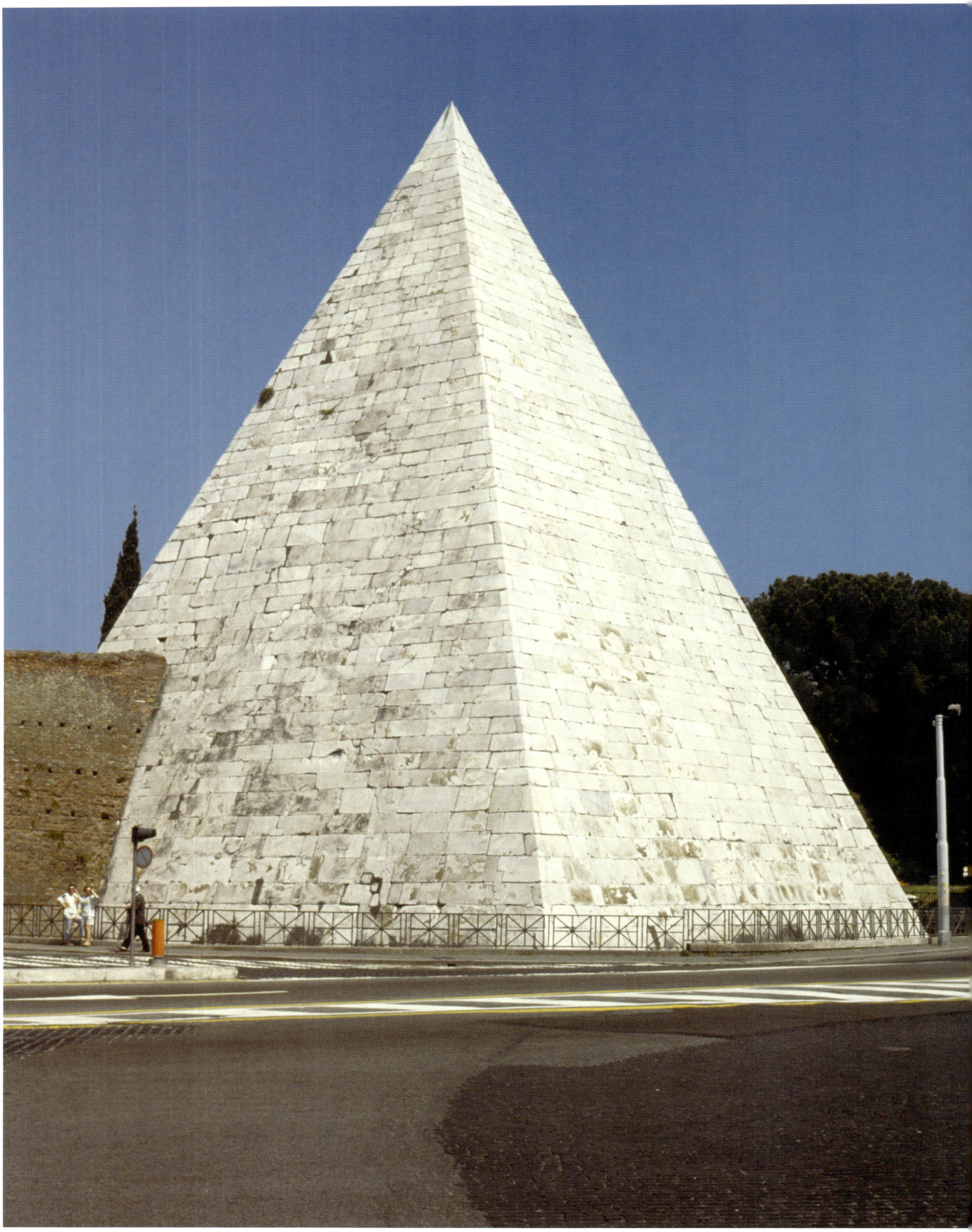

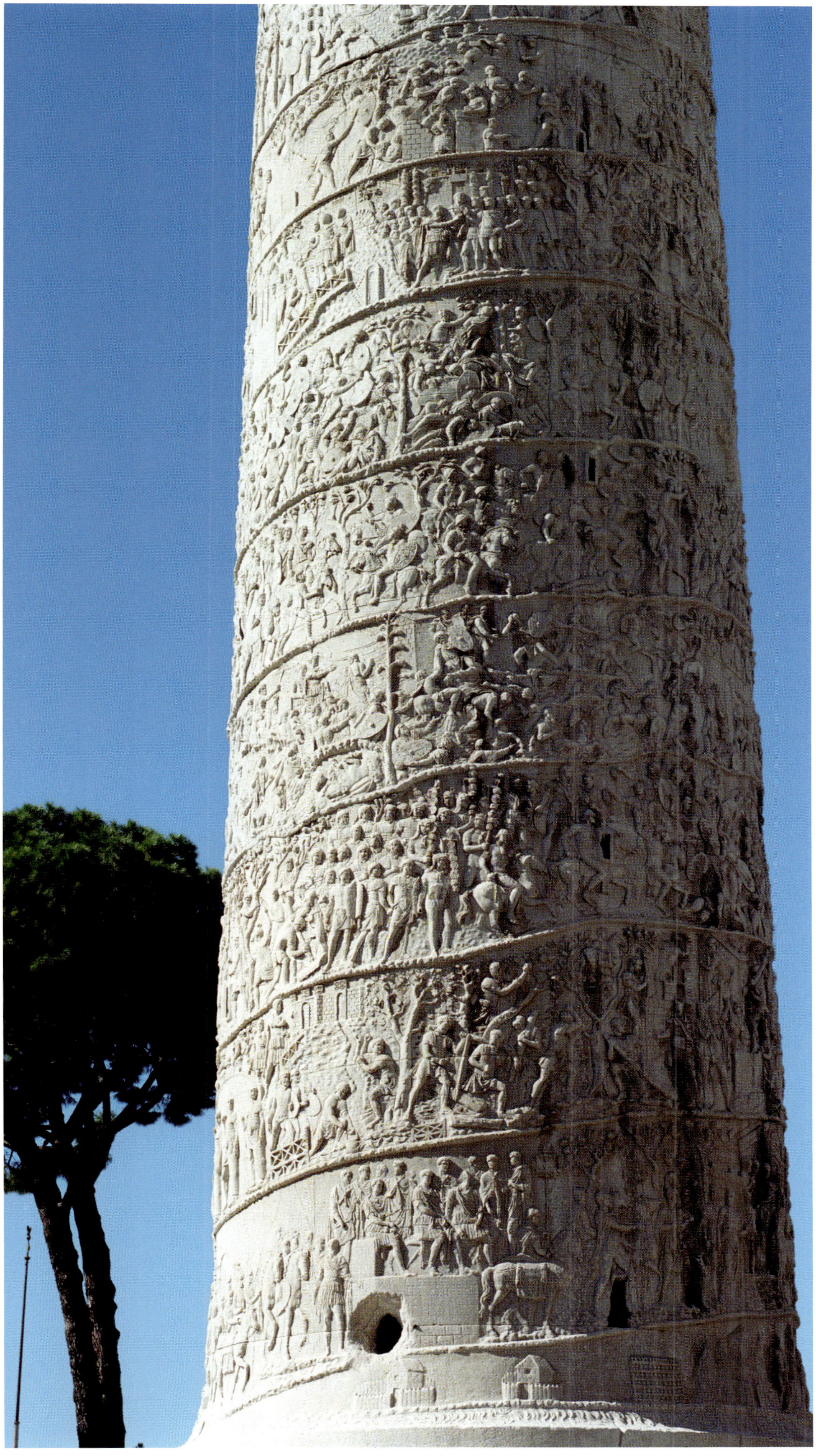

FAR LEFT: The memorial pyramid of Caius Cestius was built in about 12 B.C. and is constructed from brick-clad concrete covered with white Carrara marble slabs. It stands around 72 feet square and 88 feet high and contains burial chamber for Caius Cestius reached by a passage on the northern side. He was a rich elected magistrate—a *praetor*—and a member of the *Septemviri epulonum,* one of the four great religious corporations of Rome with responsibility for sacred banquets. The pyramid was incorporated into the Aurelian wall in 275 B.C. *Dorling Kindersley/Getty Images*

LEFT: Trajan's Column was erected in the second century A.D. *Fred Mayer/Getty Images*

Right: Trajan's Column is 130 feet tall and tells a visual account of his victorious wars against the Dacians (101–106 A.D.). Starting at the bottom, the story is shown in spiral relief (details shown here) 656 feet long around the column. Trajan is shown 60 times in the reliefs while his ashes were placed in a golden urn buried in the base. The column stands intact in the Forum of Trajan. *Gjon Mili/Time Life Pictures/Getty Images; National Geographic/Getty Images*

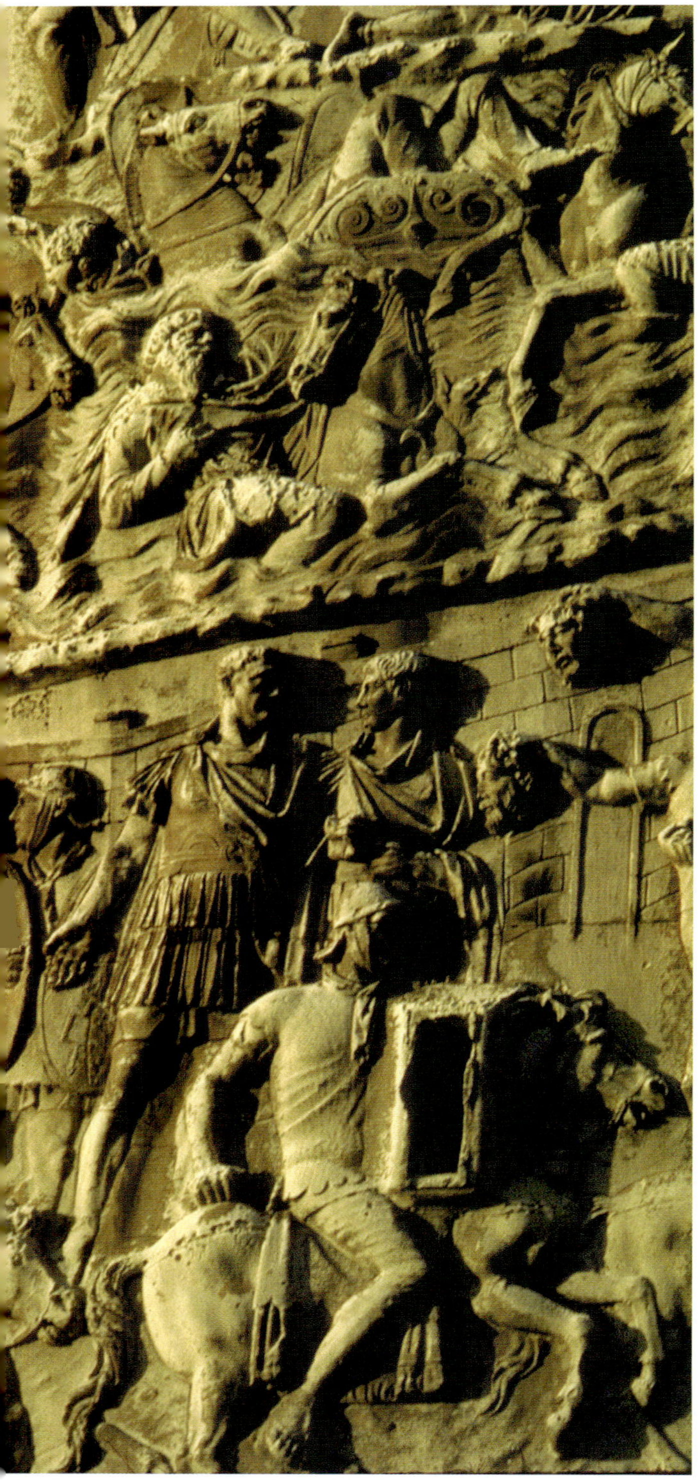

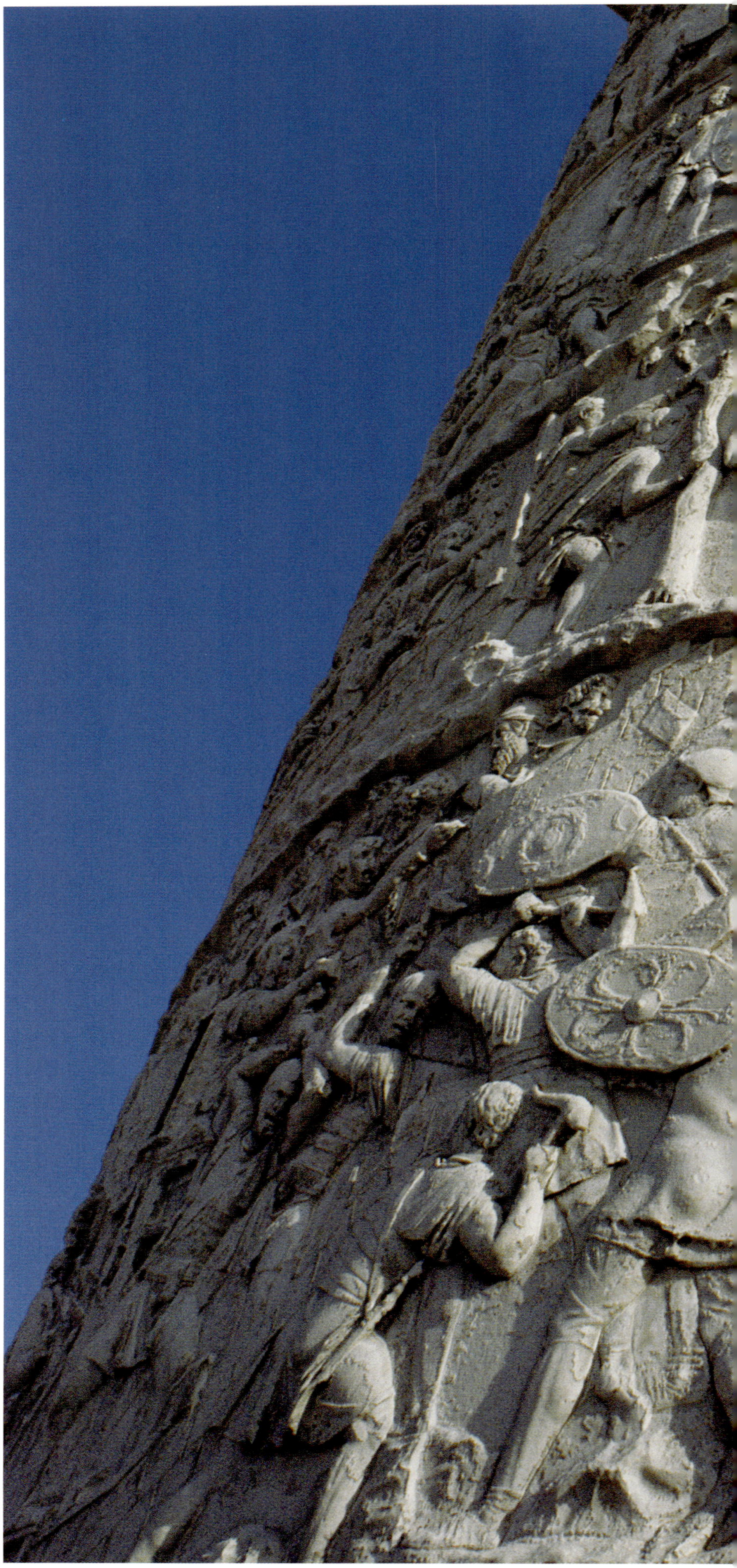

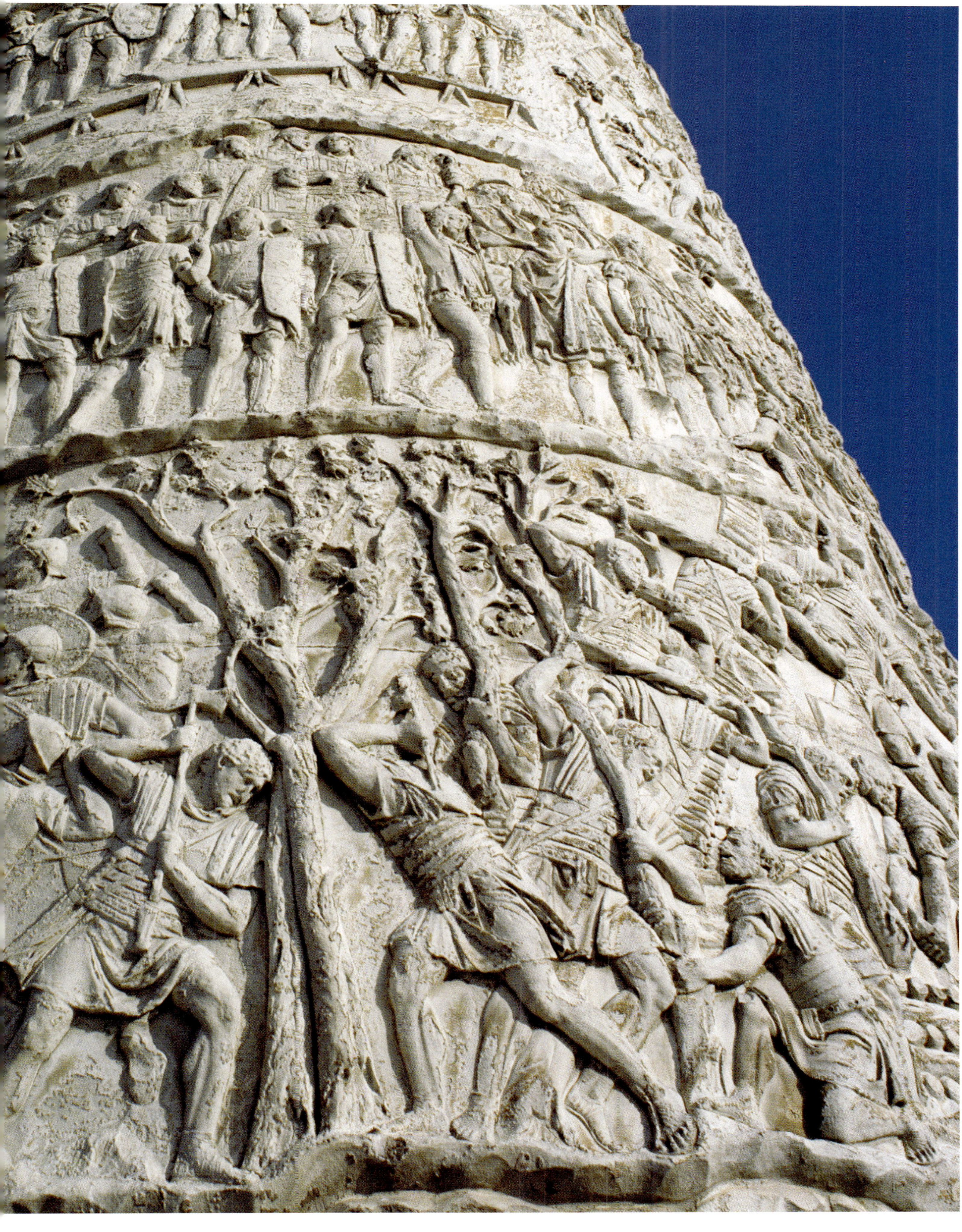

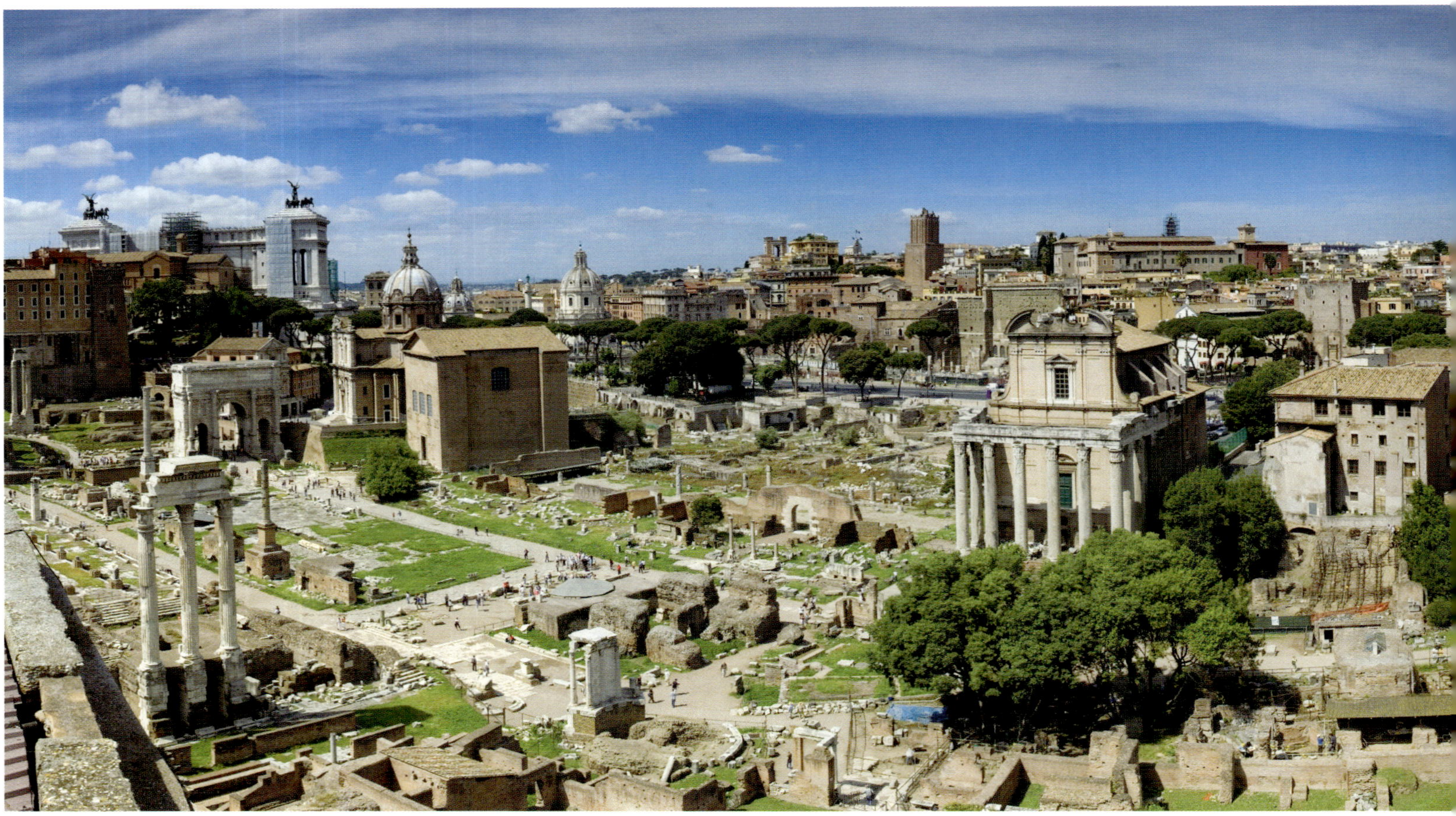

Above: Panoramic view of the Roman Forum from the Arch of Septimus Severus at extreme left, to the Arch of Titus at extreme right. Note the Colosseum at right; the large brick arches of the Basilicaof Maxentius center right; Temple of Antoninus and Faustina (with columns and steps at center right) and the Temple of Castor and Pollux in the foreground center left. The Temple of Antoninus and Faustina was converted into the church of San Lorenzo in Miranda as early as the seventh century.

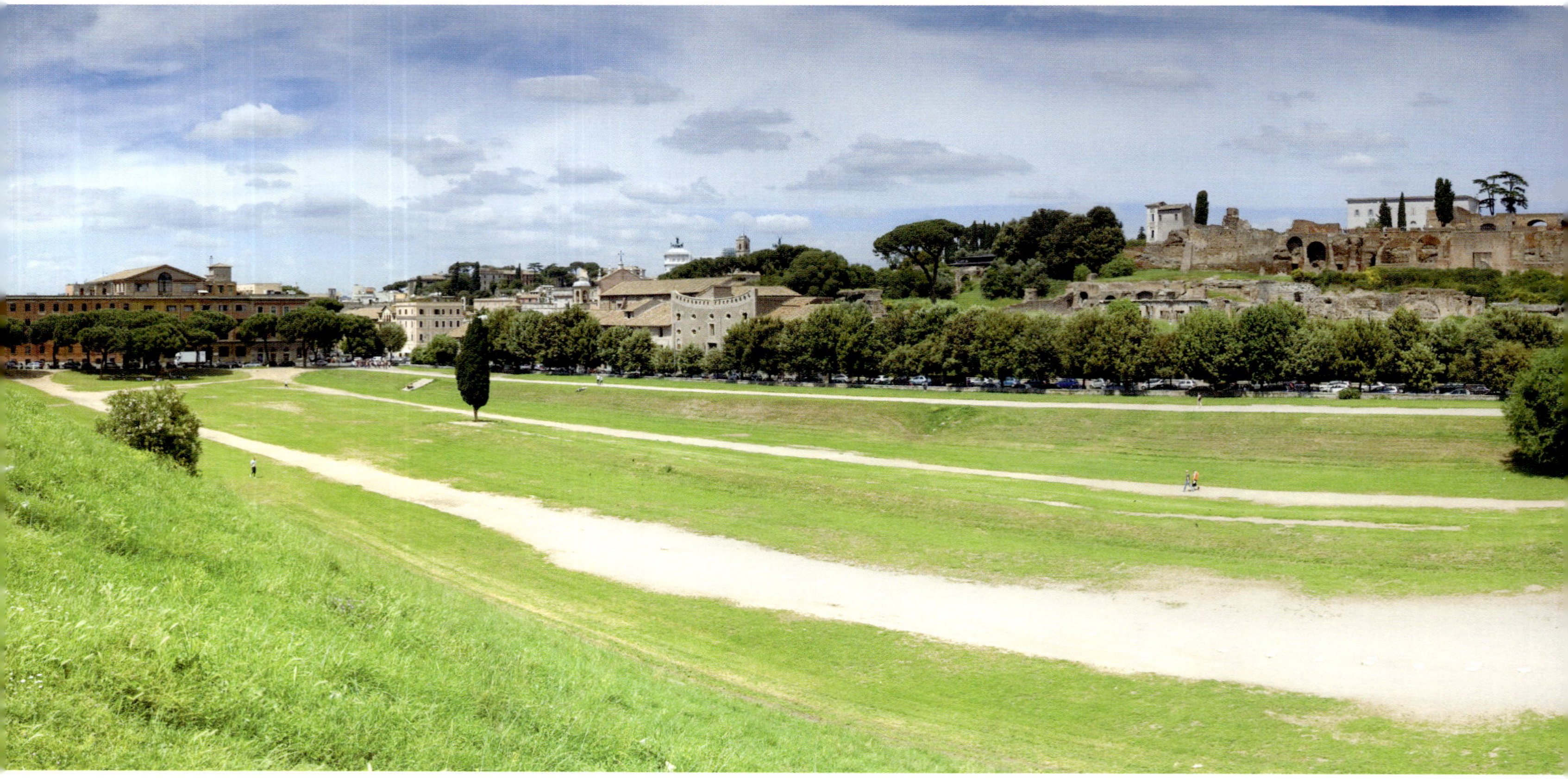

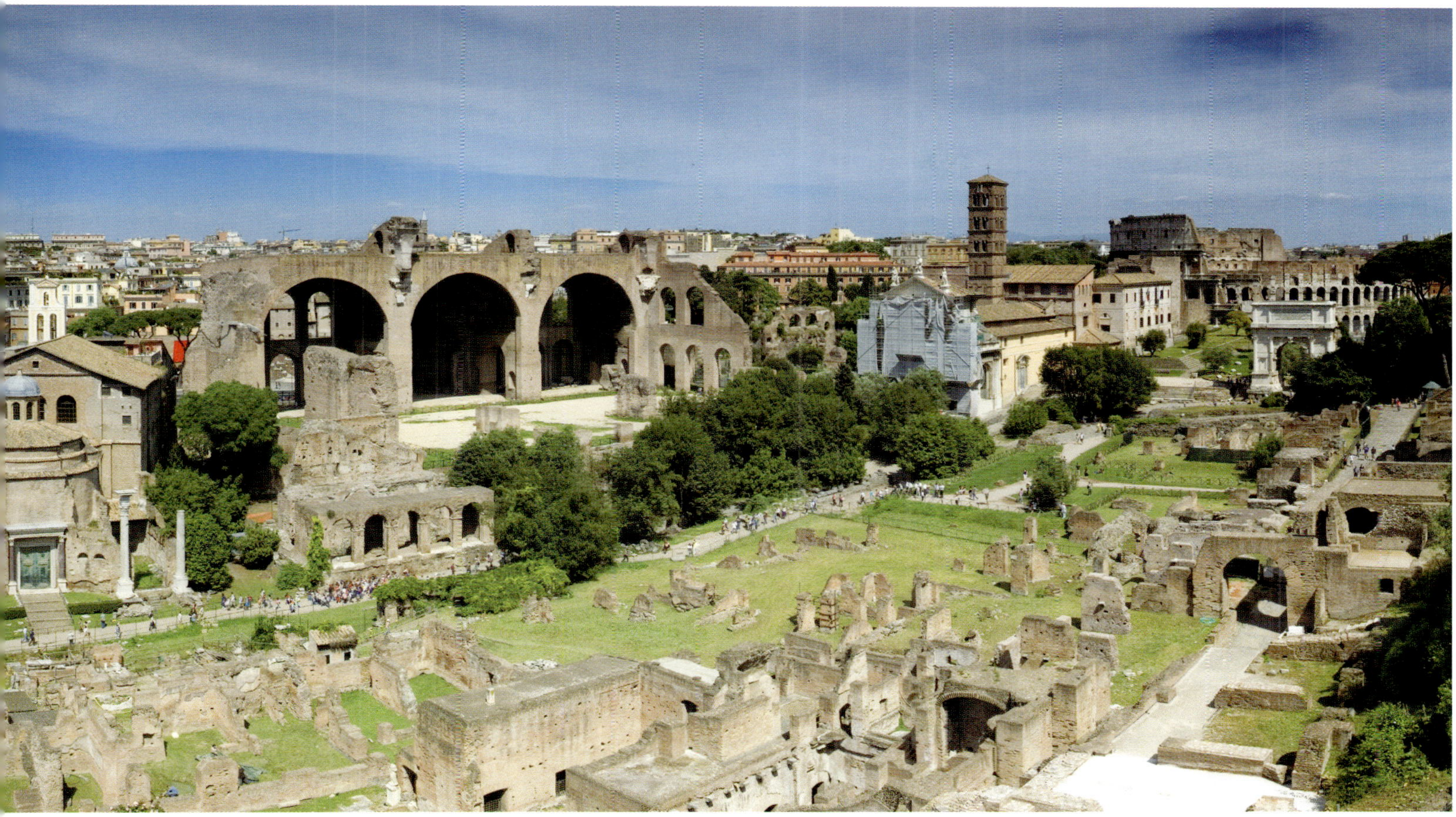

BELOW: Panoramic view across the grassy esplanade of Circus Maximus—the ancient Roman chariot racing arena—to the historic palaces of Palatine beyond. The Circus Maximus was the first arena in Rome to be built for chariot racing, according to legend by Tarquin the Elder in the 7th century B.C. After a number of enlargements and improvements the circus was nearly 2,000 feet long and could contain a crowd of around 300,000 spectators. The turing posts were the obelisk of Ramses II brought from Heliolopolis, and (added much later) the obelisk of Tutmoses III from Thebes.

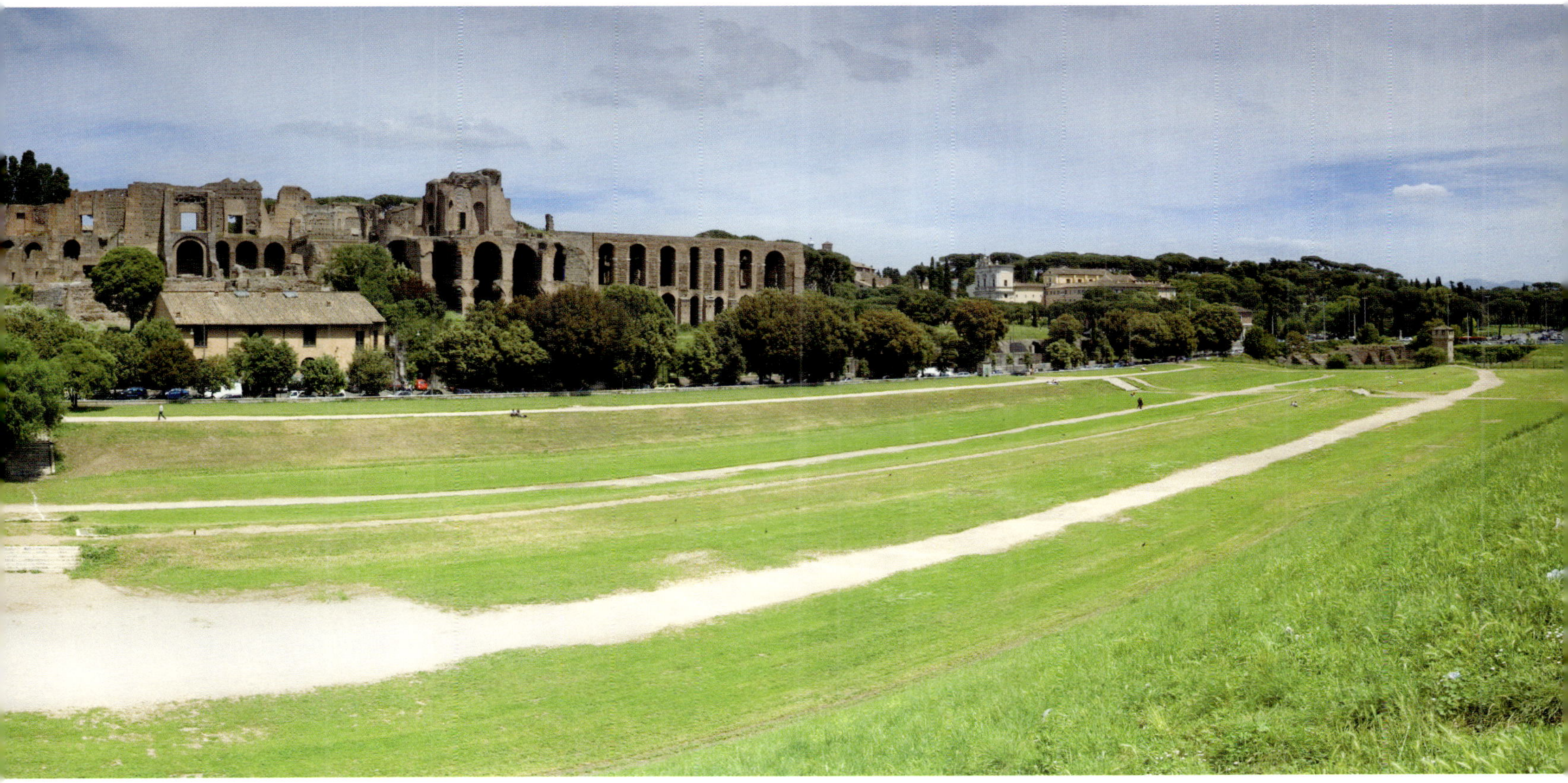

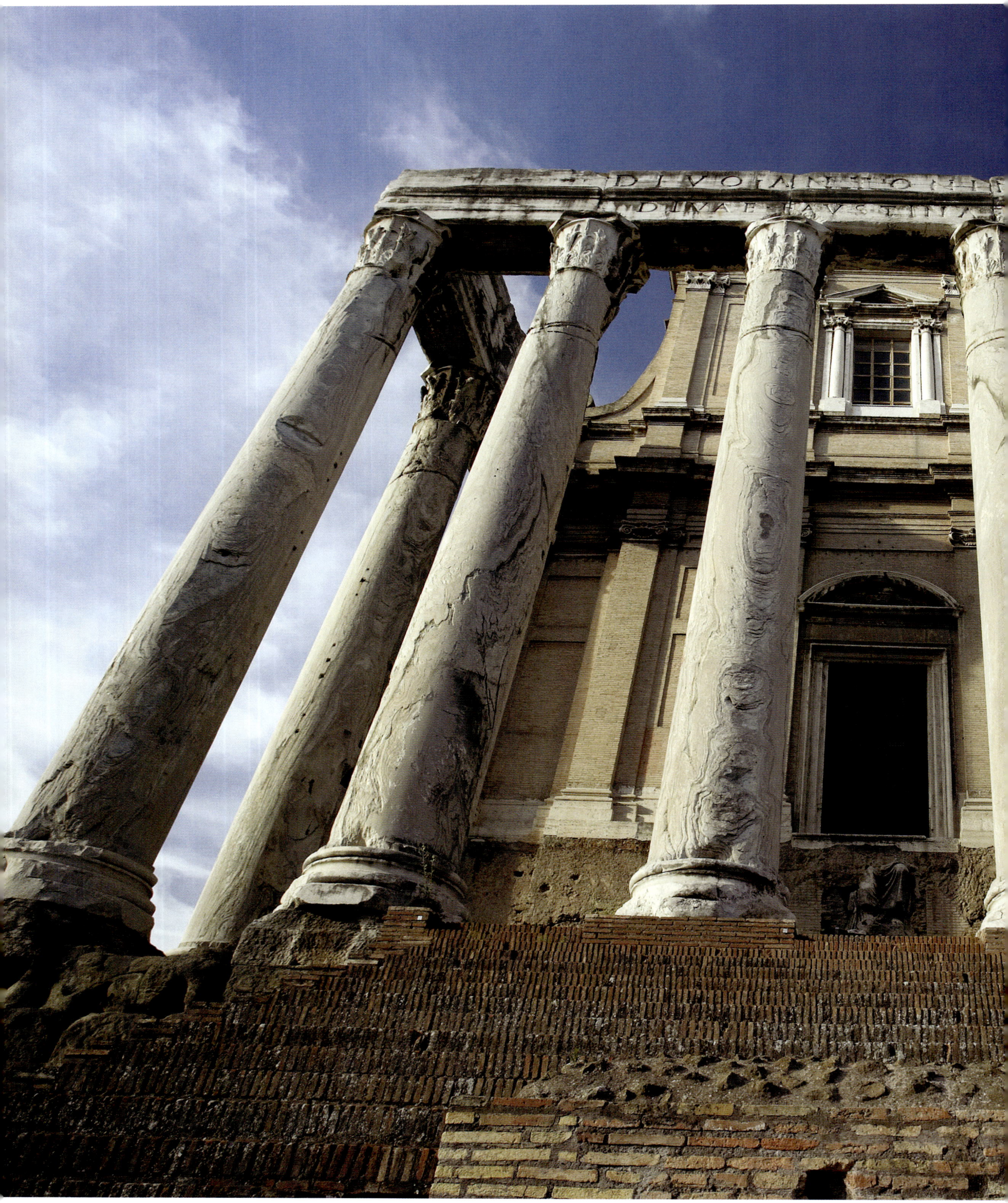

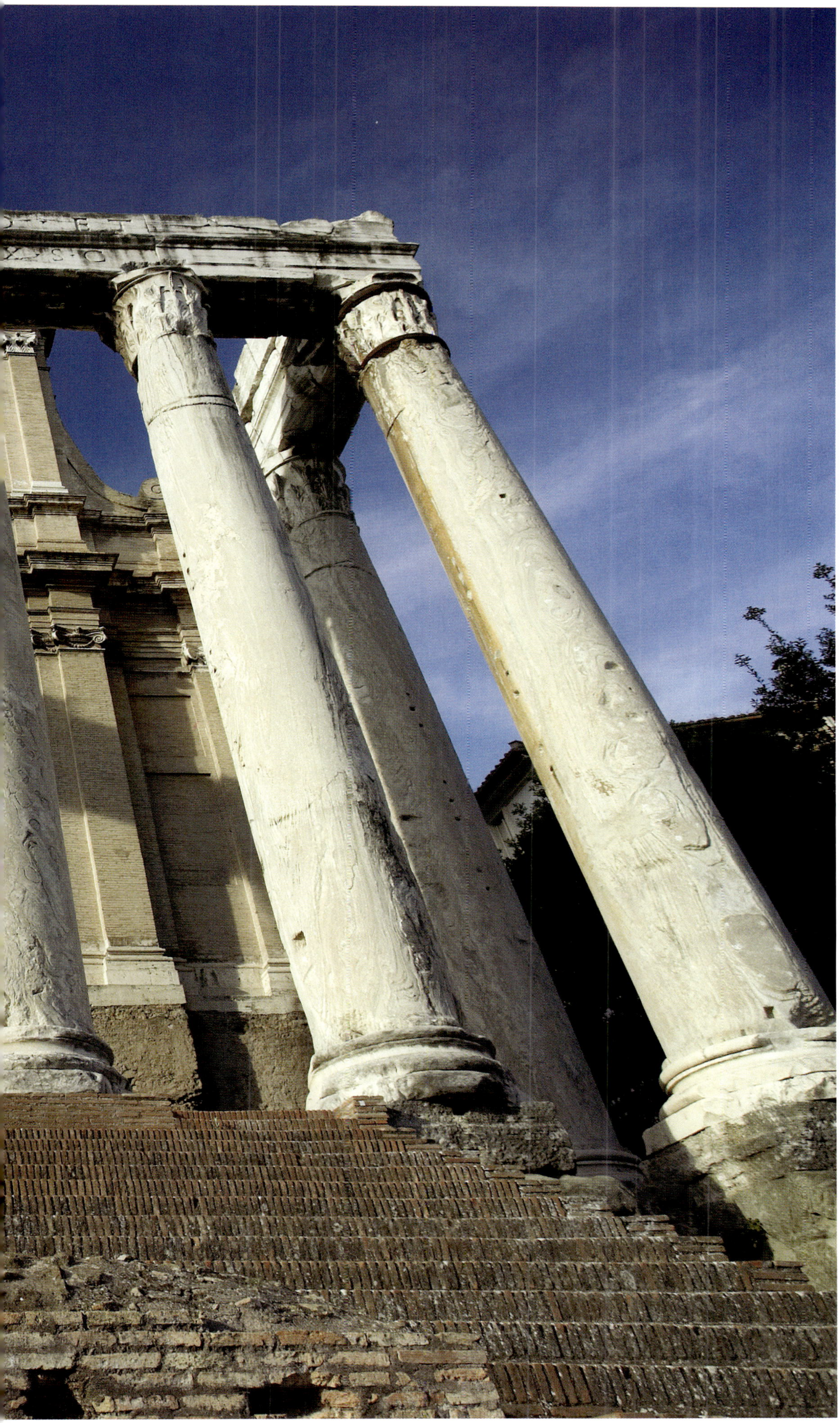

LEFT: In 141 A.D. Antoninus Pius erected this temple—the Temple of Antoninus and Faustina—in memory of his wife Faustina. The building became the Church of San Lorenzo in Miranda in the 15th century which almost certainly saved it from destruction. *Allan Baxter/Digital Vision/Getty Images*

Right: The Arch of Titus on the Via Sacra in the Forum was probably built by Emperor Domitian for his brother Titus and commemorates the capture and sack of Jerusalem in 70 A.D. It escaped almost inevitable decay and demolition by becoming a tower when it was incorporated into medieval fortifications built by the Frangipani family. It was restored in 1822.

Opposite, above and below: Spanning the Via Triumphalis between the Colosseum and the Palatine Hill lies the Arch of Constantine which was built to celebrate Constantine I's victory in 312 A.D. at the Battle of Ponte Milvio. The arch itself is made up from decorative elements taken from other monuments—known as "spolia."

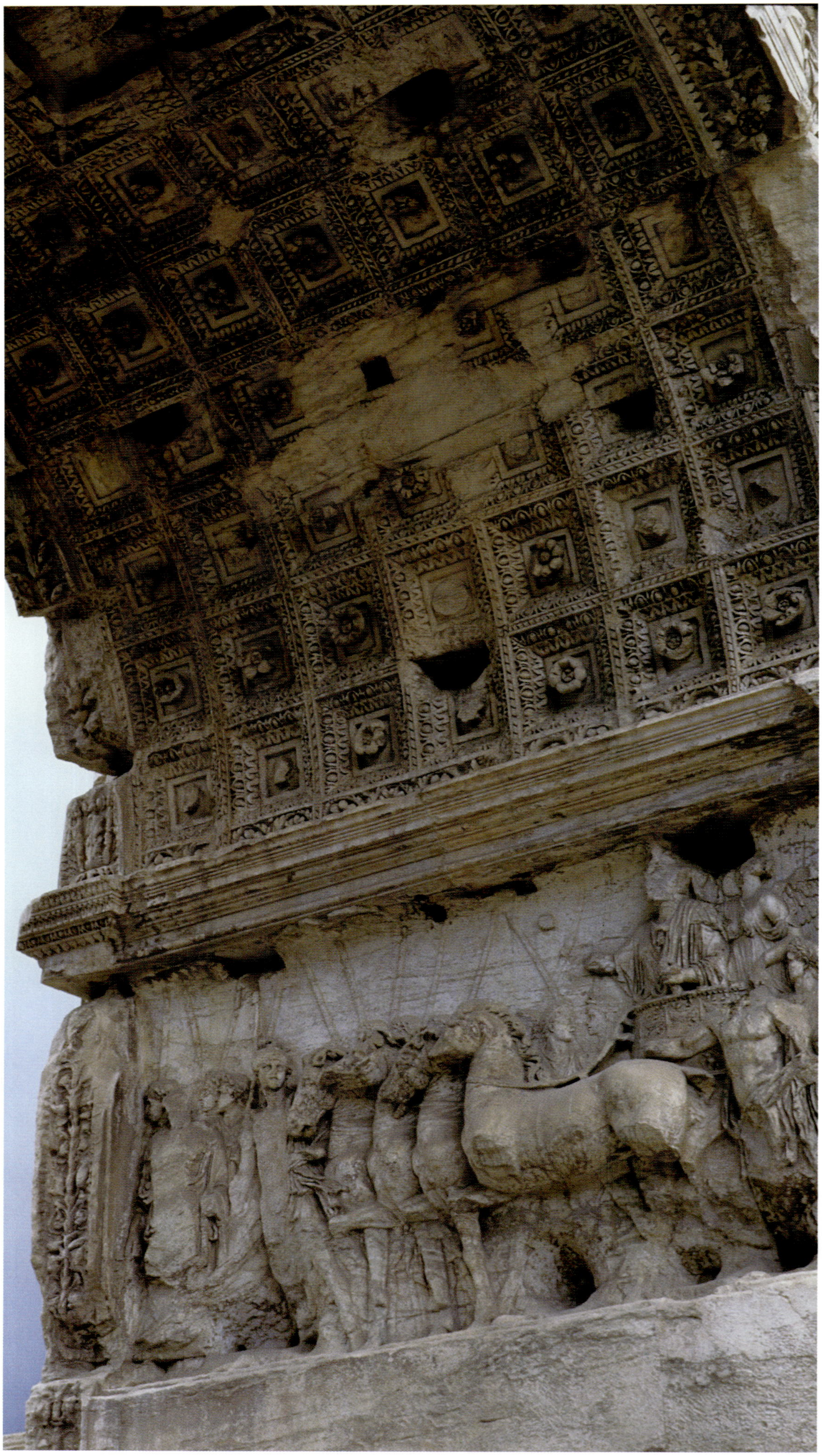

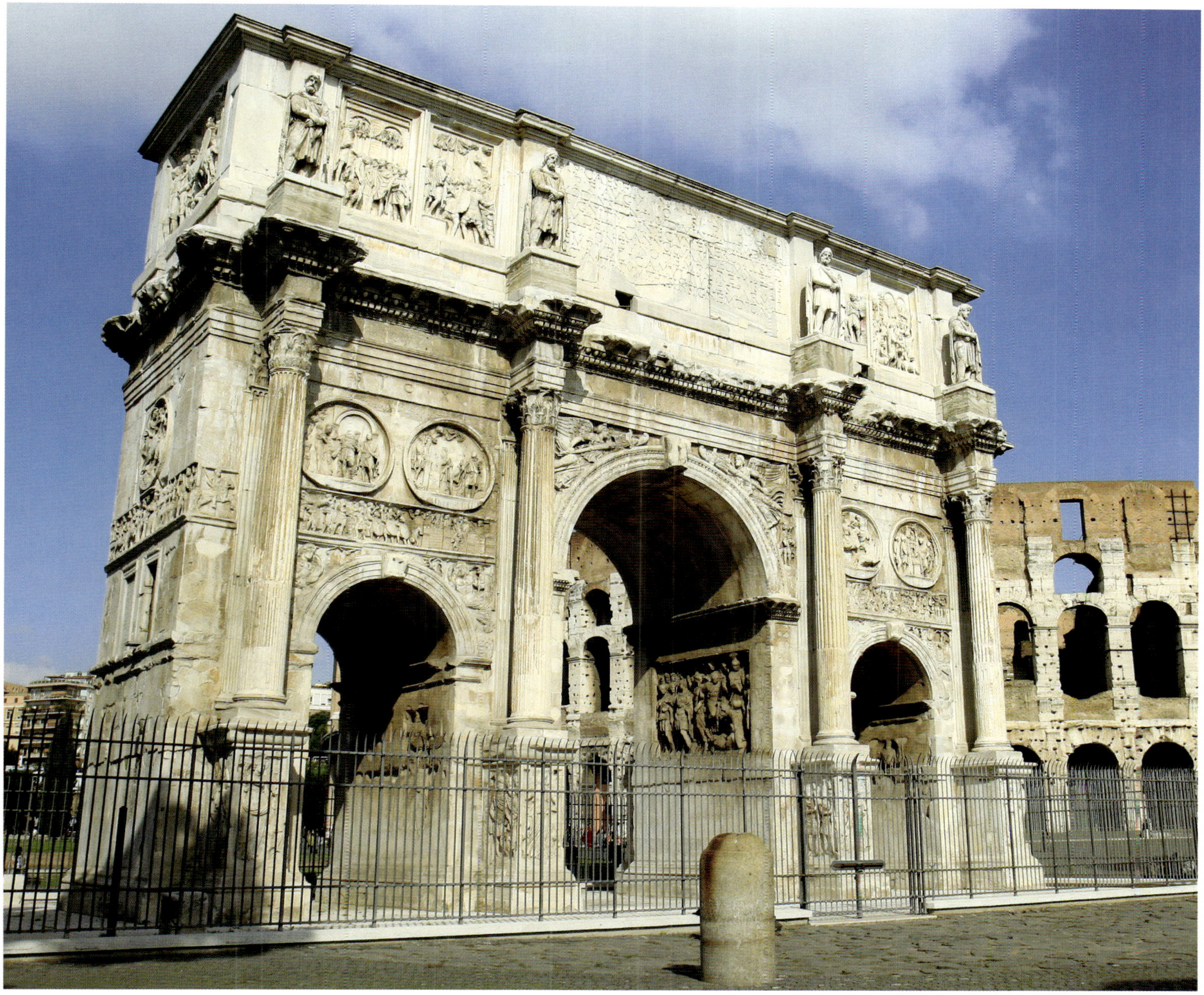

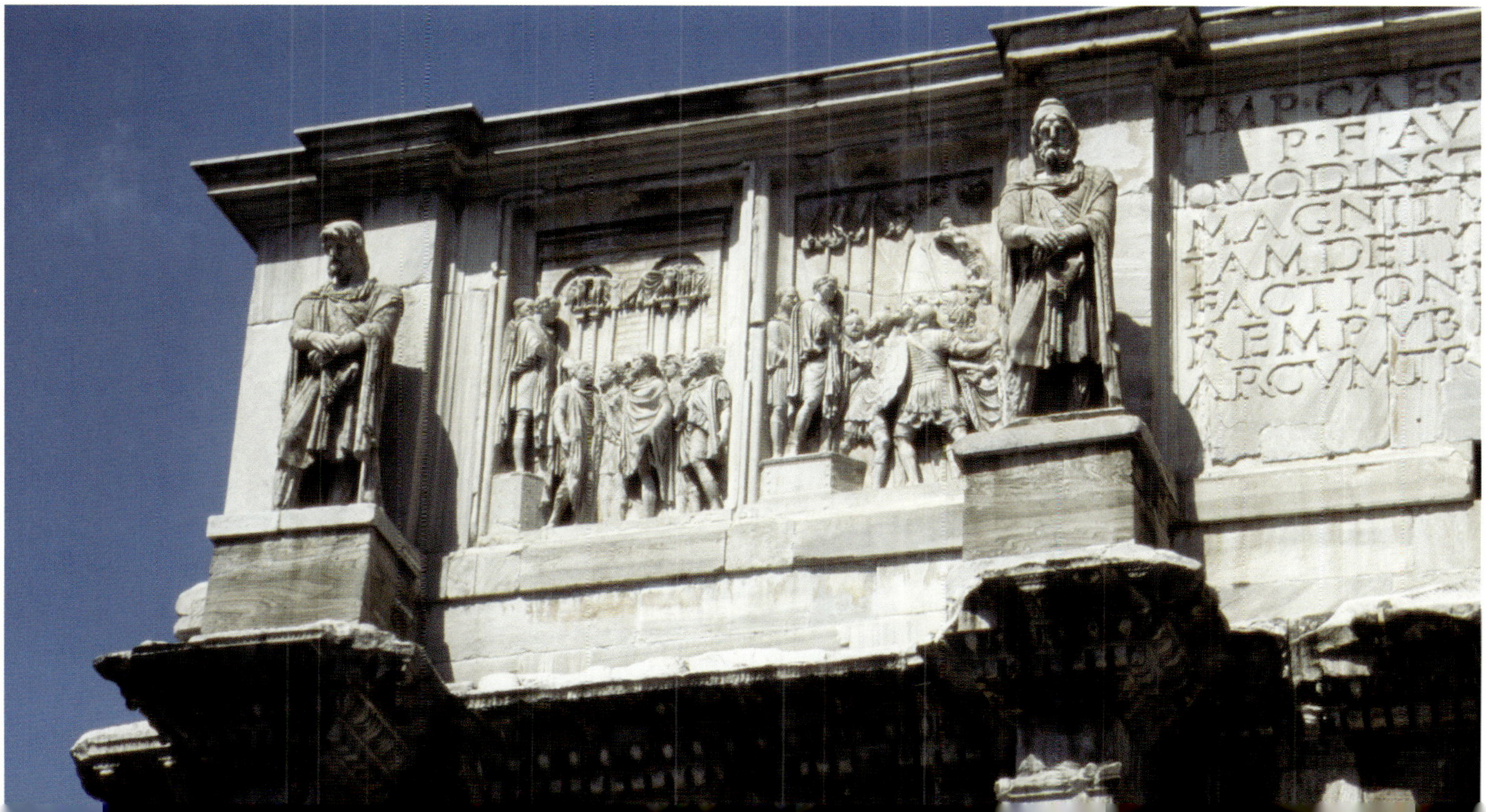
IMP·CAES
P·F·AV
QVOD INST
MAGNIT
IAM DE
FACTION
REMP
ARCVM

Right: Bright rays of light stream through the oculus at the top of the concrete dome of the Pantheon.

Far right: Sormani's sixteenth century fountain—the Fontana del Pantheon—in front of the ancient portico of the temple, built 2,000 years ago temple built by Hadrian in the heart of Rome.

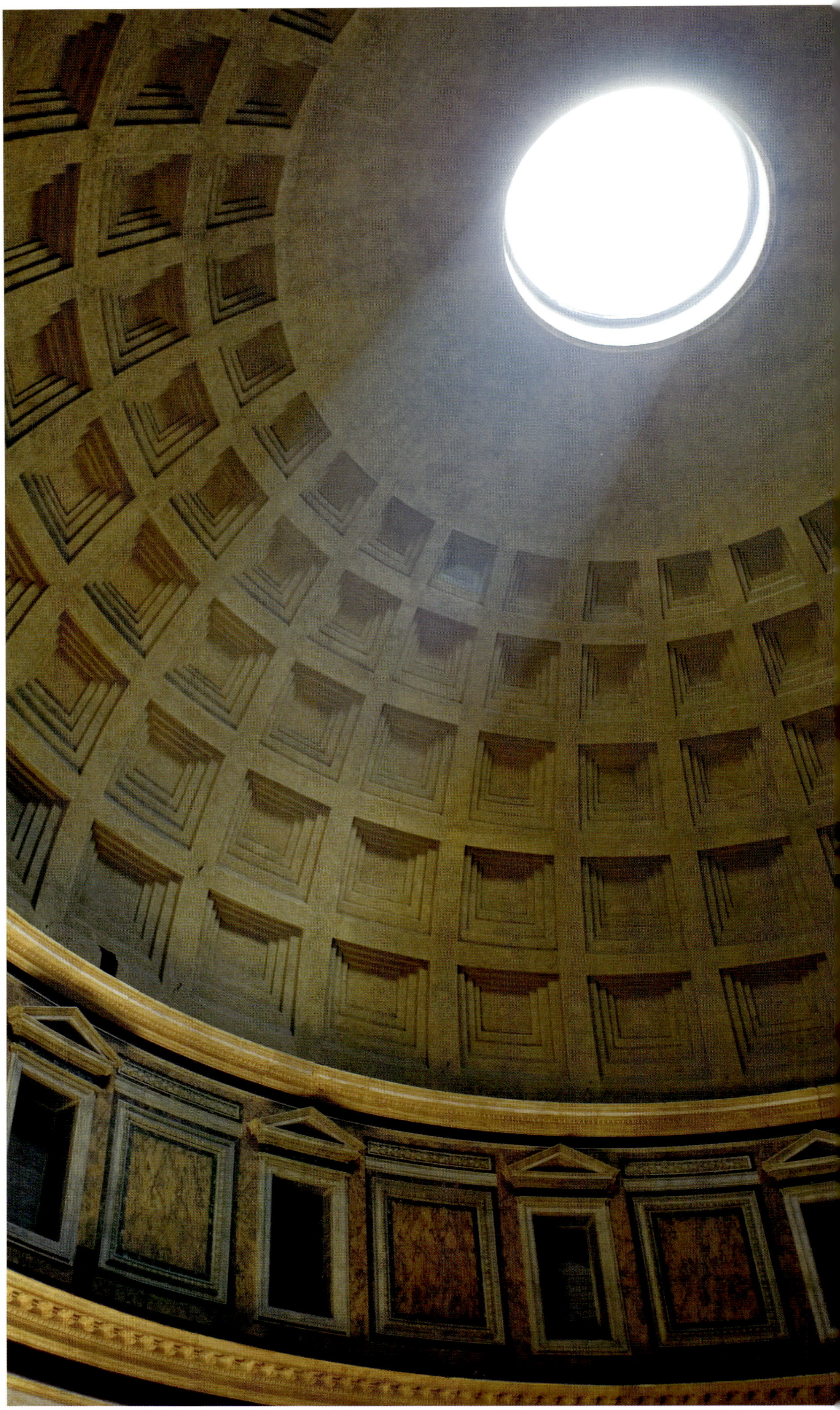

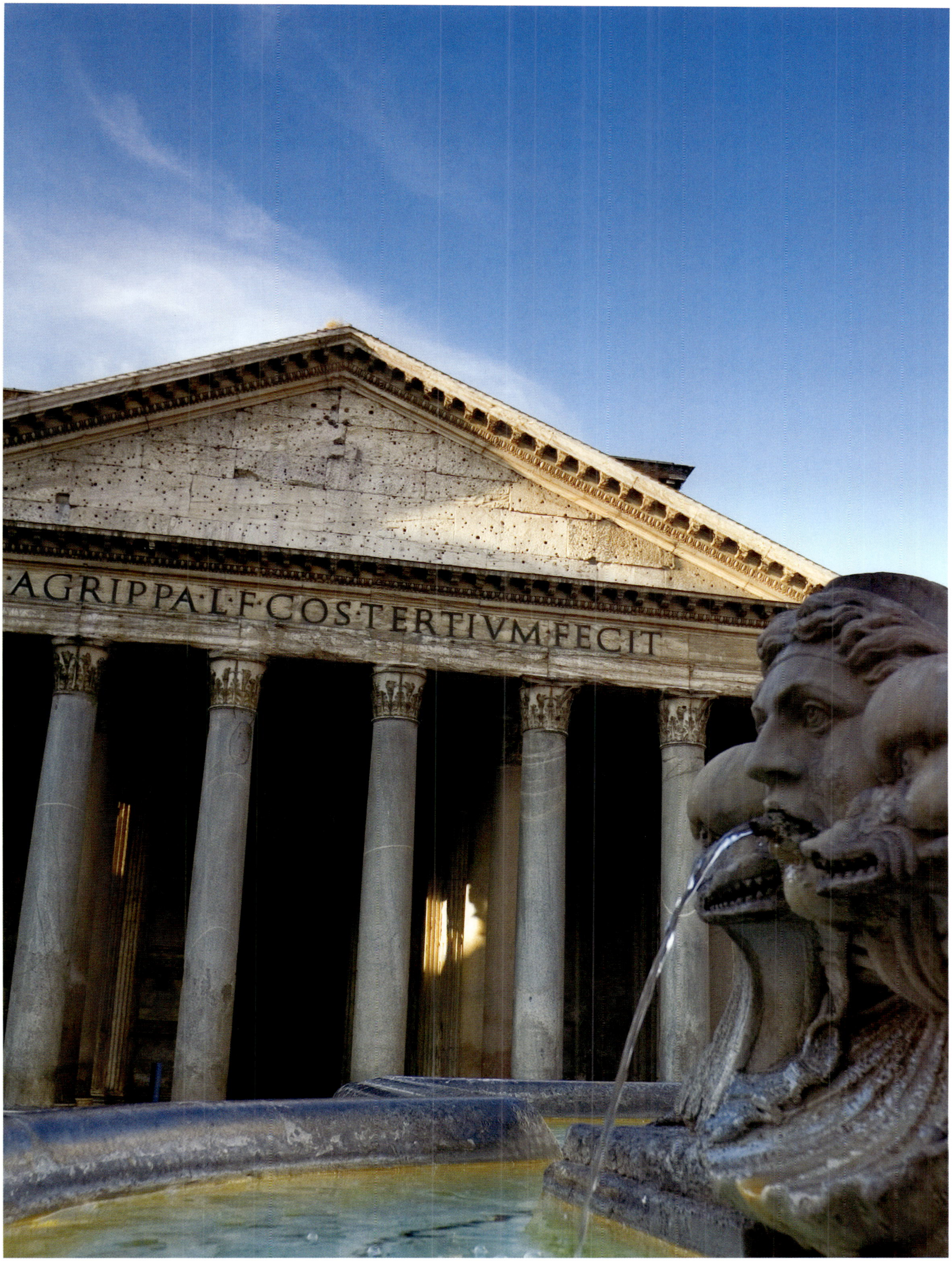
AGRIPPA·L·F·COS·TERTIVM·FECIT

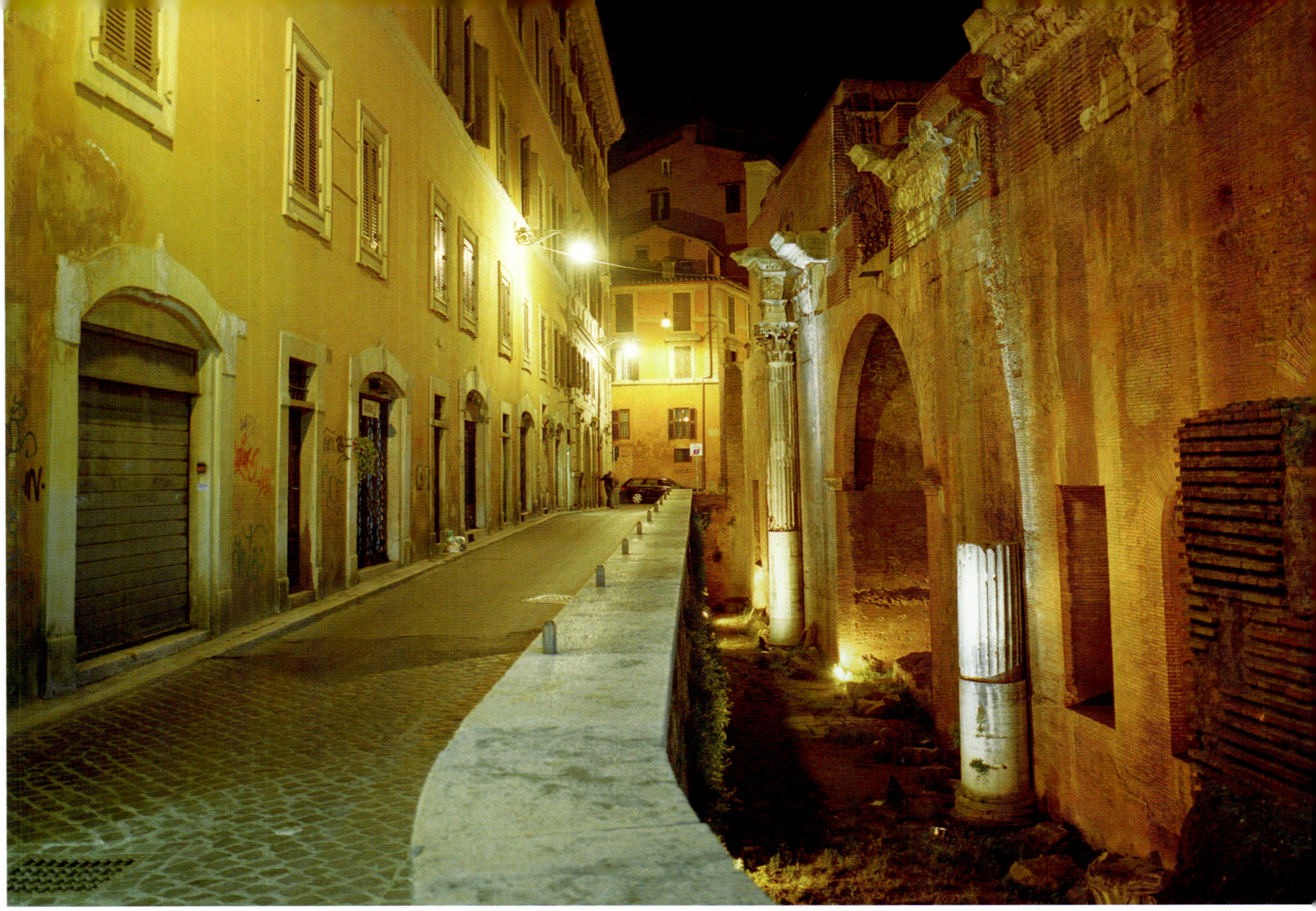

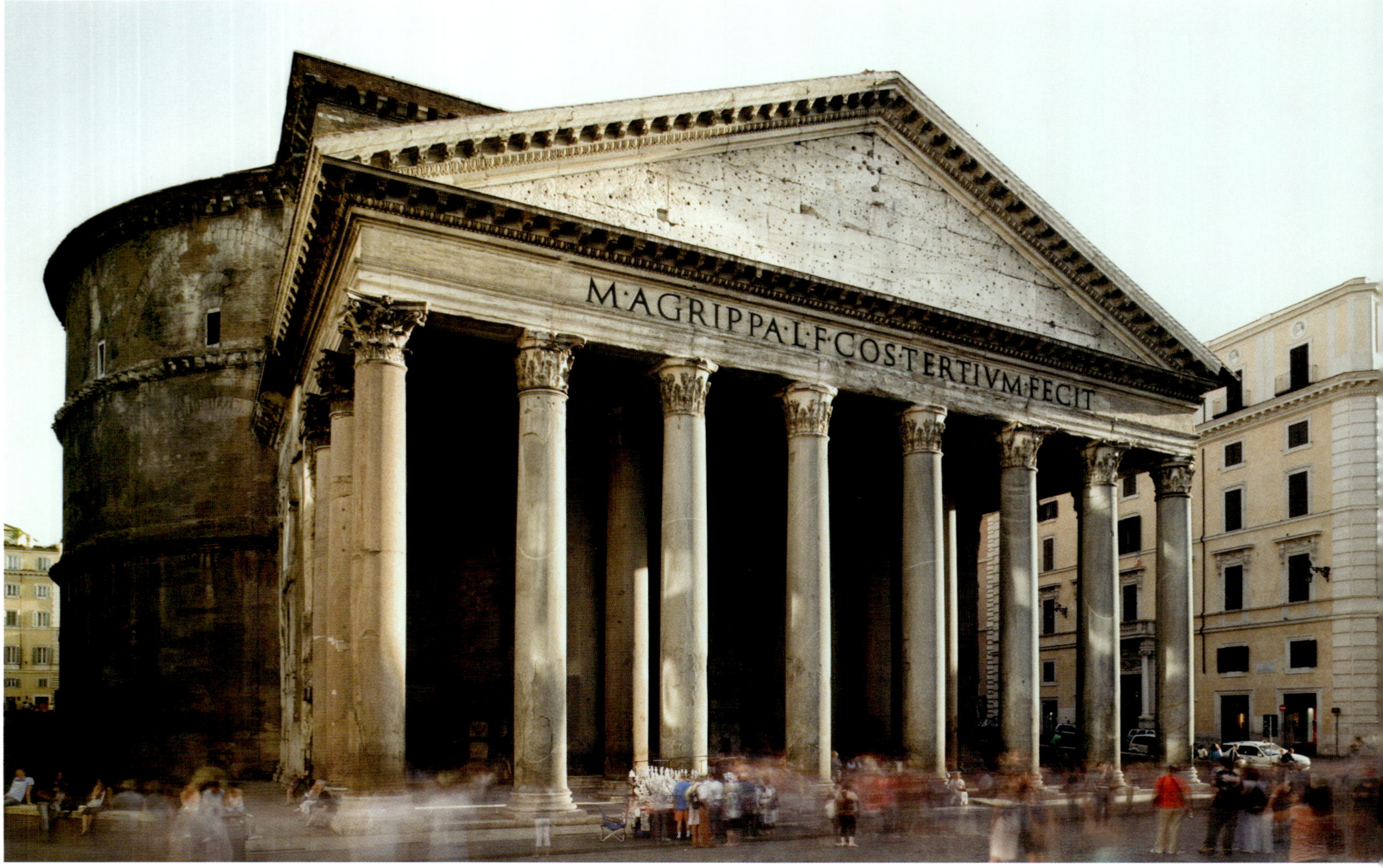
M·AGRIPPA·L·F·COS·TERTIVM·FECIT

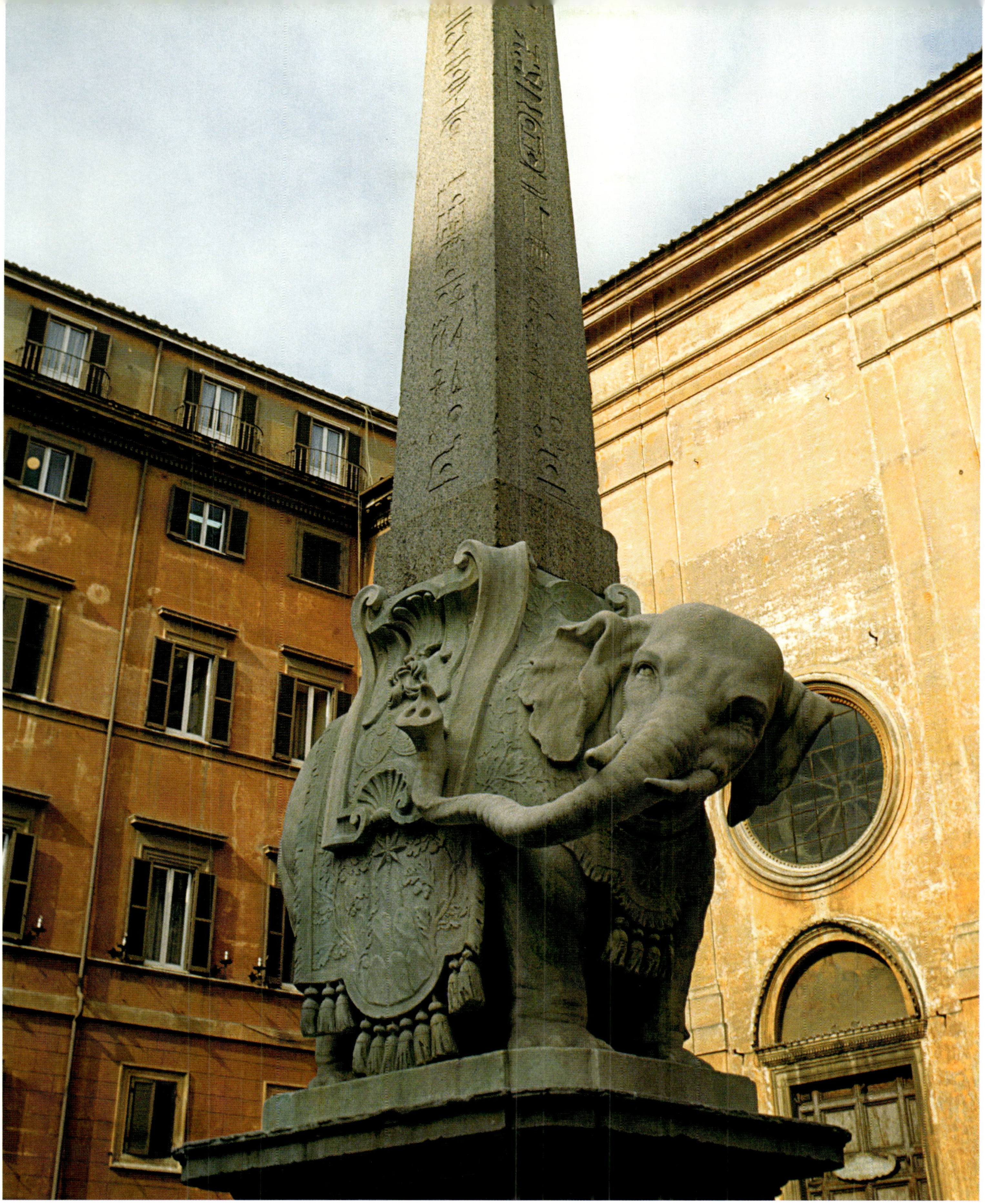

ABOVE LEFT: Night view of the rear of the Pantheon. *Silvia Otte/Photonica/Getty Images*

LEFT: Pantheon means Temple of all the Gods and was originally built as a temple to the seven deities of the seven planets in the state religion of Ancient Rome. It is the best preserved of all Roman buildings, and perhaps the best preserved building of its age in the world. *Jorg Greuel/Photonica/Getty Images*

ABOVE: The Monument of the Elephant in Piazza Della Minerva against the Pantheon in Rome. Originally one of a pair from Sais. Brought to Rome by Diocletian for the nearby Temple of Isis. Found in 1655 and erected in 1667 by Pope Alexander VII on an Elephant base by Bernini, behind the Pantheon. The other of the pair is in Urbino. *Roger Viollet/Getty Images*

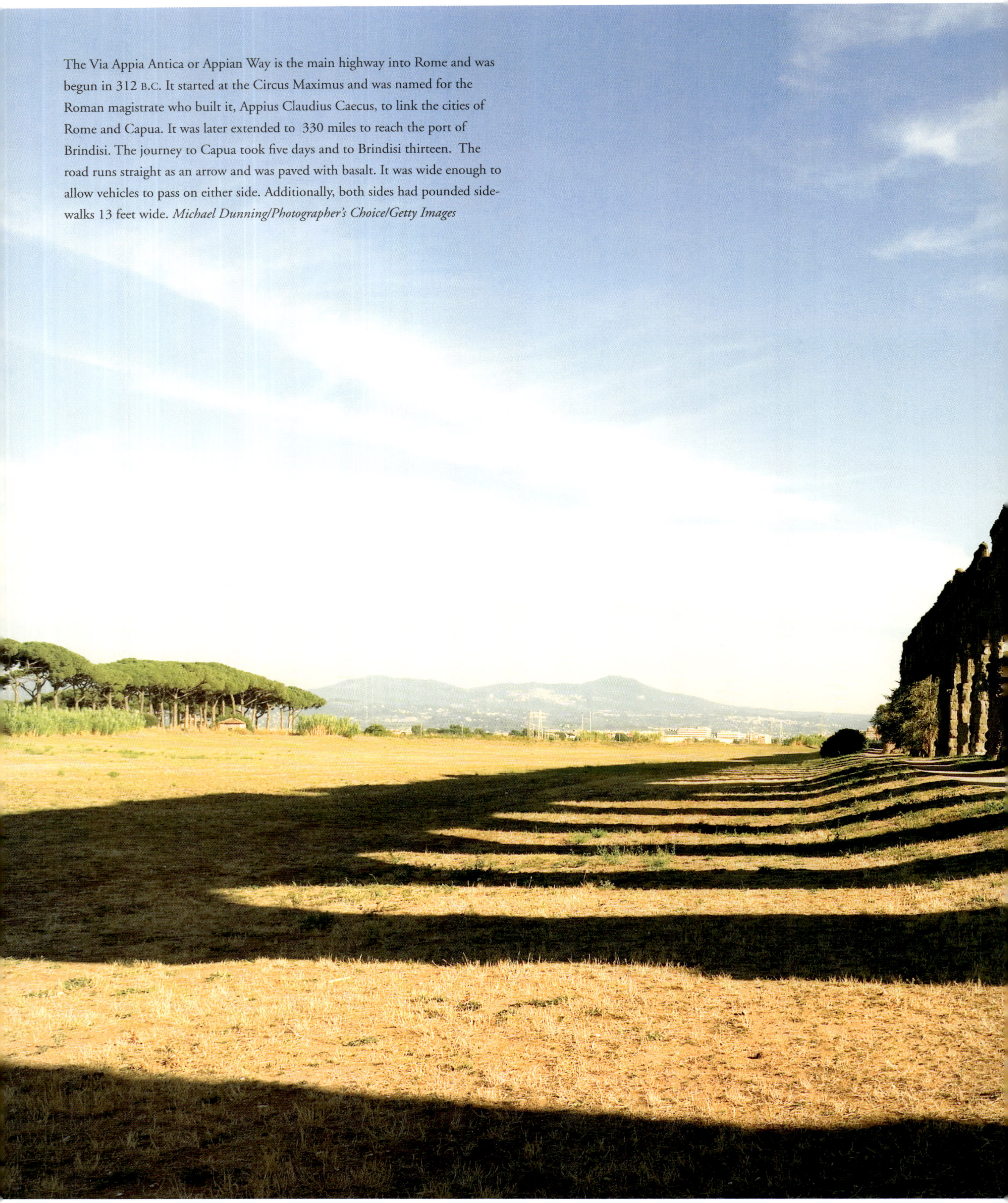

The Via Appia Antica or Appian Way is the main highway into Rome and was begun in 312 B.C. It started at the Circus Maximus and was named for the Roman magistrate who built it, Appius Claudius Caecus, to link the cities of Rome and Capua. It was later extended to 330 miles to reach the port of Brindisi. The journey to Capua took five days and to Brindisi thirteen. The road runs straight as an arrow and was paved with basalt. It was wide enough to allow vehicles to pass on either side. Additionally, both sides had pounded sidewalks 13 feet wide. *Michael Dunning/Photographer's Choice/Getty Images*

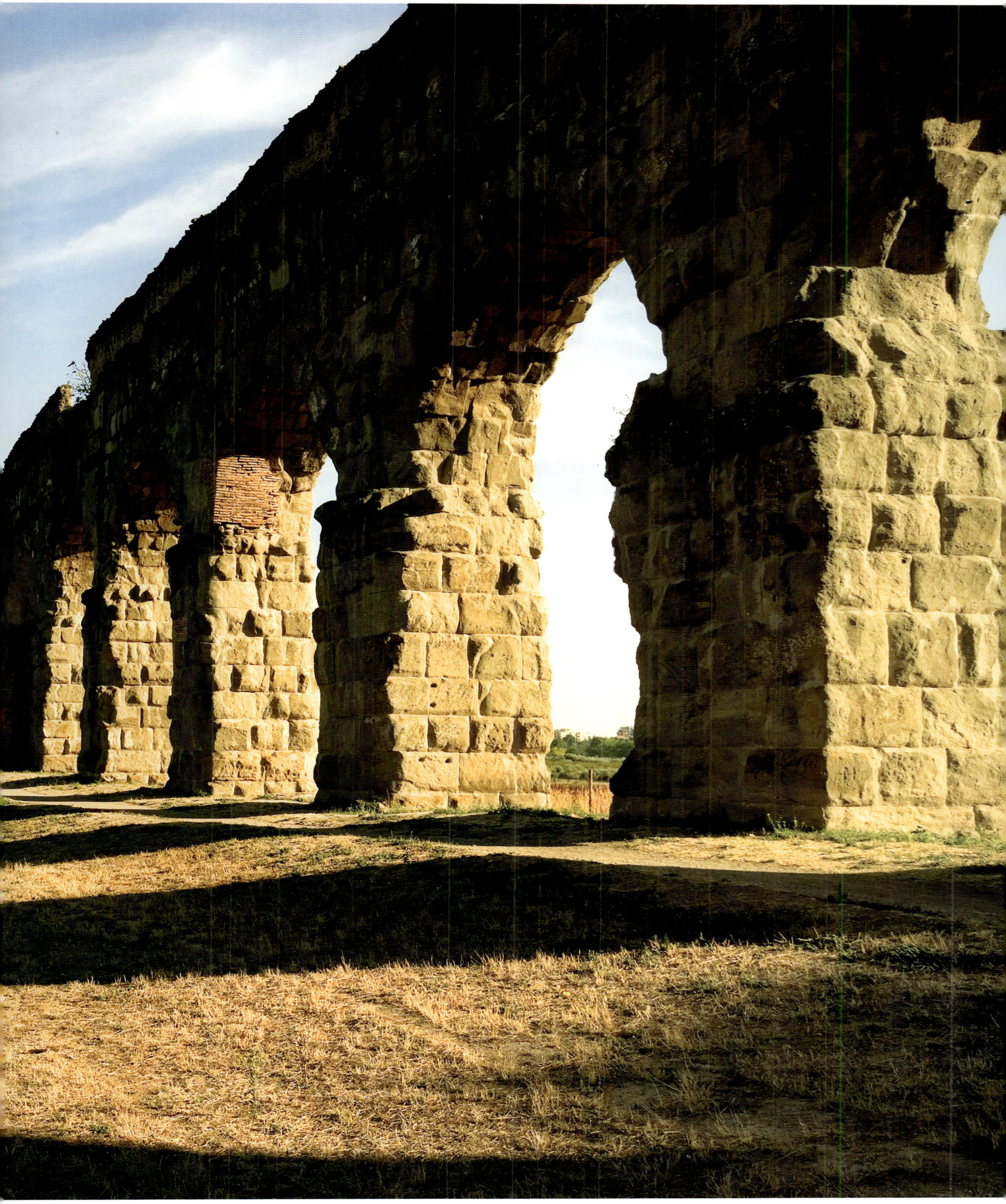

Medieval and Renaissance Rome

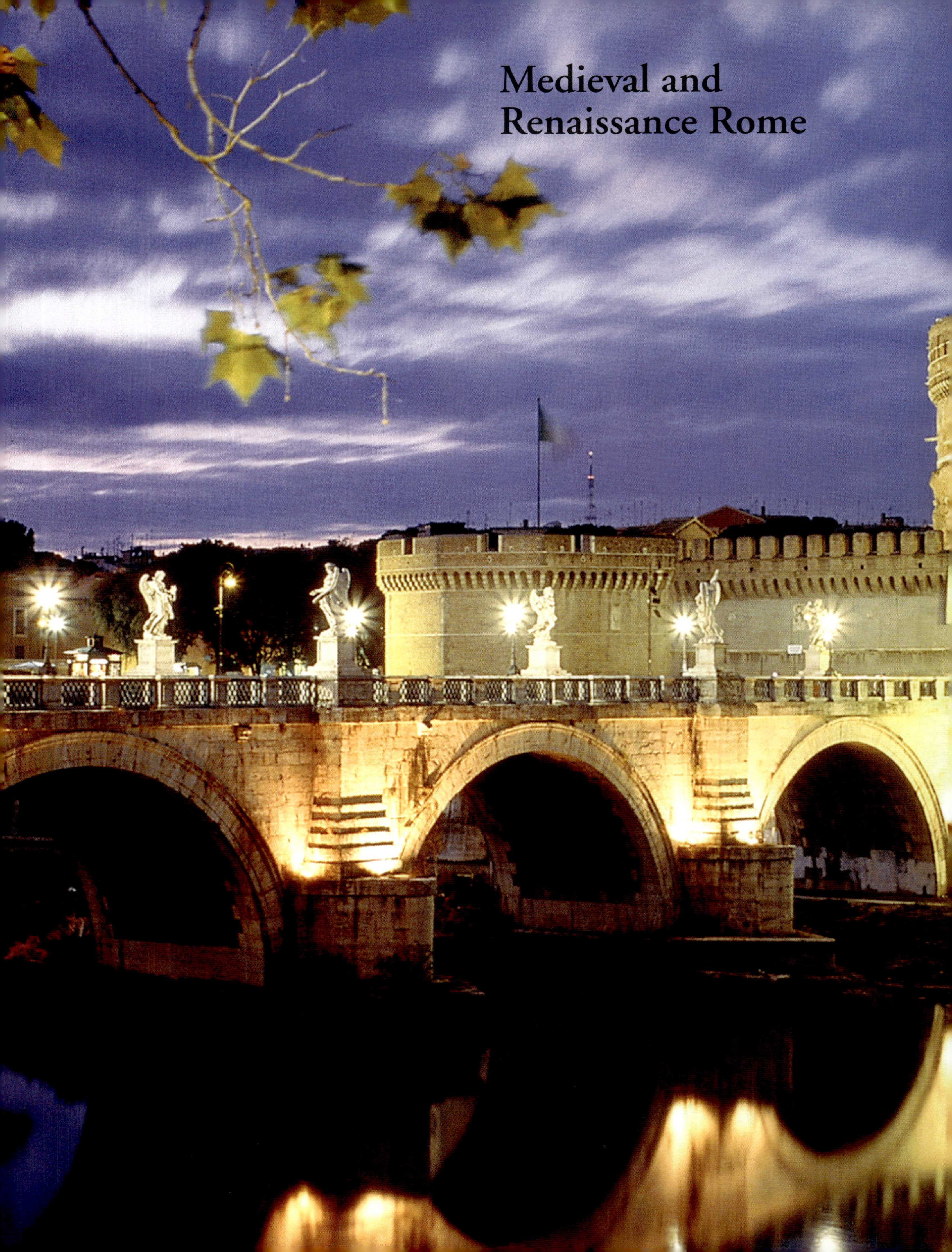

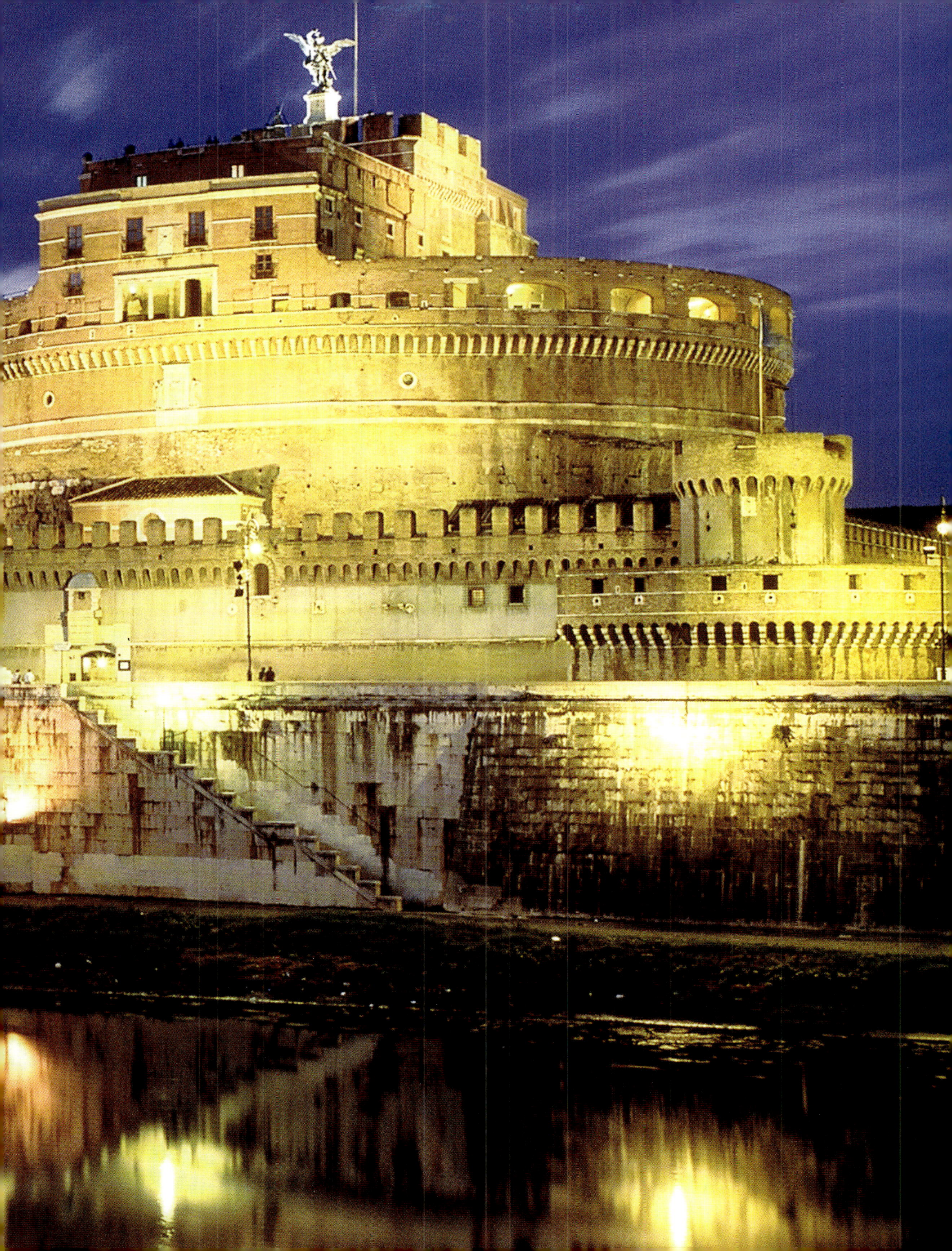

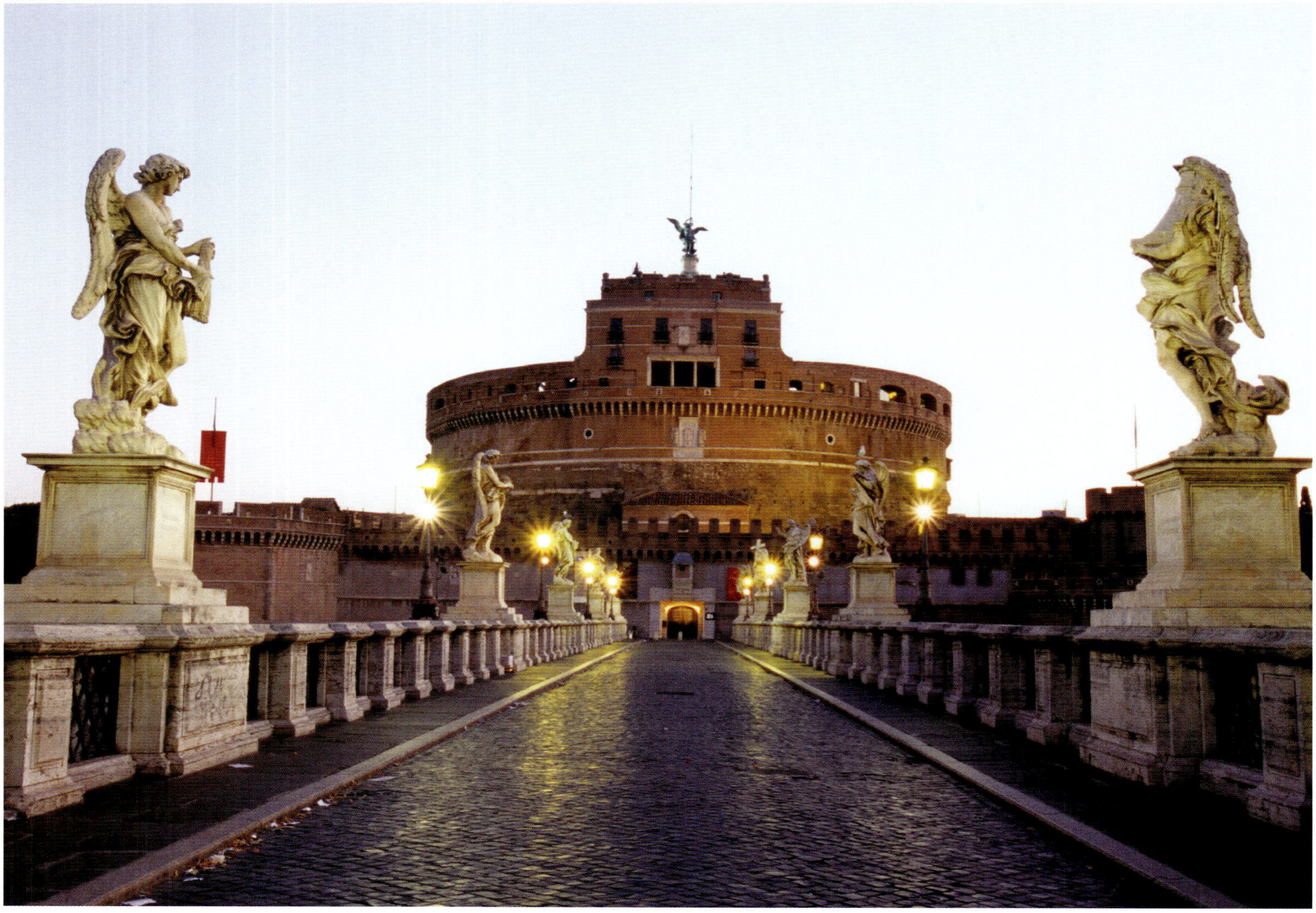

Above, Below, and Pages 102–103: The Ponte S. Angelo was built to link Castel Sant' Angelo with the Campus Martius. As well as the ten statues of angels that line the bridge there is a statue of St. Paul by Paulo Romano and another of St. Peter by Lorenzetto Lotti. The castel was originally the mausoleum built by Emperor Hadrian for himself and his successors and known as the Hadrianeum. This was changed in the Middle Ages when towers and defensive walls were erected during the reign of the Emperor Aurelian to become an almost unassailable fortress in a strategic position that defended the northern entrance of the city. *Murat Taner/zefa/Corbis*

Right: The Fontana dell'Acqua Paola on the Janiculum is a monumental fountain named after Pope Paul V. It was constructed in 1612 from marble taken from the Nerva Forum by Giovanni Fontana and Flaminio Ponzio. It is fed by spring water flowing for just over 30 miles from Lake Bracciano through the subterranean Aqueduct of Trajan. The original fountain fed into five small basins but in 1690 these were replaced by a huge granite basin created by Carlo Fontana. *Dorling Kindersley/Getty Images*

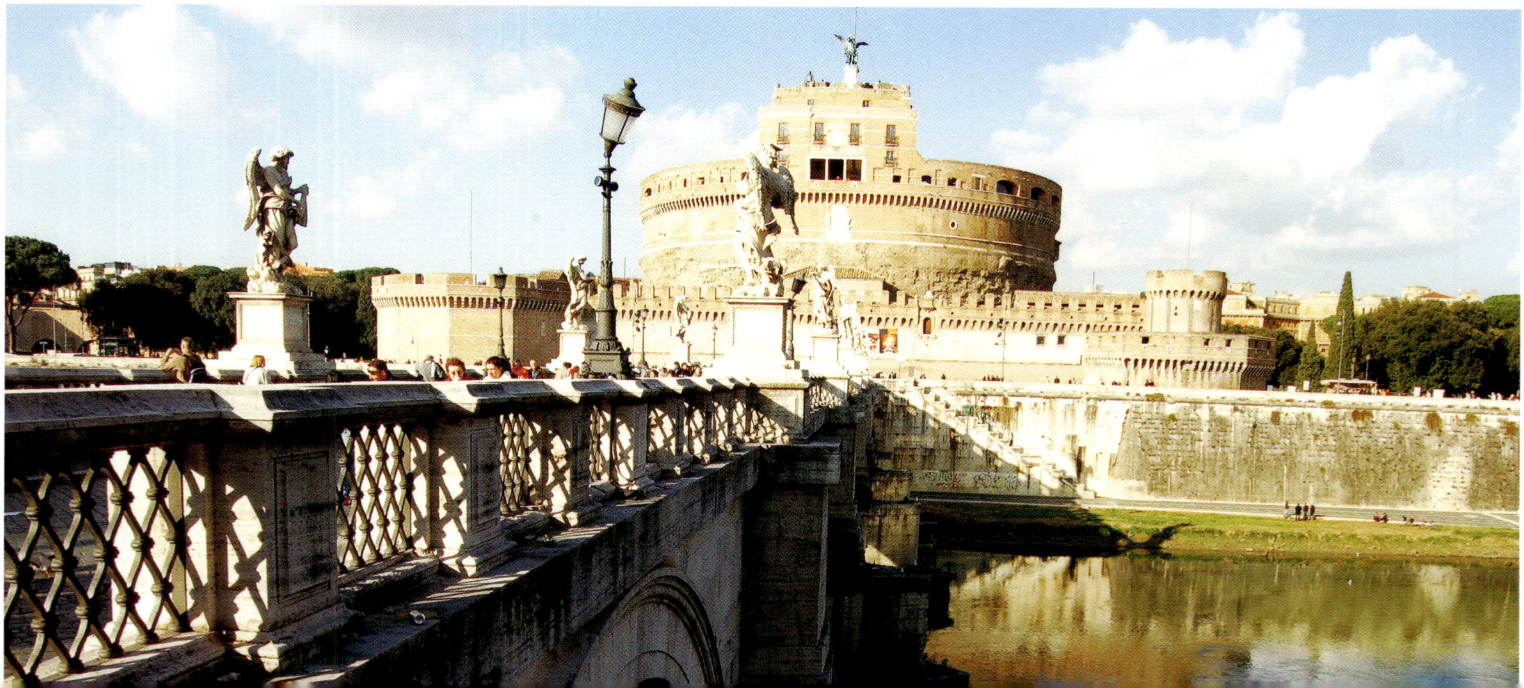

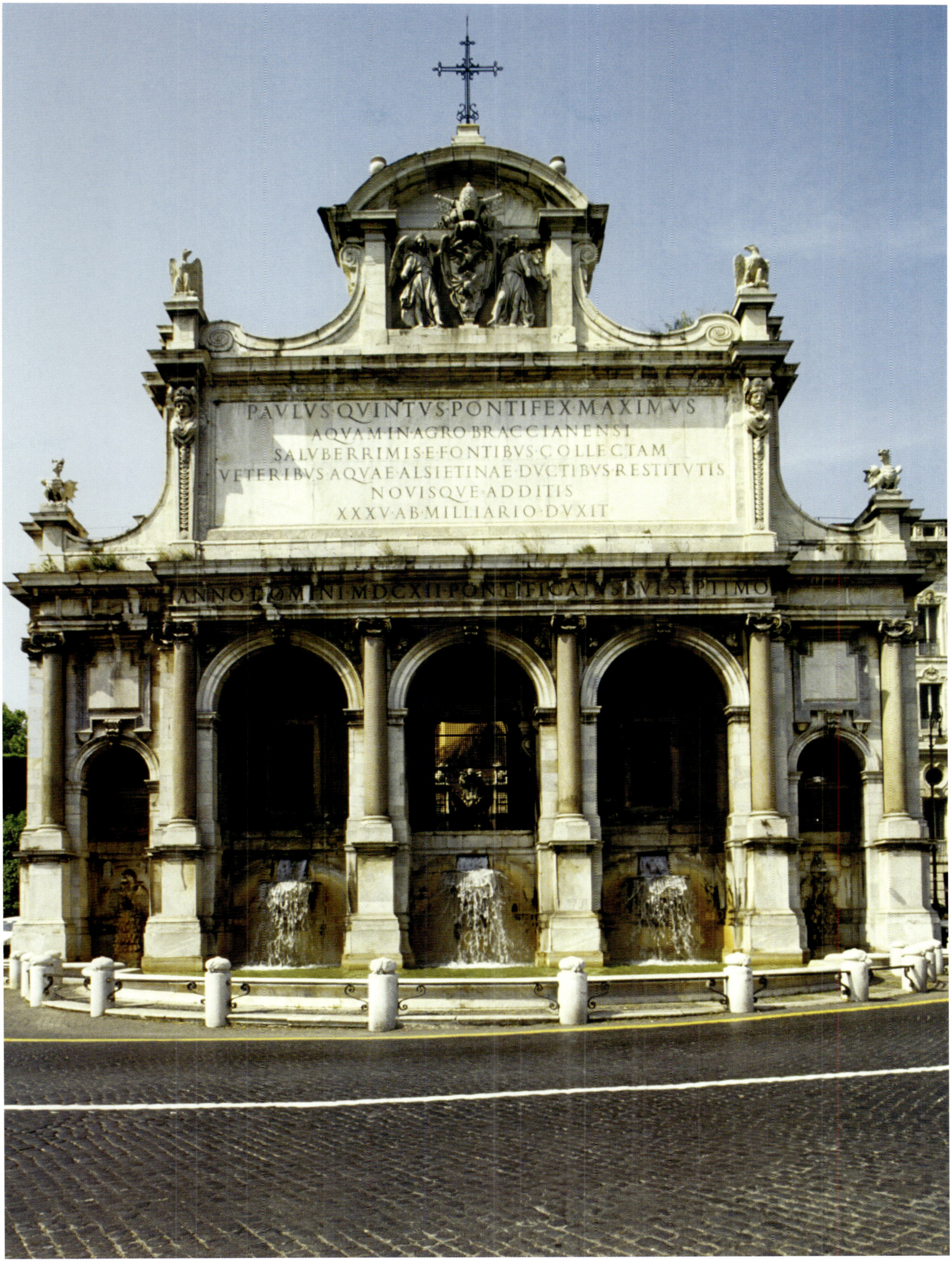
PAVLVS·QVINTVS·PONTIFEX·MAXIMVS
AQVAM·IN·AGRO·BRACCIANENSI
SALVBERRIMIS·E·FONTIBVS·COLLECTAM
VETERIBVS·AQVAE·ALSIETINAE·DVCTIBVS·RESTITVTIS
NOVISQVE·ADDITIS
XXXV·AB·MILLIARIO·DVXIT
ANNO DOMINI MDCXII PONTIFICATVS SVI SEPTIMO

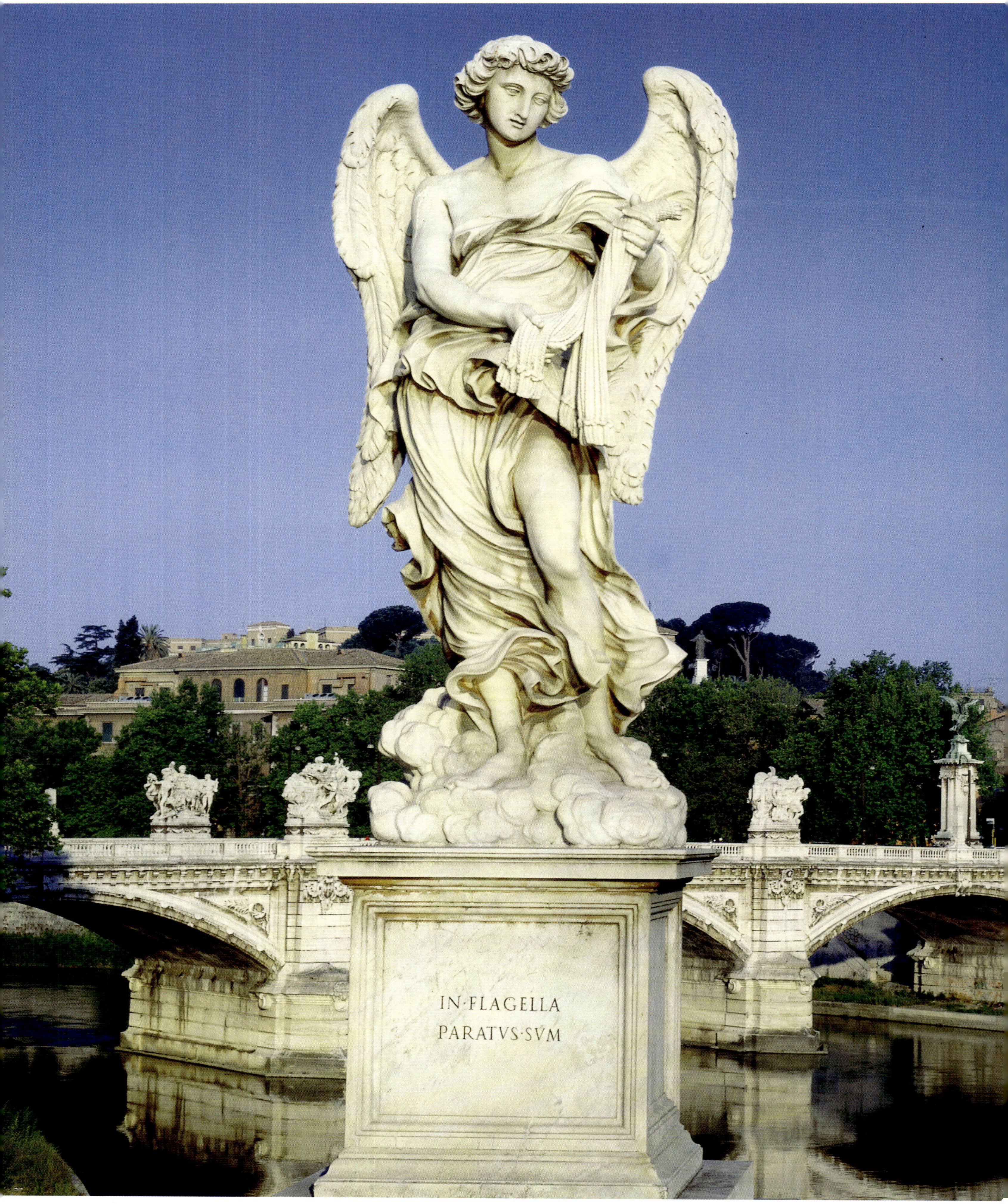
IN·FLAGELLA
PARATVS·SVM

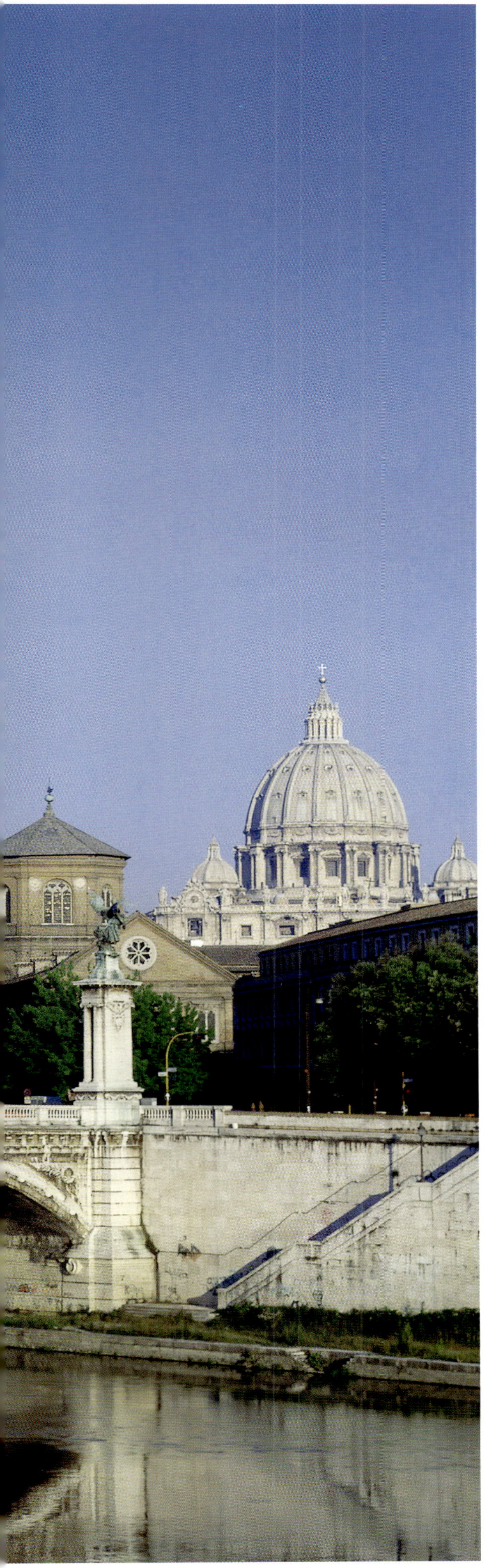

LEFT: The angels on the Ponte Sant' Angelo hold elements from the Passion of Christ; this angel holds the scourge and is by Lazzaro Morelli, after a design by Bernini. *Purestock/Getty Images*

BELOW: The poor vestment by Cosimo Fancelli. *Millah Adams/Fotolibra*

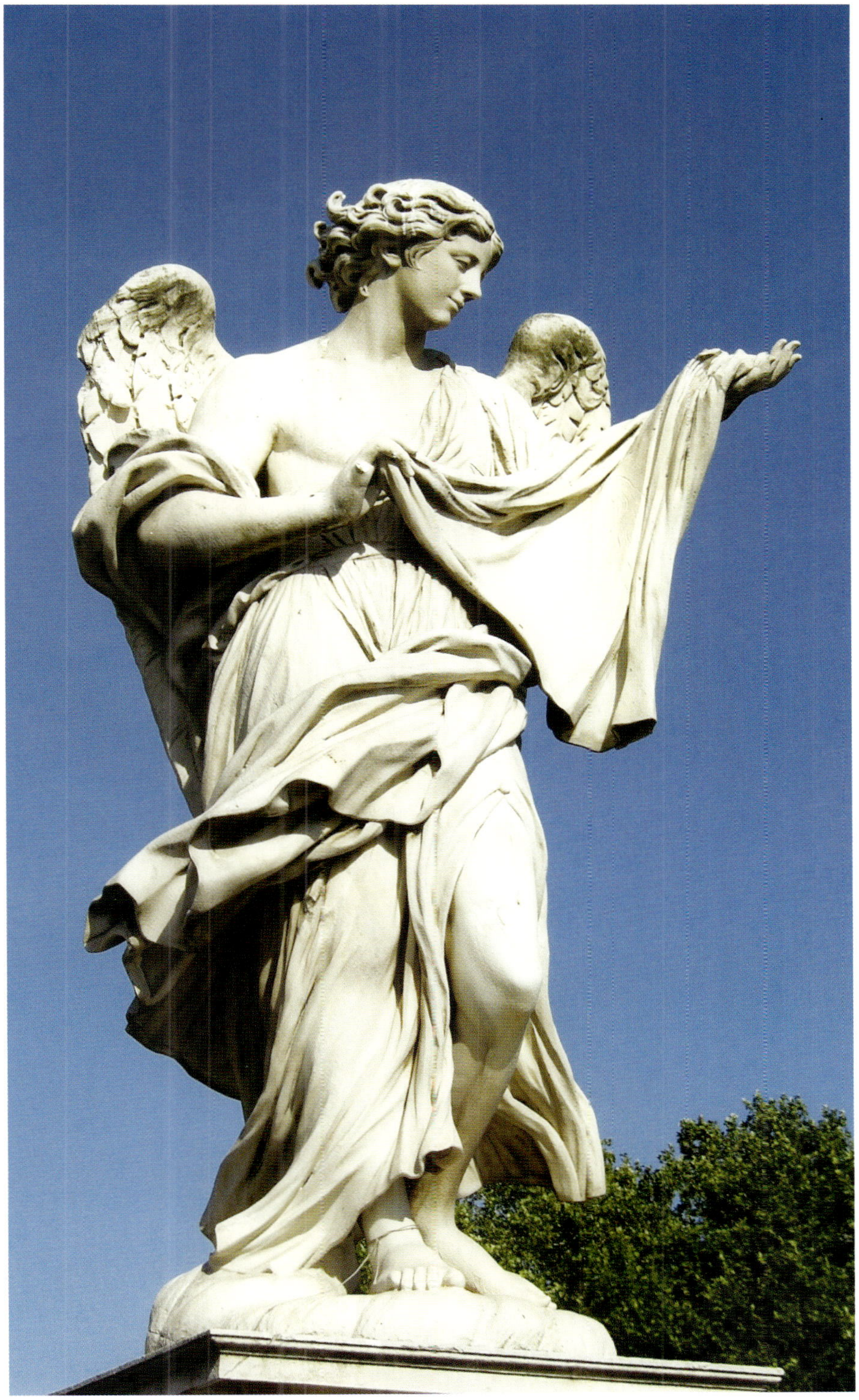

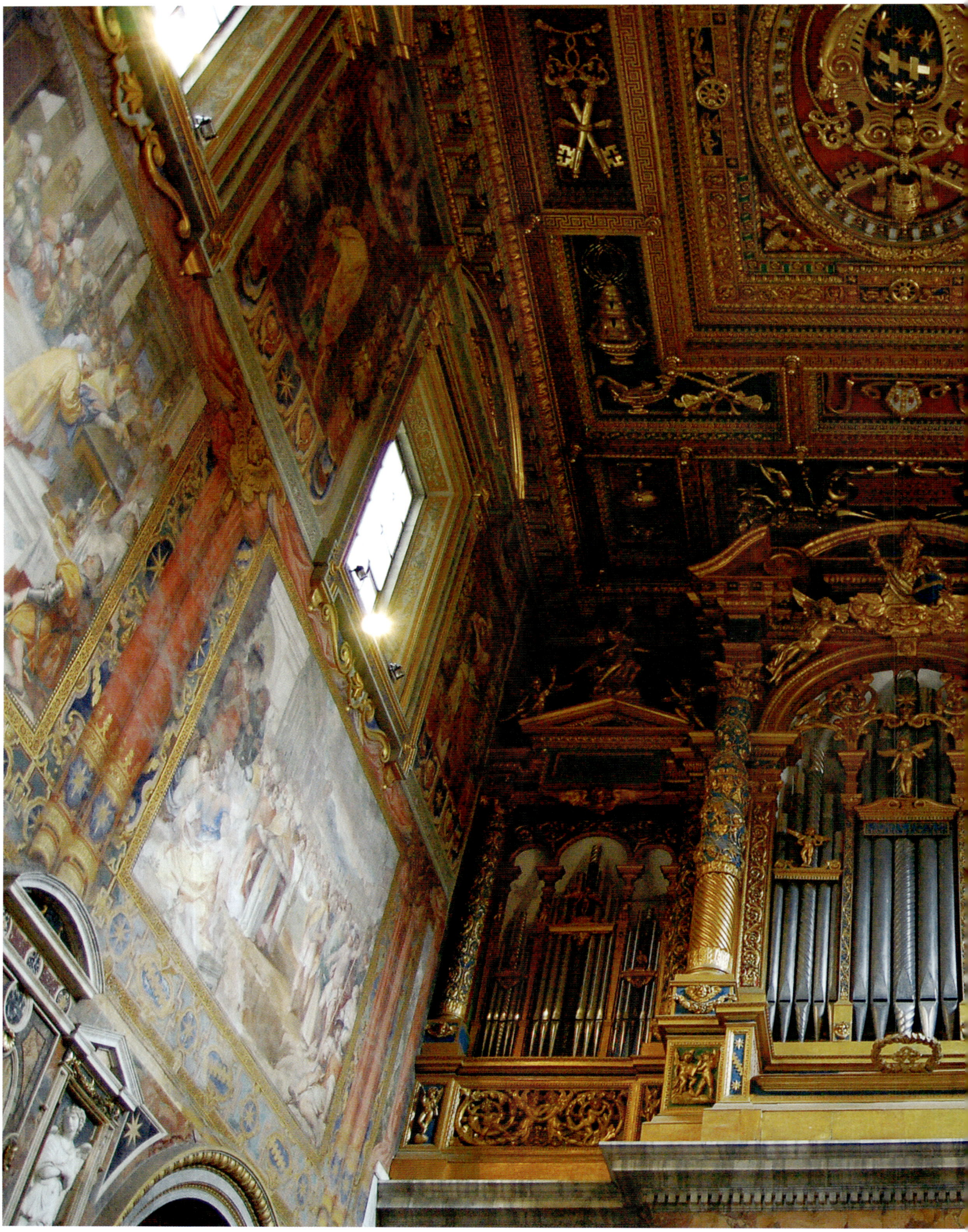

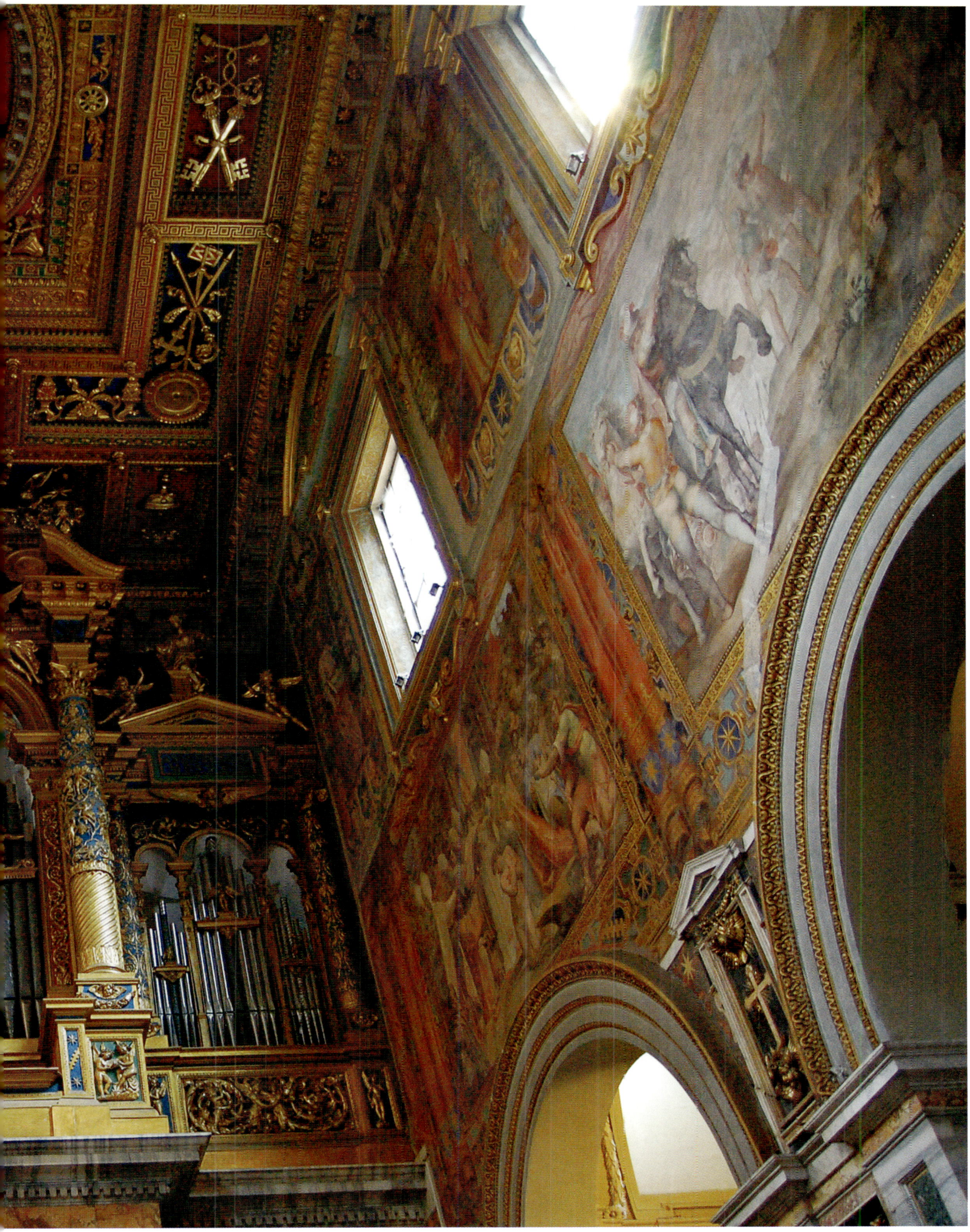

Pages 108–109: Rome is the ultimate city for elaborate church interiors, many of such are within the Vatican City itself.

Right: The interior of the dome of St. Peter's Basilica. The imposing dome was designed by Michelangelo and can be seen for miles around Rome. Internally however, is a second dome fitted into the other to create more harmonious proportions. In the space between the two domes lies a series of steps that lead right up and into the ball above the lantern. *Allan Baxter/Photographer's Choice/Getty Images*

Pages 112–113: St. Peter holding the keys to heaven. *David C Tomlinson/Photographer's Choice/Getty Images*

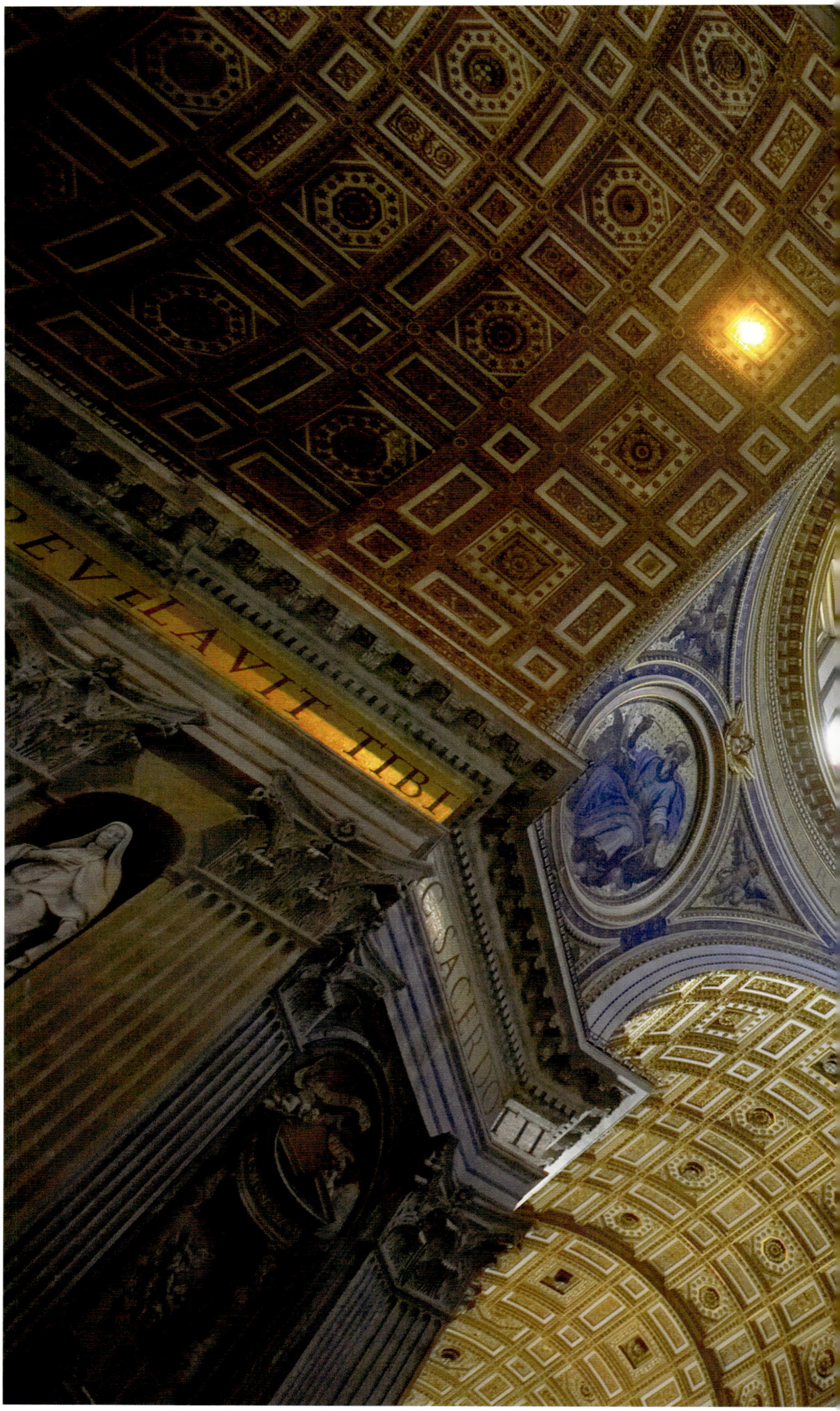

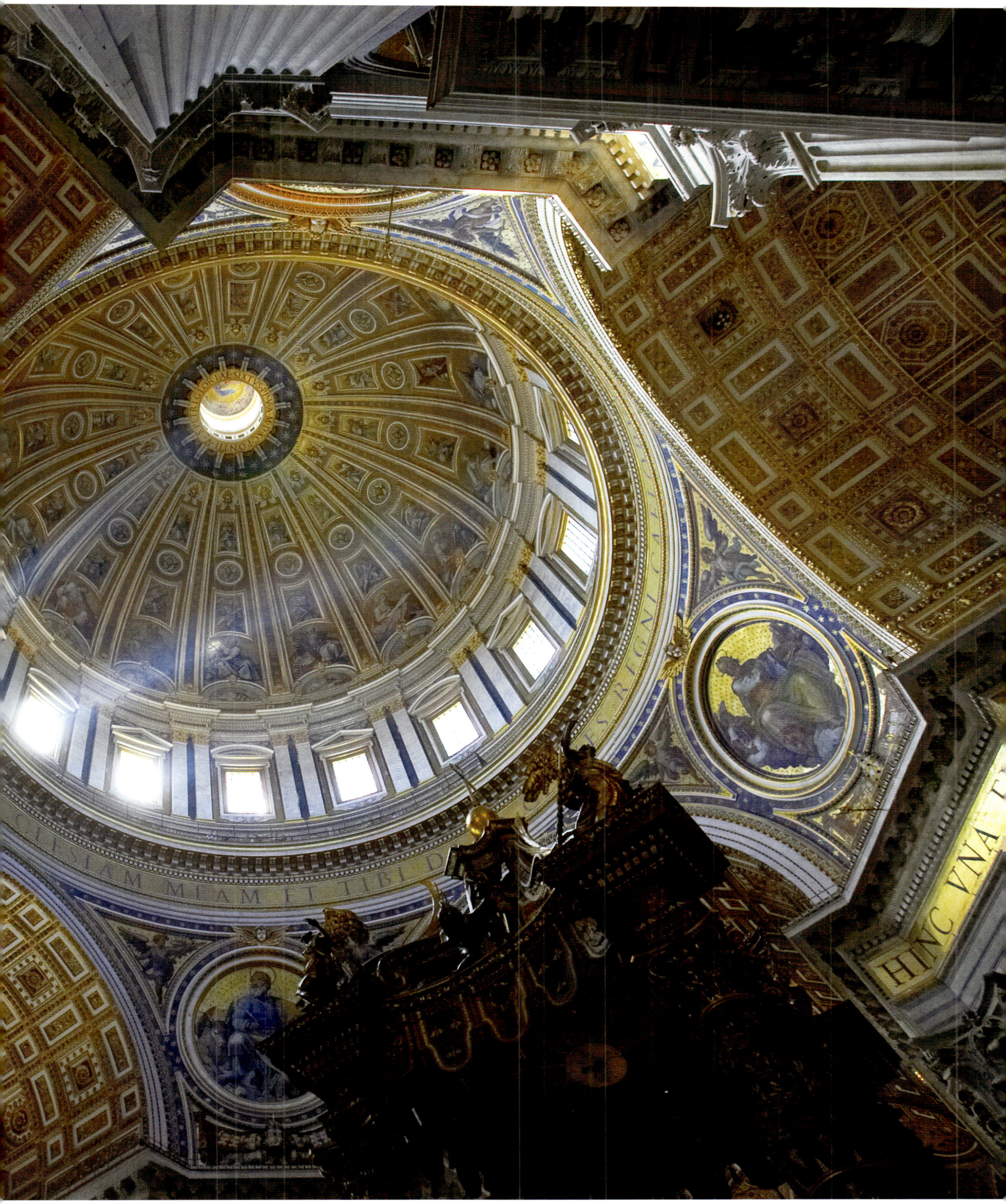
CLESIAM MEAM ET TIBI D
HINC VNA

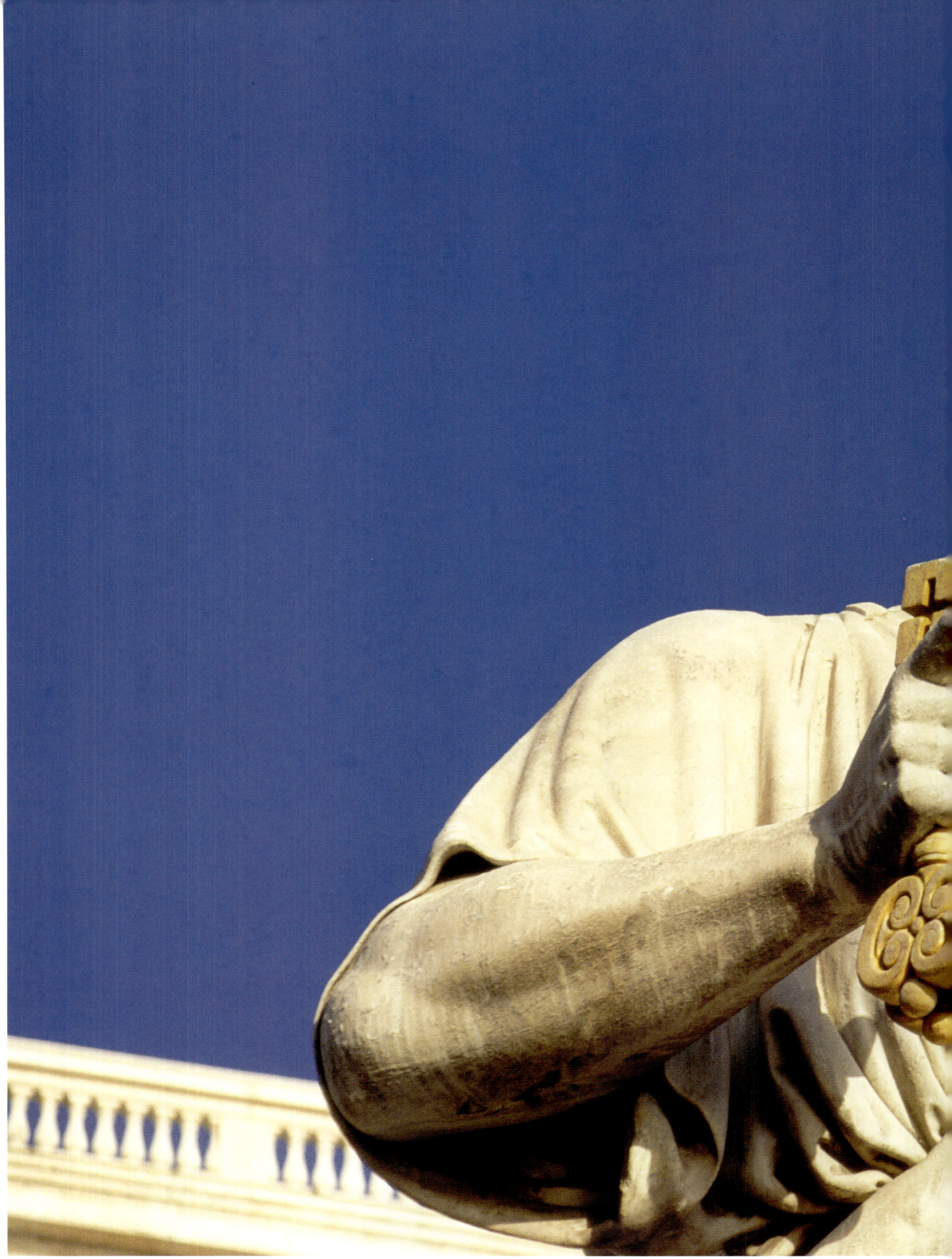

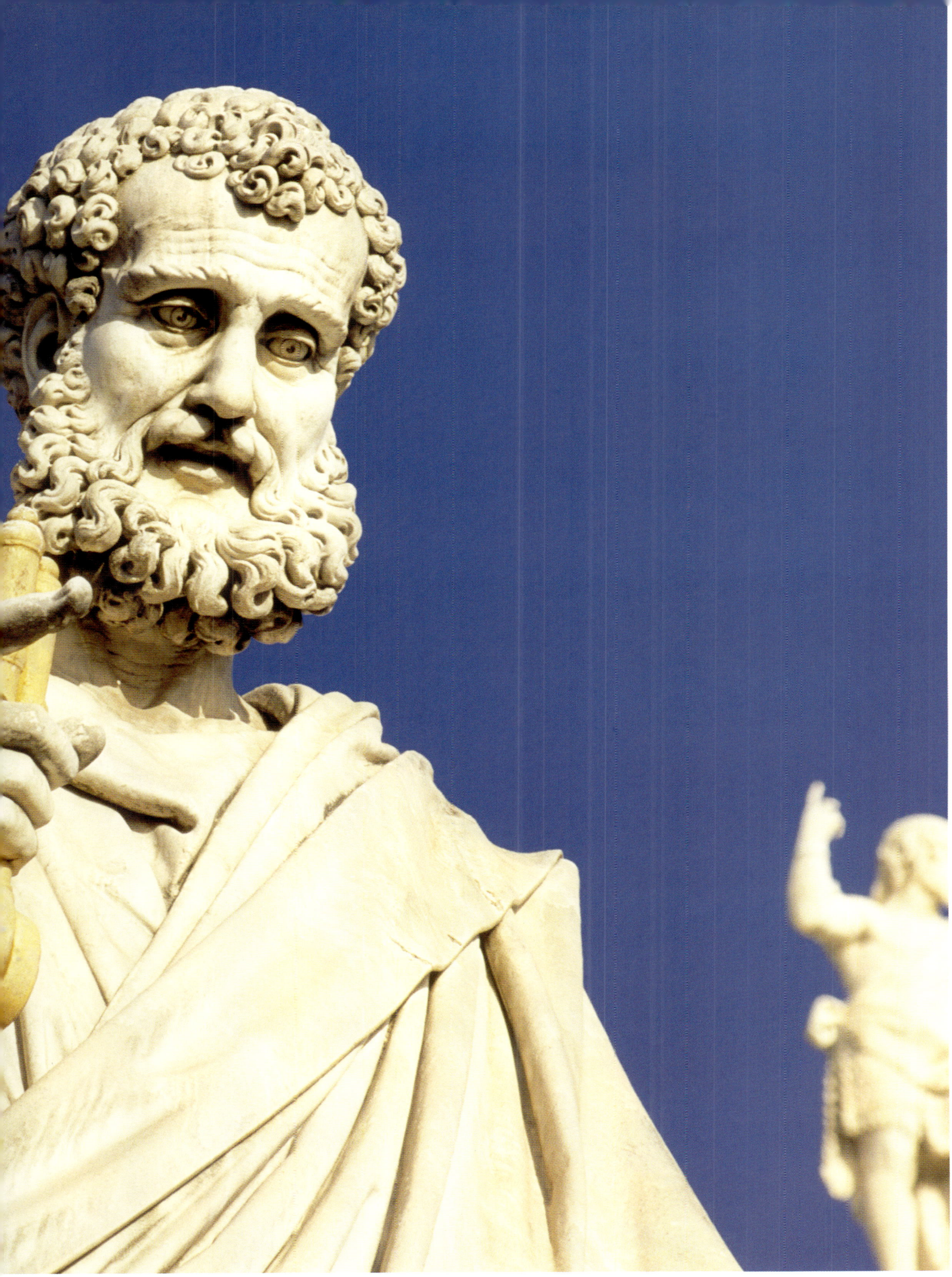

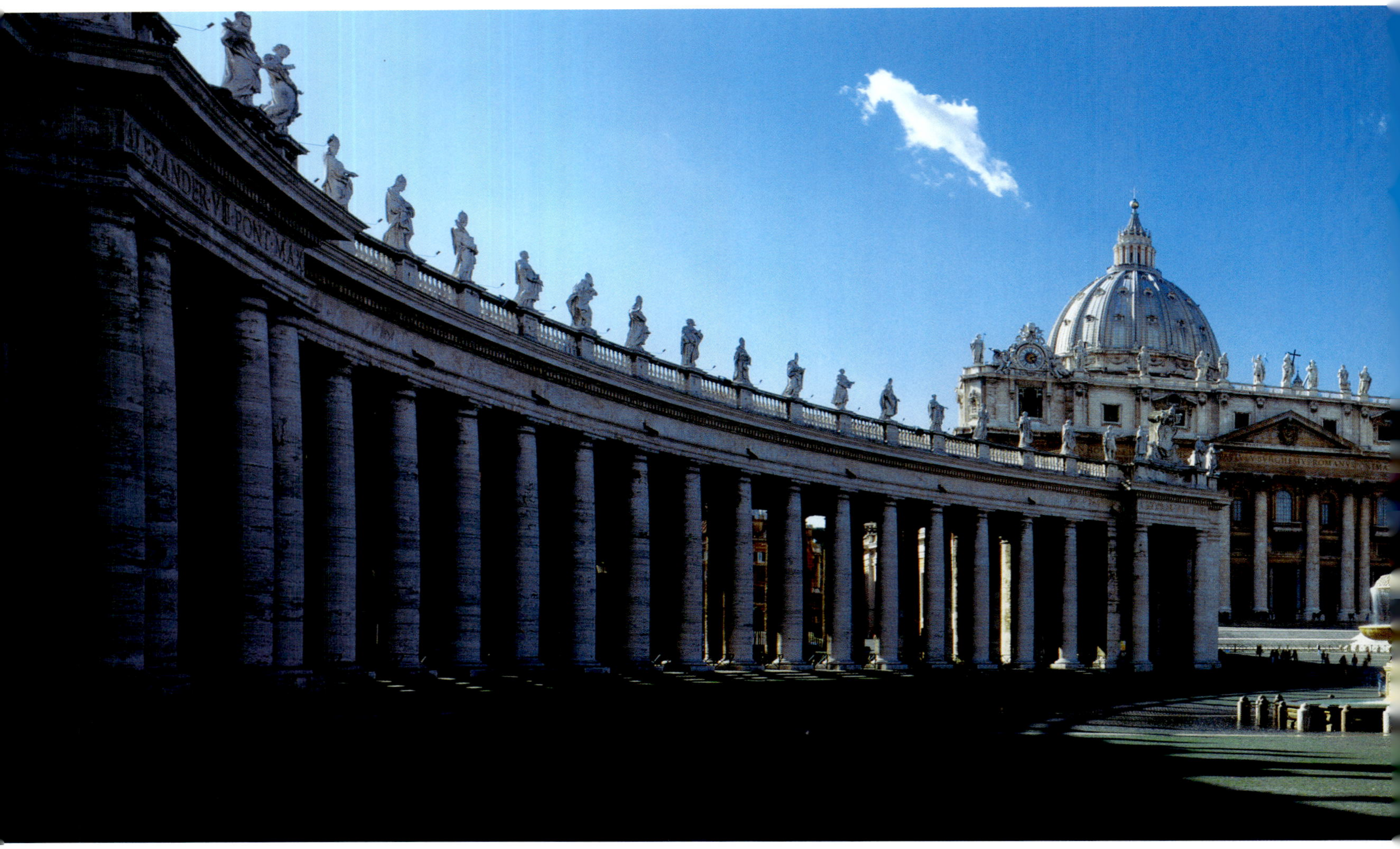

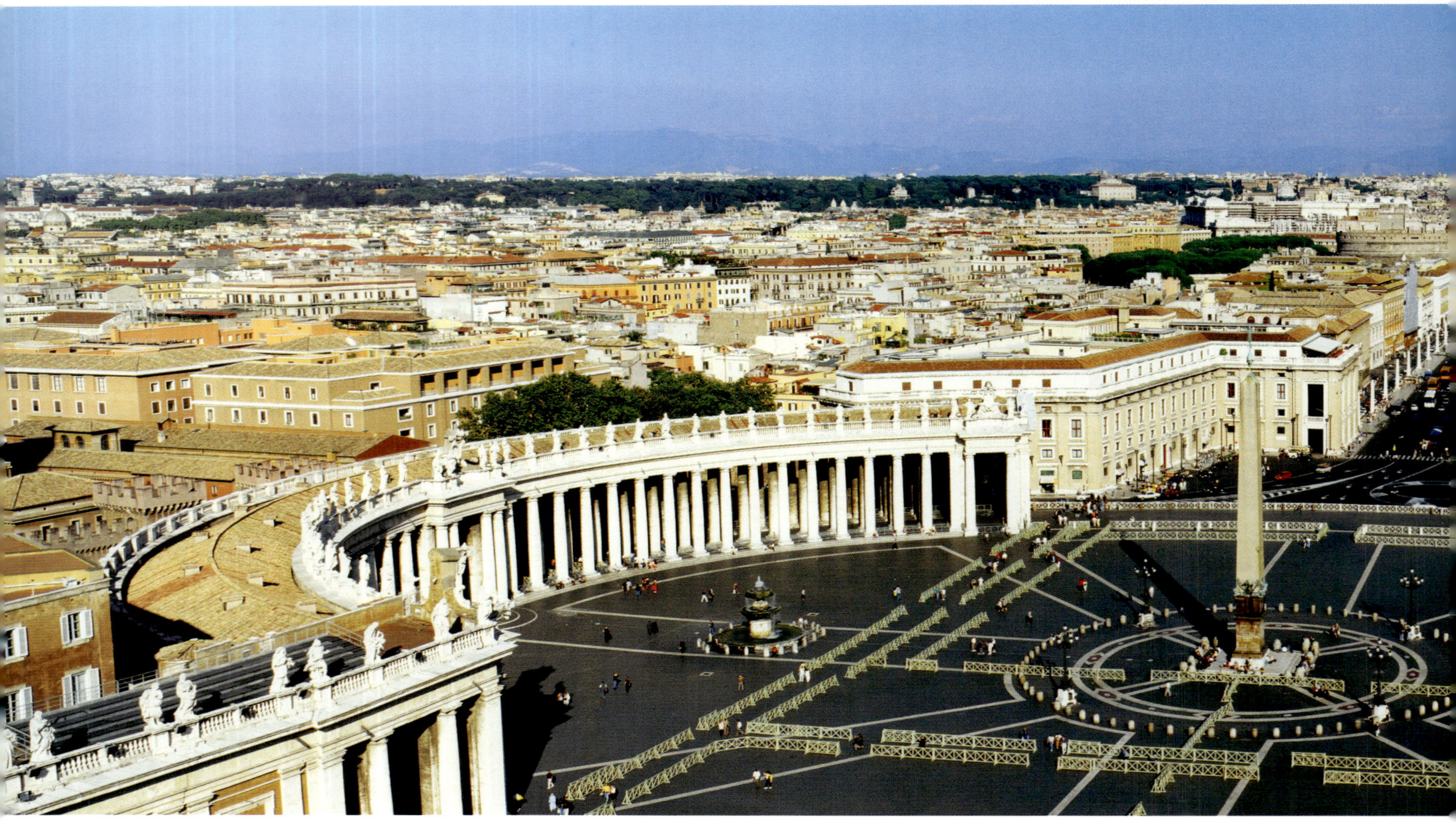

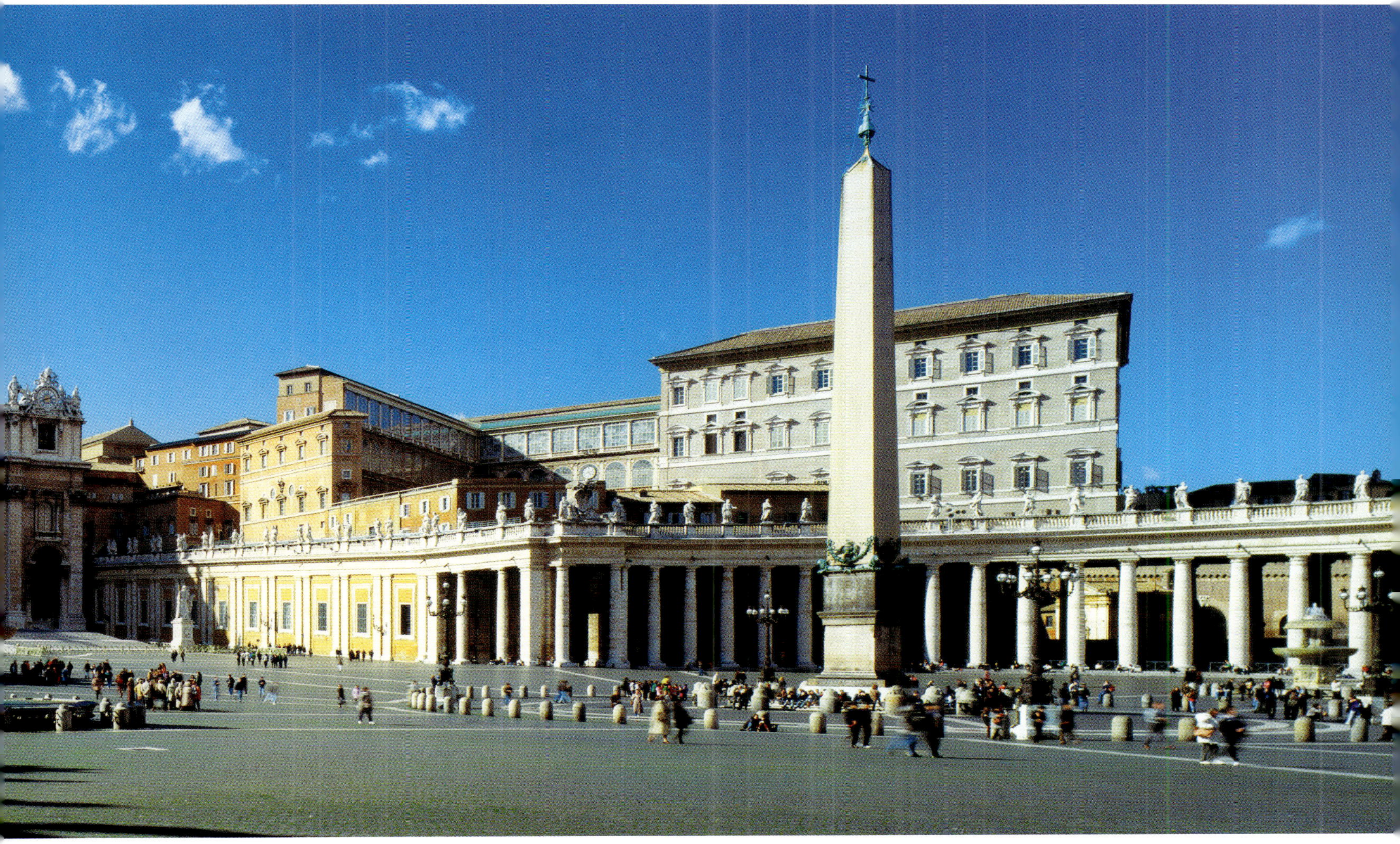

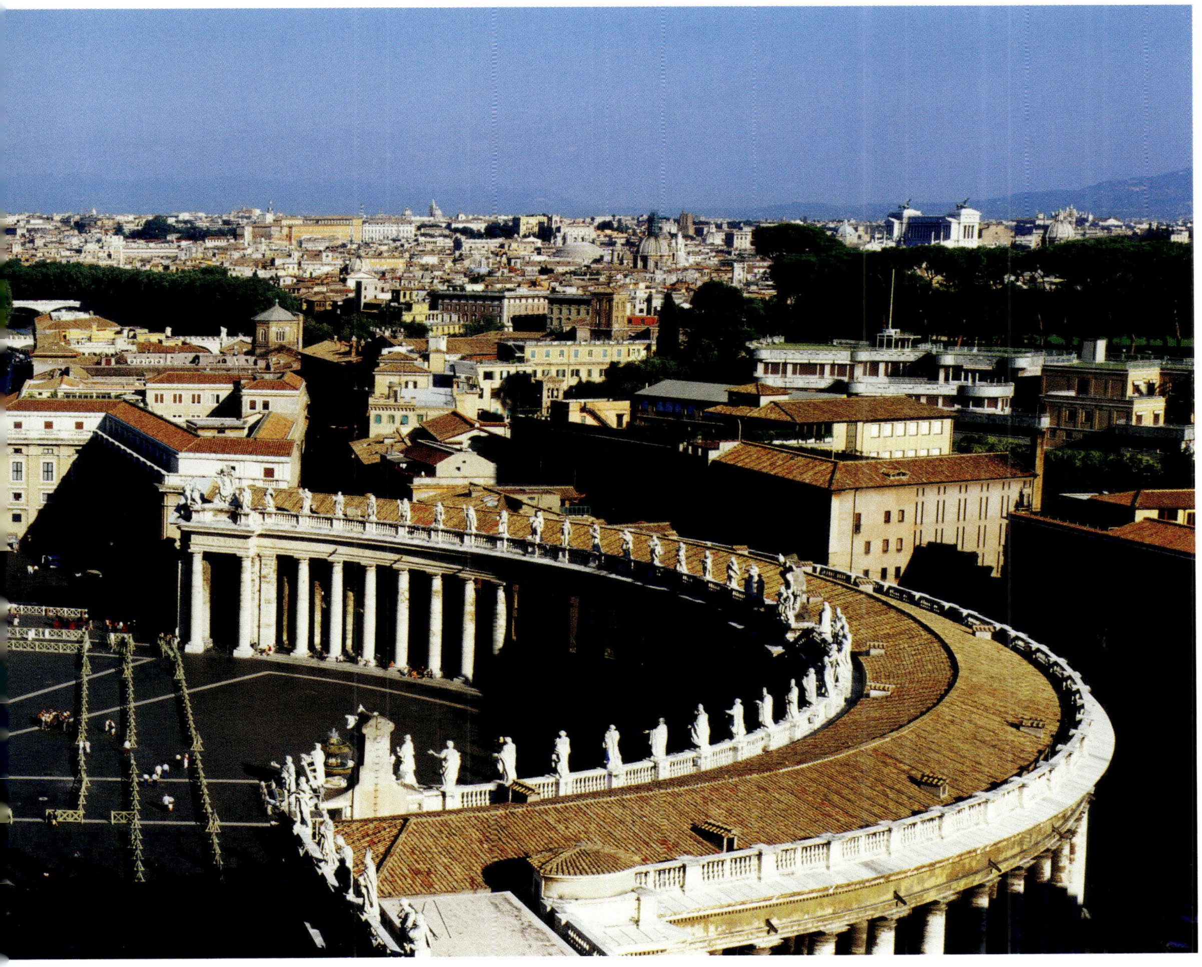

Above and Left: Panoramas of St. Peter's Square, the center of world Christianity, dominated by an obelisk from Heliopolis. Brought to Rome by Caligula in 37 A.D., it was used as part of the spine of Rome's horse-racing course. It was relocated by Pope Sixtus V in 1586 using a method devised by Domenico Fontana. It was the first monumental obelisk raised in the modern period, and it is the only obelisk in Rome that has not toppled since Roman times. *Siegfriea Layda/Stone/Getty Images; Panoramic Images/Getty Images*

Right: The view looking down into St. Peter's Square from near the top of the Basilica. The row of statues are of Christ and the Apostles.

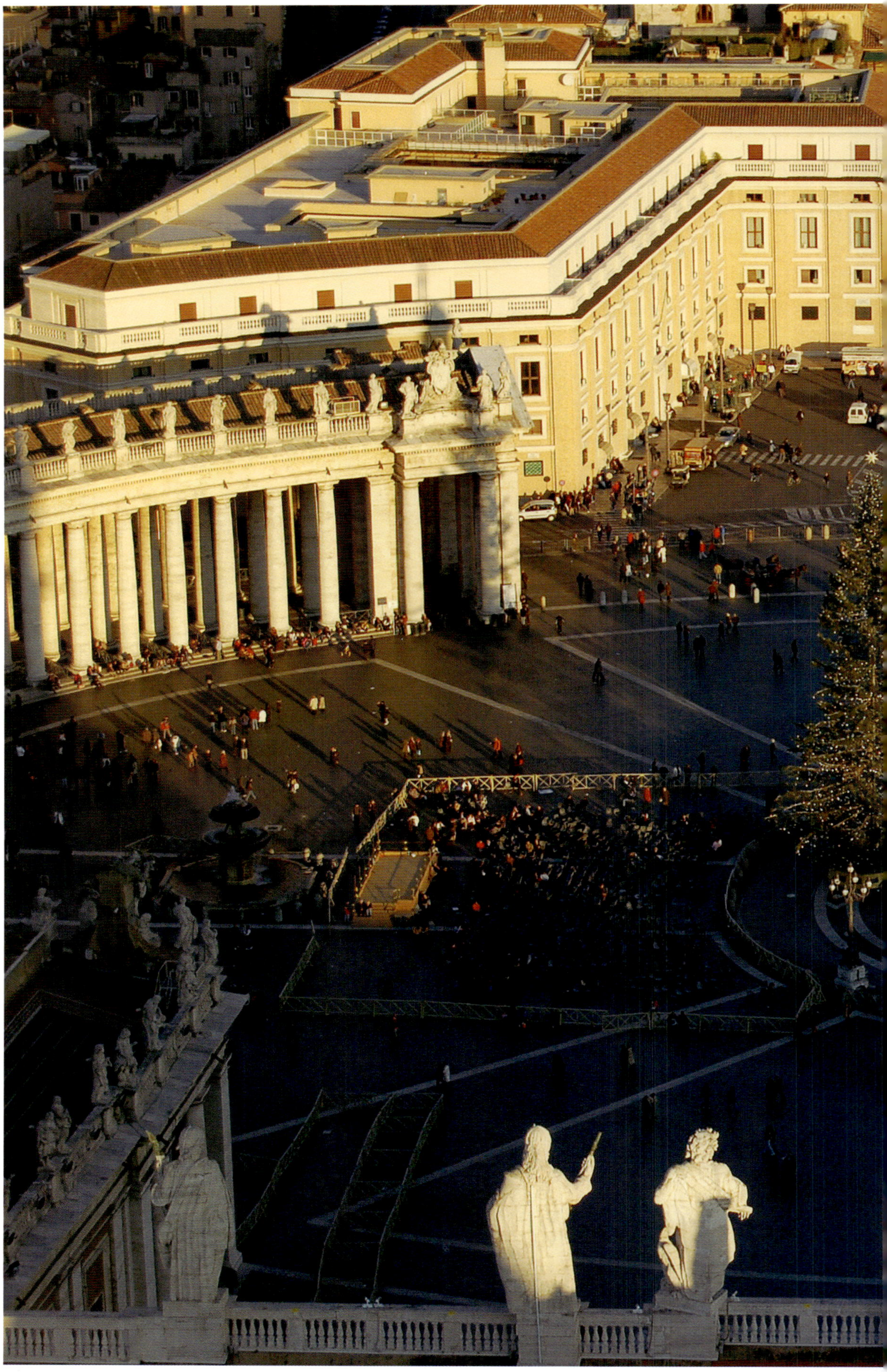

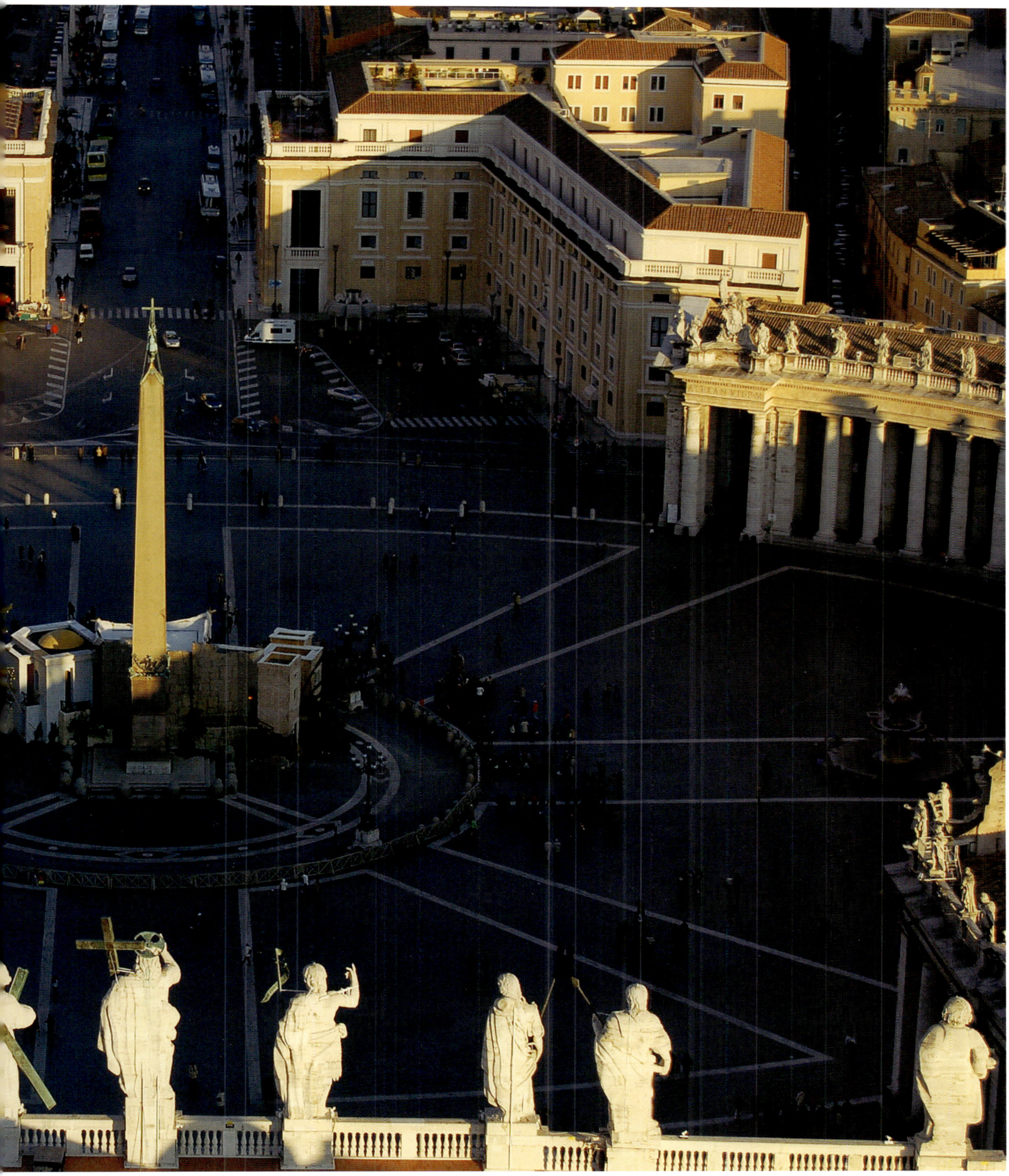

PAGES 118–119: Saint Peter's Square at dusk when most of the people have gone. Pope Alexander II commissioned Gian Lorenzo Bernini to redesign the square into the grand open plaza that still stands today. Created between 1656 and 1667 the square was intended to allow as many people as possible a good view of the Pope when he appeared to give his blessings to the faithful. *Jorg Greuel/Photonica/Getty Images*

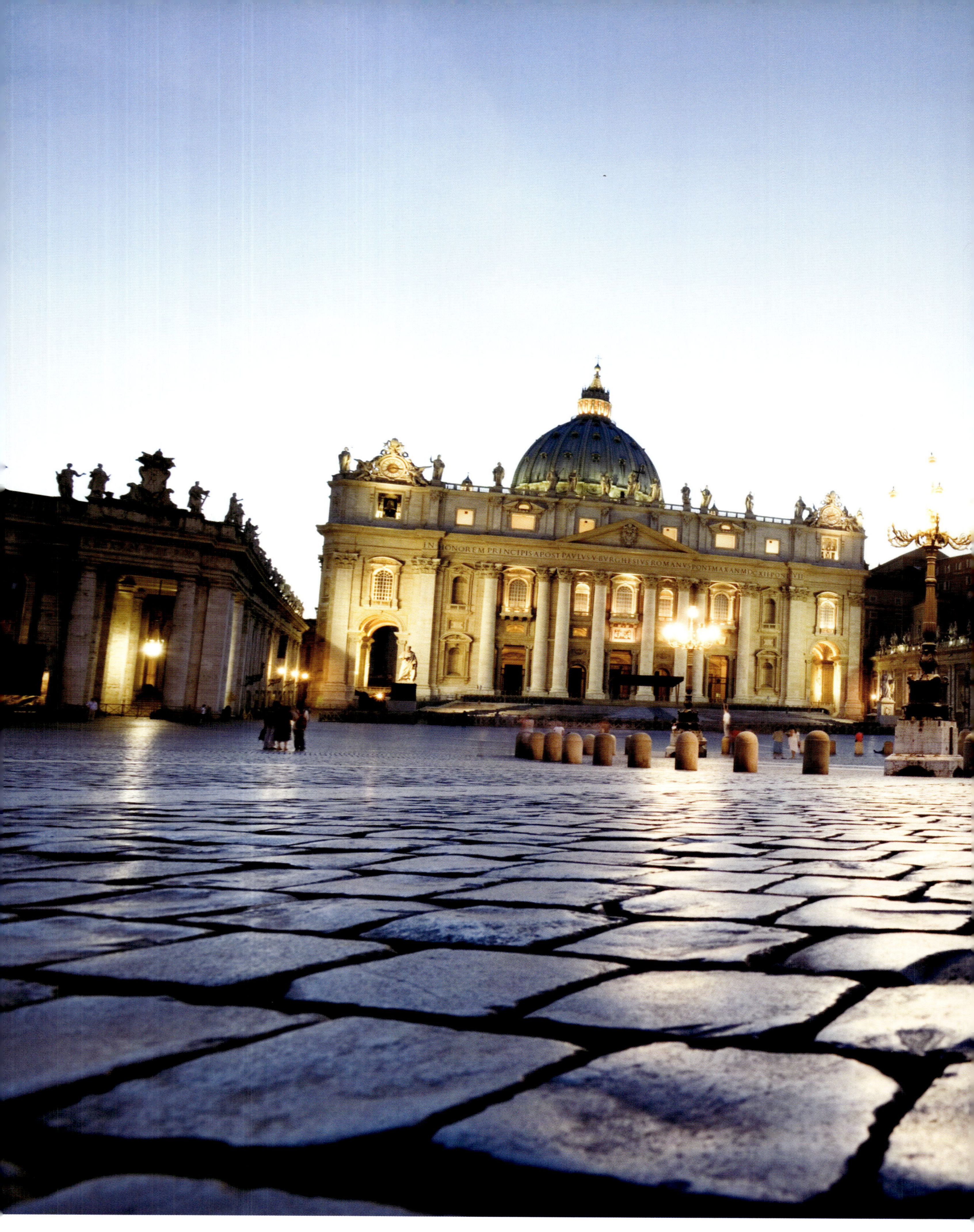
IN HONOREM PRINCIPIS APOST PAVLVS V BVRGHESIVS ROMANVS PONT MAX AN MDCXII PONT VII

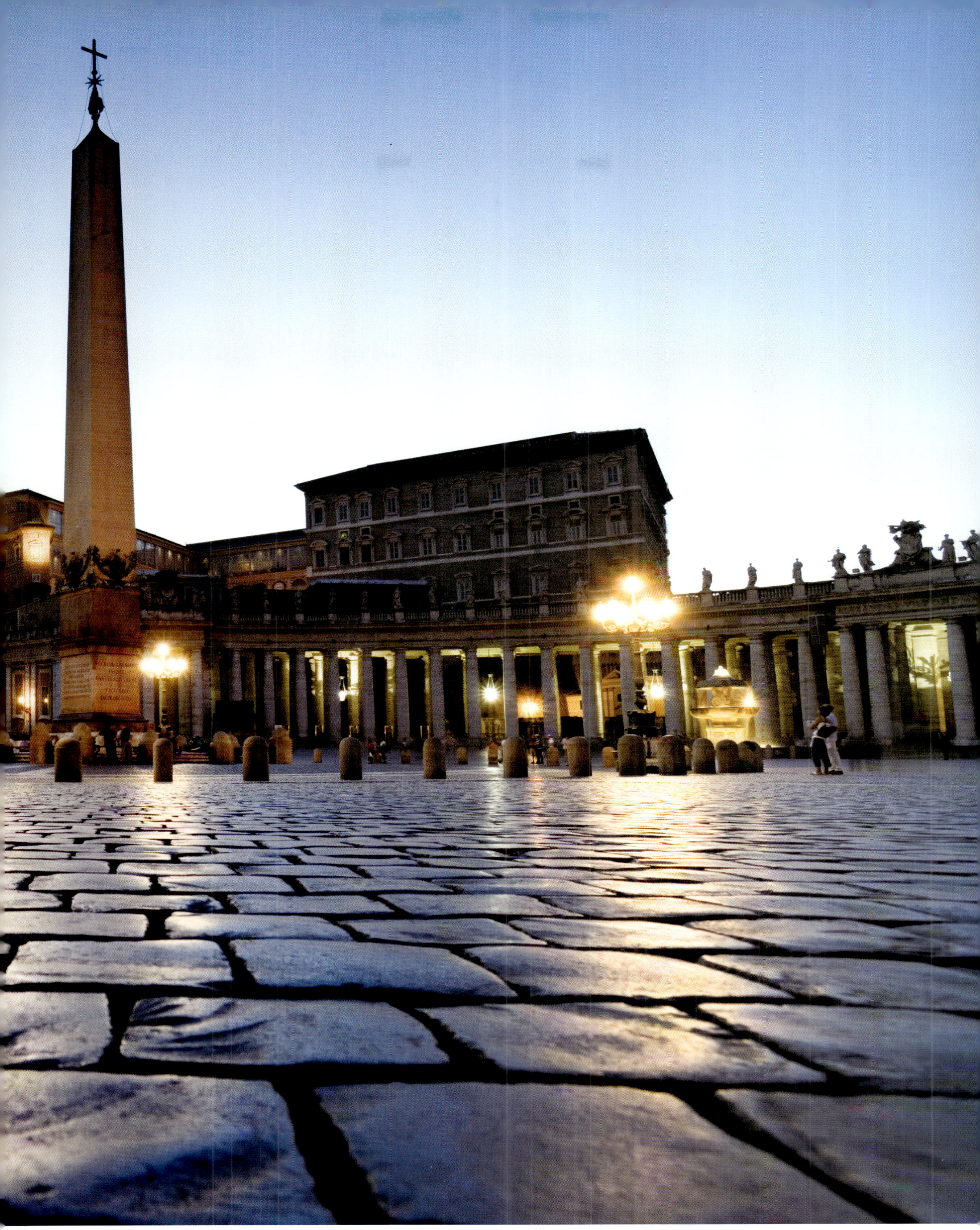

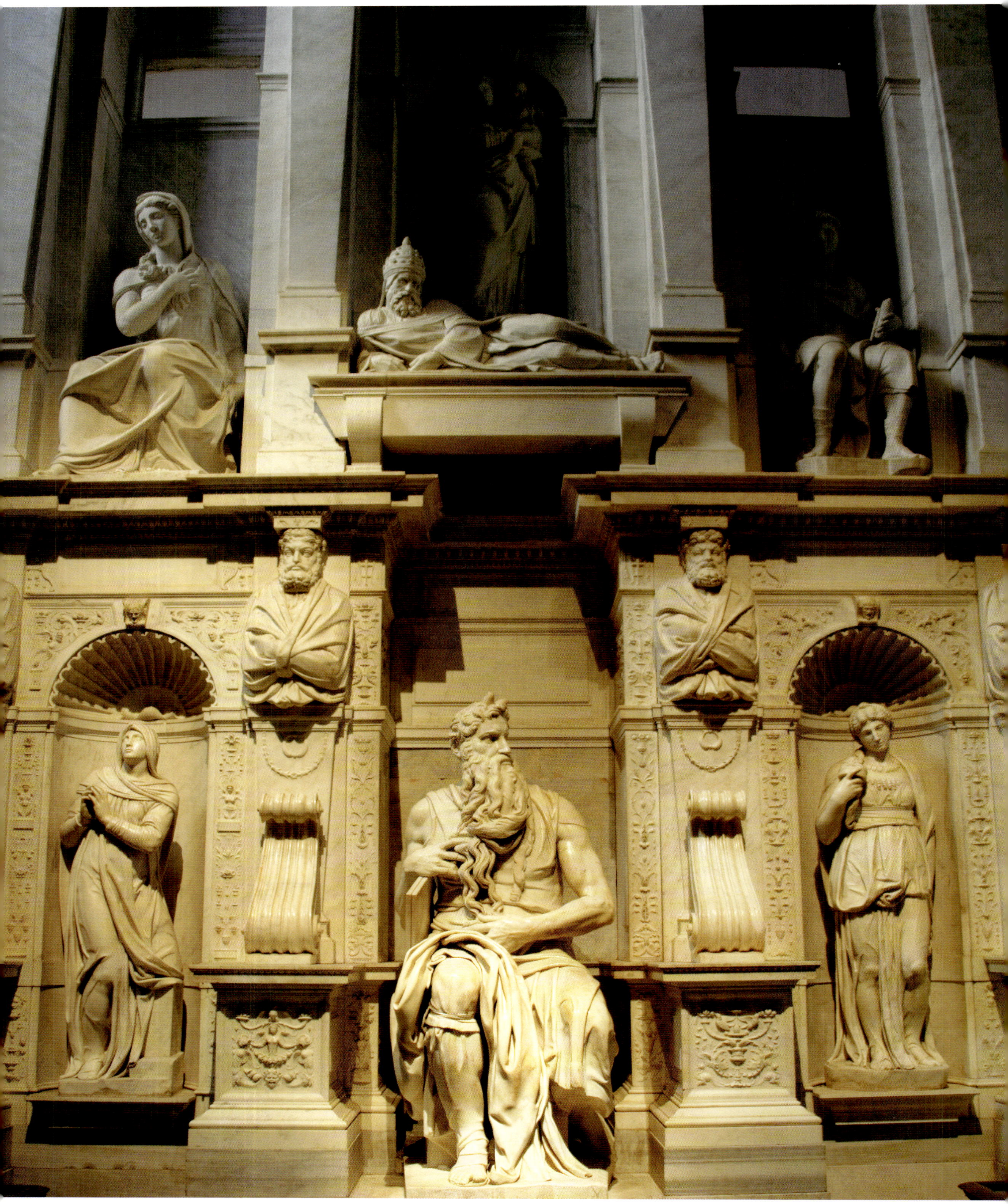

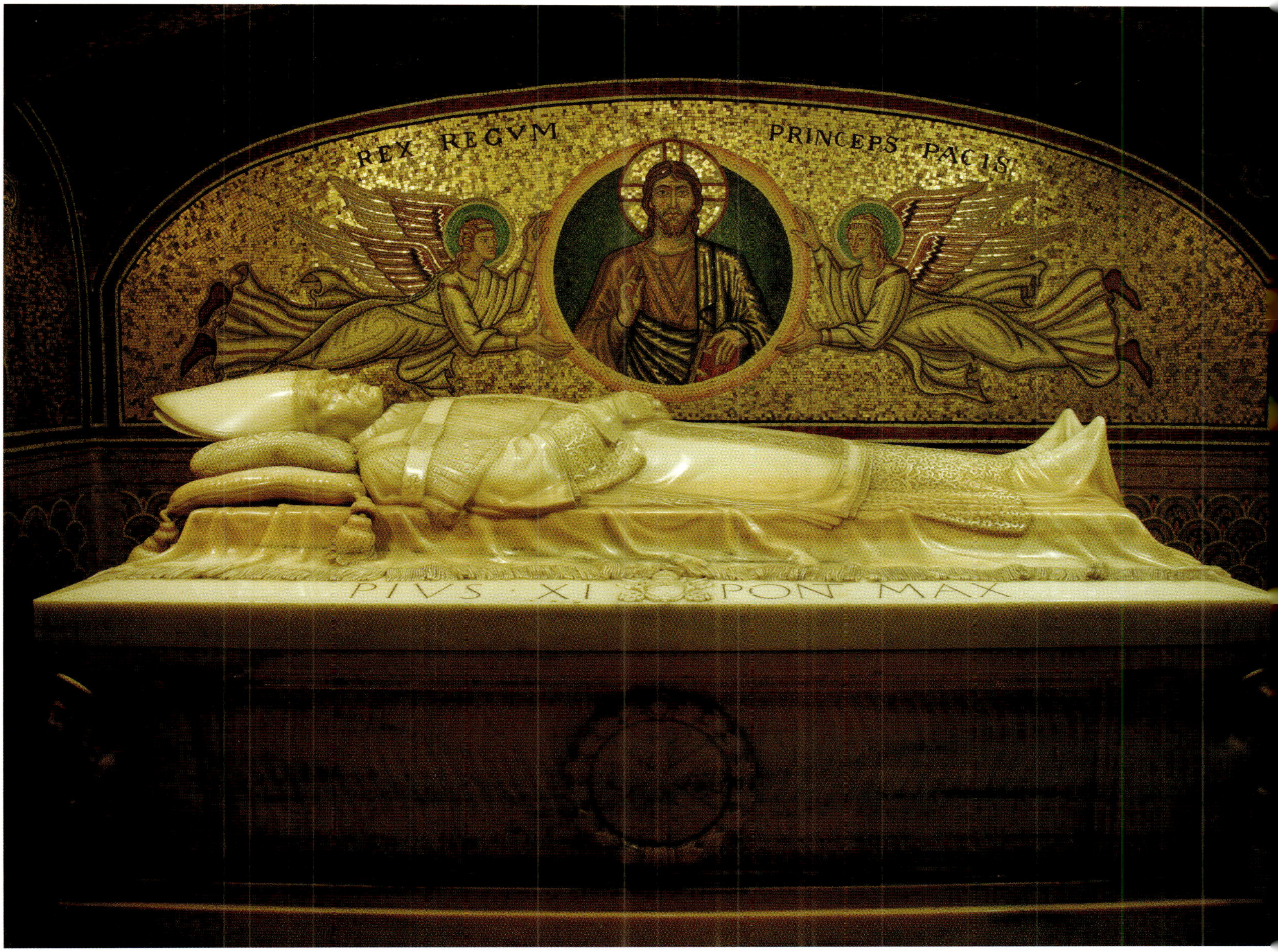

Above and Right: Medieval and Renaissance popes had grand tombs. This is that of Pius-Tomb for Pope Julius II with Michelangelo's Moses statue XI. In complete contrast the much simpler tomb of Pope John Paul II (**Right**) also lies in St. Peter's.

Left: The basilica of St. Peter in Chains was originally built in the fourth century when it was named for the precious chains of St. Peter with which he was fettered in Jerusalem and Rome. Legend says that when the two chains were brought together they miraculously joined up. Pilgrims have made their way here for centuries to see the relic. Between 1471 and 1503 Cardinal Giulano della Rovere oversaw a massive modification of the church. He was to become Pope Julius II and commissioned this tomb by Michelangelo for himself.

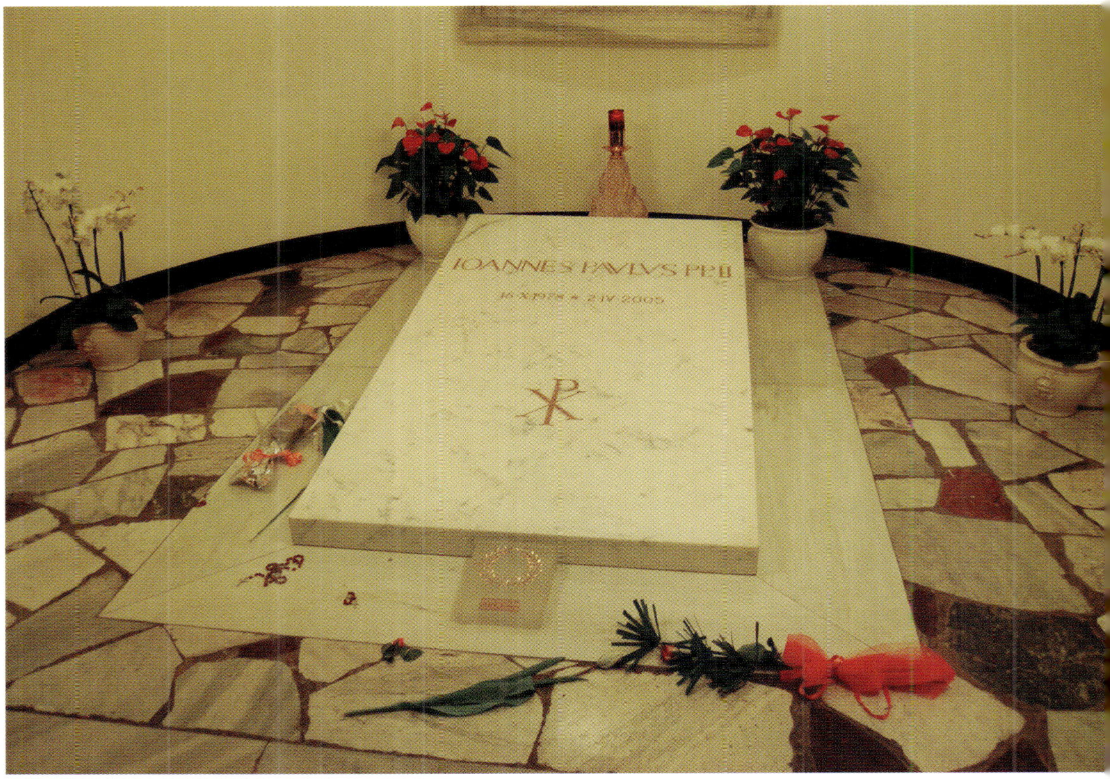

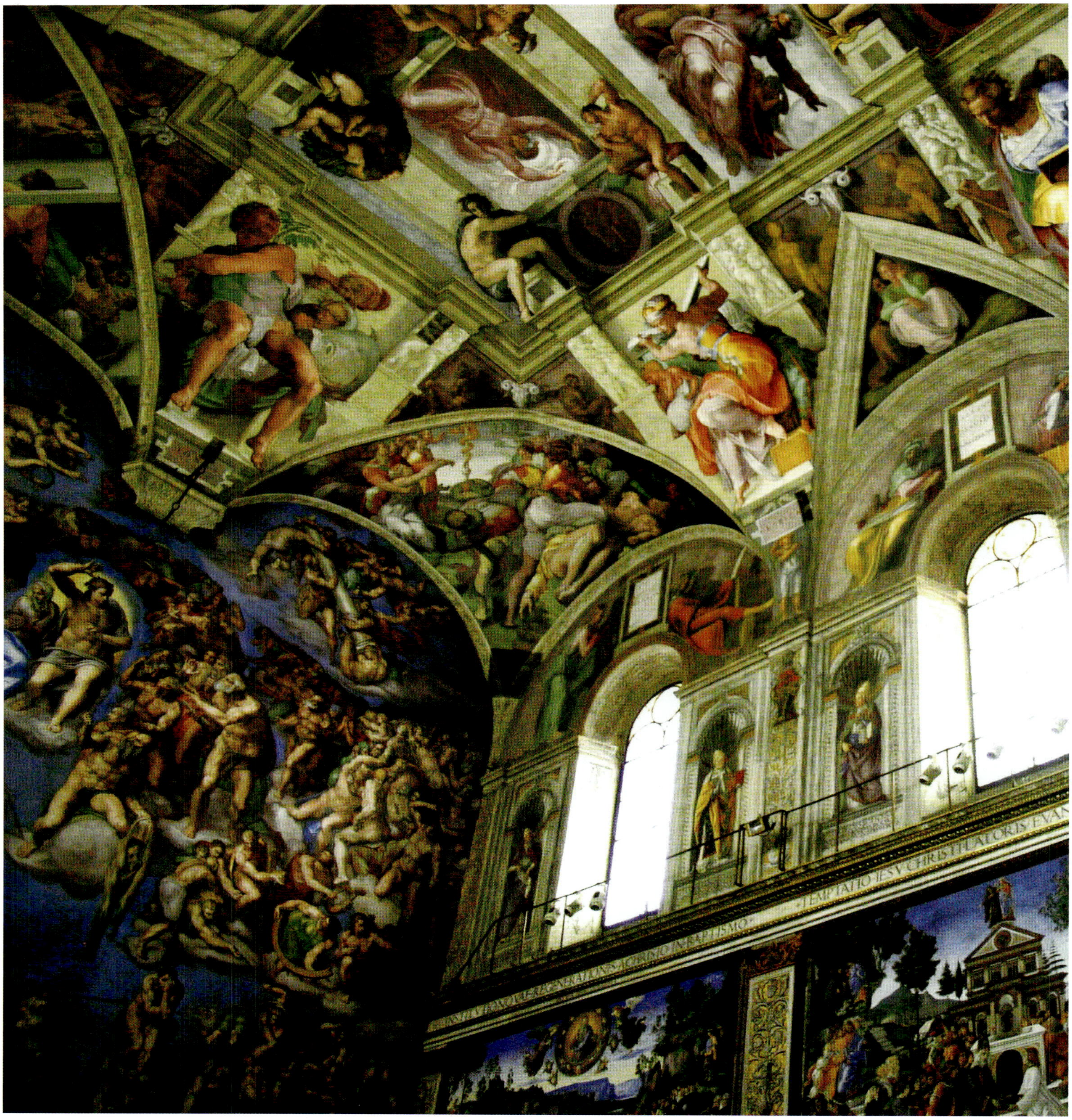

ABOVE: The Sistine Chapel in the Apostolic Palace, in the Vatican City. The fame of the chapel rests on its architecture and its decoration—particularly that of Michelangelo whose ceiling is legendary. It is also well-known for its purpose—the conclaves, at which a new Pope is selected. *fotoLibra*

RIGHT: The Pietà (1498–1499) by Michelangelo is a marble sculpture in St. Peter's. Commissioned by a French cardinal, the statue was made as part of his funeral monument, but was moved to its current location in the 18th century. It shows Jesus' dead body on the lap of his mother after the Crucifixion. *Peter Scholey/Photographer's Choice/Getty Images*

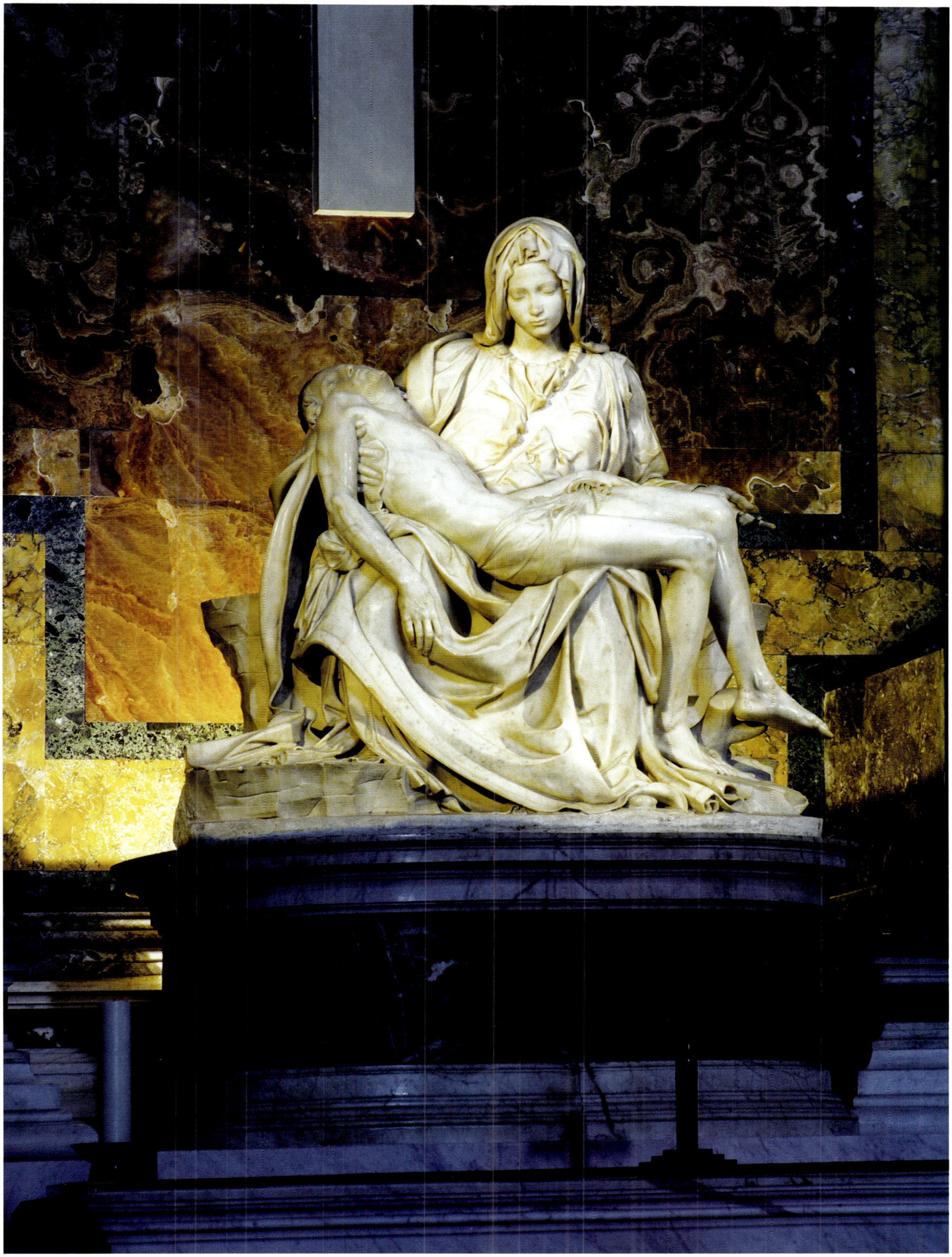

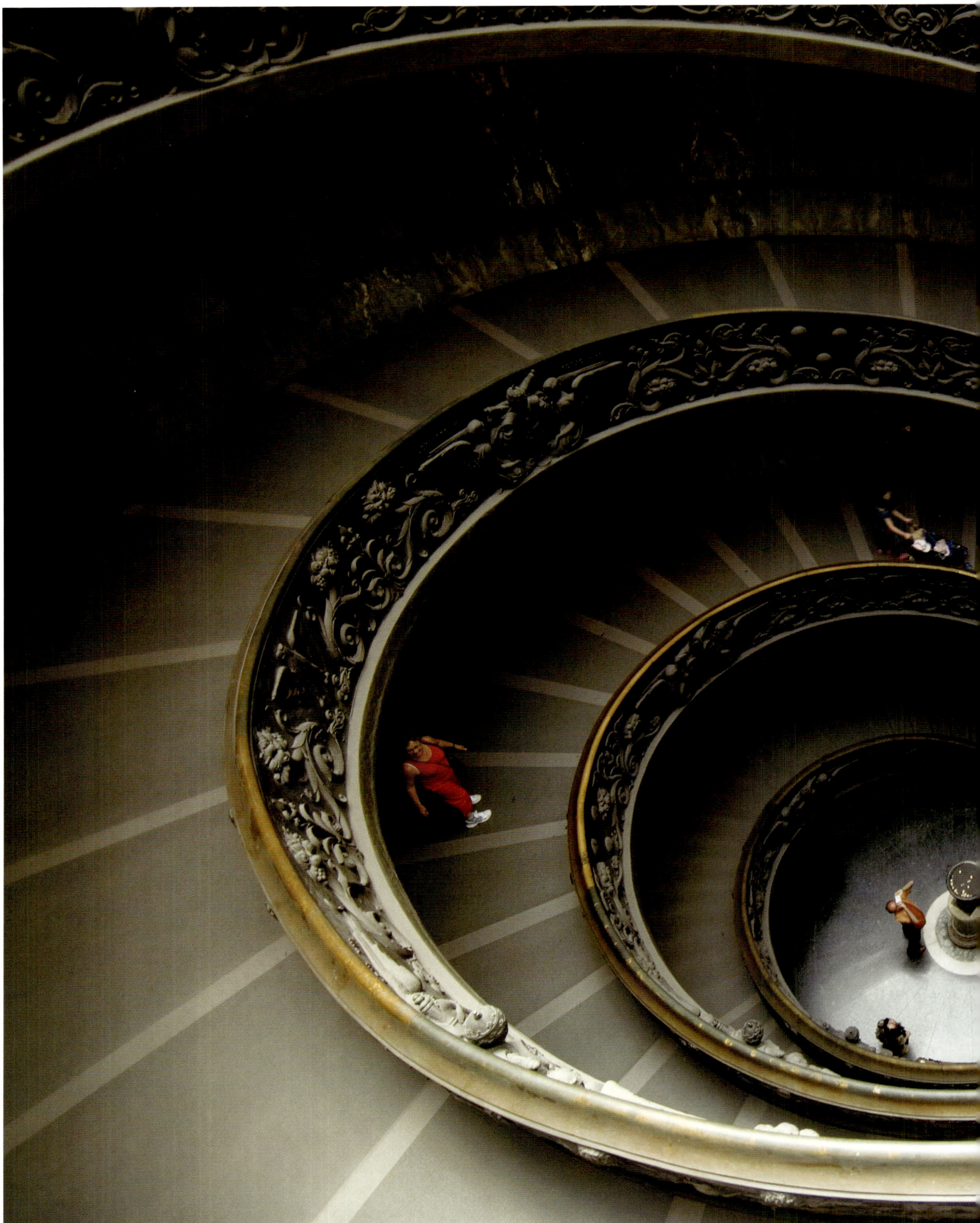

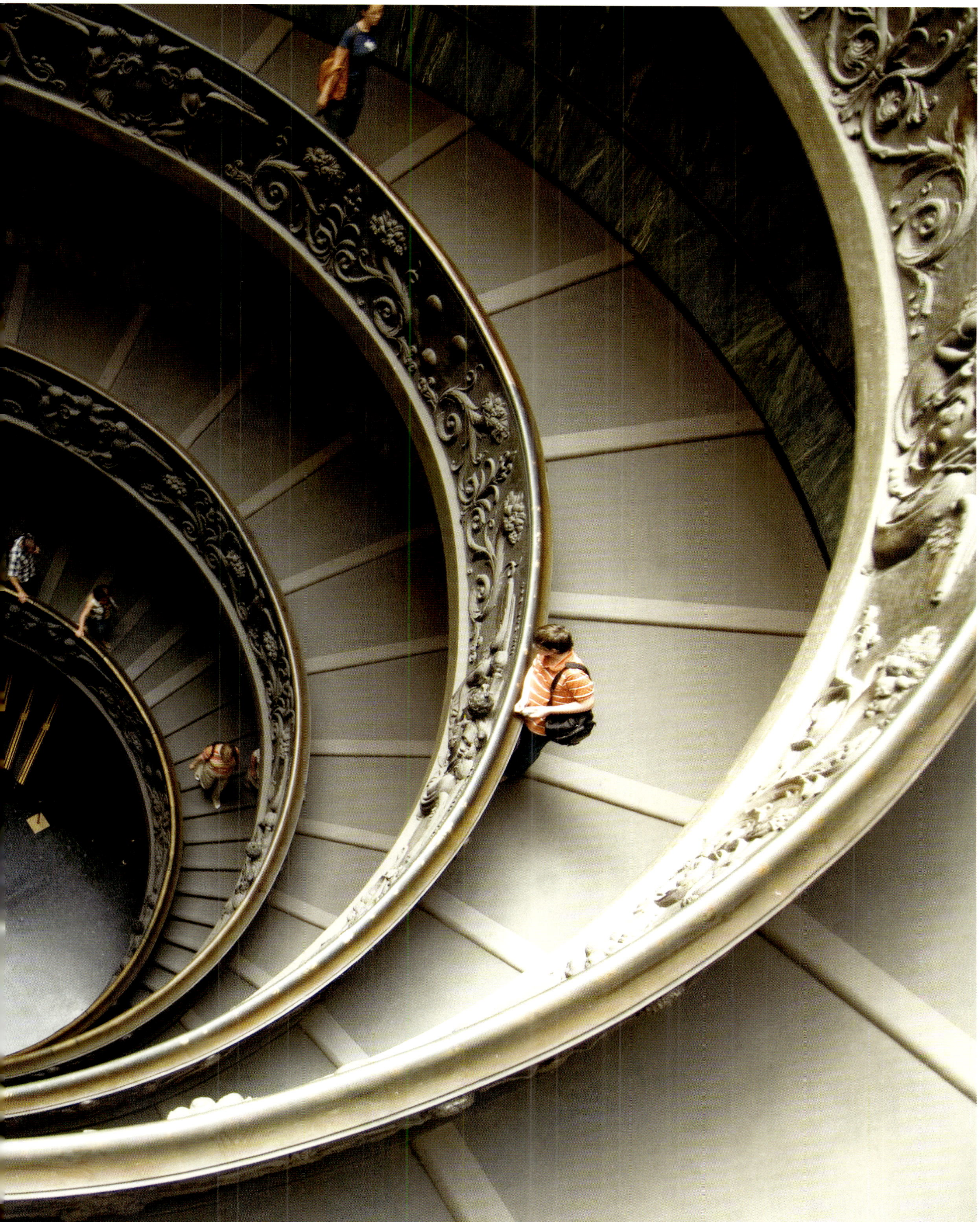

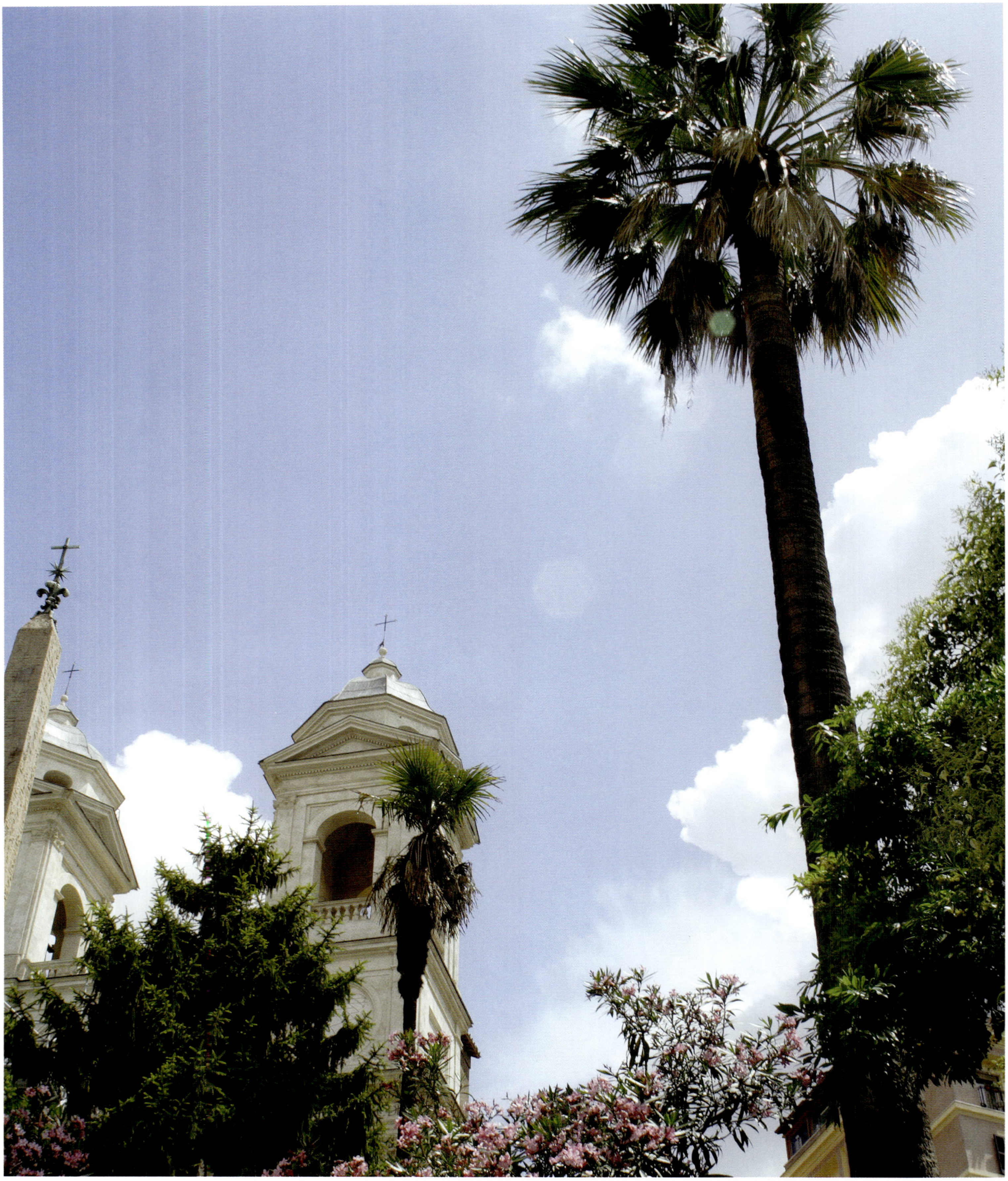

PAGES 124–125: A winding staircase in the Vatican. *Joel Sartore/National Geographic/Getty Images*

PAGES 128–129: The Spanish Steps leading up to Trinita Dei Monti church. *Simeone Huber/Stone/Getty Images*

ABOVE AND RIGHT: Trinita dei Monti church—founded in 1502—sits above the Spanish Steps which themselves lead from the Piazza di Spagna. The scalinata (flight of steps) was begun in 1723 and paid for by King Louis XV of France. At the foot of the steps are the arms of Pope Innocent VIII and the fleurs-de-lys of France.

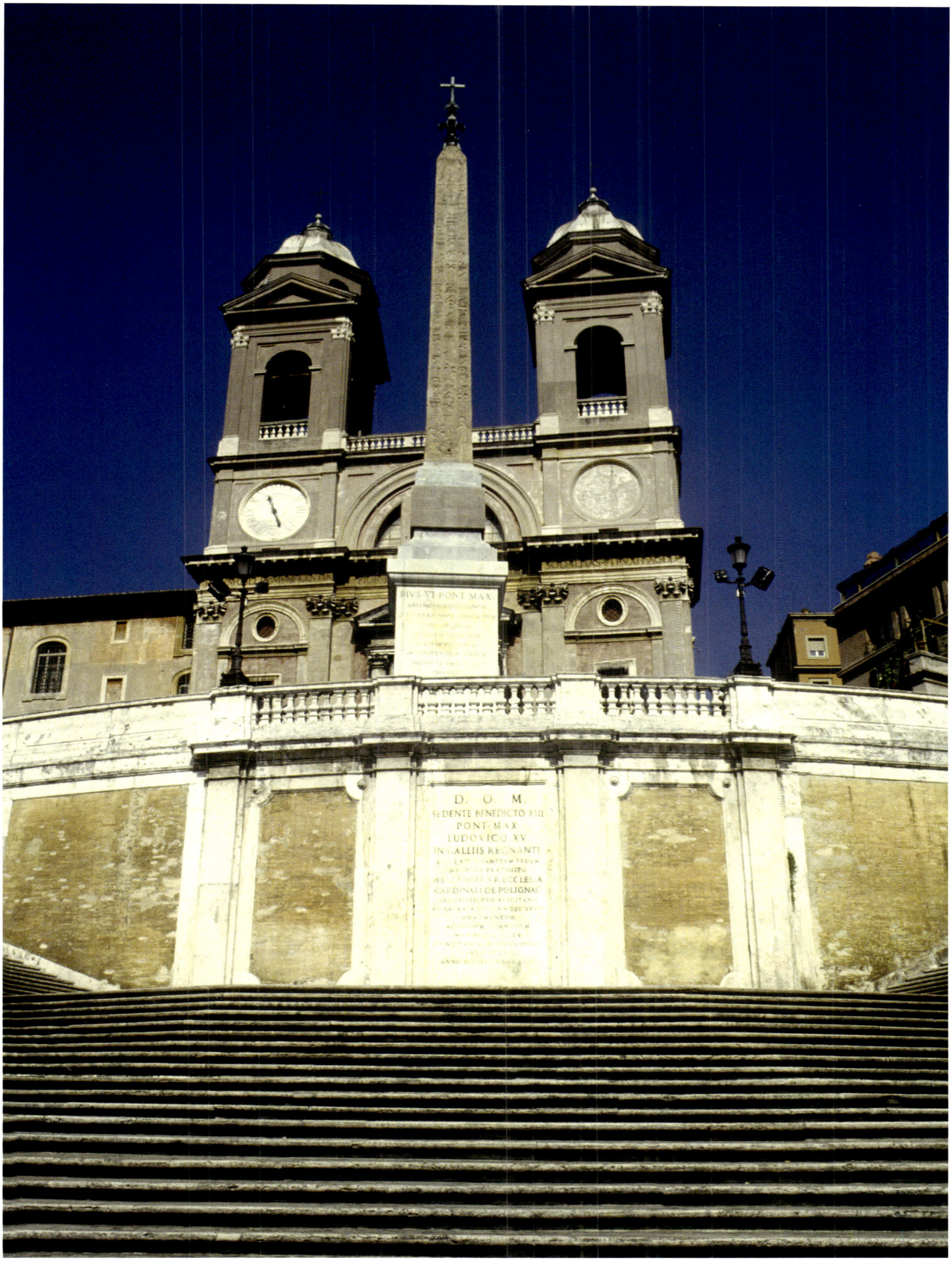
PIVS VI PONT MAX
D. O. M.
SEDENTE BENEDICTO XIII
PONT MAX
LUDOVICO XV
IN GALLIIS REGNANTE
CARDINALI DE POLIGNAC

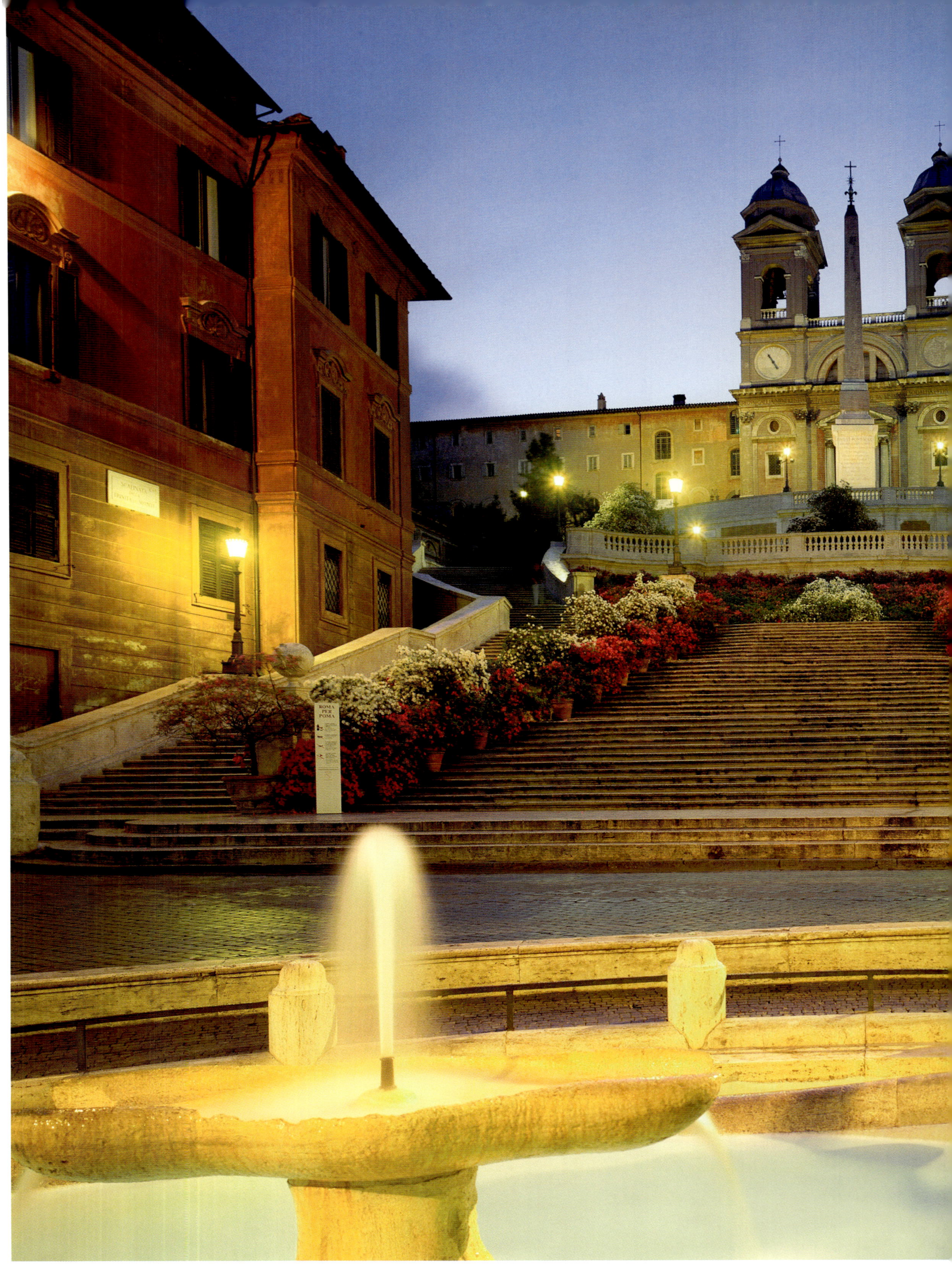

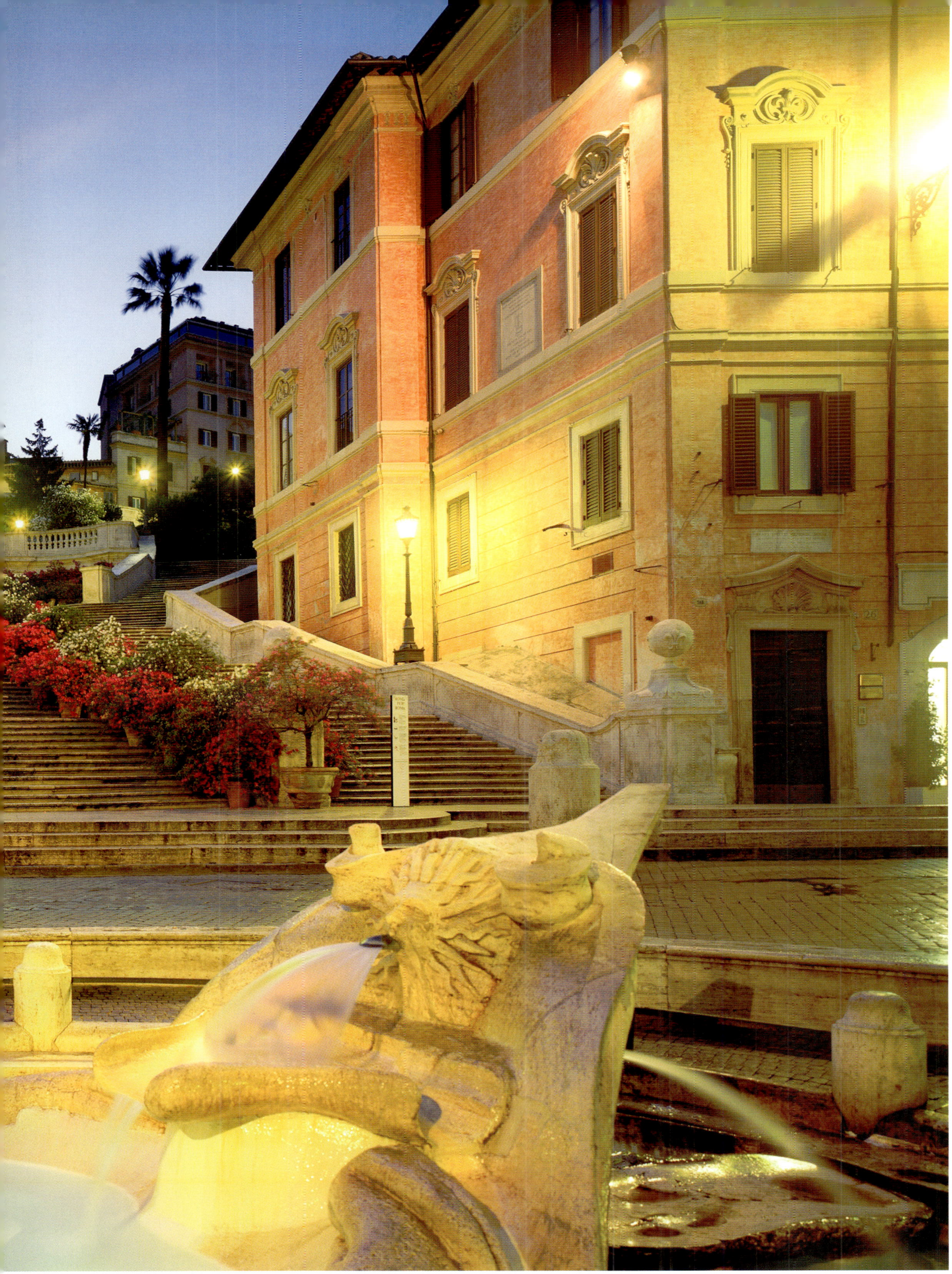

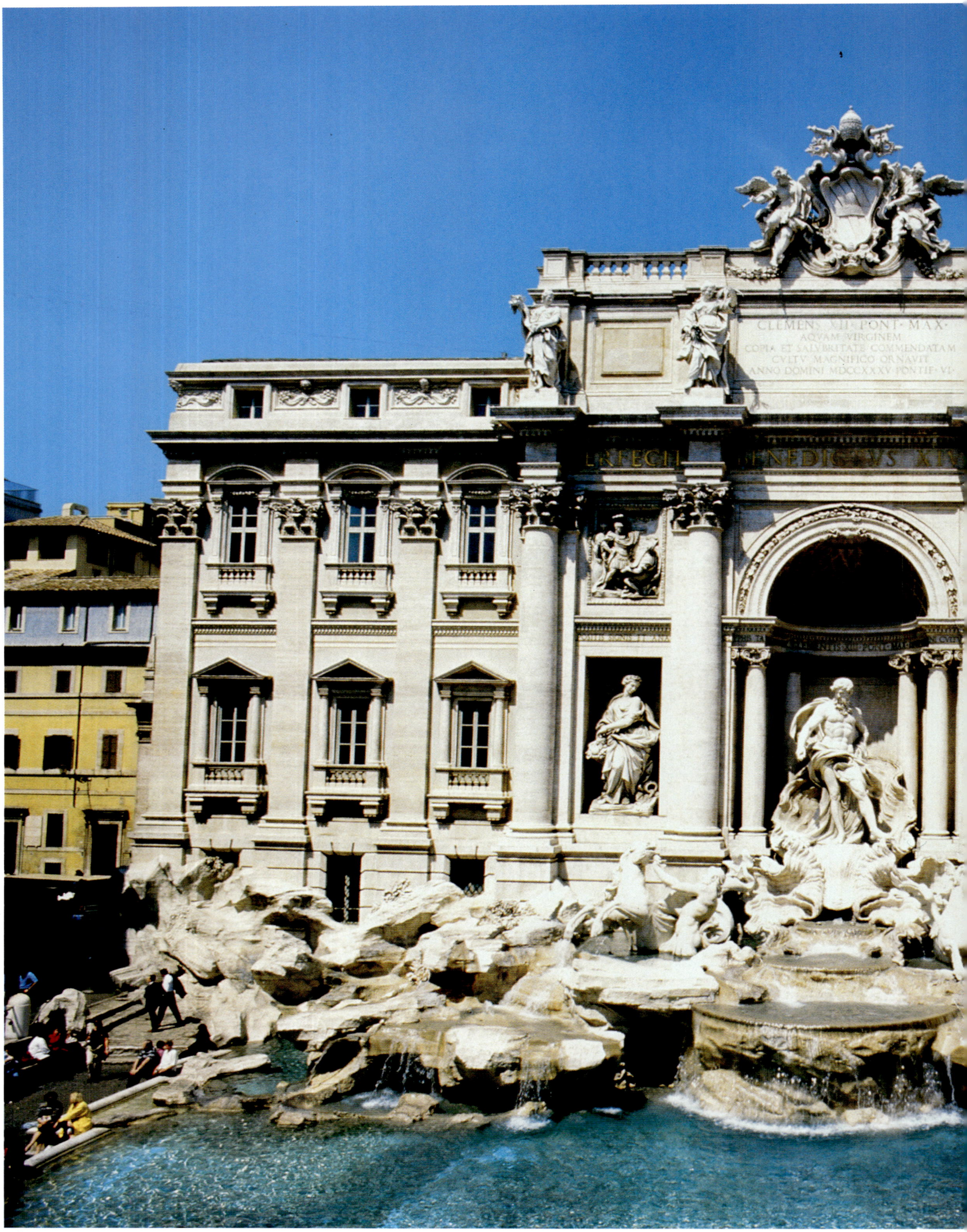
CLEMENS XII PONT MAX
AQVAM VIRGINEM
COPIA ET SALVBRITATE COMMENDATAM
CVLTV MAGNIFICO ORNAVIT
ANNO DOMINI MDCCXXXV PONTIF VI

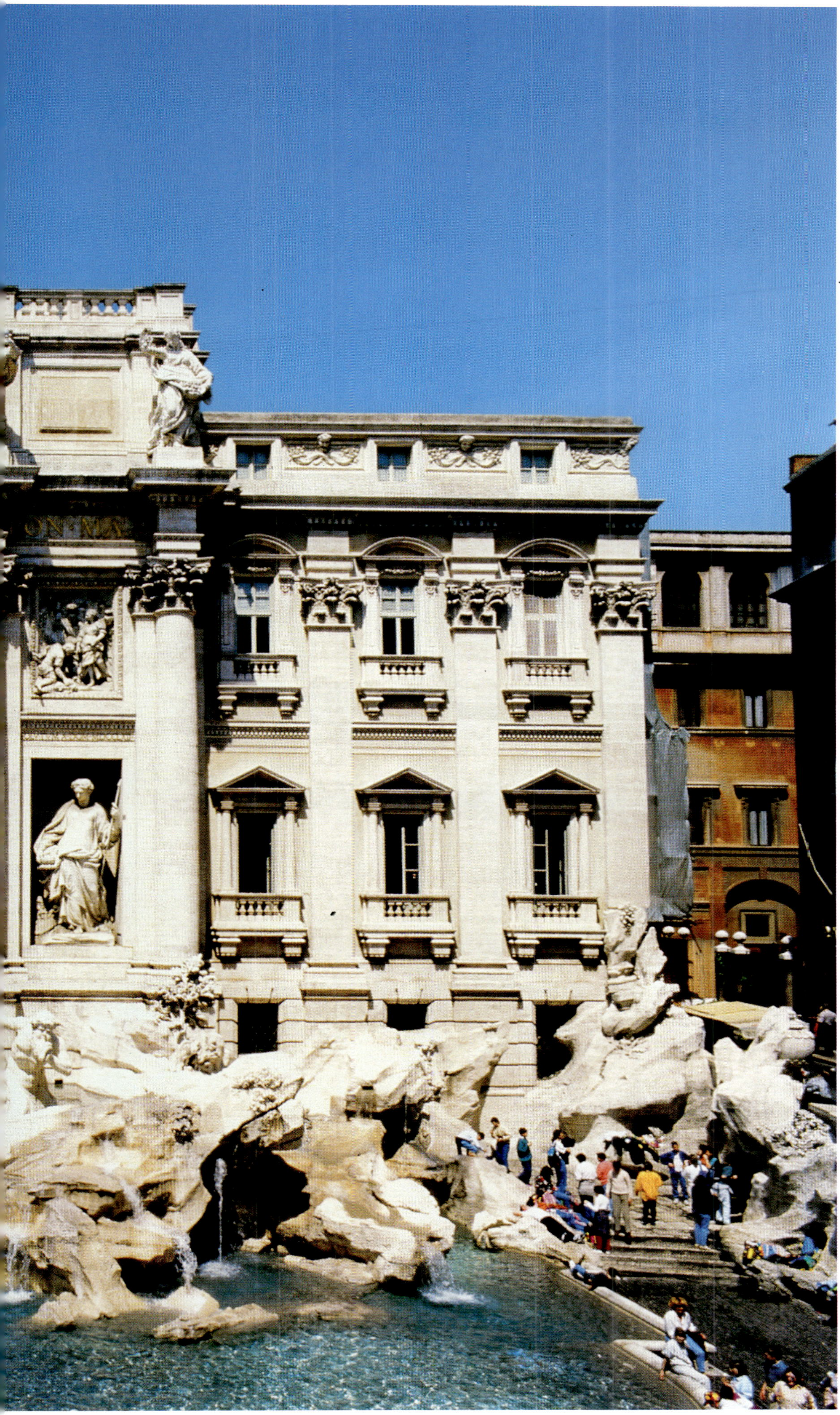

LEFT: In the Quirinal lies the most famous fountain in Rome and maybe even the world—the Fontana di Trevi (Trevi Fountain). It sits on the site of a former fountain that spewed the waters of the Aqua Virgo. The central figure is by Pietro Bracci and shows Ocean commanding sea horses and Tritions with (on the left) the figure of Abundance and (on the right) the figure of Health watching on. The latter two figures were sculpted by Filippo della Valle.

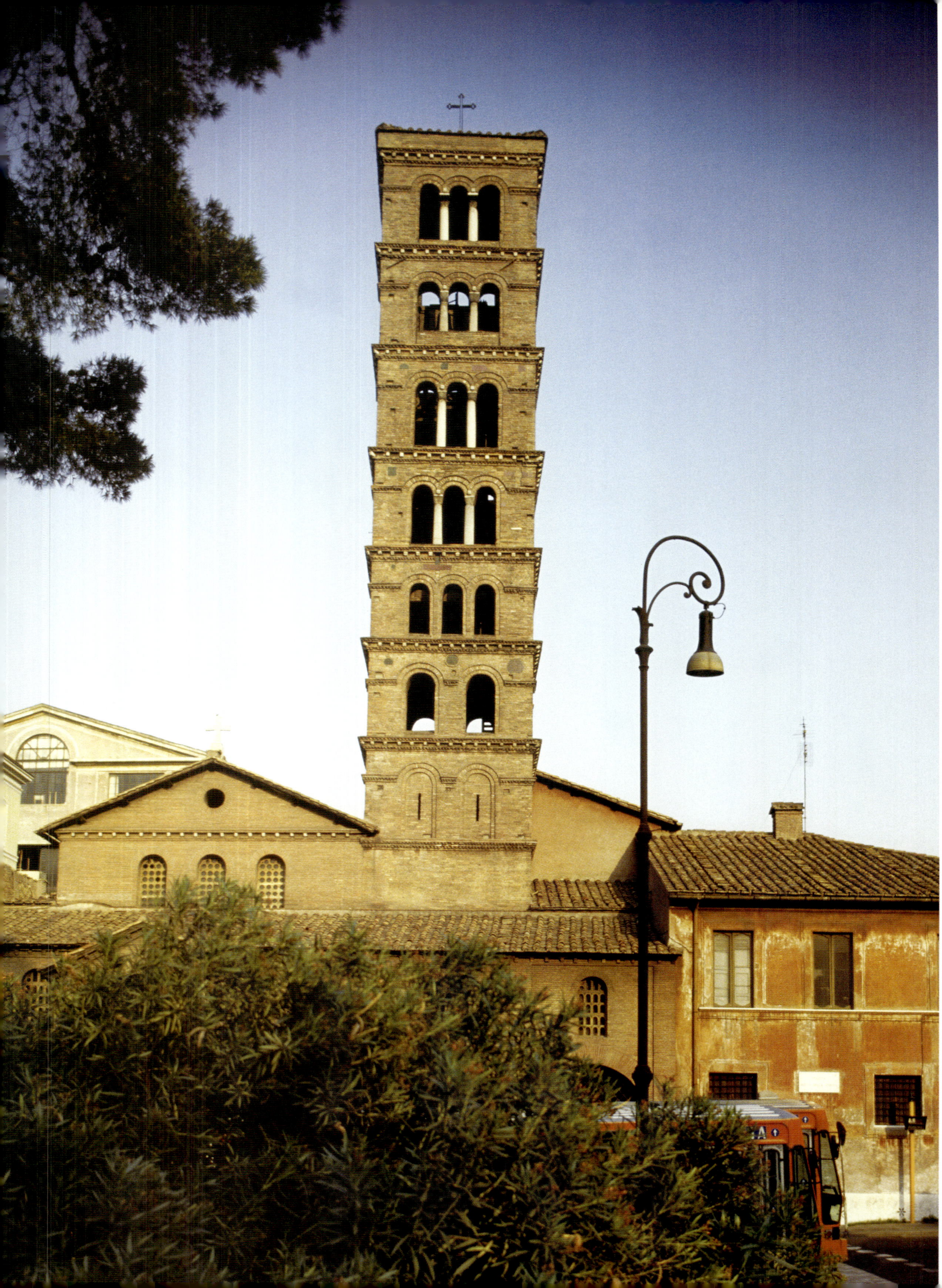

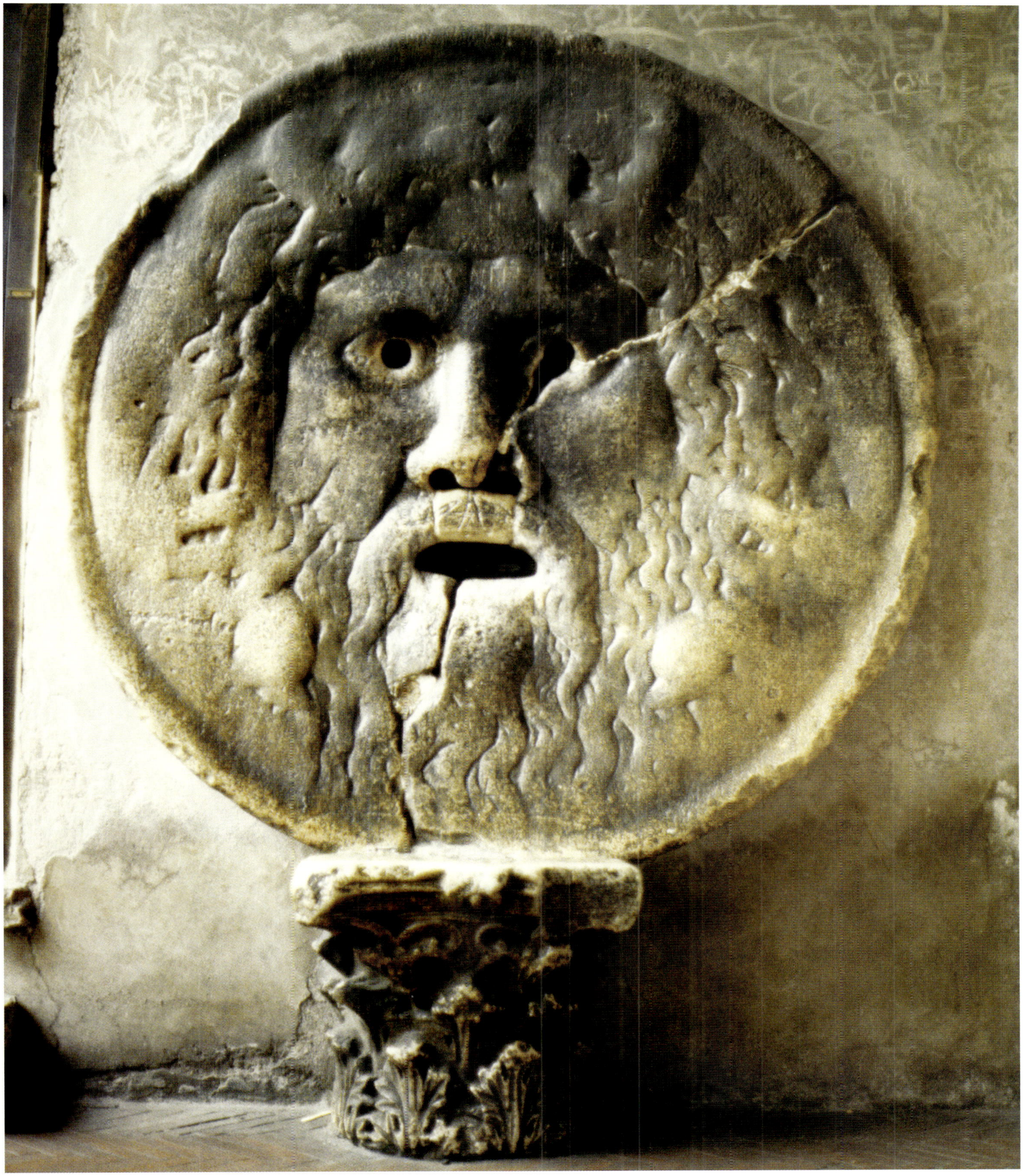

LEFT: The tower of Santa Maria in Cosmedin in Piazza Bocca della Verita. The church was founded in the sixth century in the heart of ancient Rome. In the eighth century the church was enlarged and given by Pope Hadrian I to the Greek community for their worship, and hence "Cosmedin"—the name of a Constantinople neighborhood.

ABOVE: Beneath the portico of Santa Maria in Cosmedin lies the Bocca della Verita —the Mouth of Truth—which was placed here in the seventeenth century. The carving with the face of the sea god Oceanus, is probably an ancient drain cover or fountain head made from Pavonazzetto marble. Roman legend has it that it was used as a lie detector—anyone placing their hand into its mouth who told a lie would have their hand bitten off. *Dorling Kindersley/Getty Images (both)*

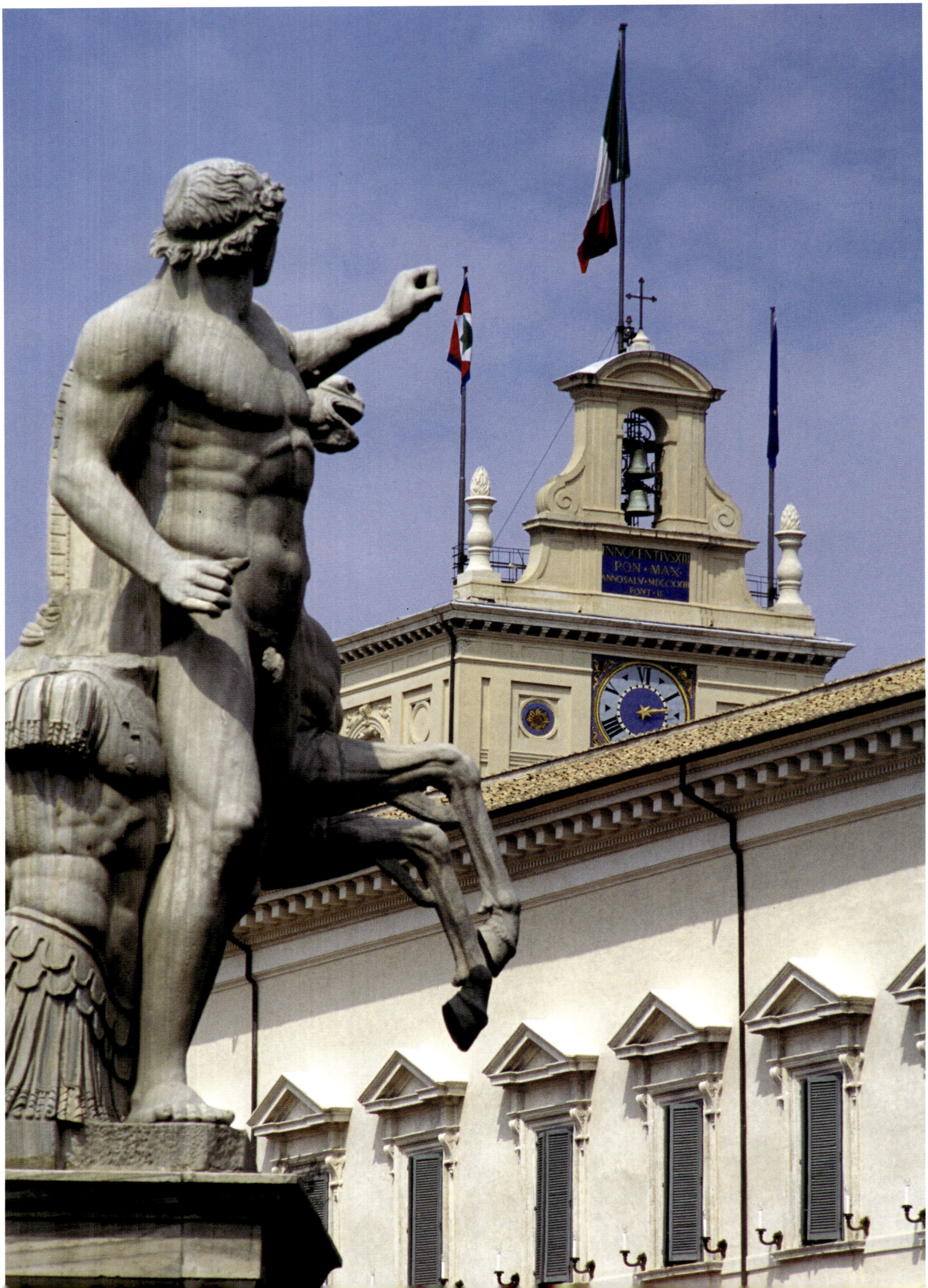
PON • MAX

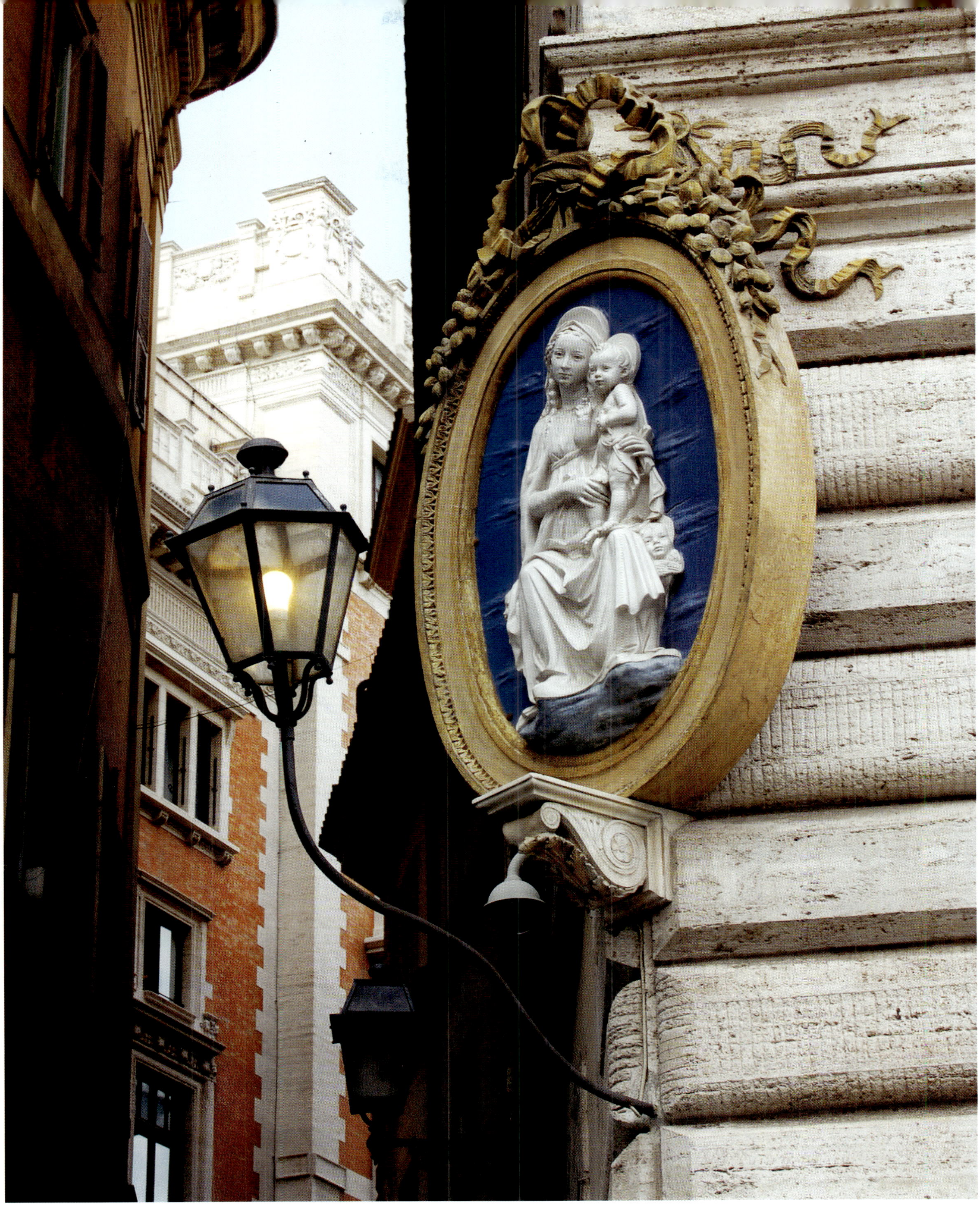

LEFT: Between 1870 and 1944 the Quirinale Palace was used by successive popes as their summer residence but on the proclomation of the Republic of Italy it became the official residence of the president. *Vincenzo Lombardo/Taxi/Getty Images*

ABOVE: The Madonna and Child are very important figures in the Roman Catholic Church and their image is used everywhere, even, as here, on the side of a building.

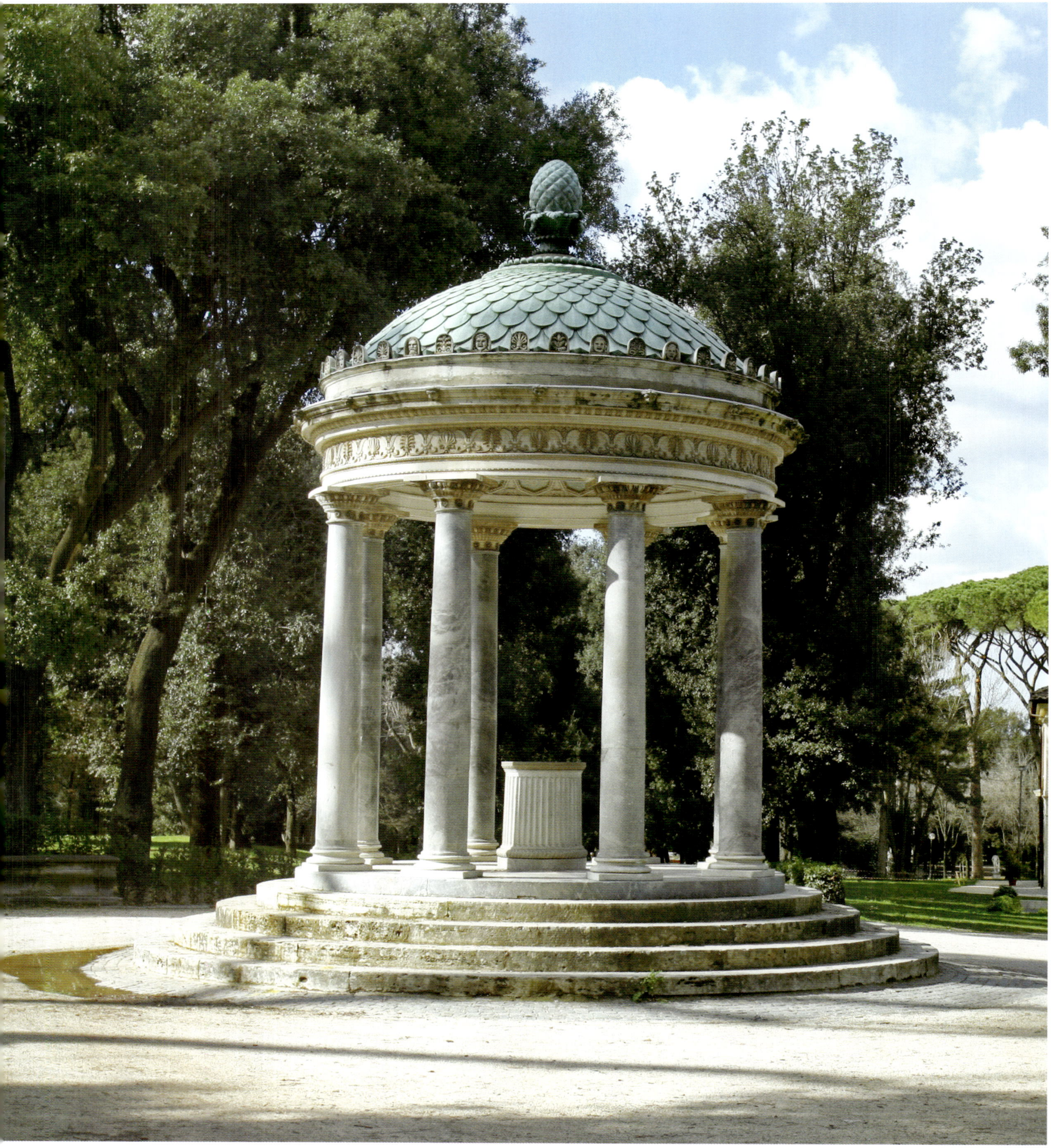

Above: A small temple in Parco Villa Borghese, one of the largest villas in Rome which became the property of the Italian State in 1901. The grounds are full of follies, fountains, small temples, and artistic ruins.

Right: Near Piazza Navona is the smaller Campo dei' Fiori—or Field of Flowers, named for a time when this area was a meadow and in complete contrast to its later use as a place for public executions. The piazza contains a monument to the philosopher Giordano Bruno who was burned alive here by the Inquisition in February 1600. This monument erected on the site of his death was dedicated in 1887 and his status as a martyr to freedom.

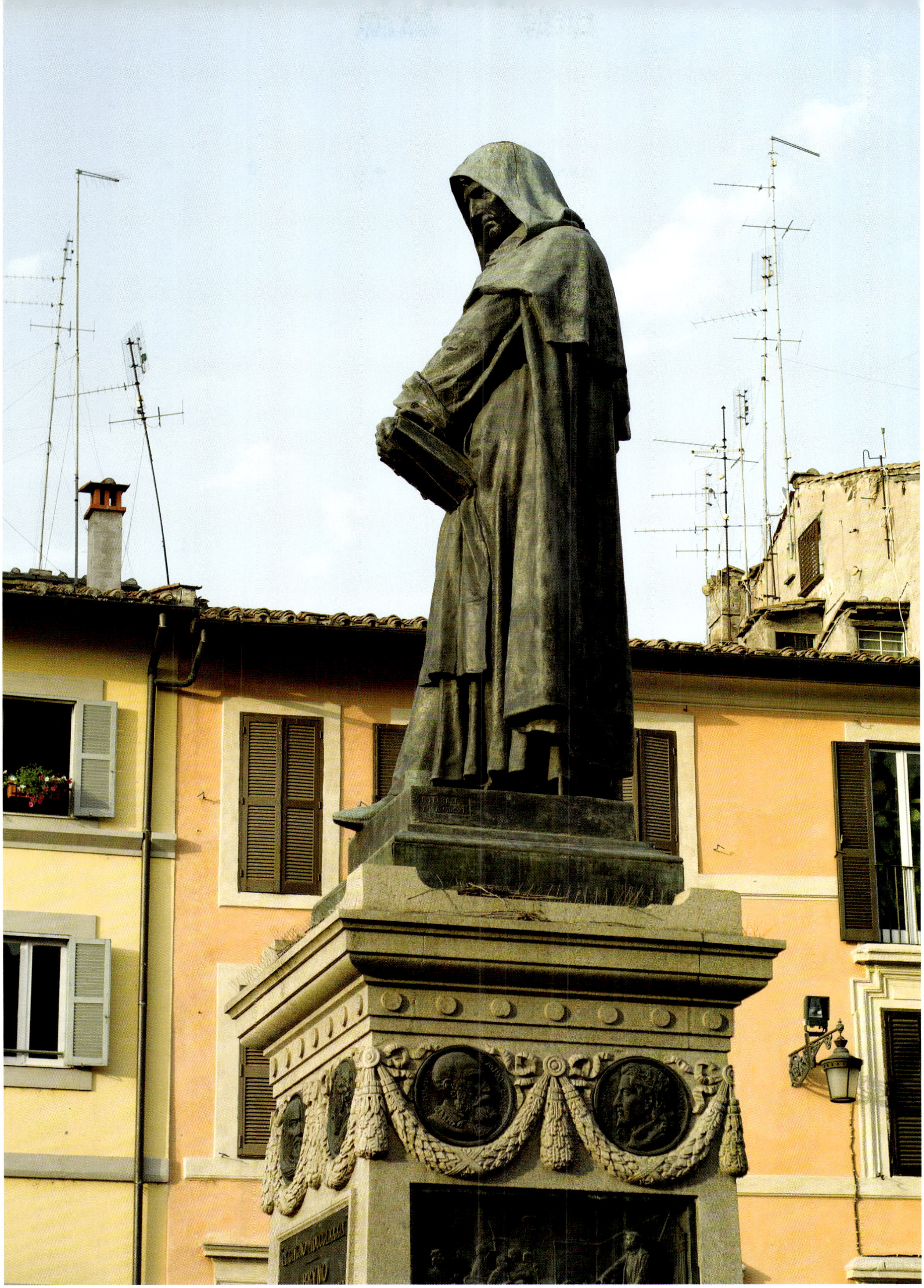

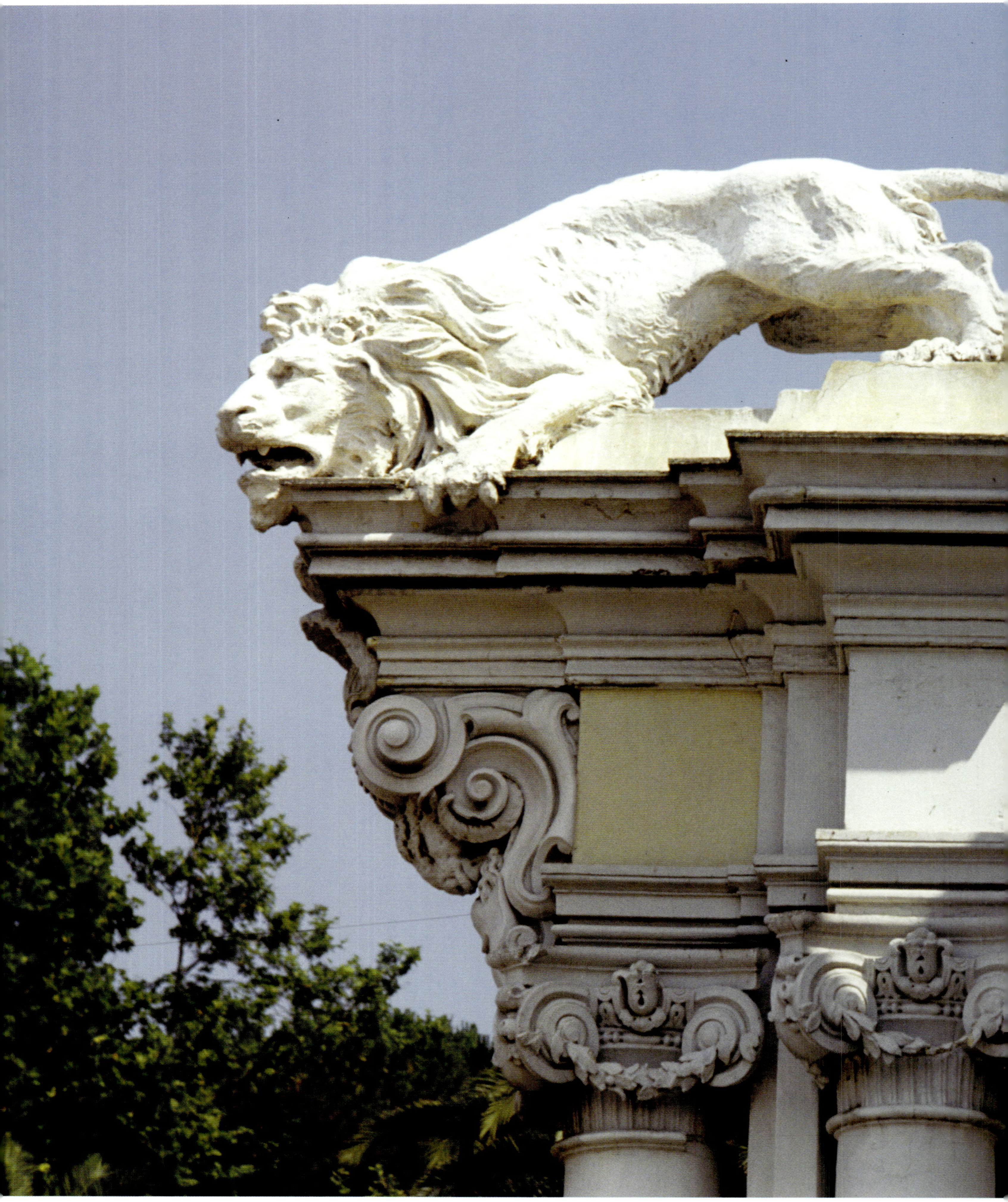

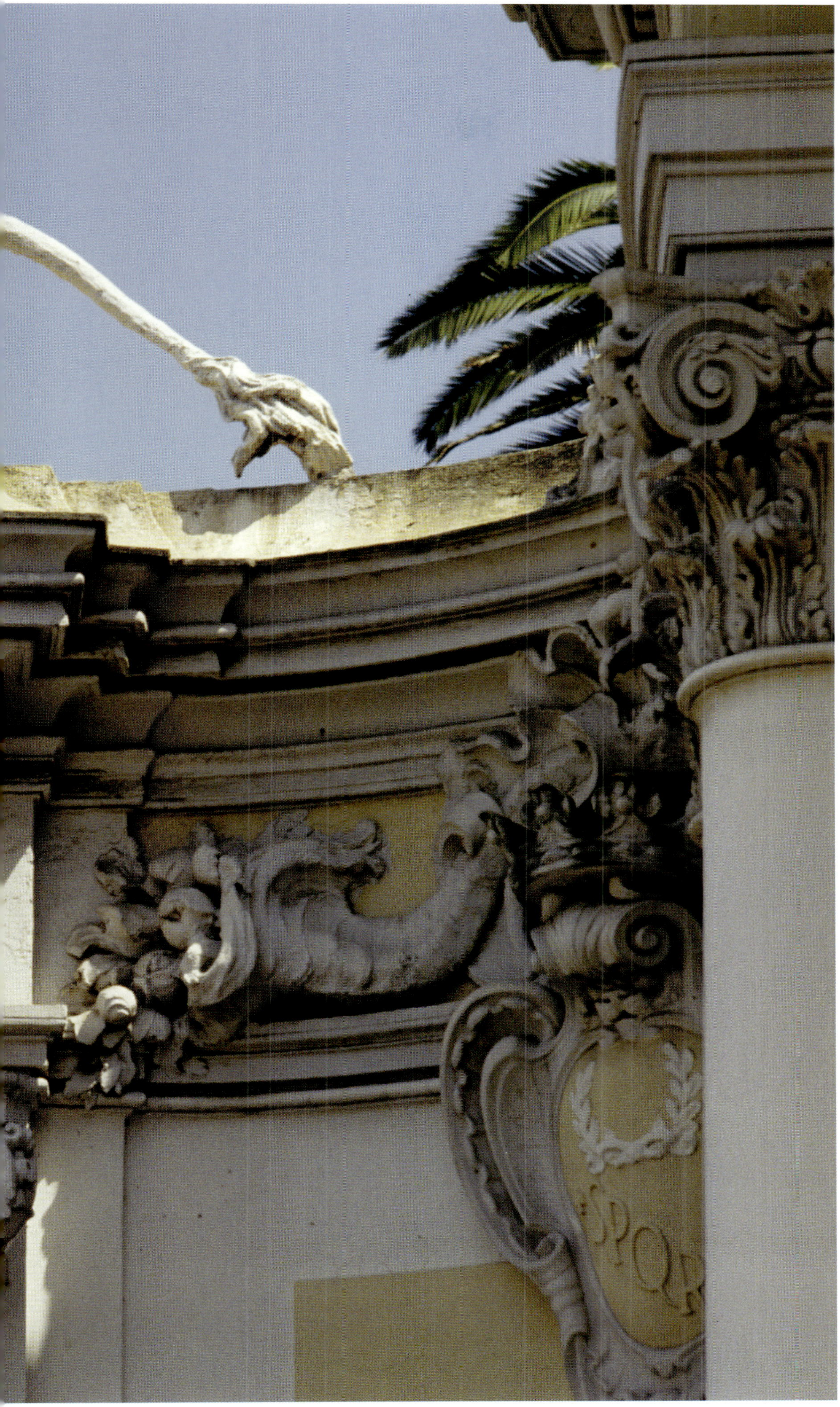

LEFT: A stone lion guarding the ornate entrance to the zoo at the Villa Borghese. This is just one of many animal statues that adorn the grounds. The villa was originally commissioned by Cardinal Scipione Borghese, a ruthless art and antiques collector who used his power to arrest and confiscate the collections of his rivals. *Dorling Kindersley/Getty Images*

Right: The *Campidoglio*—or Capitol—is the hill on which Rome was first built and the center of political power where all the most important ceremonies took place. Now called the Piazza del Campidoglio, it was once dominated by the Temple of Juno Moneta and the Temple of Jupiter Capitolinus although almost nothing remains of them now. Today's piazza was initially designed by Michelangelo around the statue of Marcus Aurelius for the visit of Charles V to Rome in 1536. The piazza contains many other monuments including this one of Constantine. *Andrew Gunners/Digital Vision/ Getty Images*

Pages 142–143: In front of the Senatorial Palace in Piazza del Campidoglio stands a replica of the equestrian statue of Marcus Aurelius. The restored original now stands in the Capitoline Museum. *De Agostini Picture Library/Getty Images*

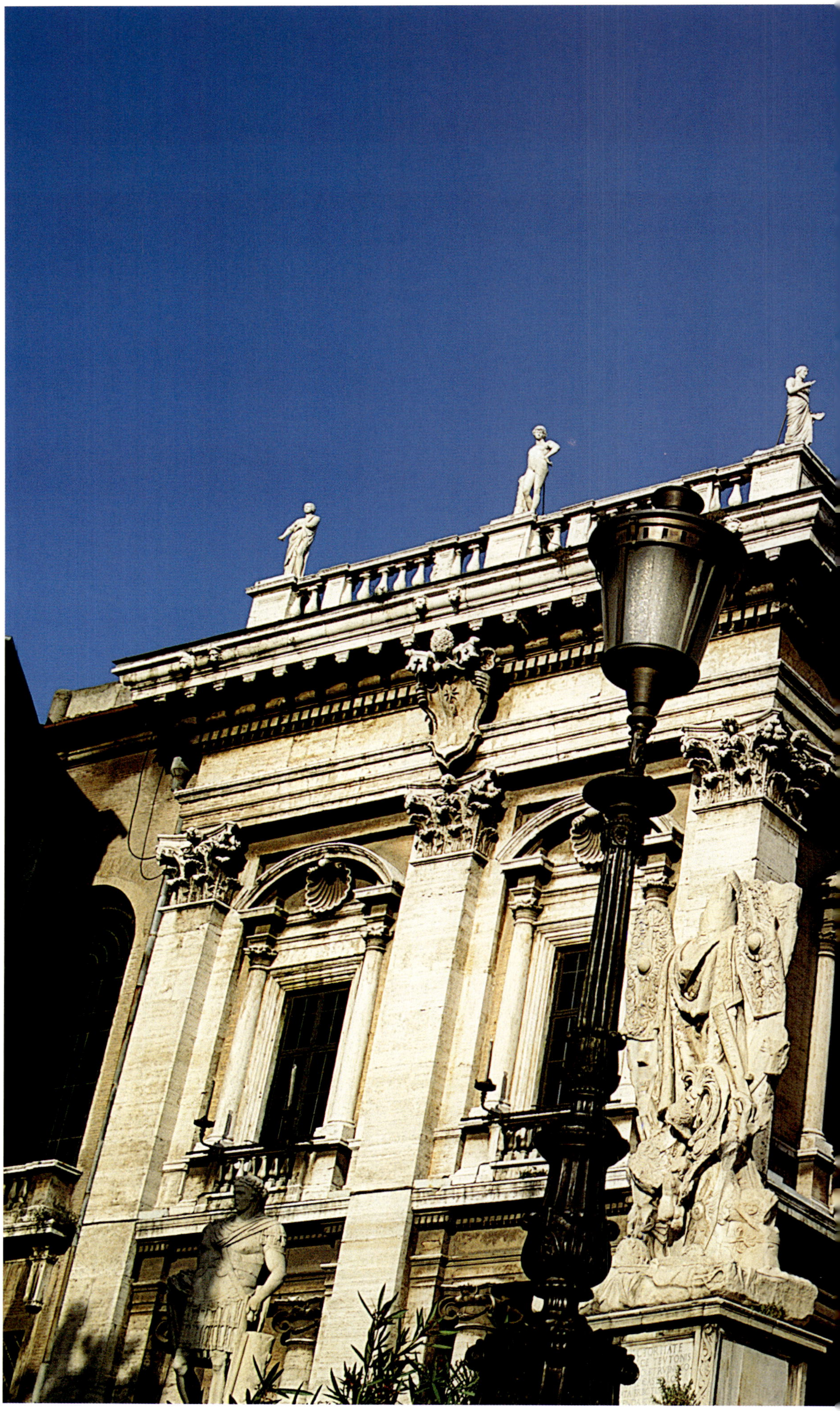

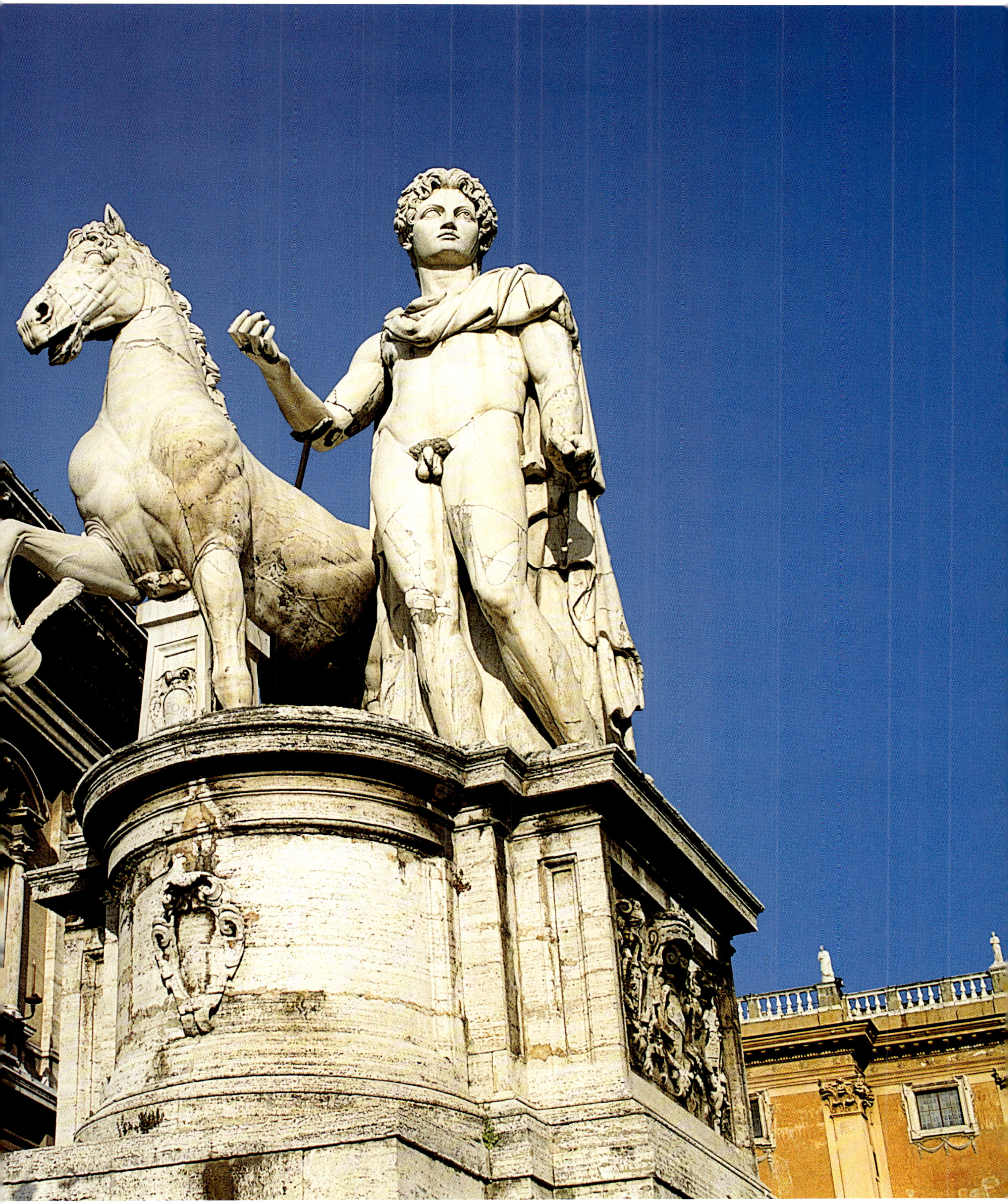

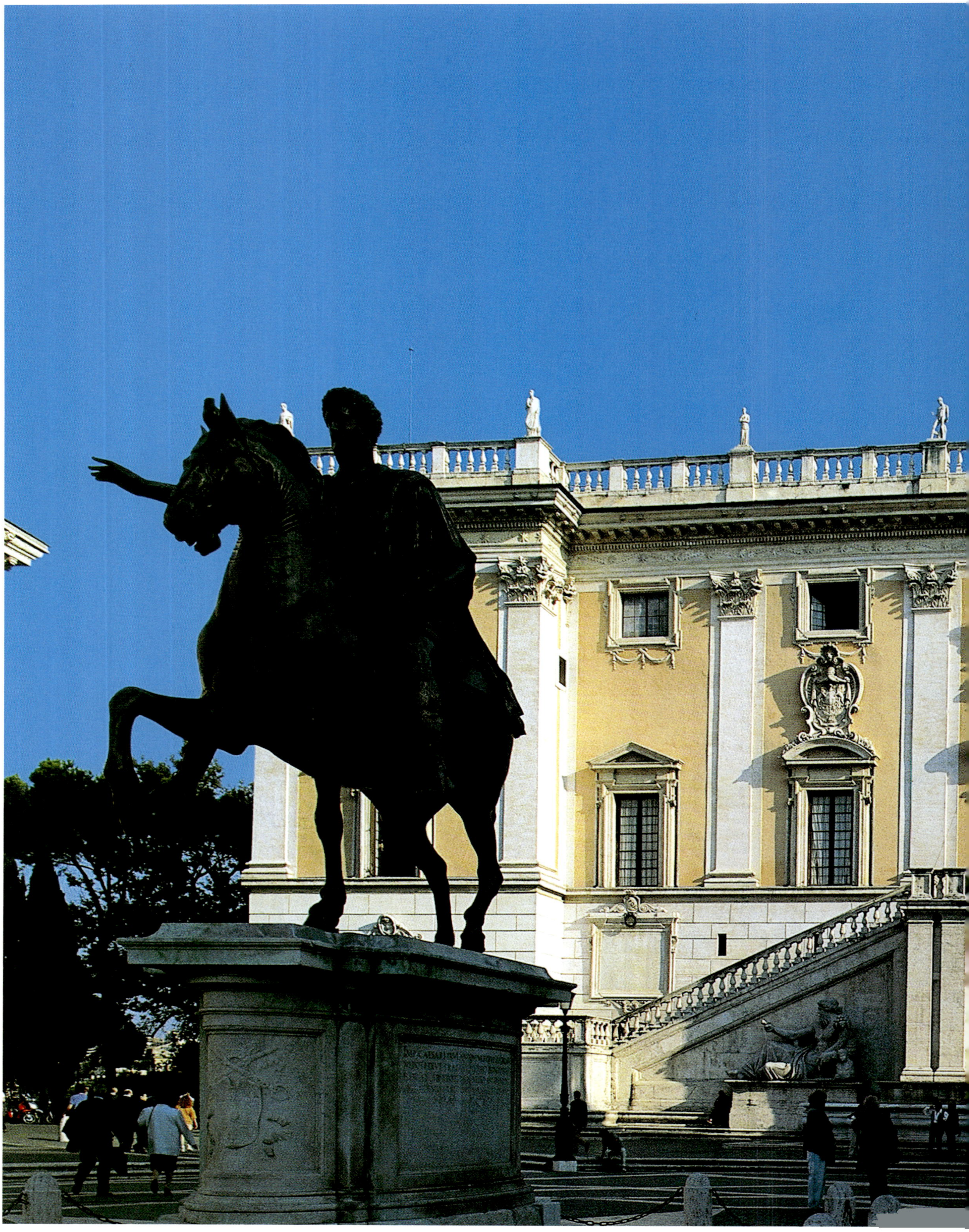

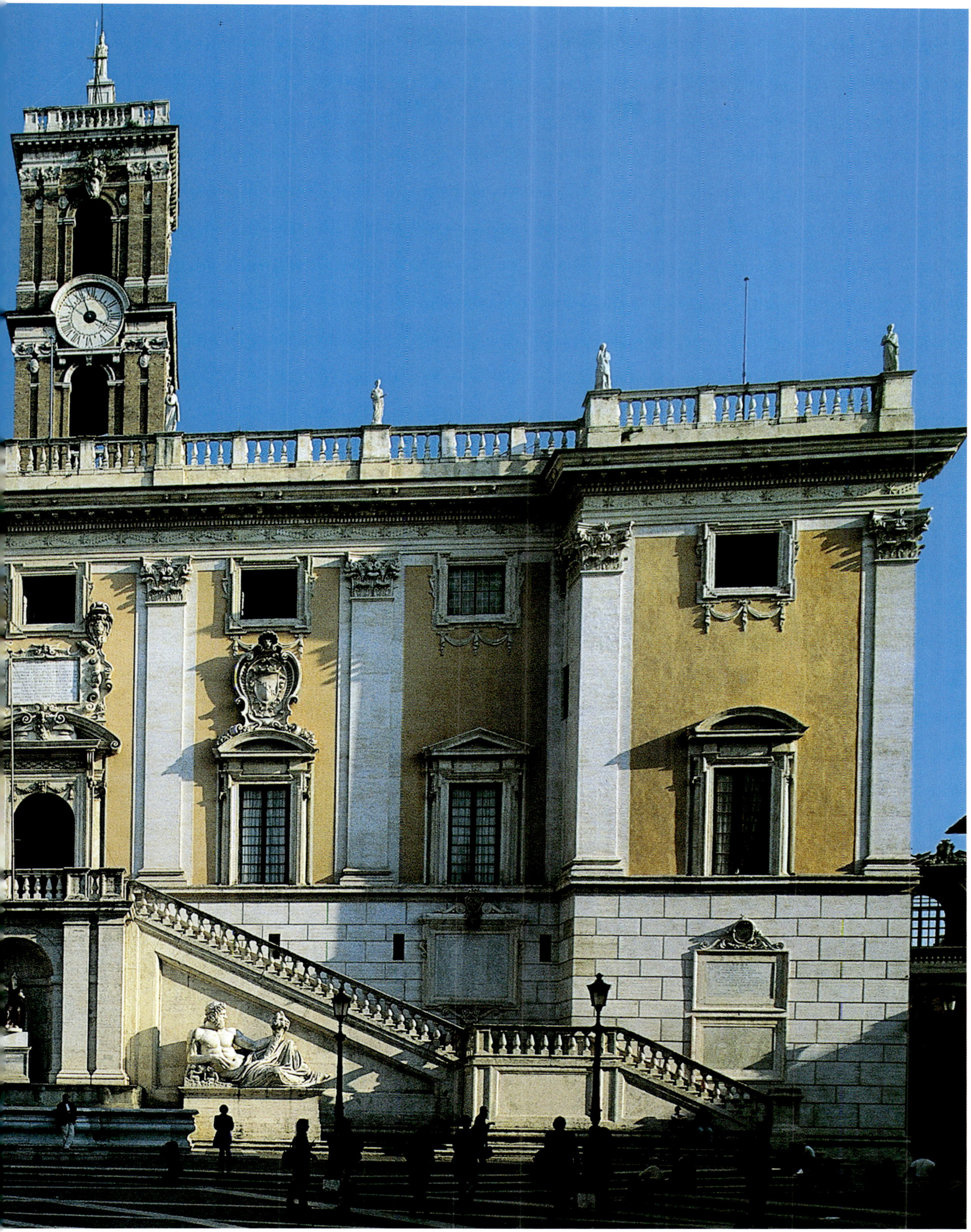

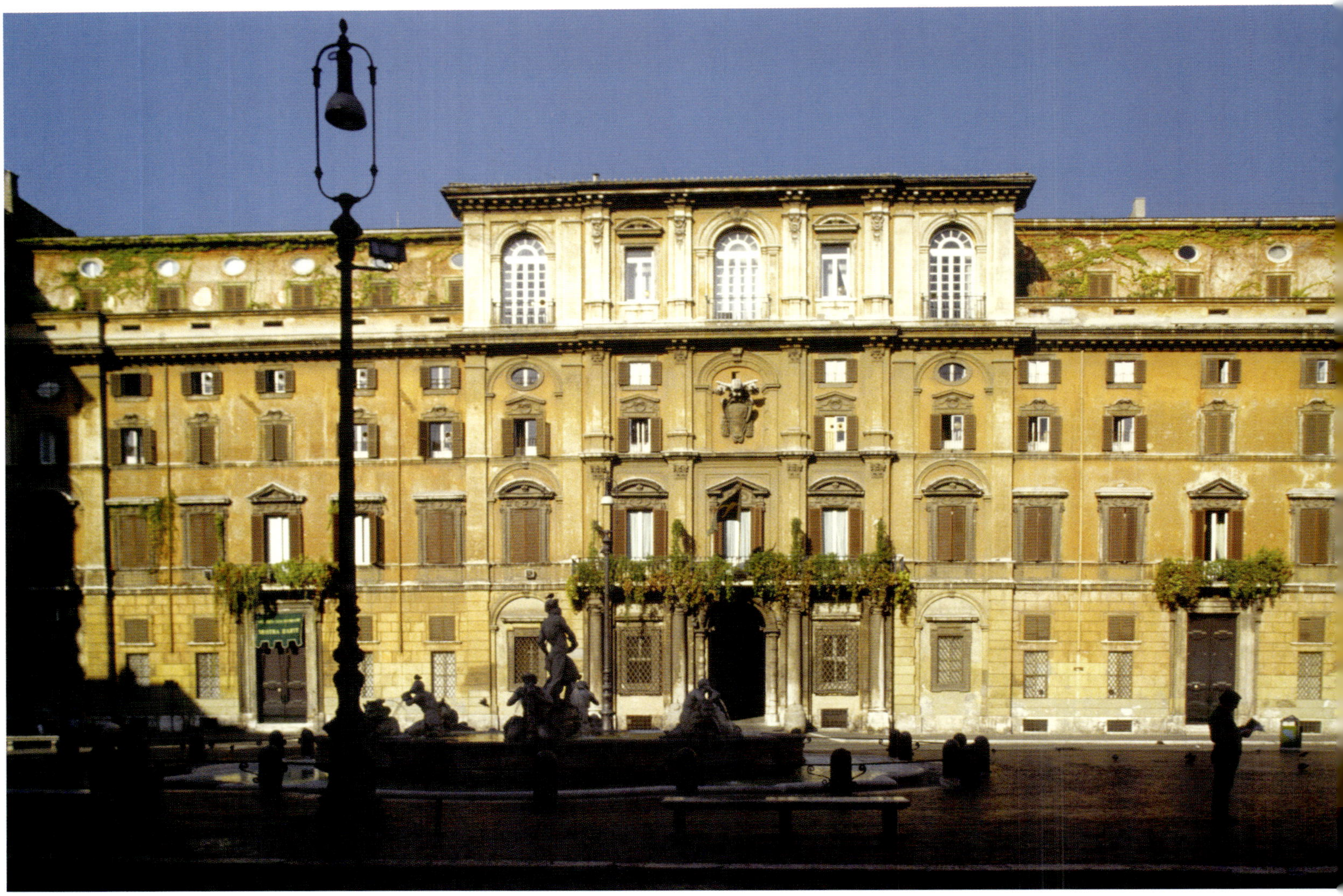

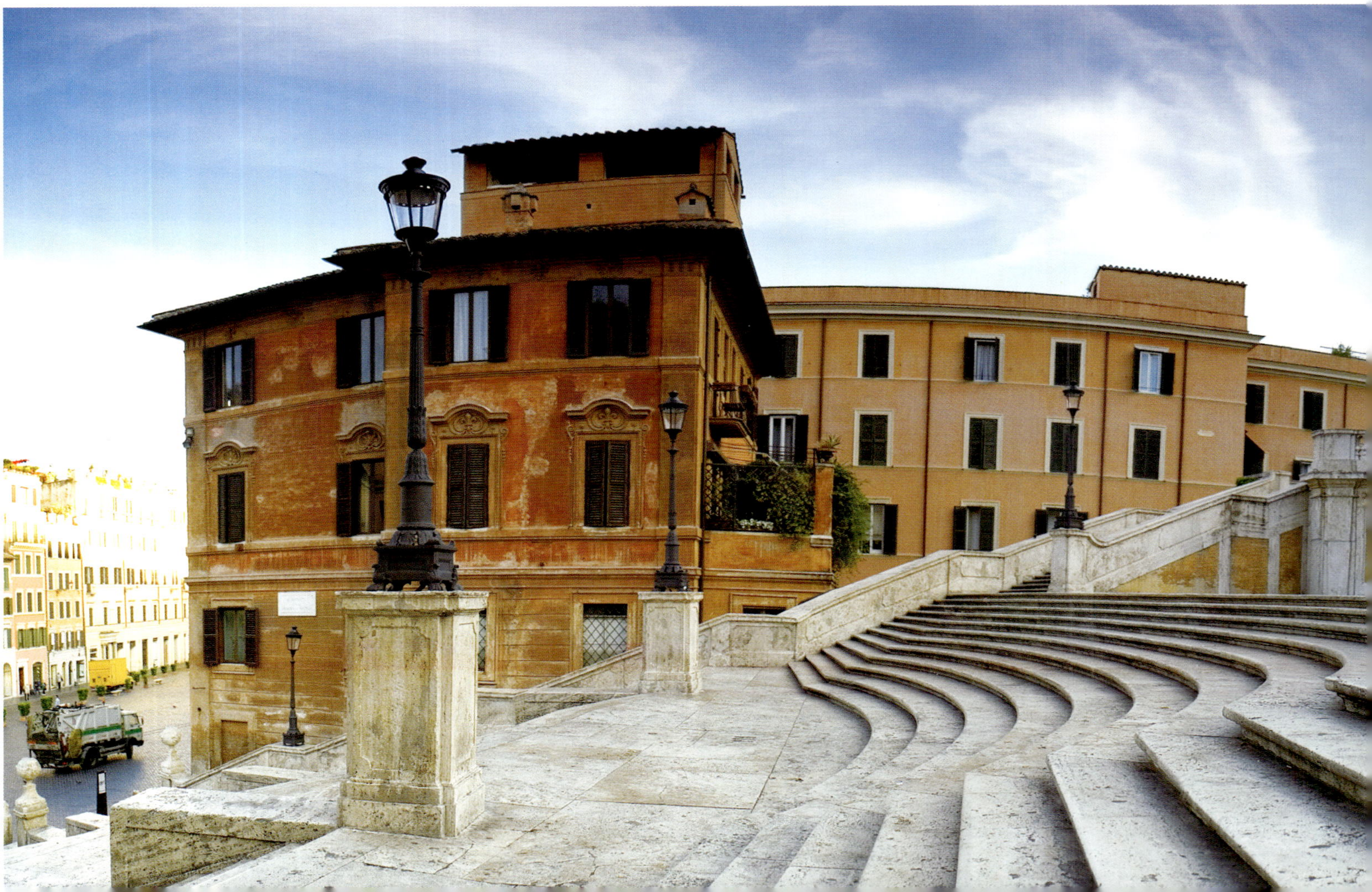

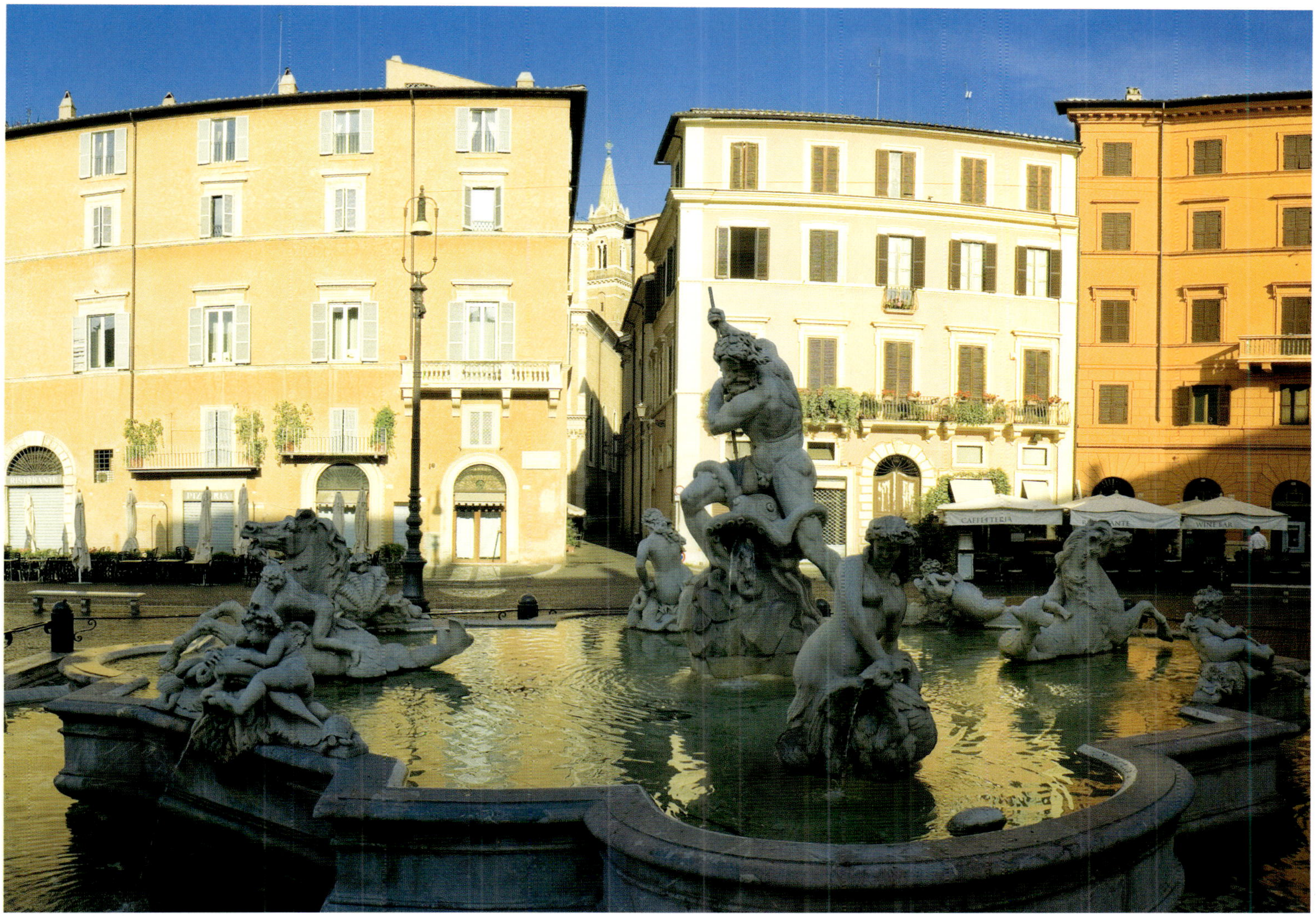

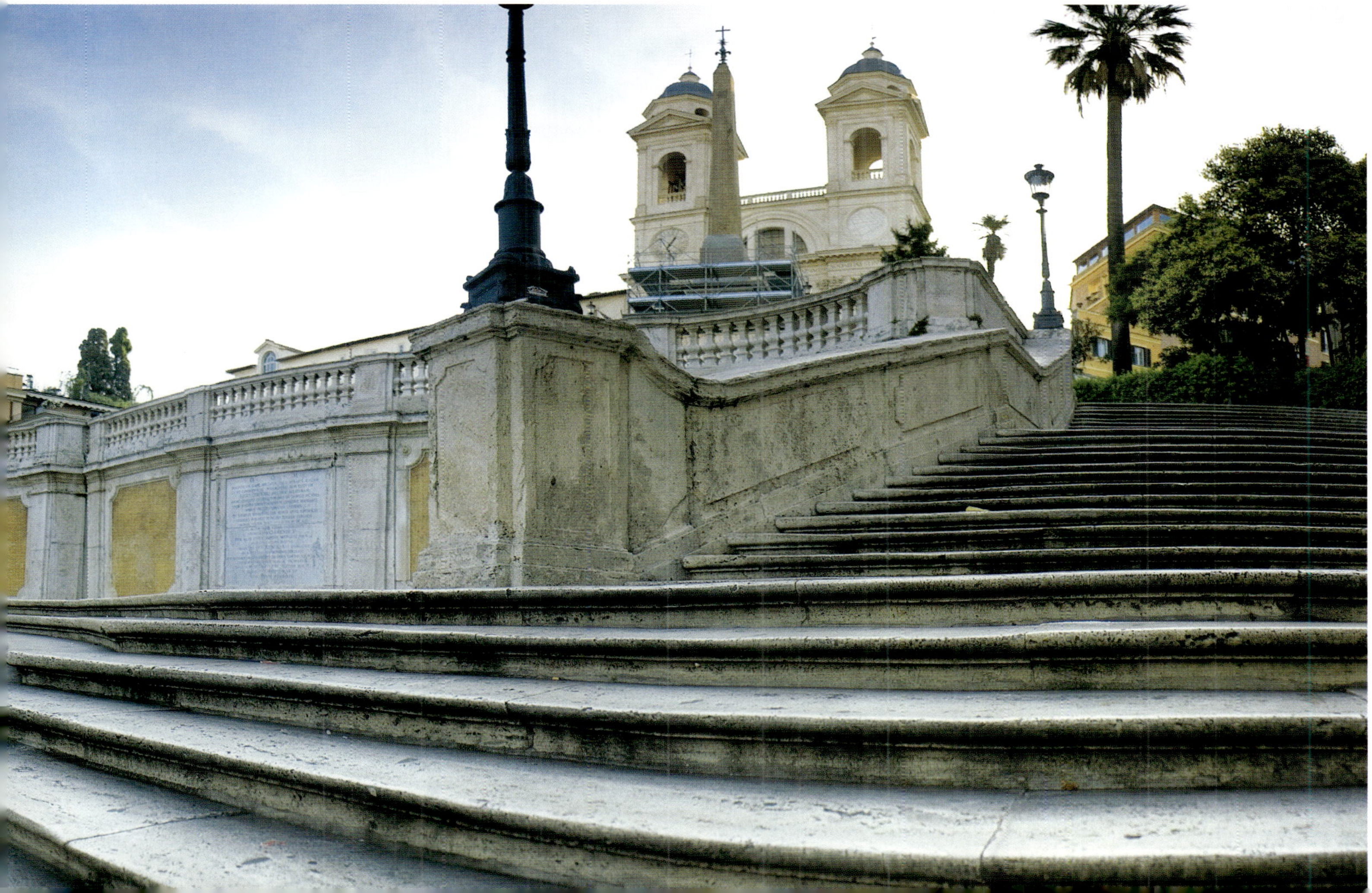

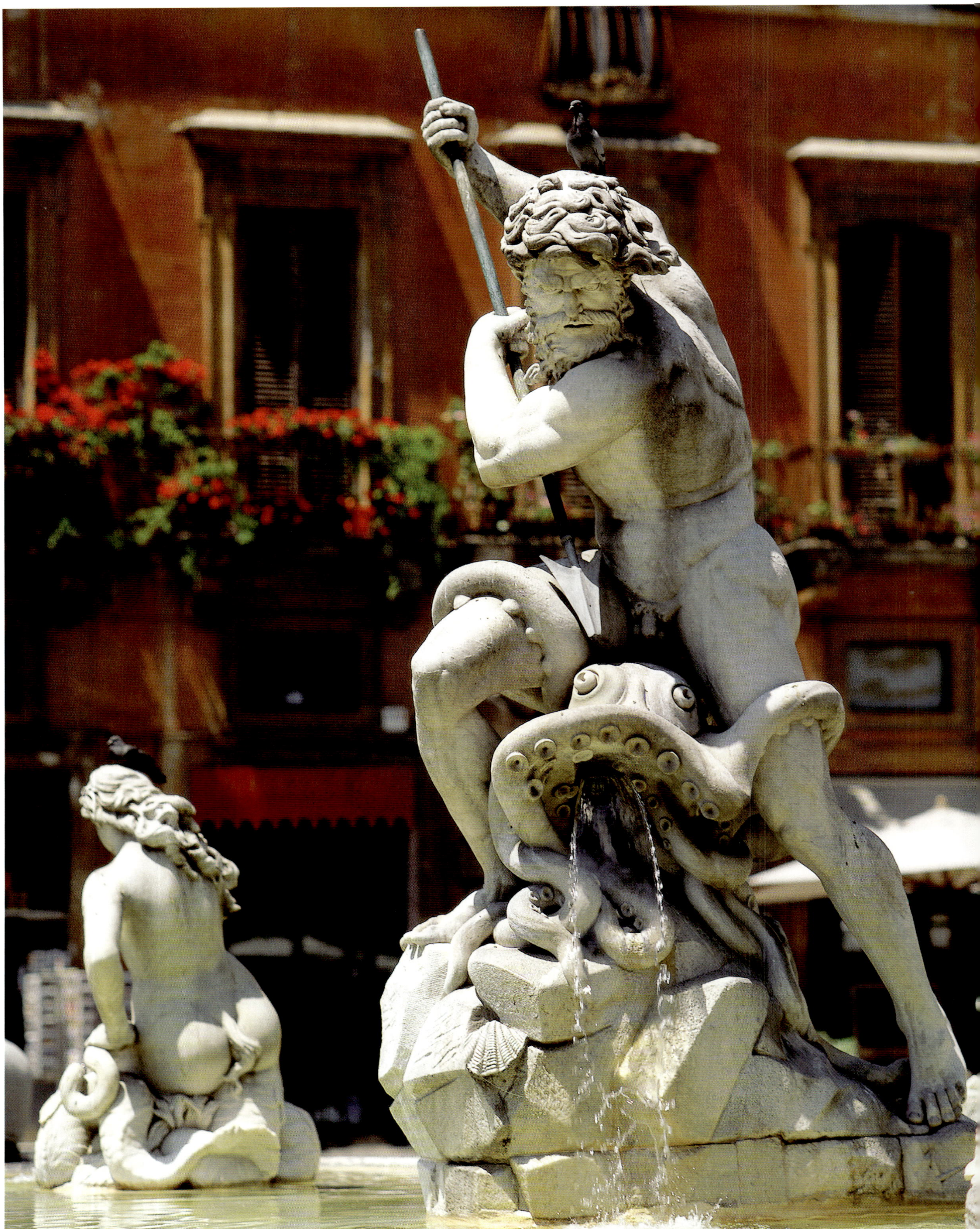

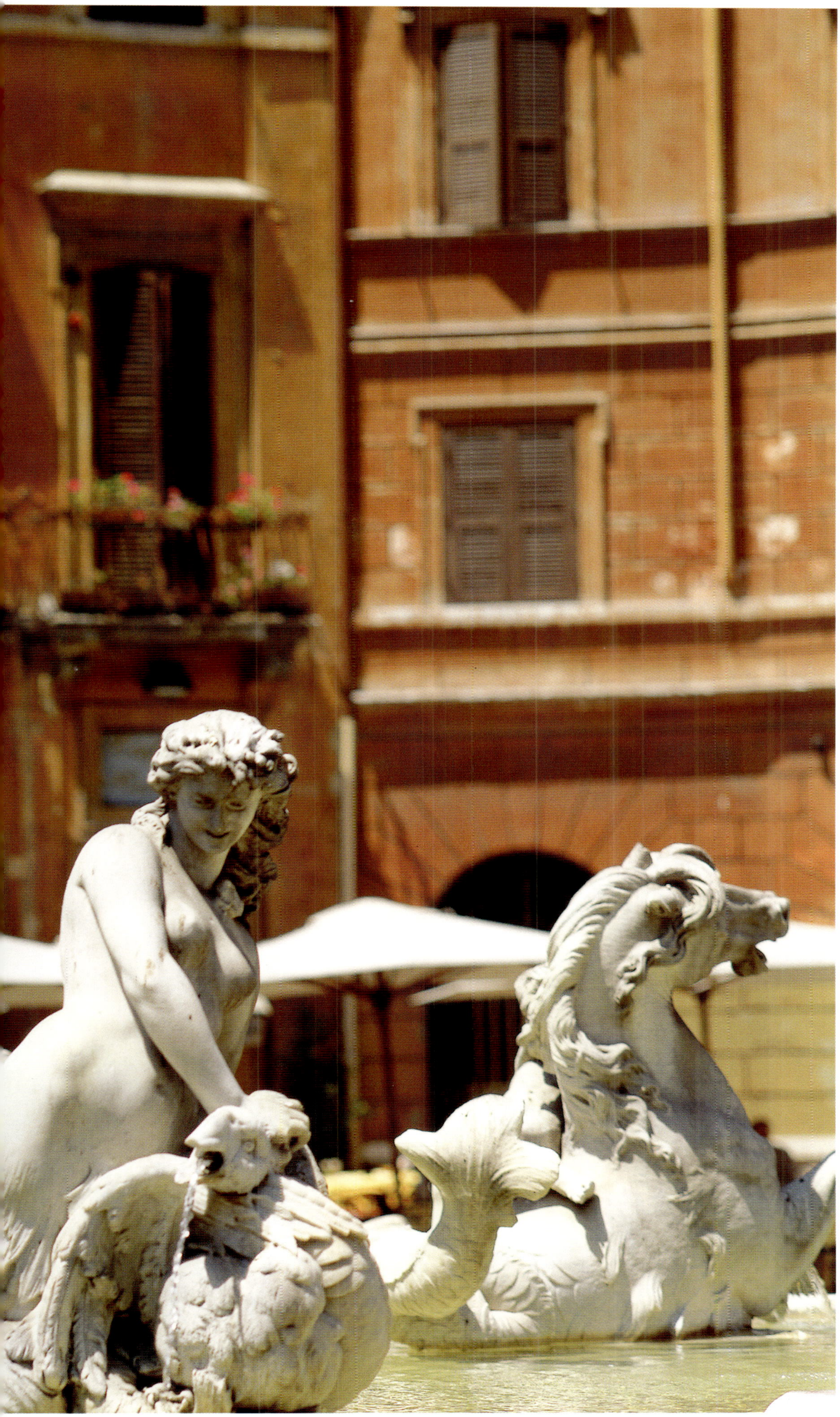

PAGES 144–145:

ABOVE LEFT: The front elevation of the Palazzo Pamphili on the western side of the Piazza Navona; the palace is now the Brazilian embassy. Much of the building dates from its resoration which started in 1646. *Dorling Kindersley/Getty Images*

ABOVE RIGHT: The Baroque Piazza Navona in the Centro Storico district of central Rome is the great metropolitan meeting center of Rome. It is embellished by three incredible water features.

BELOW: The famous terraced staircase, Scalinata della Trinità dei Monti, connecting the Piazza di Spagna below to the Piazza Trinità dei Monti on the hill above.

LEFT: The Fontana di Nettuno (Neptune Fountain) in the Piazza Navona. The basin was designed in the sixteenth century by Giacomo della Porta while the statues were added in 1873. *Purestock/Getty Images*

Modern Rome

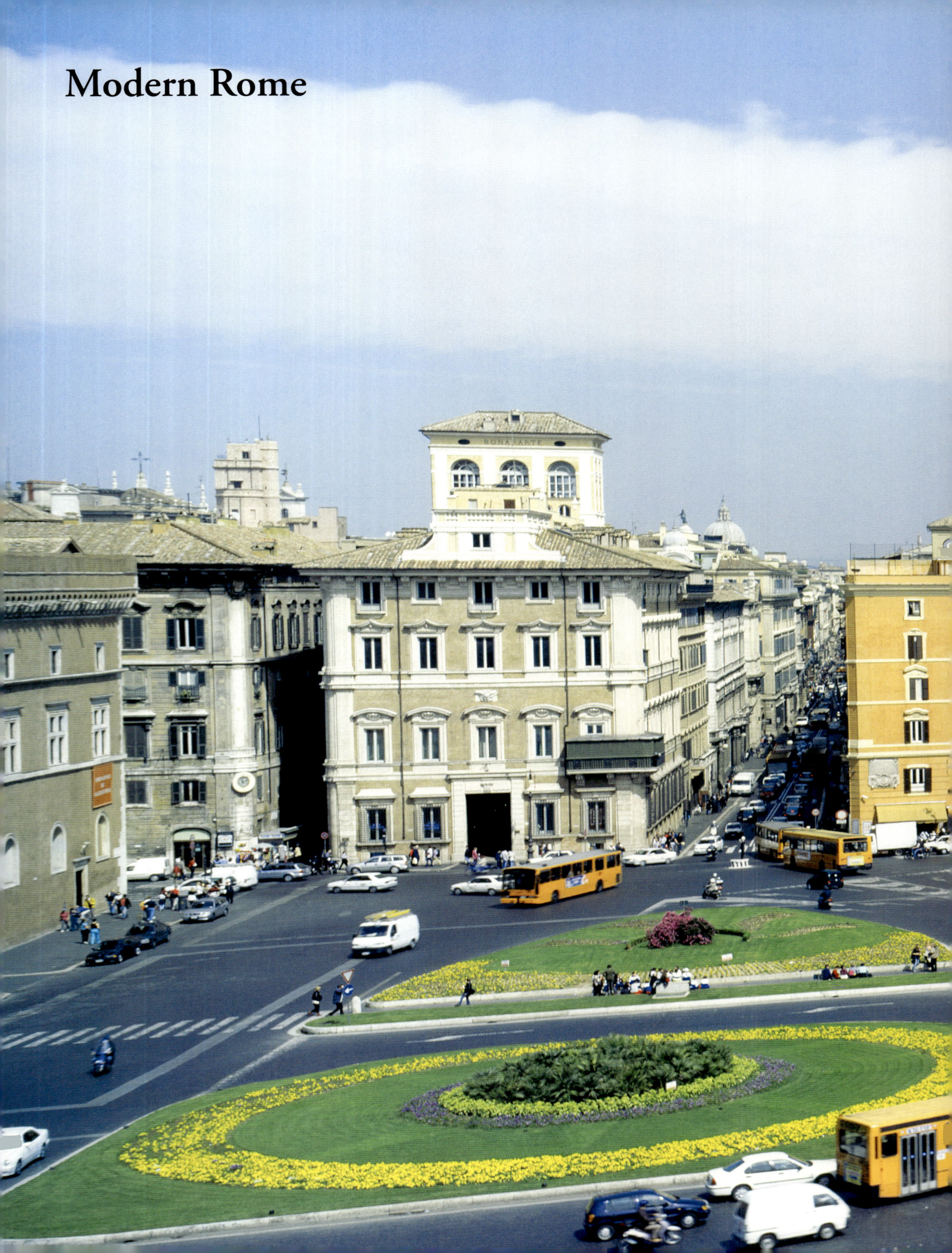

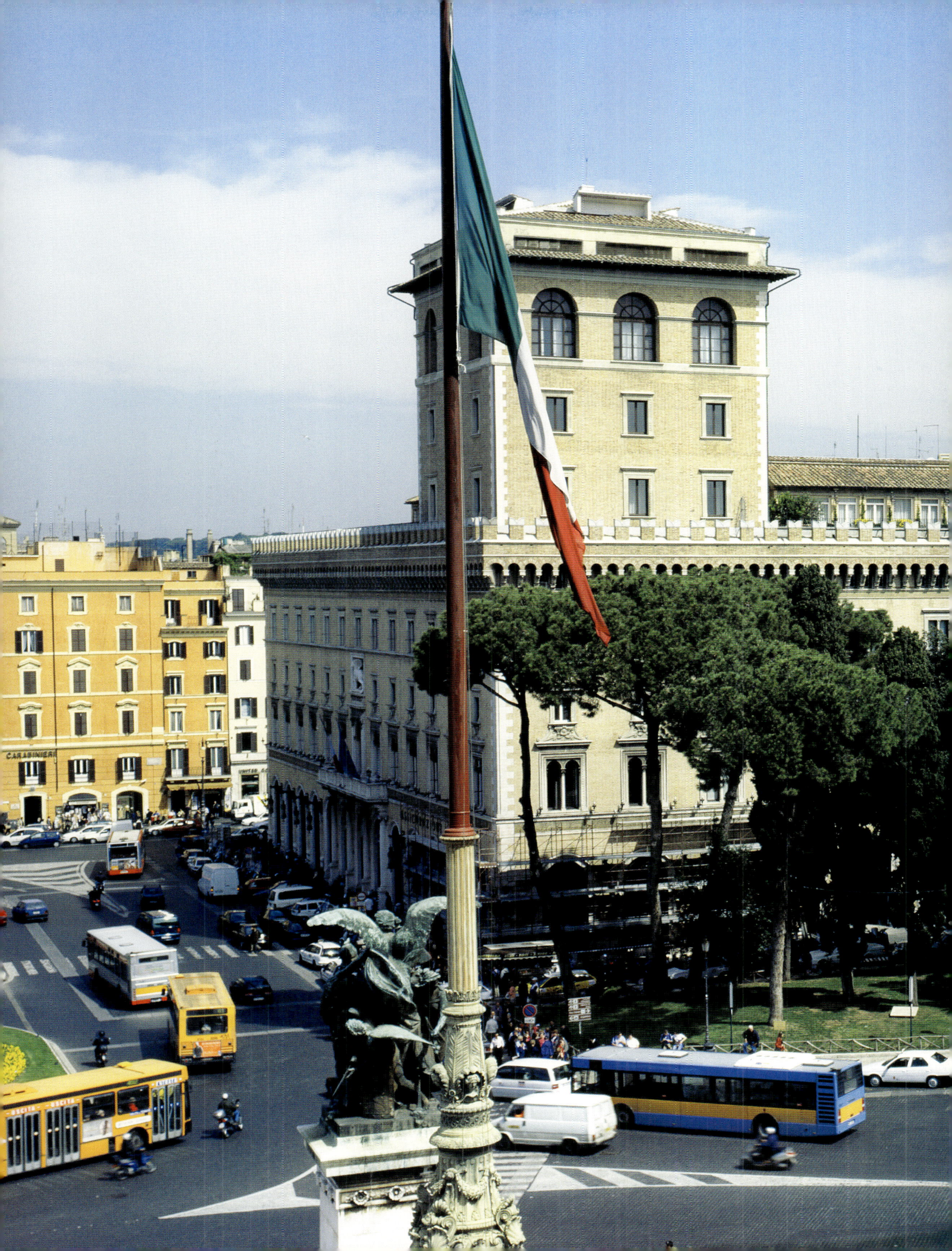
CARABINIERI

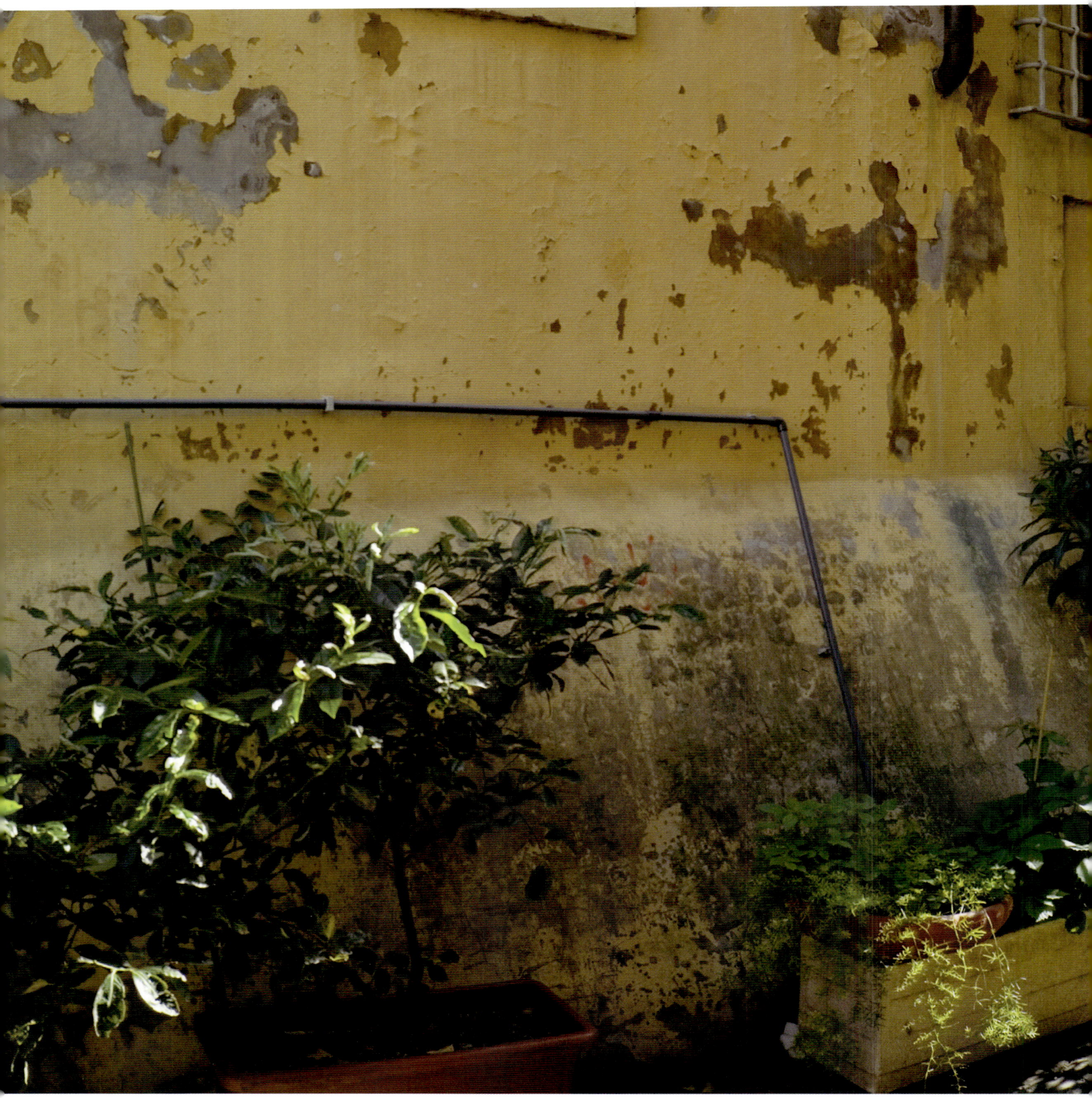

Previous page: Modern Rome is one of the world's great capital cities. It has its own distinct character with practically no hi-rise buildings. Beautiful piazzas—this is the Piazza Venezia seen from the Vittoriano—give it a feeling of space and, remarkably amidst all the helter skelter, a feeling of calm. *Panoramic Images/Getty Images*

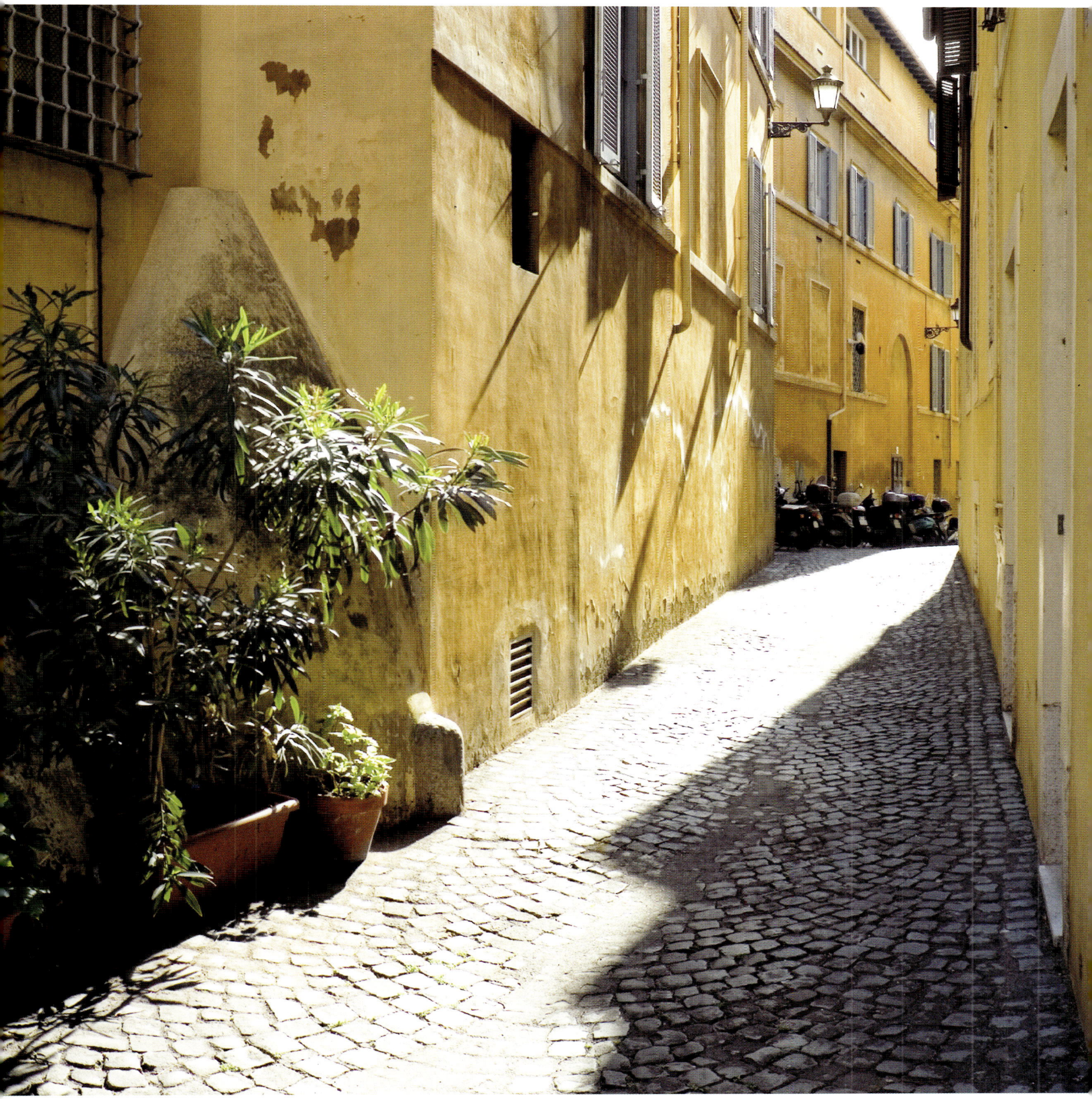

ABOVE: In complete contrast to the open piazzas and wide avenues, there are still small lanes and back alleys that give Rome its true personality. Here sunlight illuminates a typically atmospheric Roman alleyway right in the heart of the city, complete with characteristic scooters parked at the end of the street. The wooden-shuttered houses are painted in warm complimentary colors that have mellowed beautifully with time. *iStockphoto*

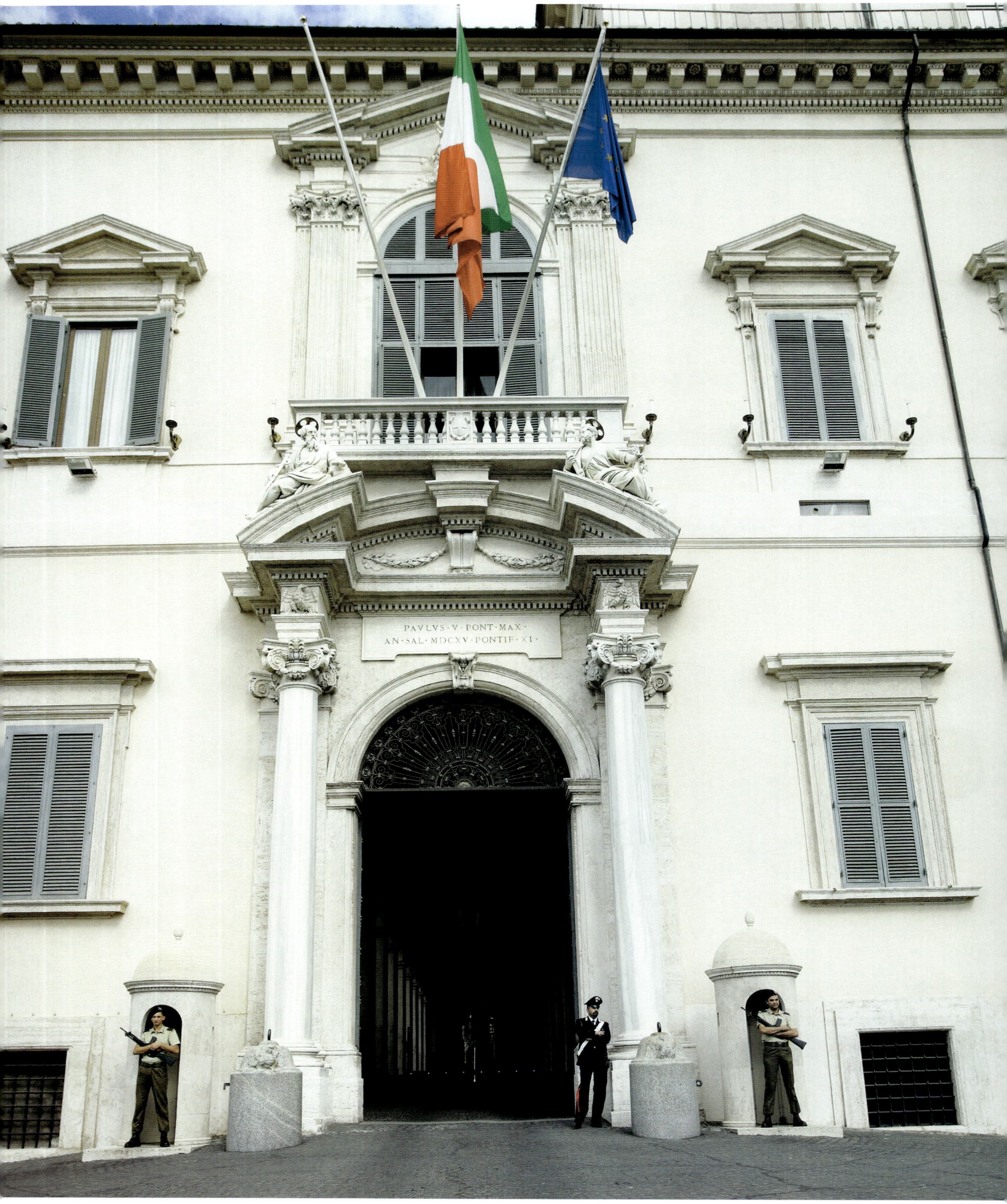
PAVLVS·V·PONT·MAX·
AN·SAL·MDCXV·PONTIF·XI·

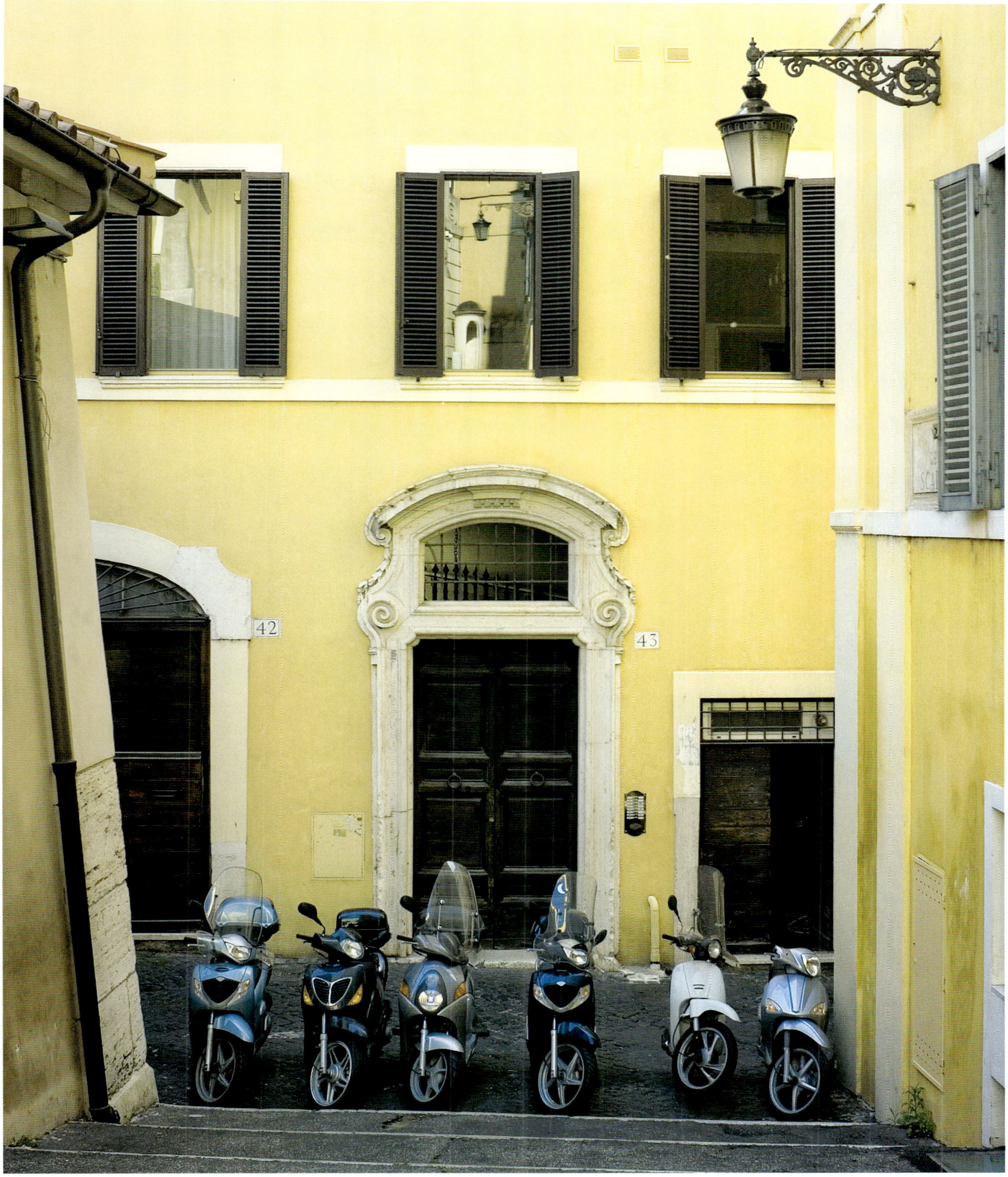

LEFT: The Entrance to the Palazzo del Quirinale—Quirinal Palace—the official residence of the President of the Republic of Italy. When first built in the late sixteenth century the Quirinal was the summer palace for the popes; then between 1870 and 1944 it served as a royal palace before becoming the official residence of the President when the Republic of Italy was declared in 1944. *Altrendo travel/Getty Images*

ABOVE: Scooters parked in a line at the bottom of stone steps in a typical Quirinale district back street. *iStockphoto*

Right: Victor Emmanuel III (1869–1947) inherited the throne of Italy from his father Umberto I in 1900. Originally a popular monarch his decision-making during World War II lost him public support. In an attempt to retain his throne he abdicated in 1945 hoping that the referendum called for May 1946 would reinstate him. However, the Italian public came out in favor of a Republic and the royal family exiled itself to Egypt. Victor Emmanuel died there and was buried in Alexandria.

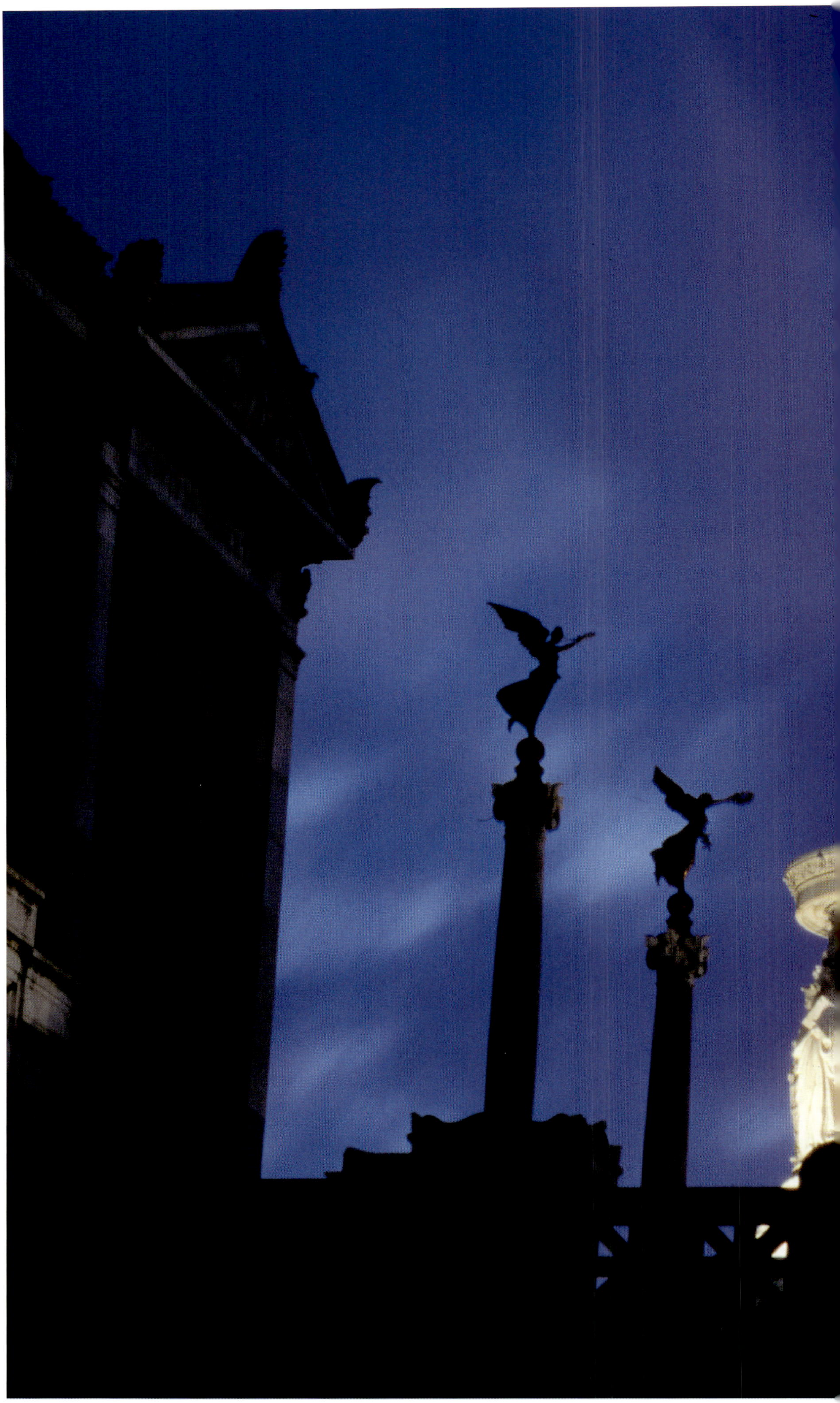

Pages 156–157: The Vittoriano, the monument to Victor Emmanuel stands in front of the Assicurazioni Generali di Venezia building and the Piazza Venezia; both were built in the late nineteenth century, as was the monument.

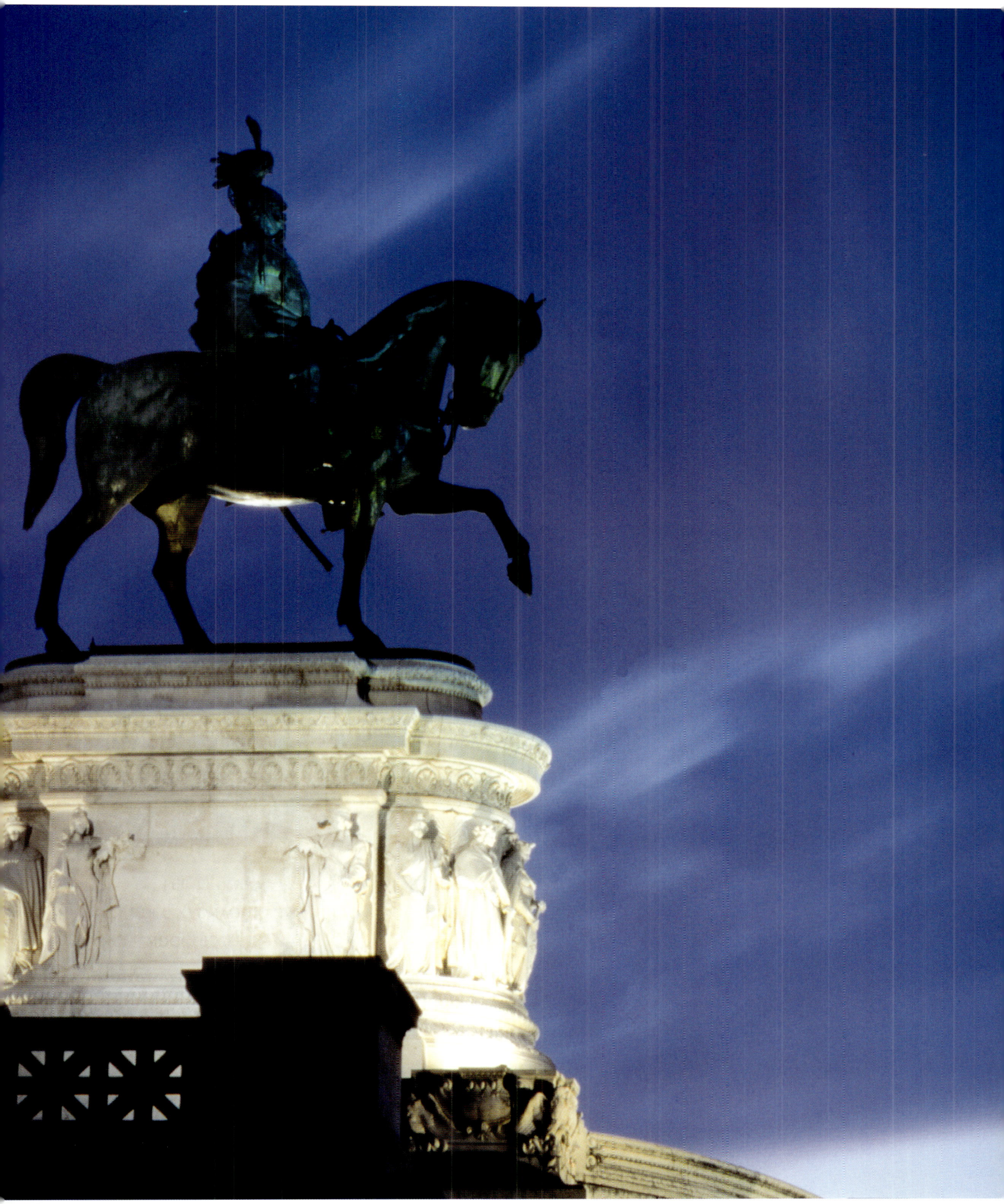

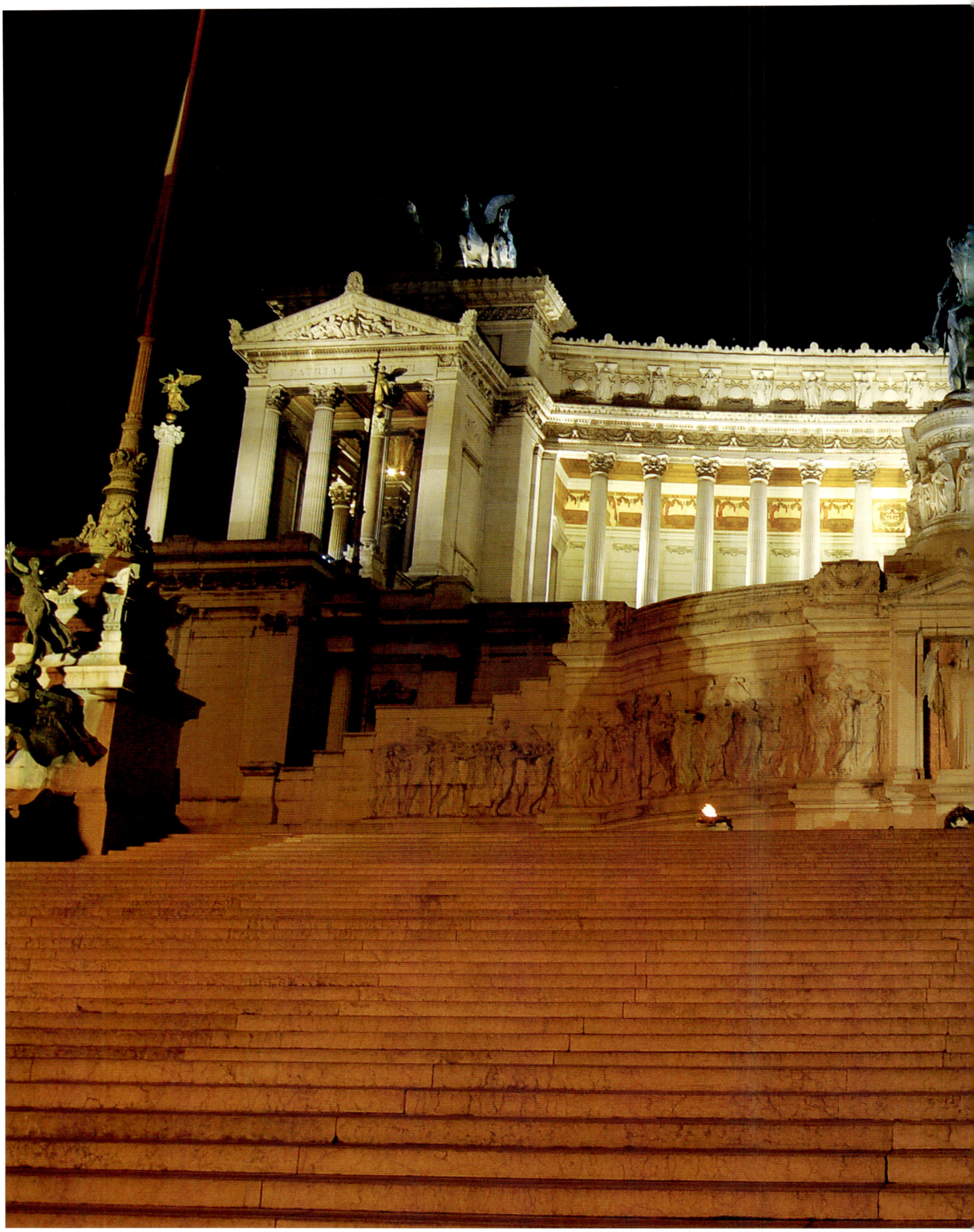

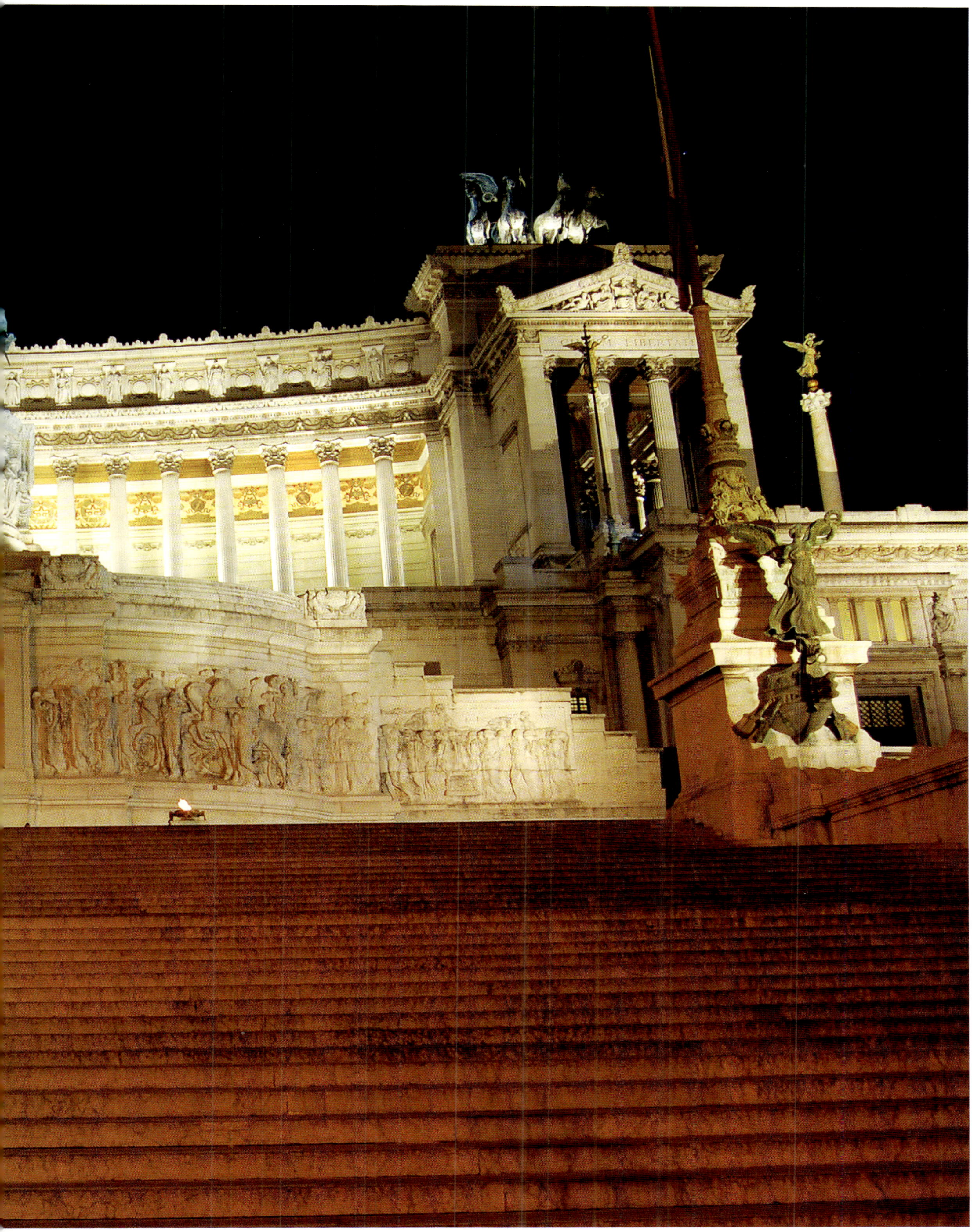

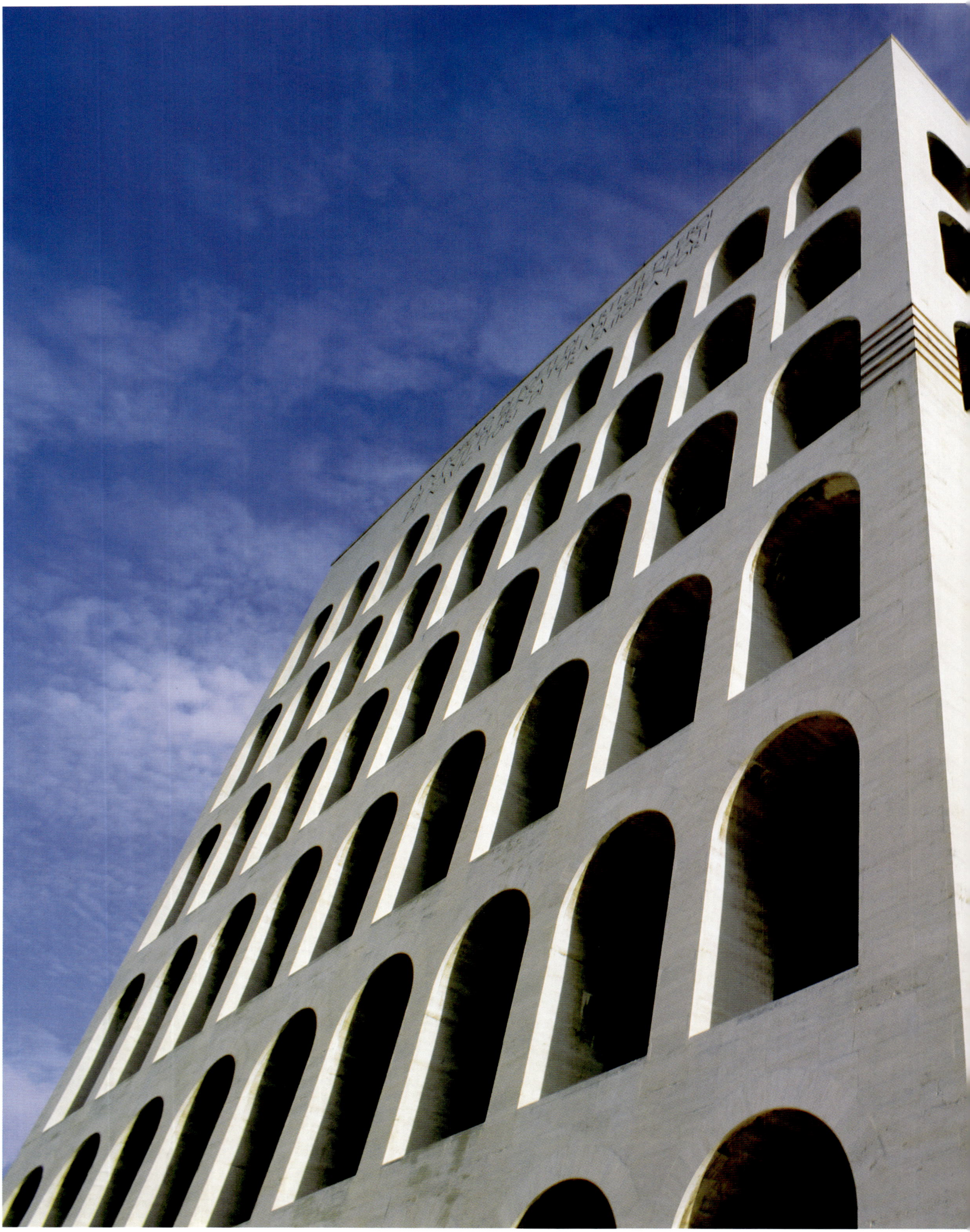

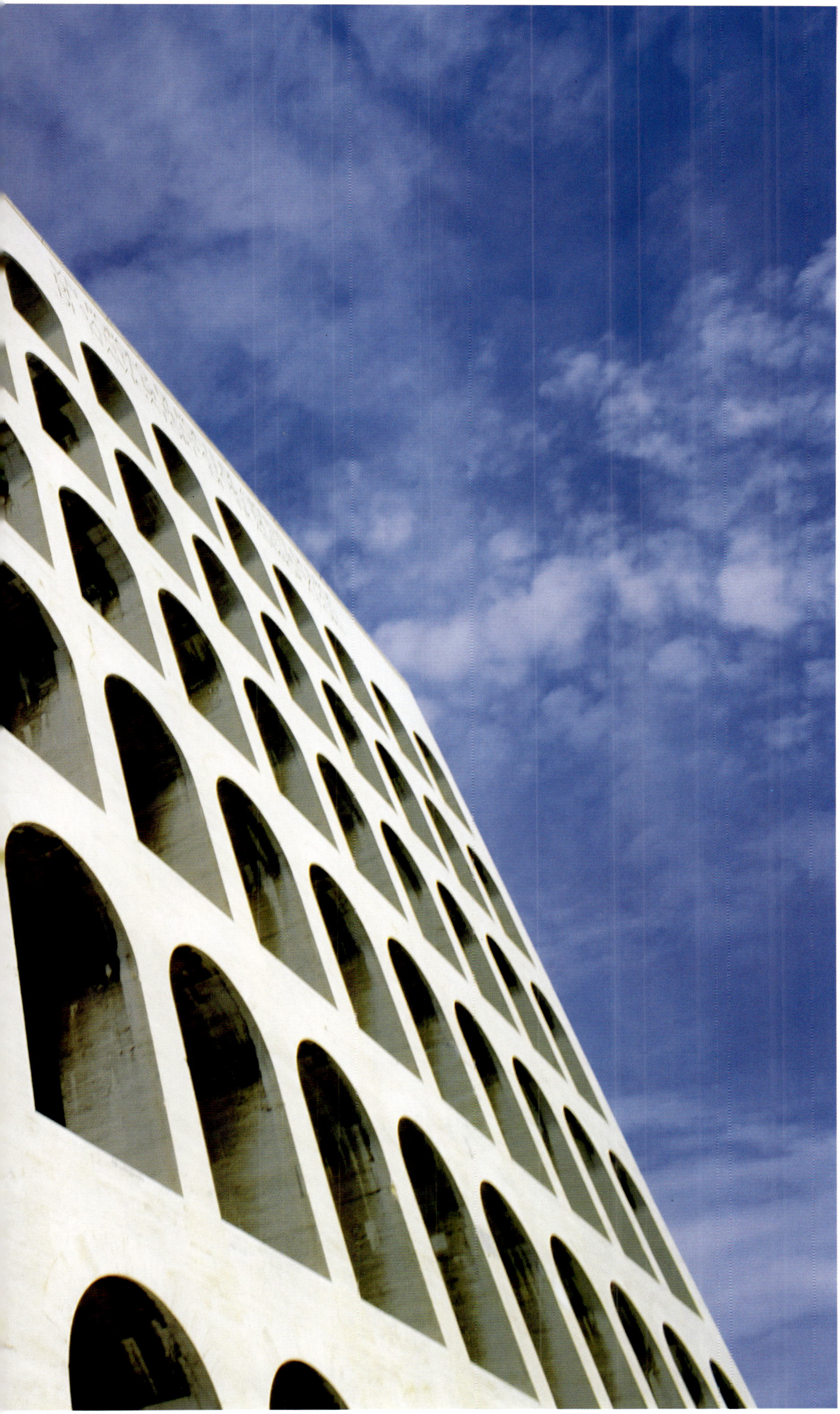

Left: In the 1930s during the Mussolini era the land between Rome and the sea was built up into a monumental administrative area known as the EUR (Esposizione Universale di Roma) as part of the dictator's vision of creating an Urbs Magna or Third Rome. The Palazzo della Civilta di Lavoro or Square Coliseum is the most magnificent and imposing of the buildings. *Oliviero Olivieri/Robert Harding World Imagery/Getty Images*

Page 160: The Foro Italico was originally called the Foro Mussolini—a vast and imposing sports complex embellished with huge white marble statues of athletes. Constructed at the foot of Mount Mario it was designed for political rallies and sporting occasions. The stadium became the Olympic Stadium for the 1956 Rome Olympics. *iStockphoto*

Page 161: The ground floor of the Palazzo della Civita del Lavoro contains statues in the ground floor arcades representing the arts and human activities. *Oliviero Olivieri/Robert Harding World Imagery/Getty Images*

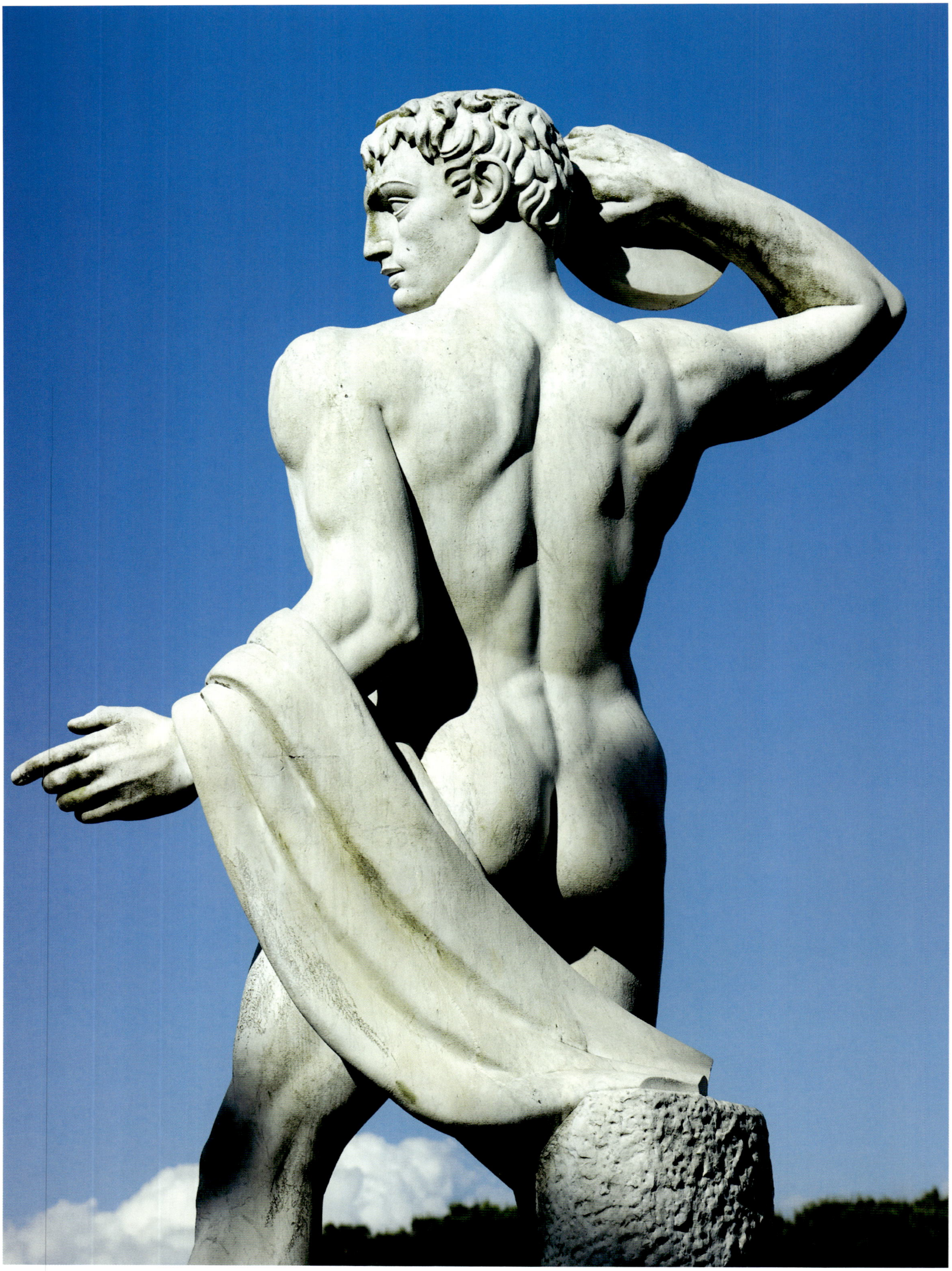

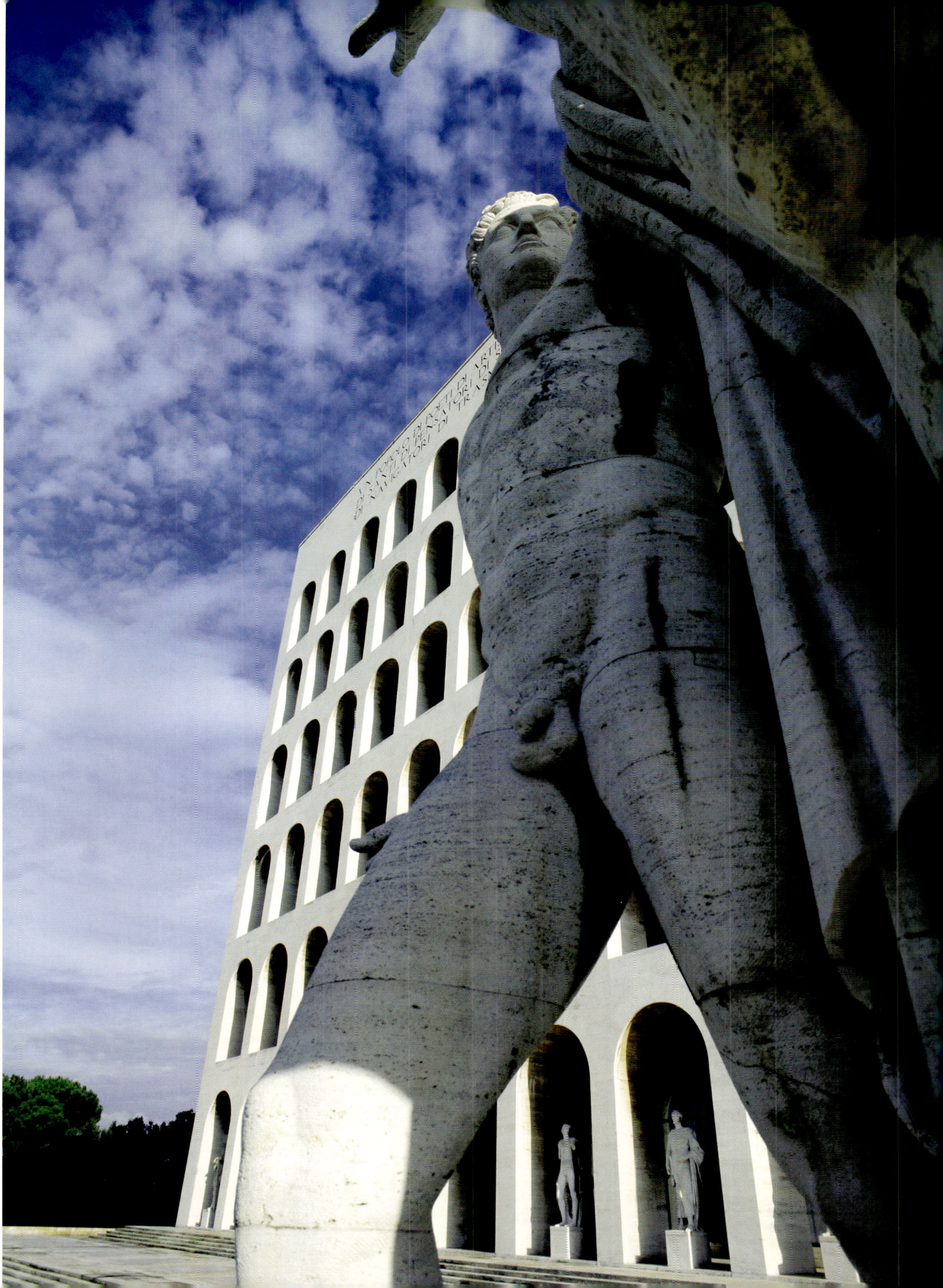

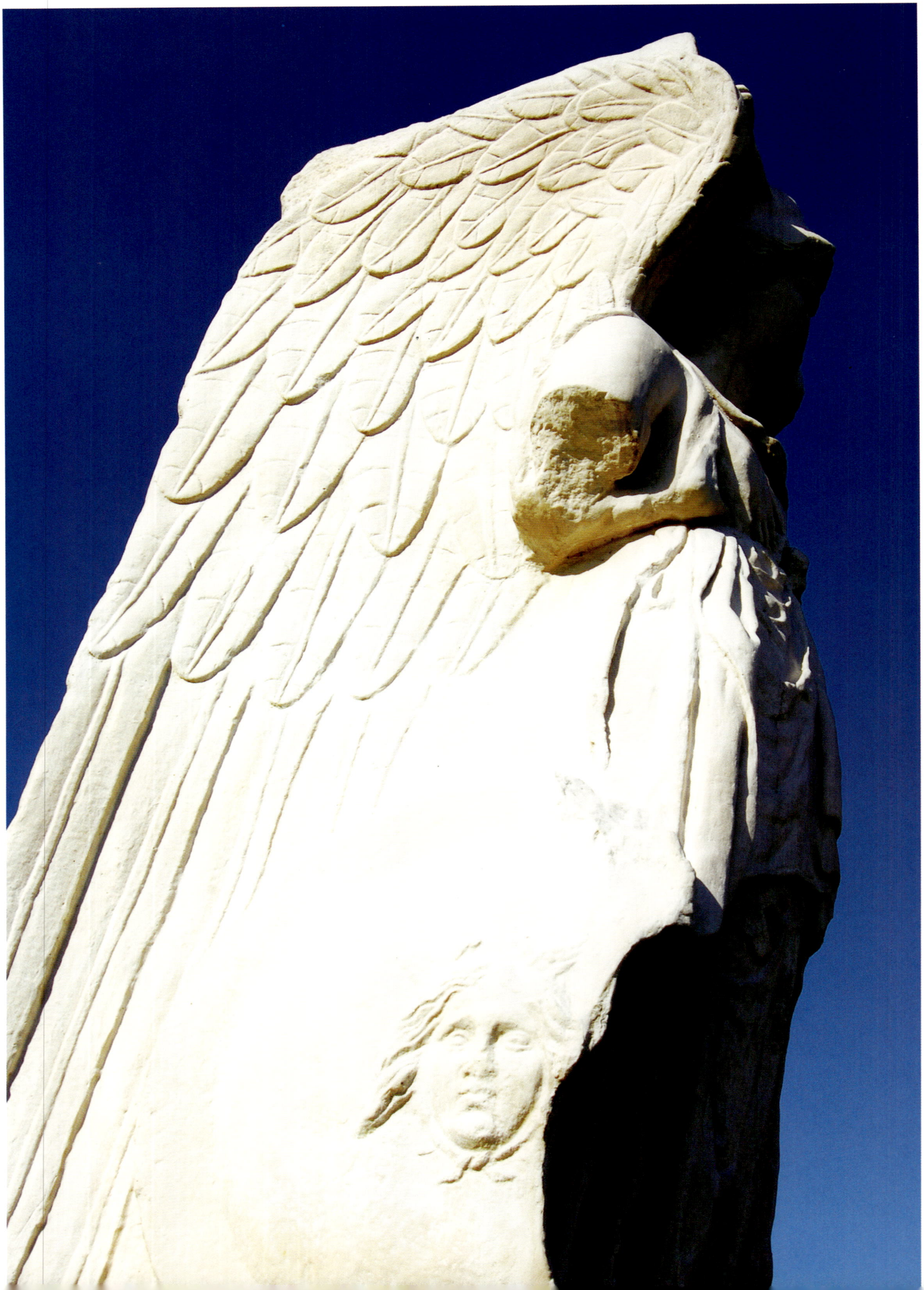

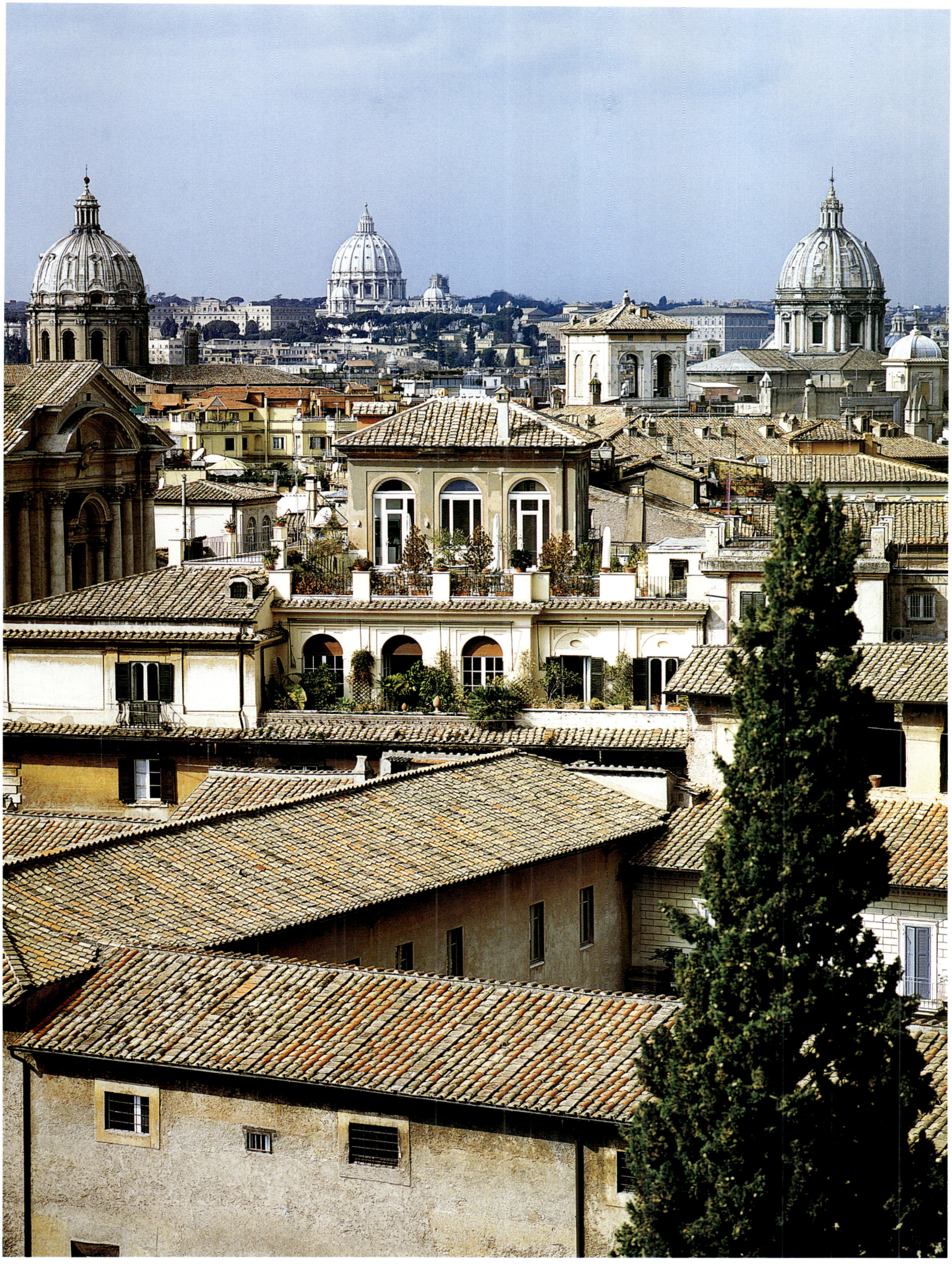

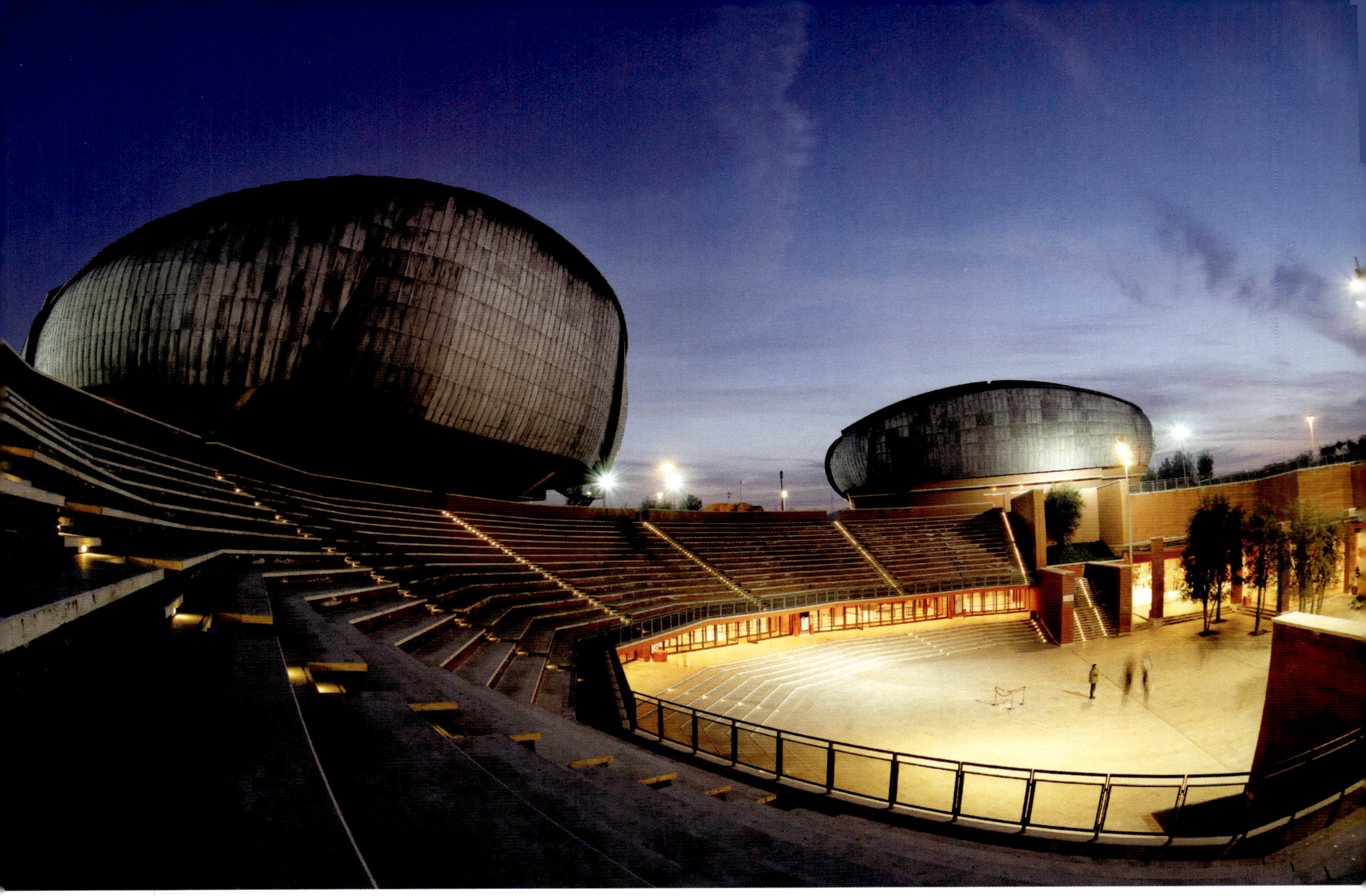

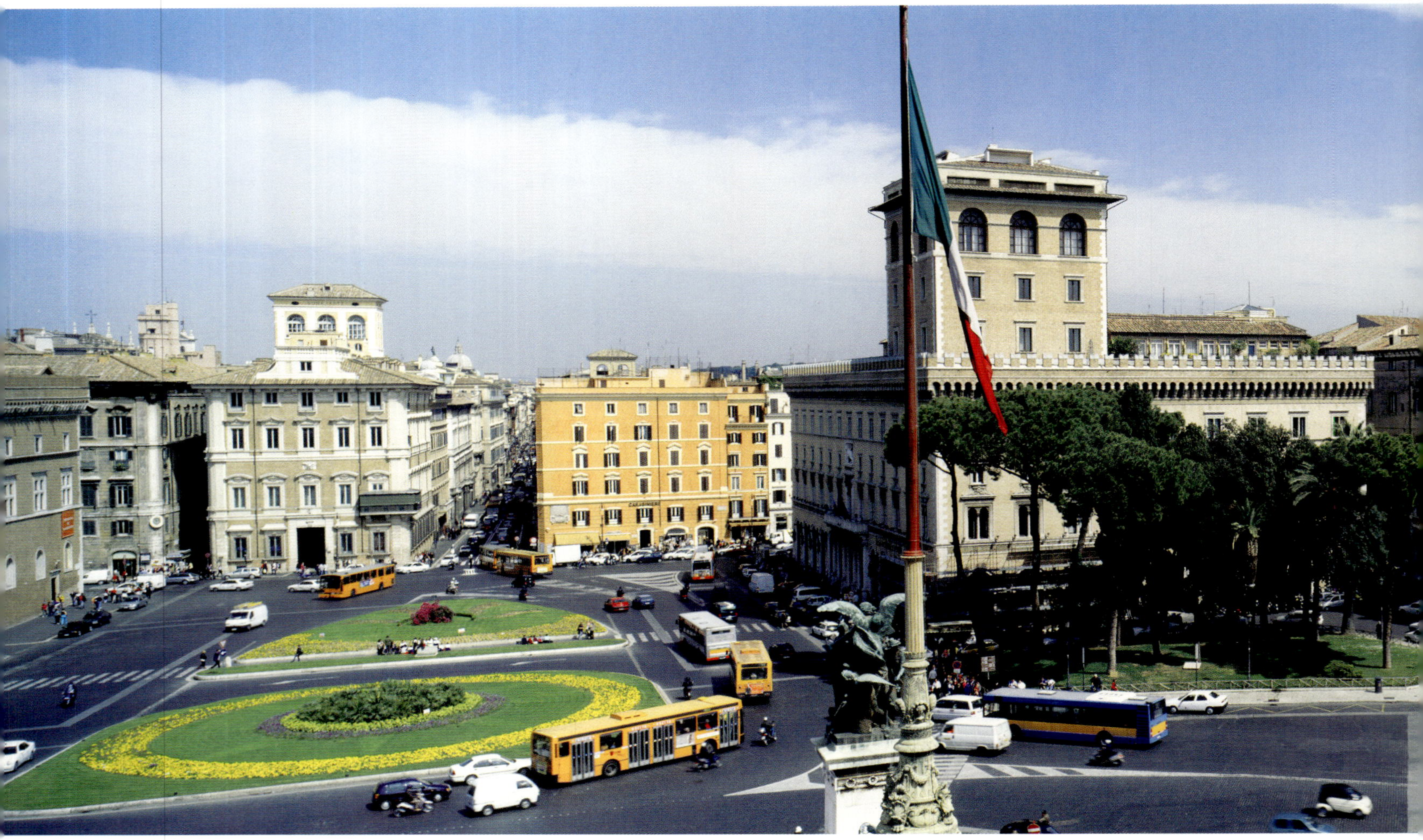

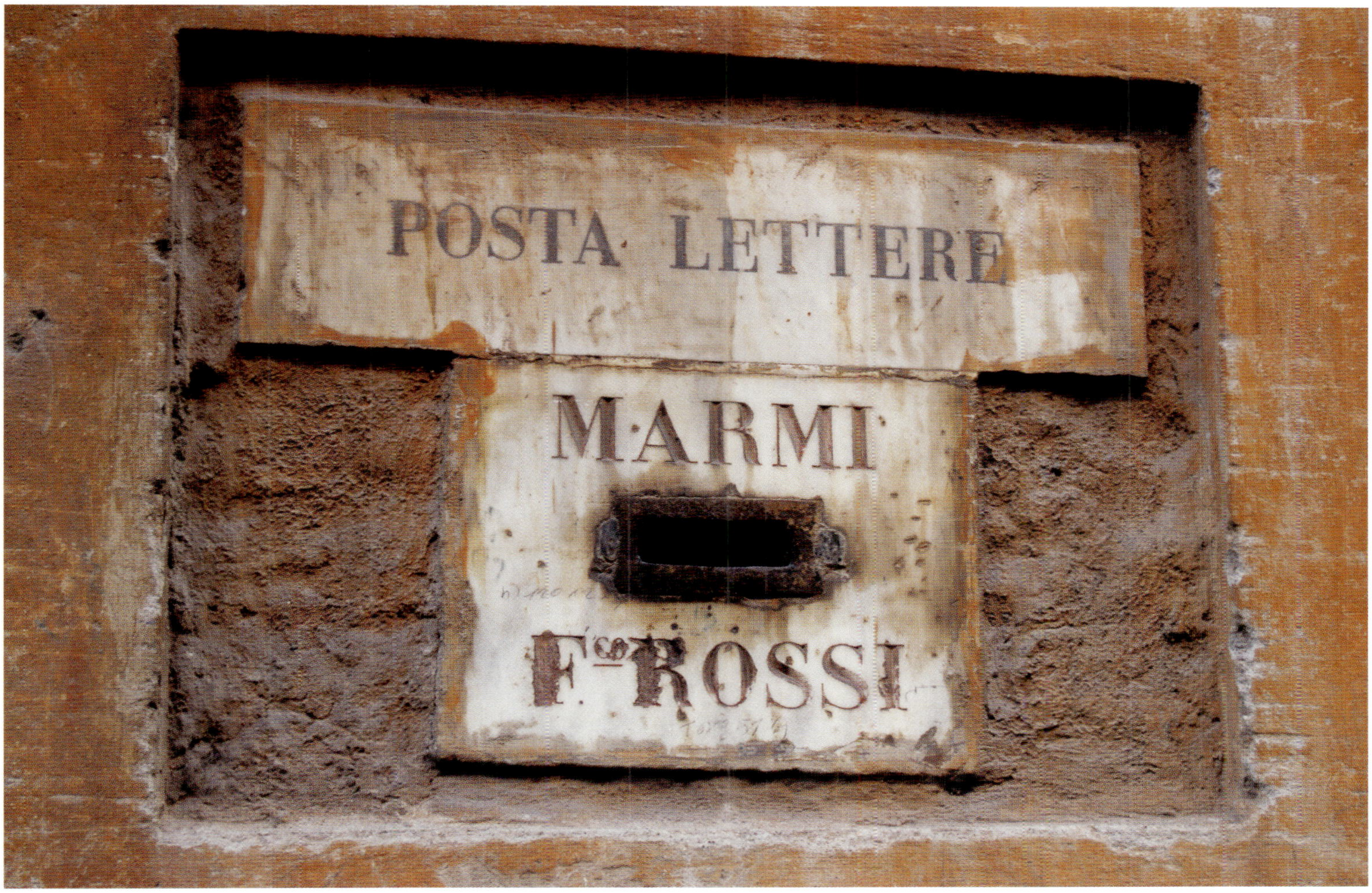

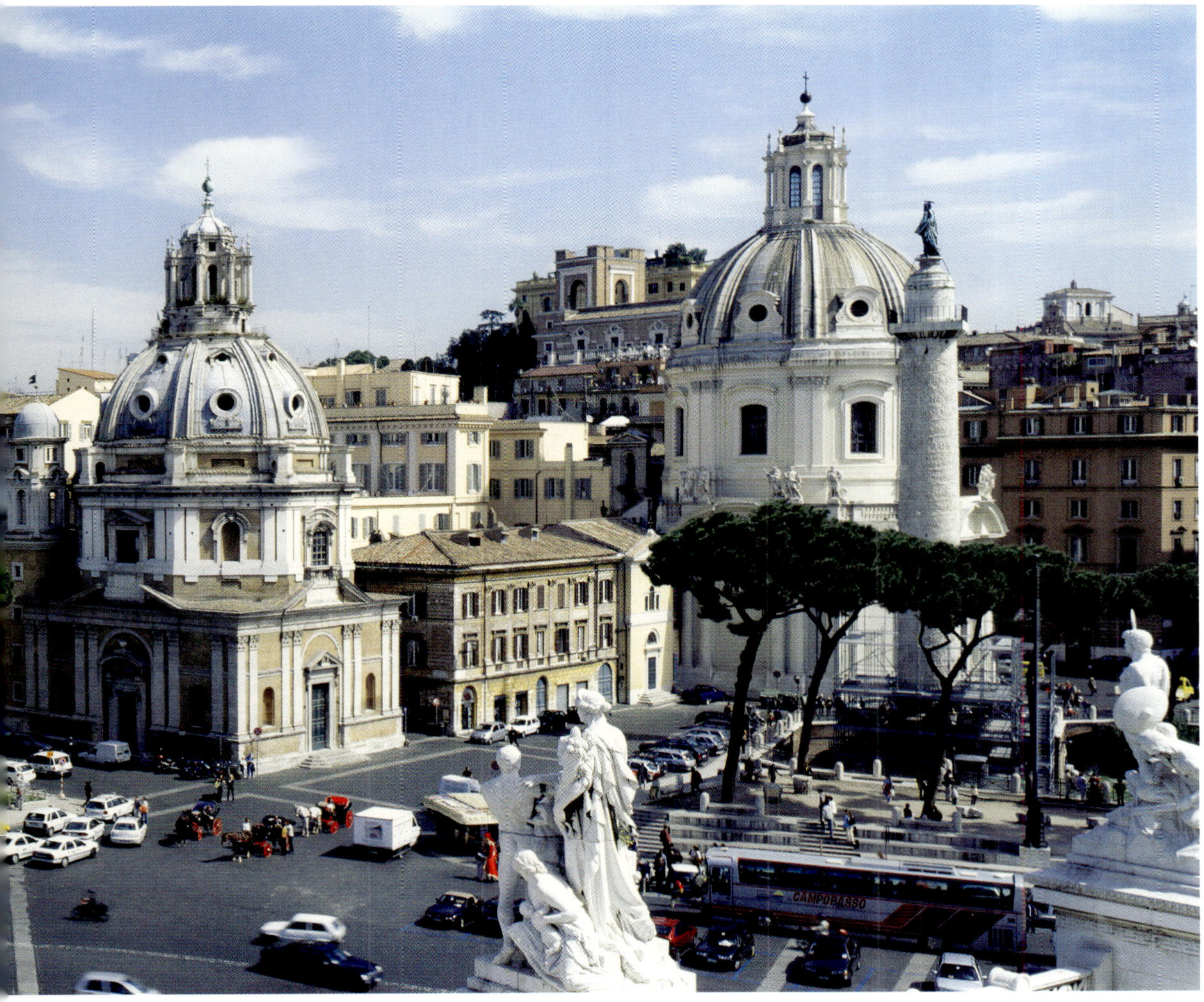

Page 162: Impressive sculpture is to be found all over Rome.

Page 163: Rome is not a hi-rise city and its skyline is still dominated by beautiful domes and spires. In the distance the daddy of all the domes—that of St. Peter's Basilica. *Martin Child/Digital Vision/Getty Images*

Top left: The Cittá della musica auditorium was completed in 2002. *iStockphoto*

Above: An old Roman post box.

Left: The full panorama shows the other side of the opening photograph of this chapter, with Trajan's Column evident at right. *Panoramic Images/Getty Images*

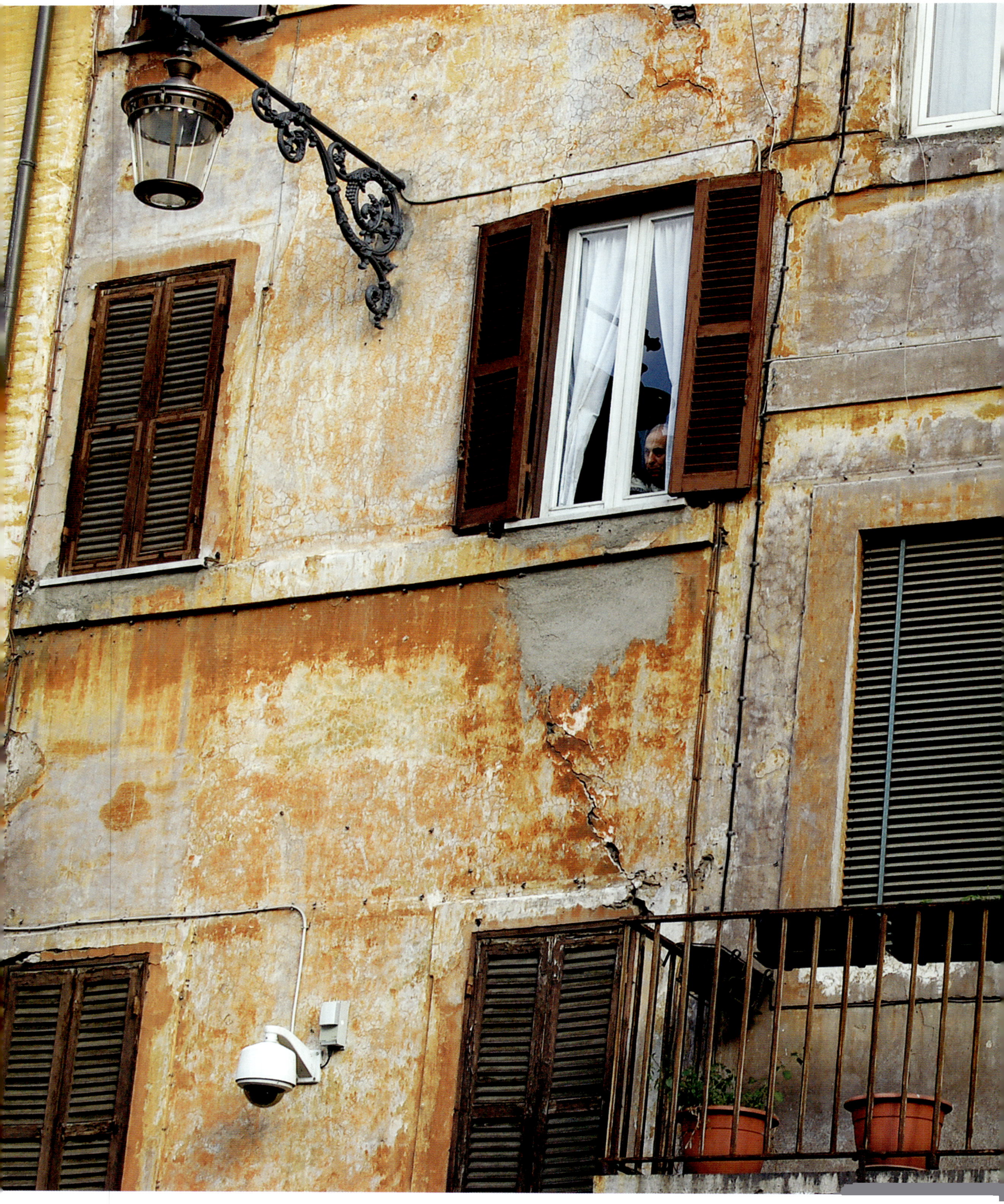

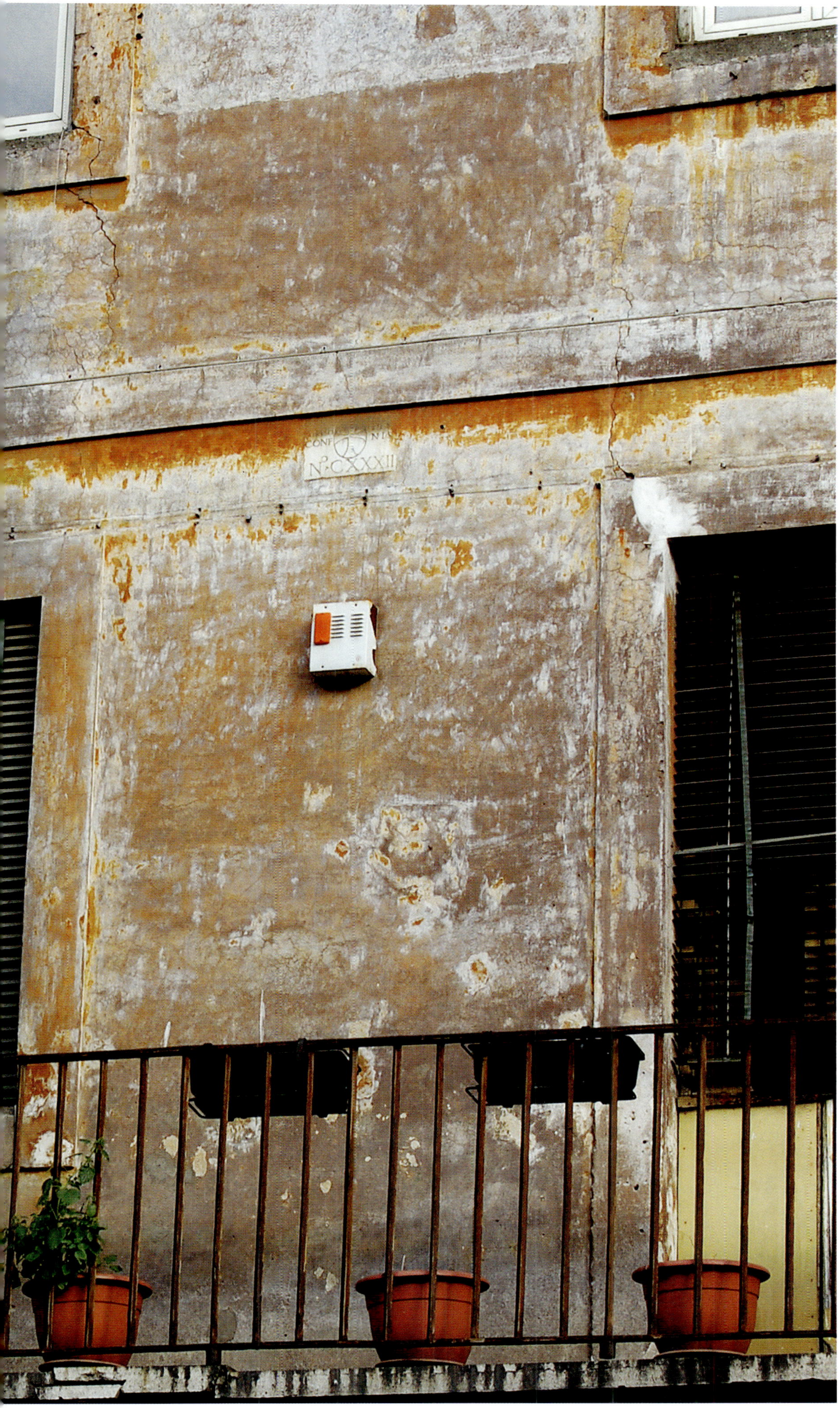

LEFT AND PAGES 168–169: Rome gets much of its character from the smaller, more personal buildings around the city in which most Romans live and work. The faded color palette—reds, ochres, terracotta—comes alive in the evening sun light to give Rome its feeling of warmth.

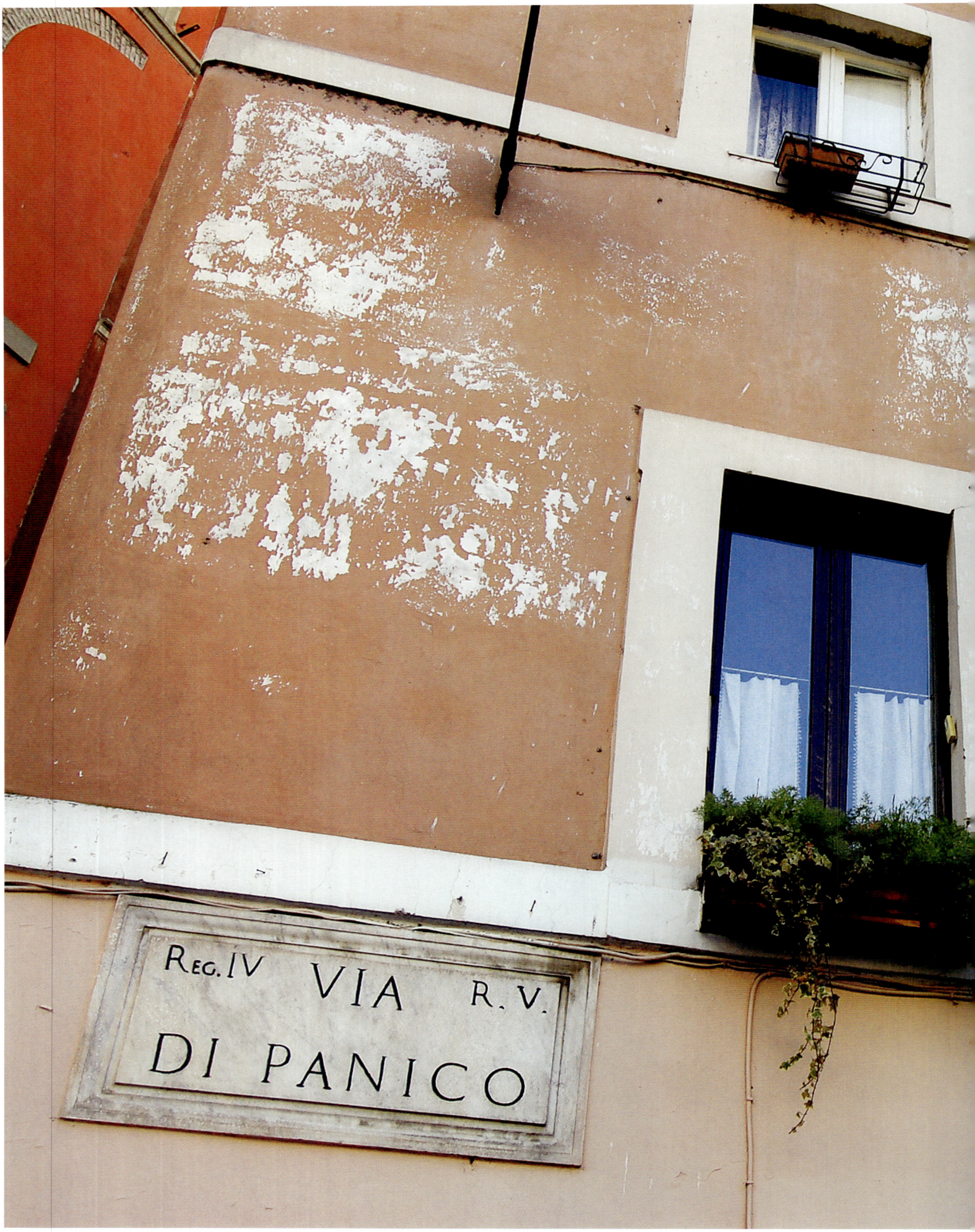
Reg. IV VIA R.V.
DI PANICO

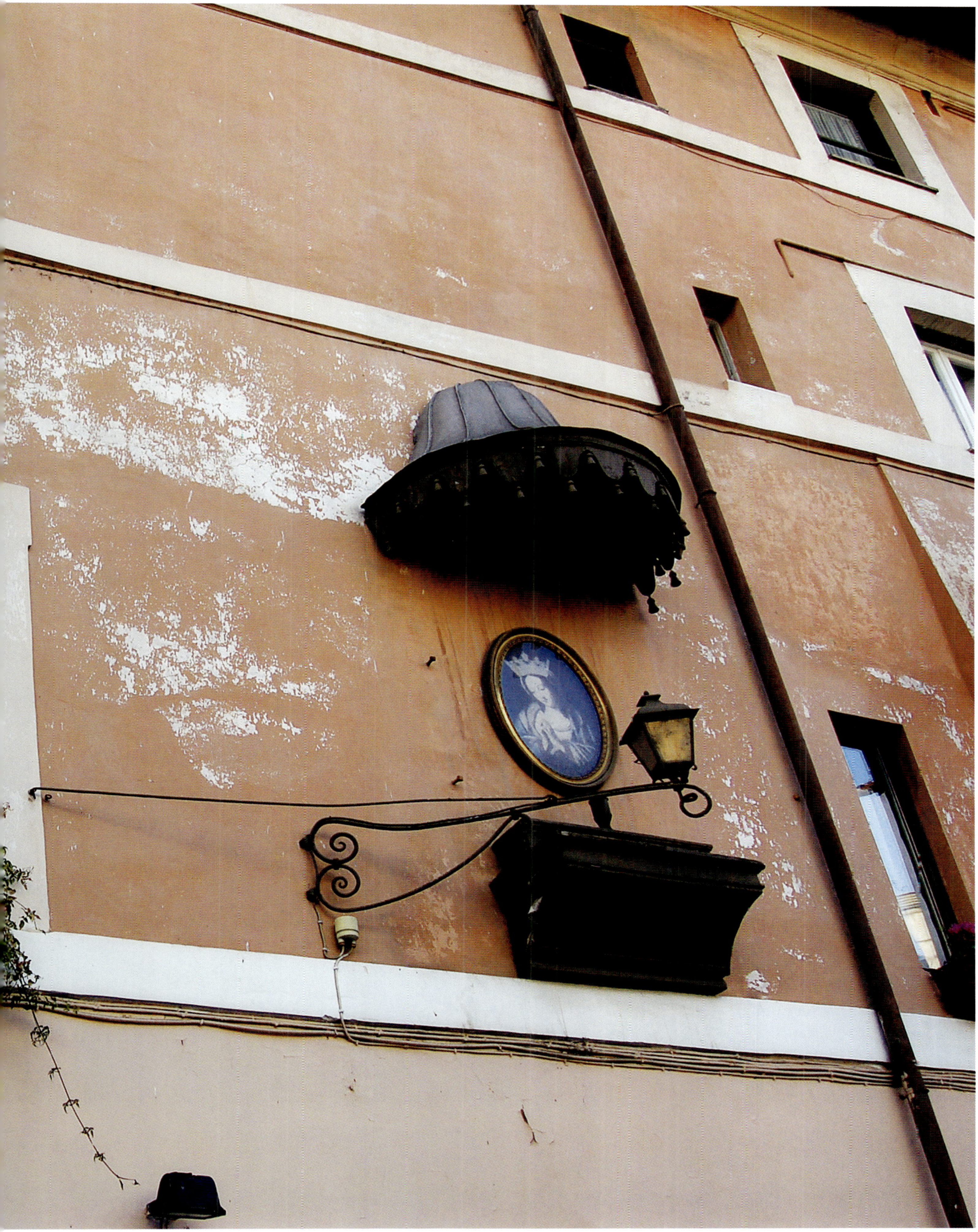

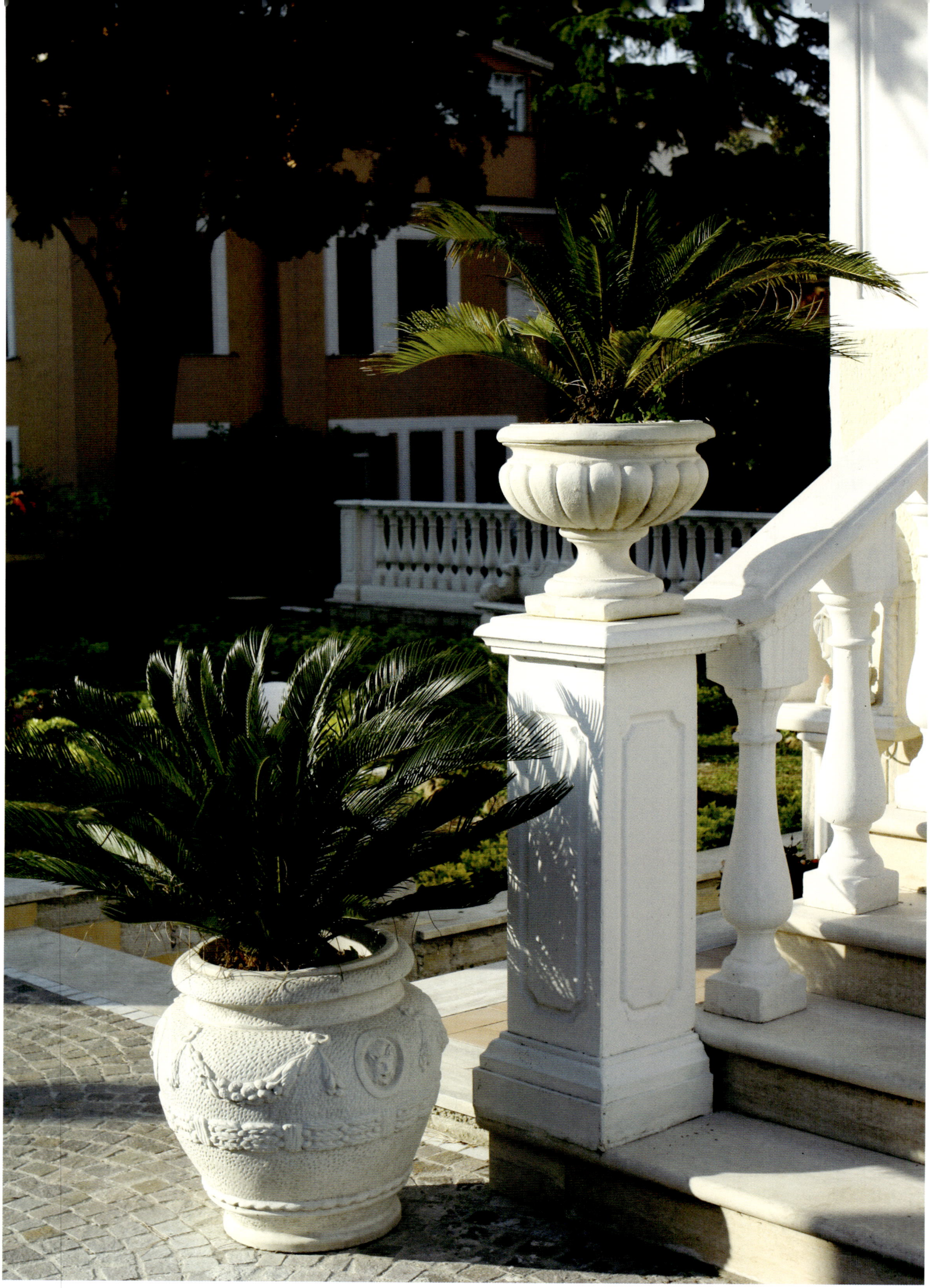

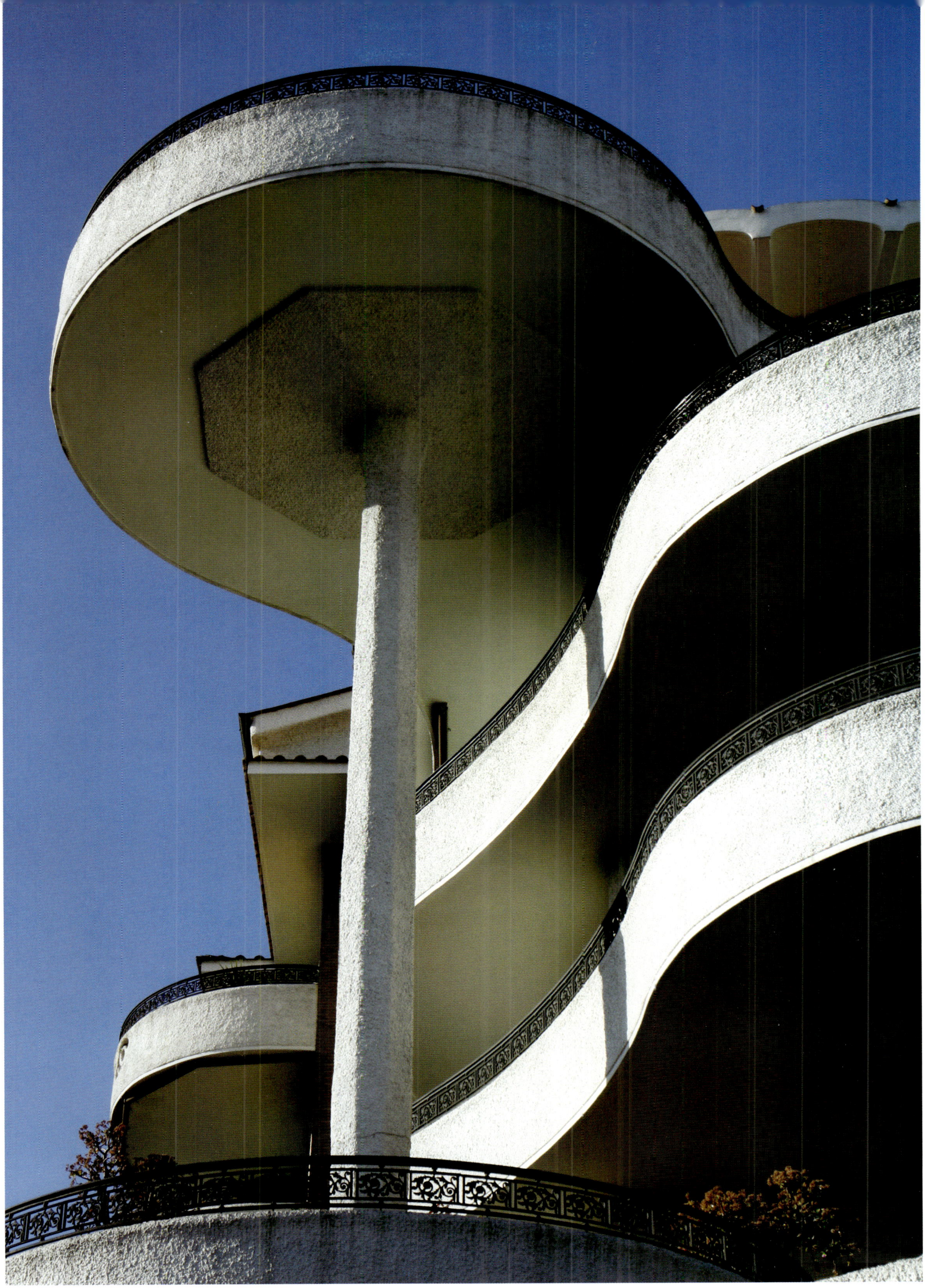

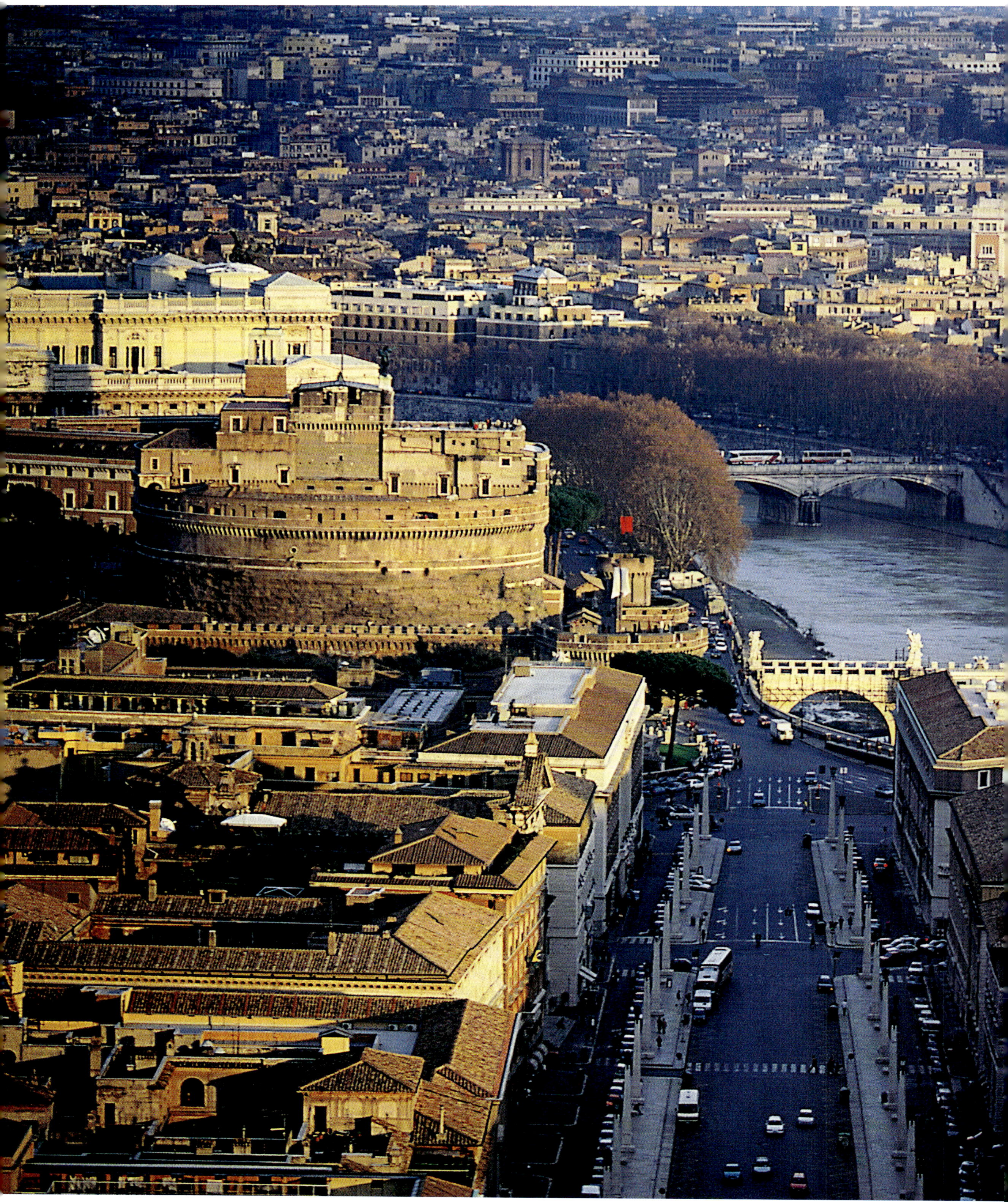

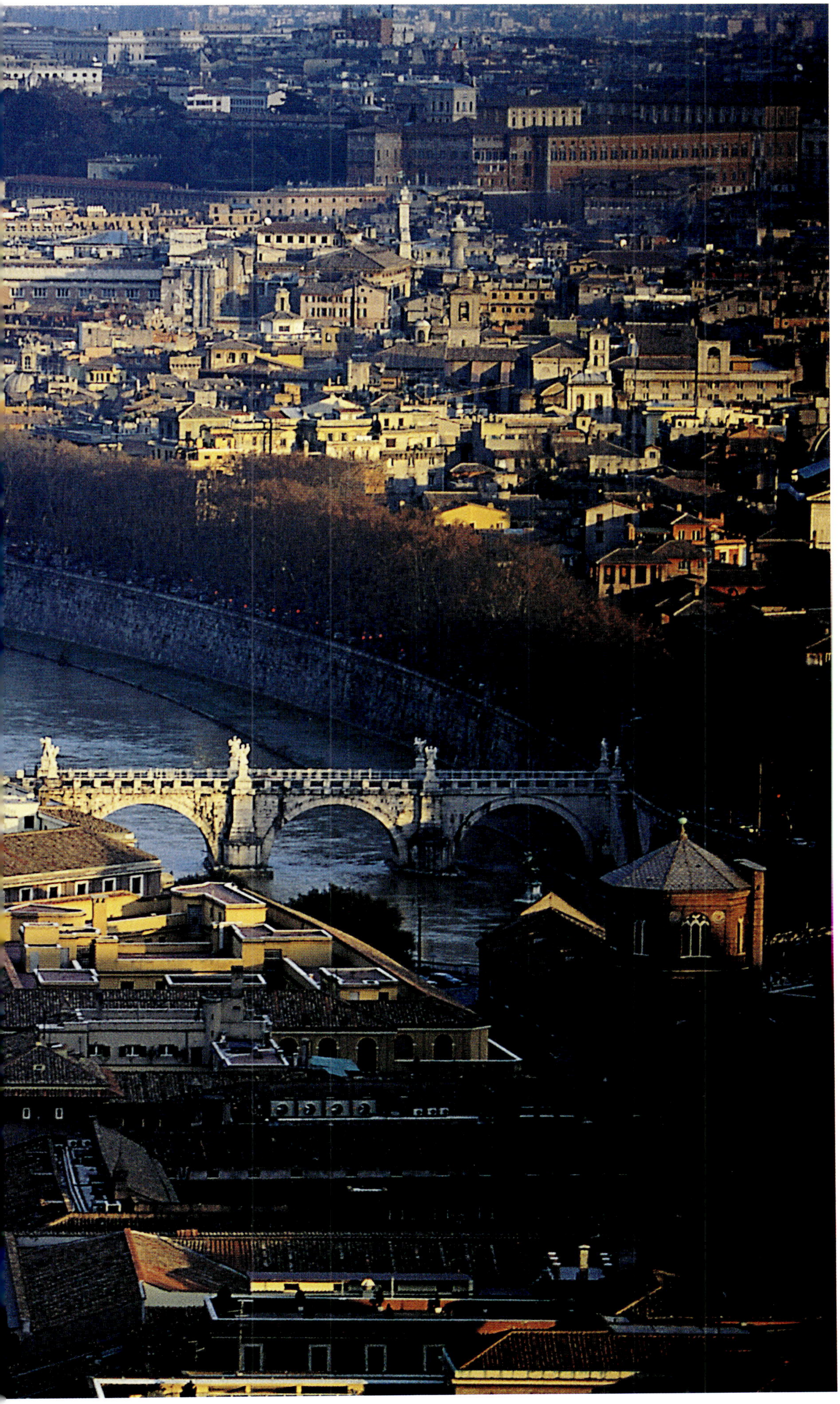

PAGES 170 AND 171: Modern apartment living in Rome—palms and balconies. *iStockphoto*

LEFT: Bird's eye view of Castel Sant' Angelo, and the rooftops of central Rome. The River Tiber is nicknamed "the blond," because its waters carry sediment that give it a yellow color. *Getty Images*

PAGES 174 AND 175:
ABOVE: The river-god Ganges by Gianlorenzo Bernini (1651), from the Fontana dei Quattro Fiumi in the Piazza Navona. *Getty Images*

BELOW LEFT: It is impossible to talk about Rome without mentioning soccer! Romans are passionate about the game and have two great teams to support—A.S. Roma and S.S. Lazio. This statue can be found near the Olympic Stadium where both teams play. *Petr Svarc/Photographer's Choice/Getty Images*

BELOW RIGHT: Pope Benedict XVI, framed by Swiss Guards, attends the Easter Sunday Mass in St. Peter's Square, April 8, 2007 in Vatican City. Founded in 1506, the Papal Swiss Guard is responsible for the security of the Apostolic Palace, the entrances to the Vatican City, and the safety of the Pope. Its official language is German and its uniform colors stem from two popes. The blue and yellow were the family (Della Rovere) colors of Pope Julius II (1443–1513); the red was added by Pope Leo X (1475–1521) who was a Medici. *Franco Origlia/Getty Images*

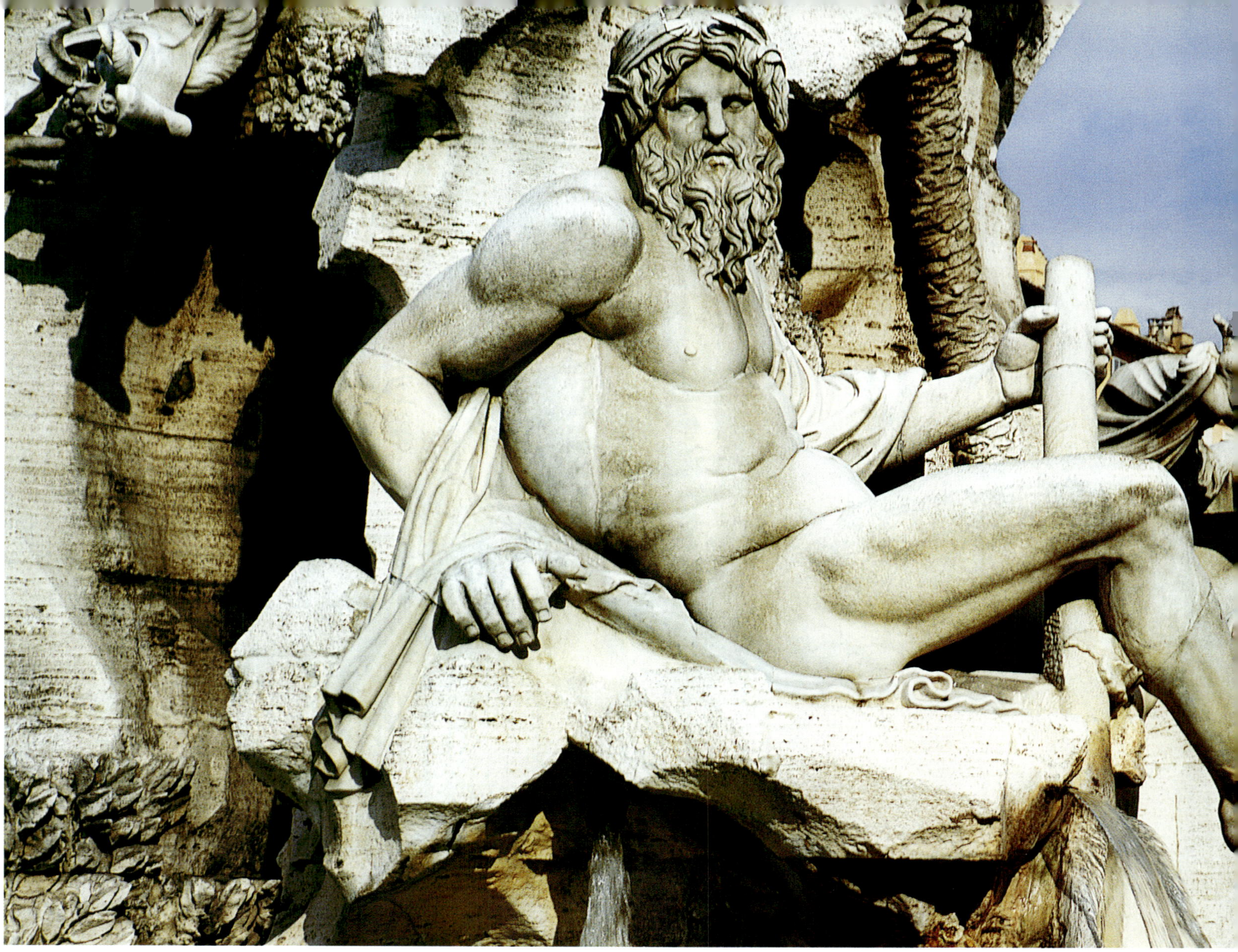

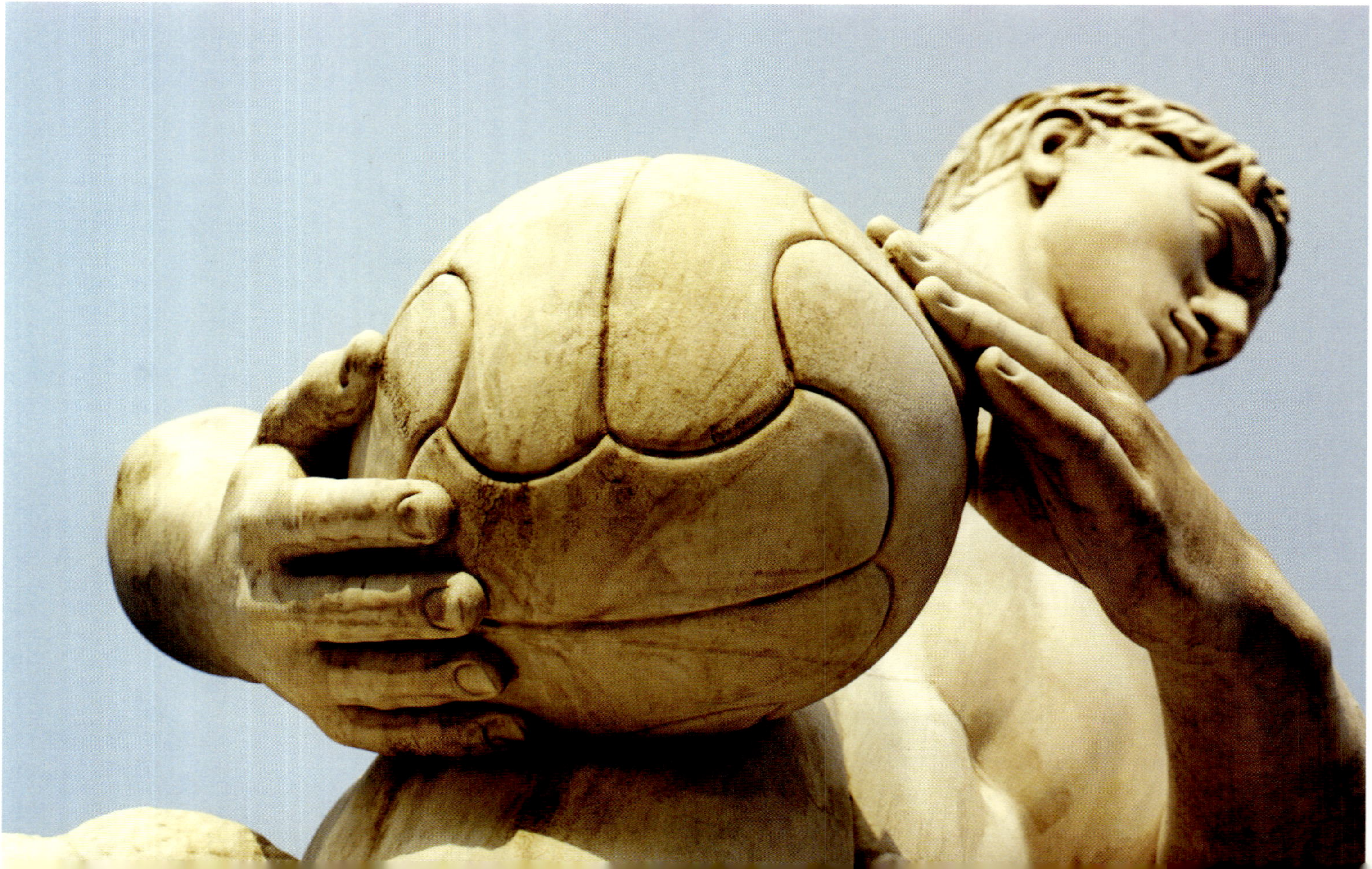

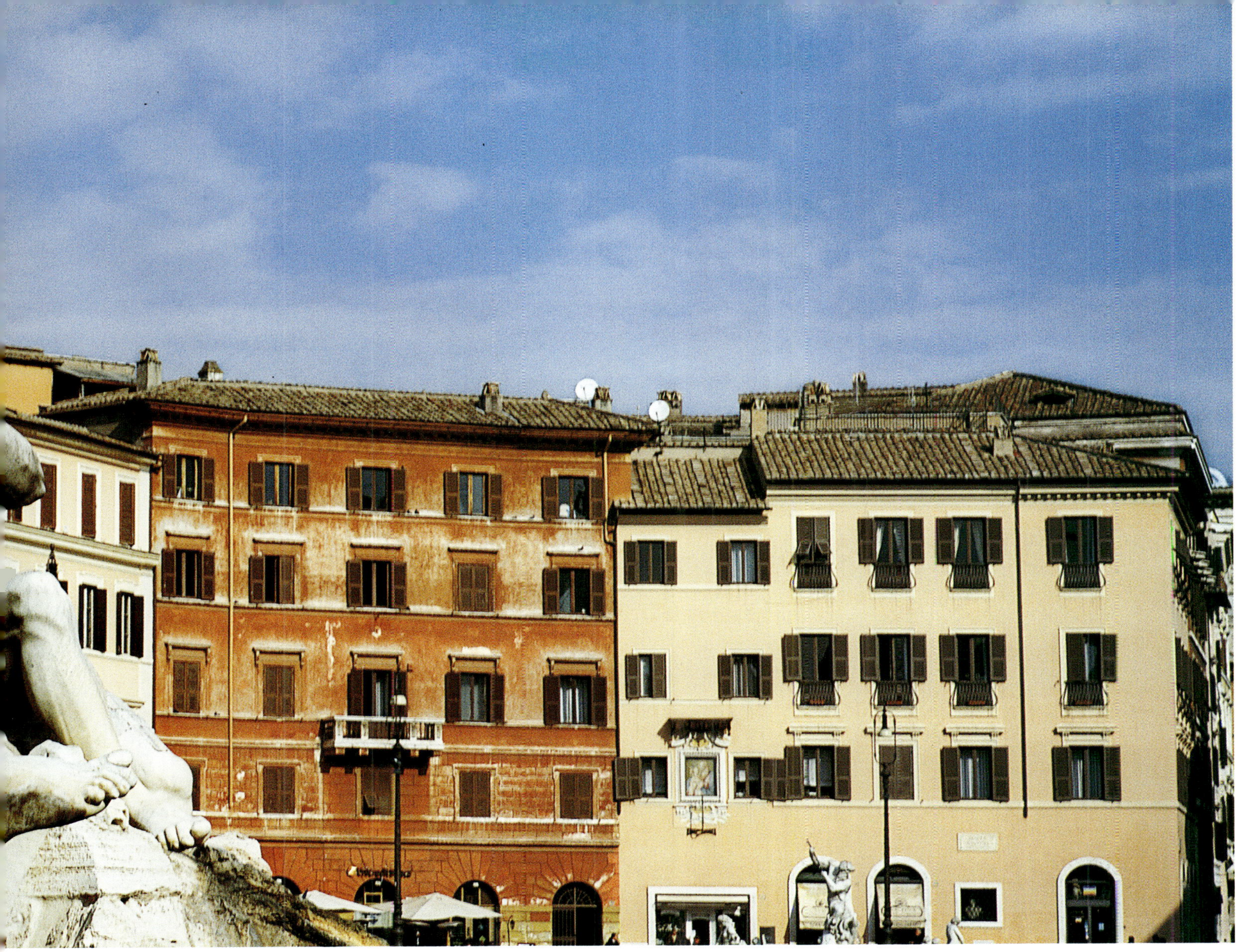

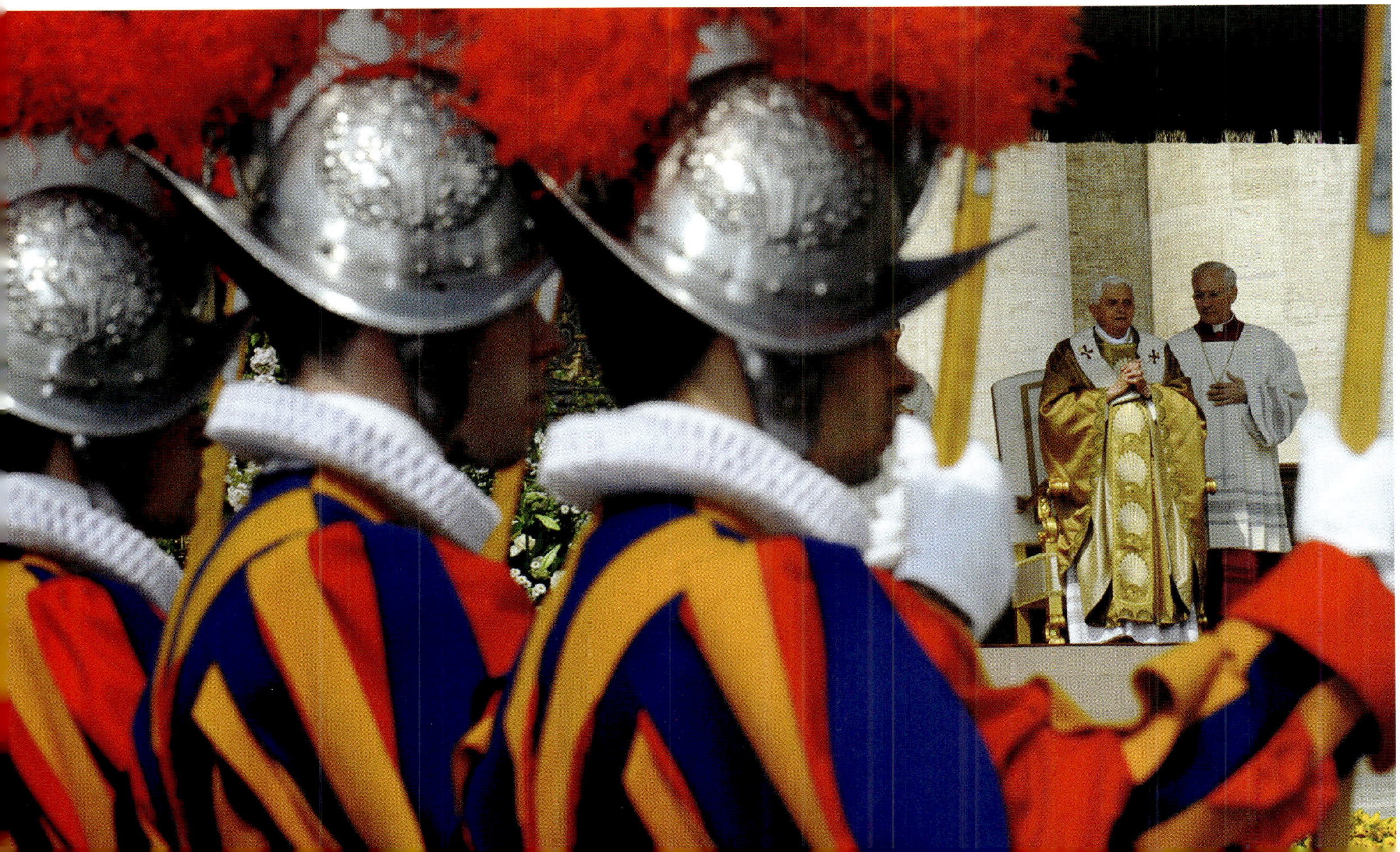

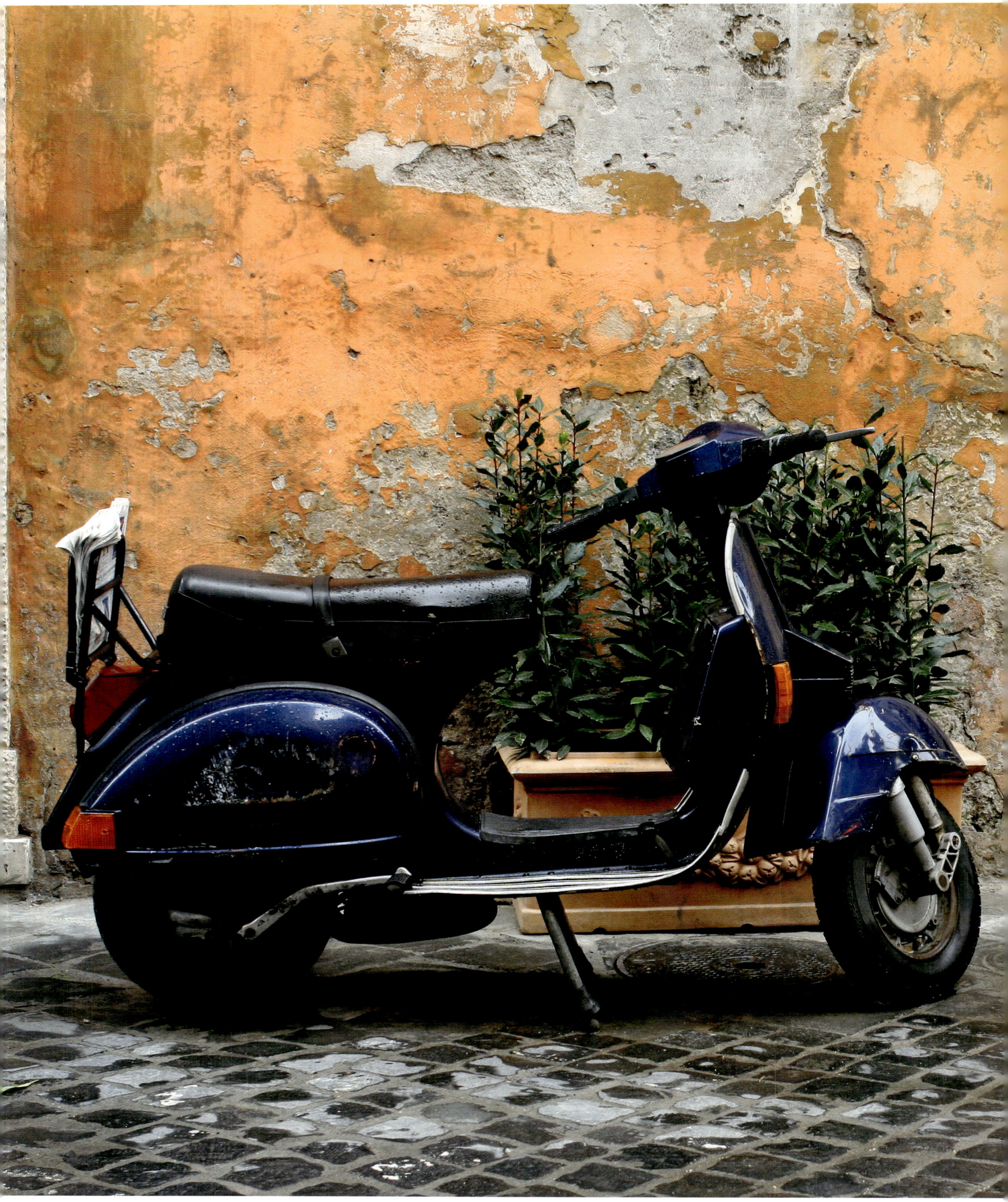

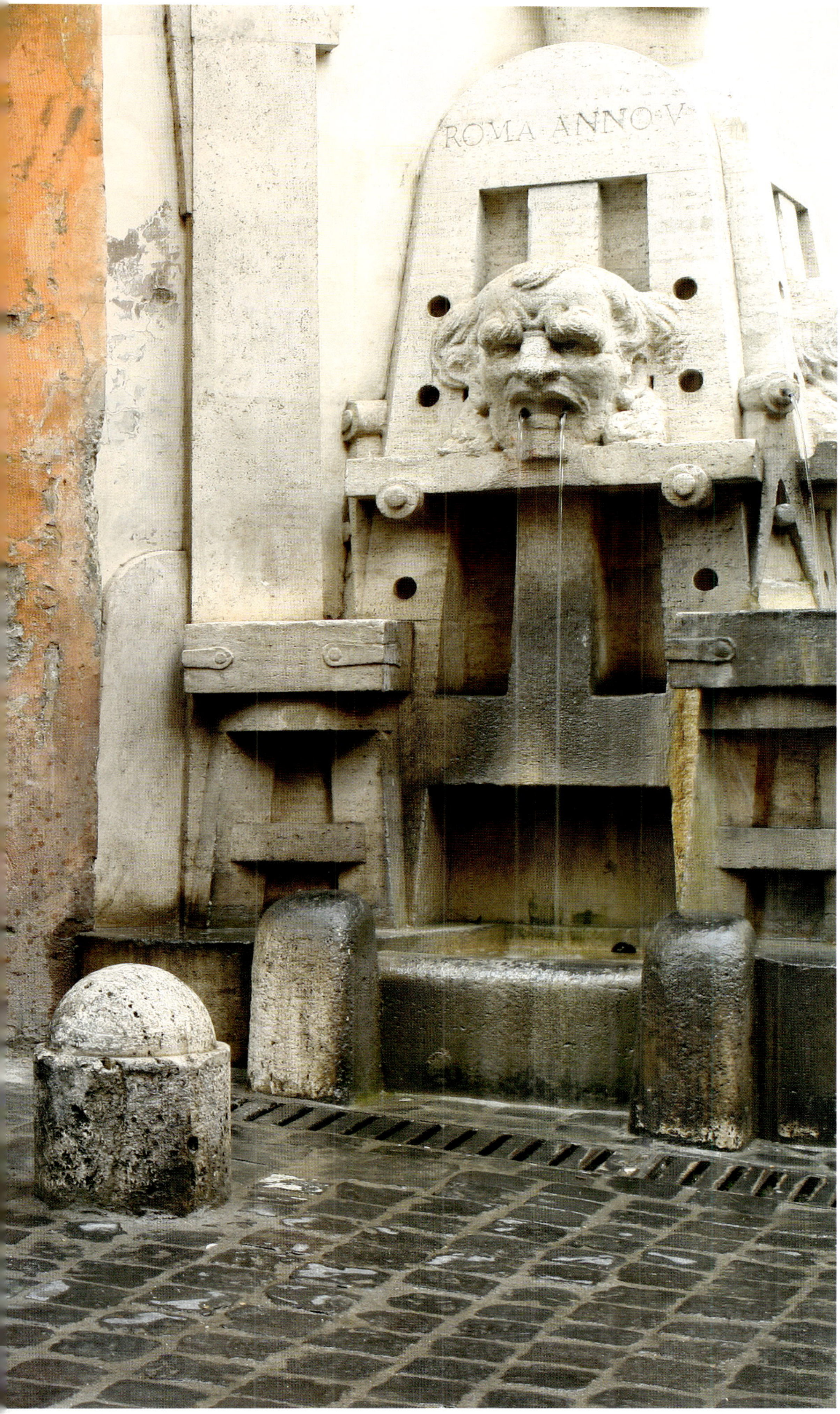

LEFT: A typical Roman scene—terracotta wall; a fountain; and a scooter. Italian manufacturers revolutionized the two-wheel industry in the post-World War II period and they became the standard urban mode of transport for many young people. The two main names were Piaggio, whose Vespa provided a model on which nearly every other scooter made since has been based, and Lambretta. *iStockphoto*

PAGES 178–179: A shield with the modern coat of arms of the city of Rome on a typical sun-washed terracotta wall. SPQR—*Senatus Populusque Romanus* (the Roman Senate and People). *Allan Baxter/Photographer's Choice/Getty Images*

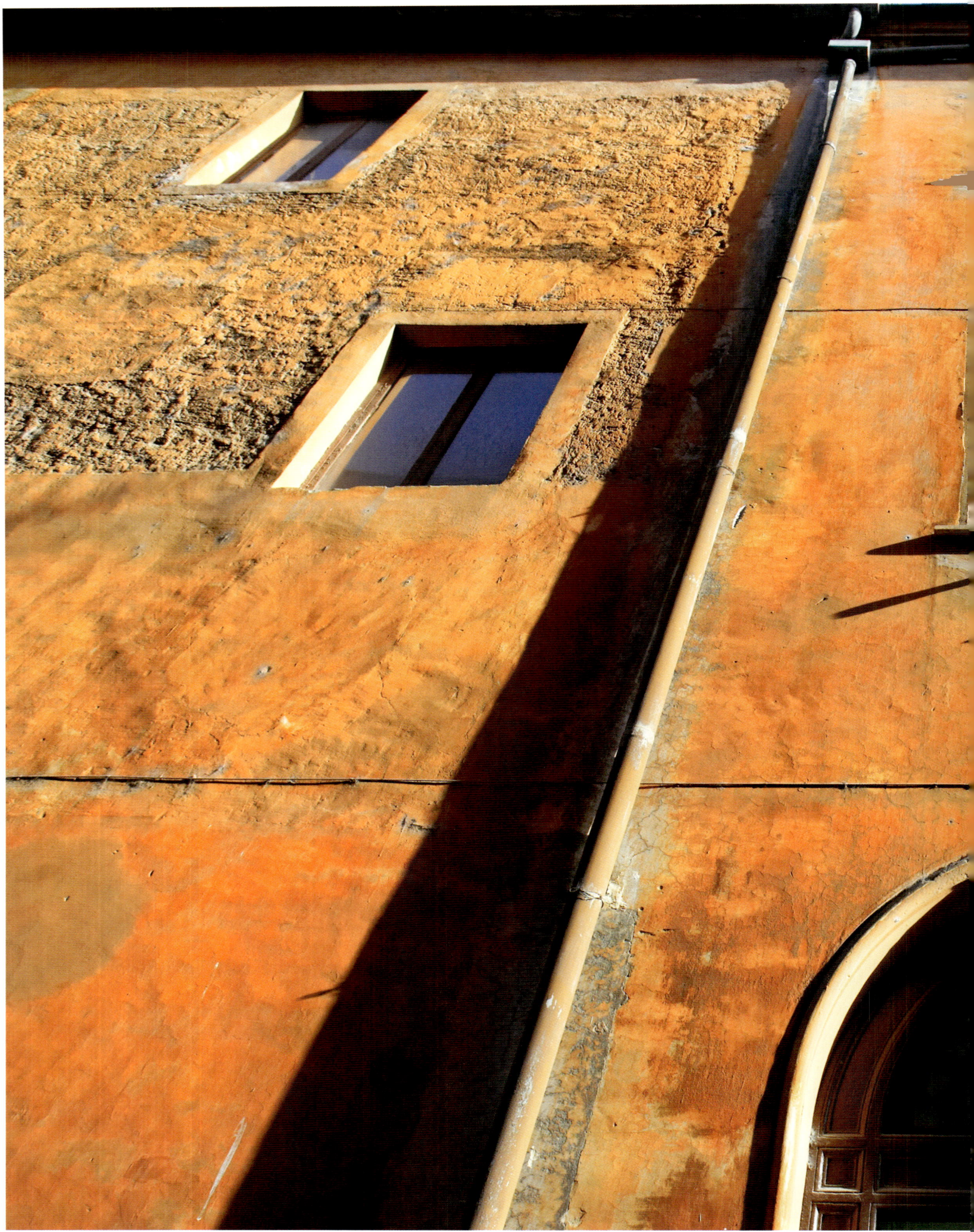

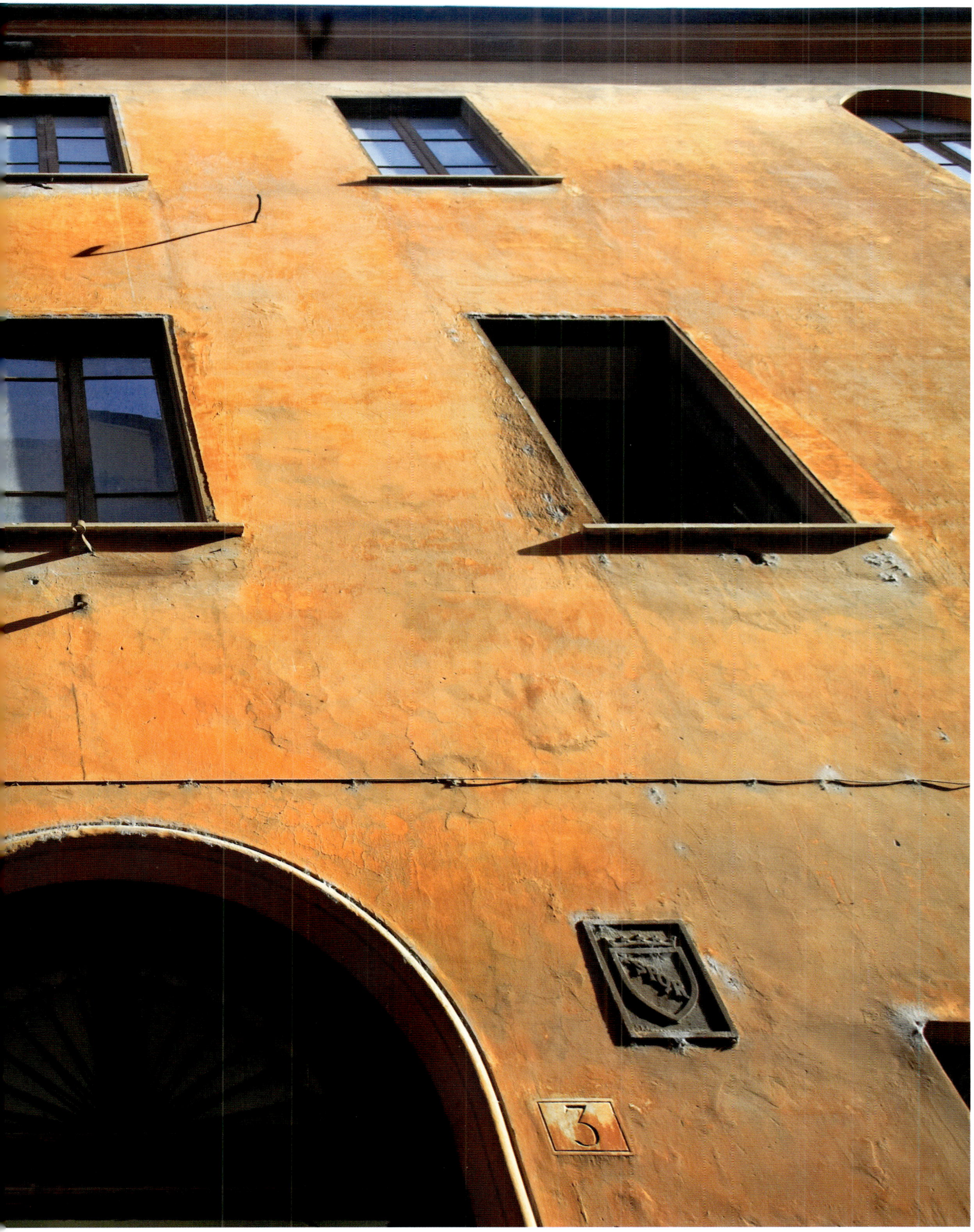
SPQR
3

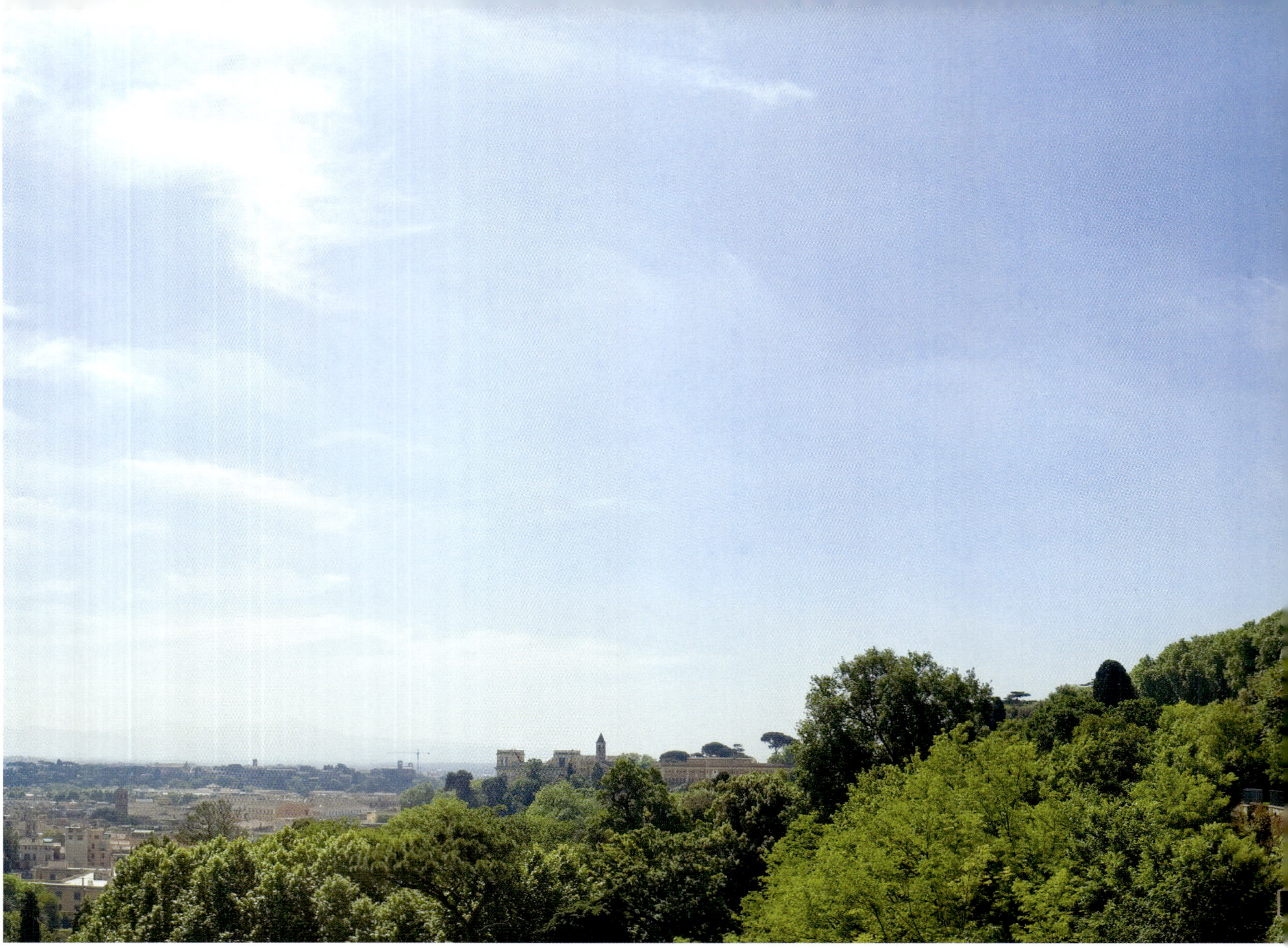

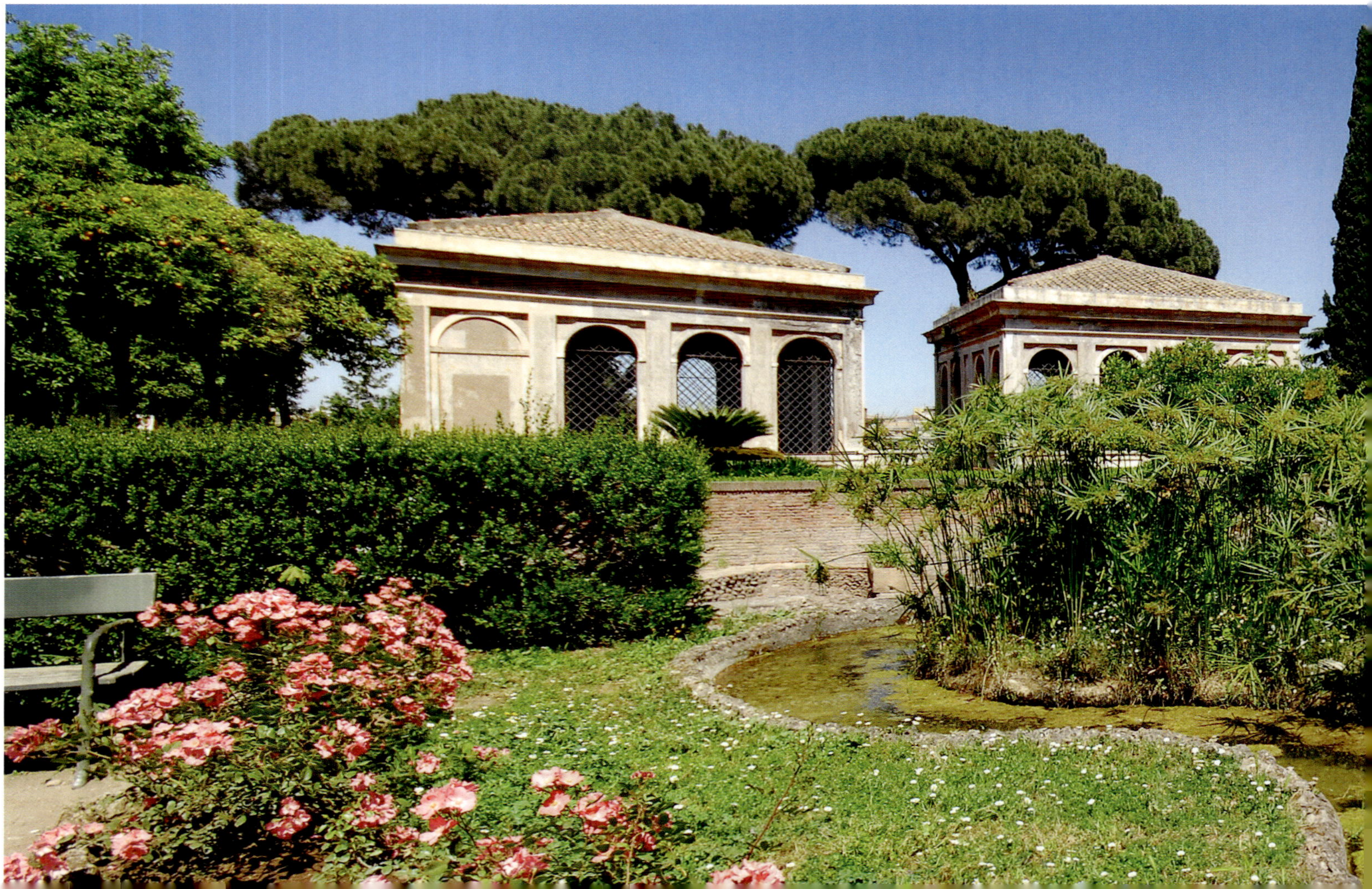

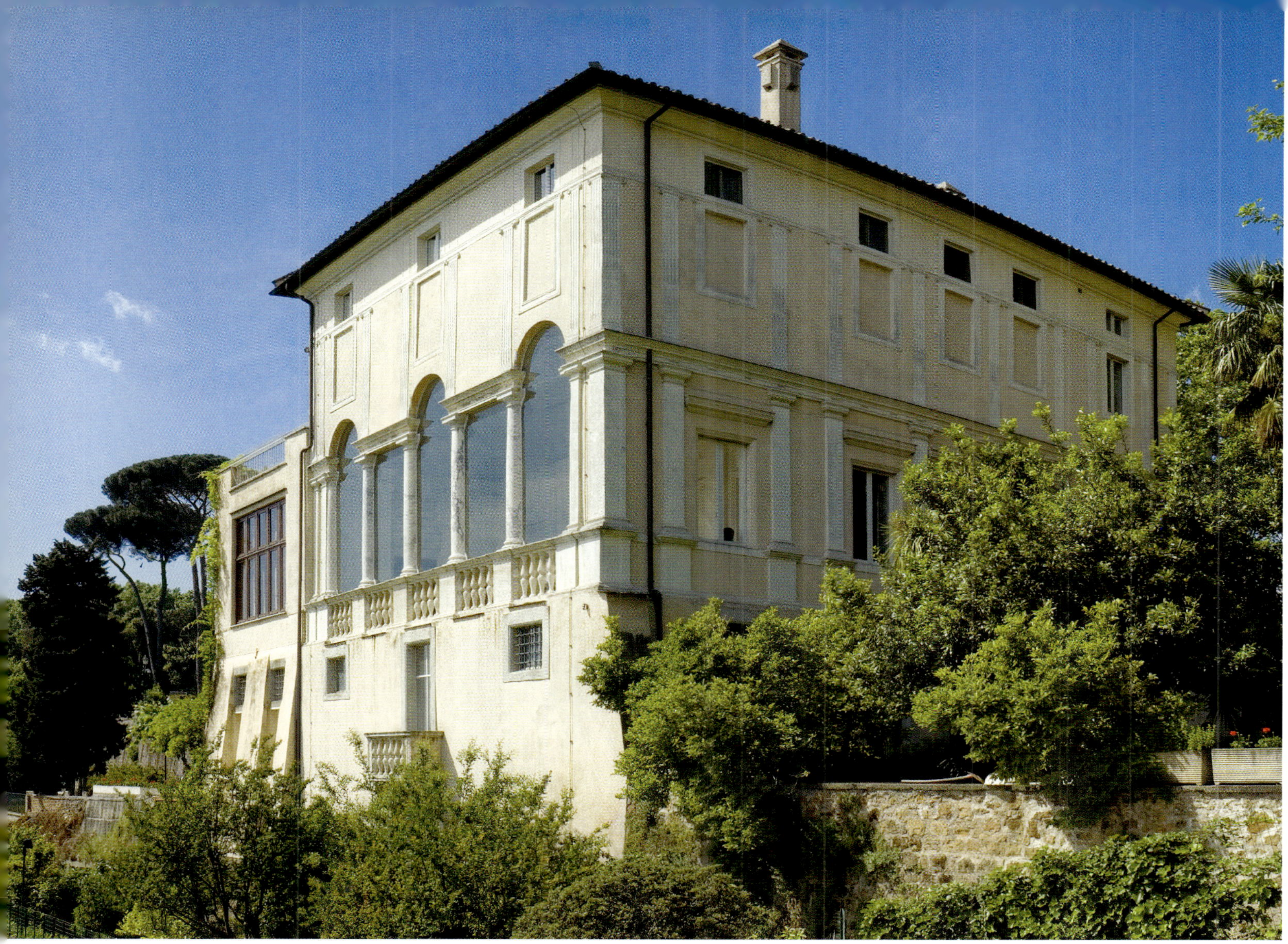

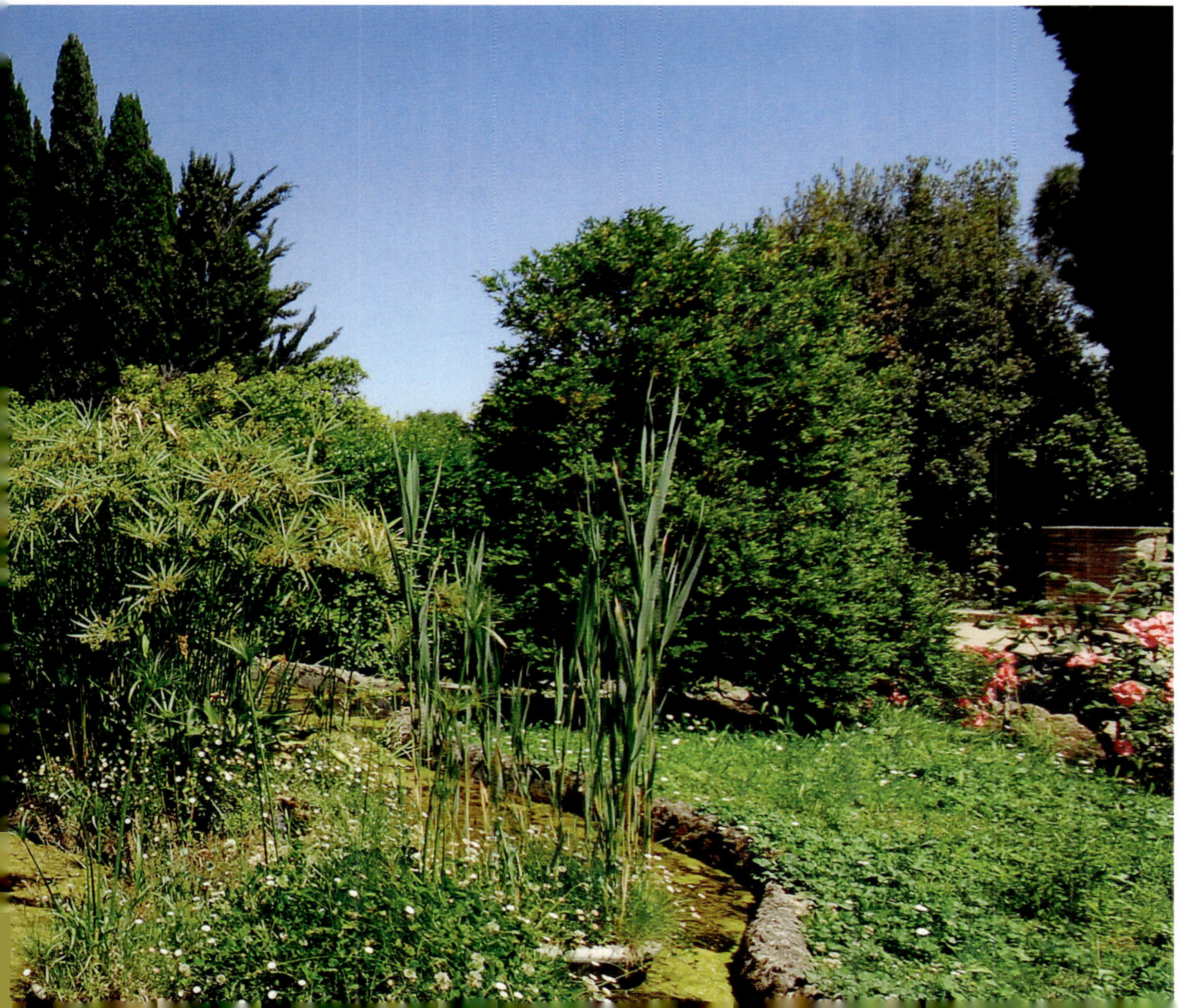

Above: The Janiculum Hill is an extremely good place from which to view the city. It is not one of the original seven hills of Rome, but is a good address today. Daily at noon, a cannon fires once from the Janiculum to signal the exact time. *iStockphoto*

Left: Seventeenth century aviaries on the Palatine Hill. As Rome developed the old buildings on the western side of the Palatine were pulled down and replaced by a number of palaces each of which had its own superbly designed garden. Many of the surviving gardens have been incorporated into public parks where local flora and flora thrive. *Aleksandar Kolundzija/iStockphoto*

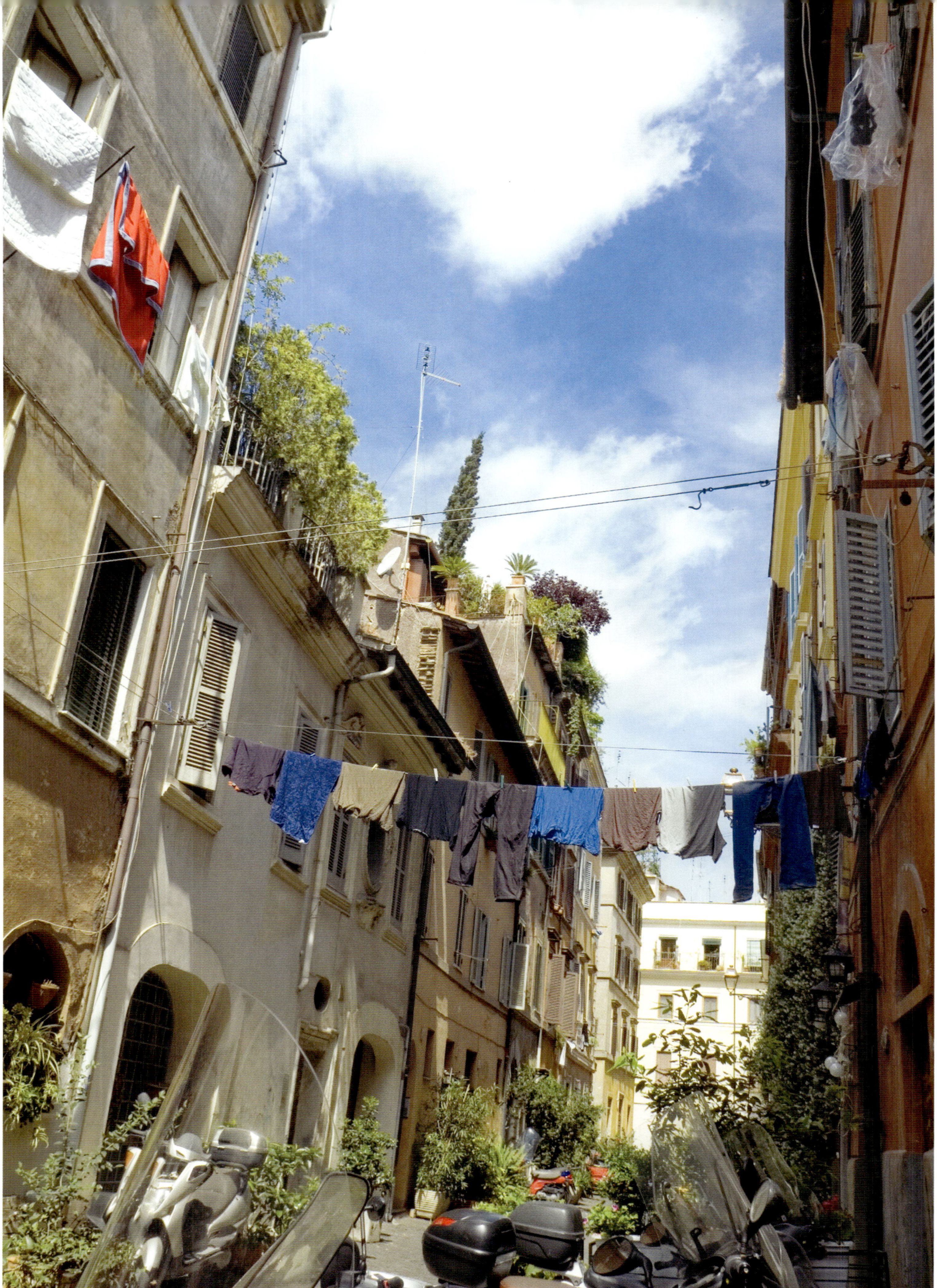

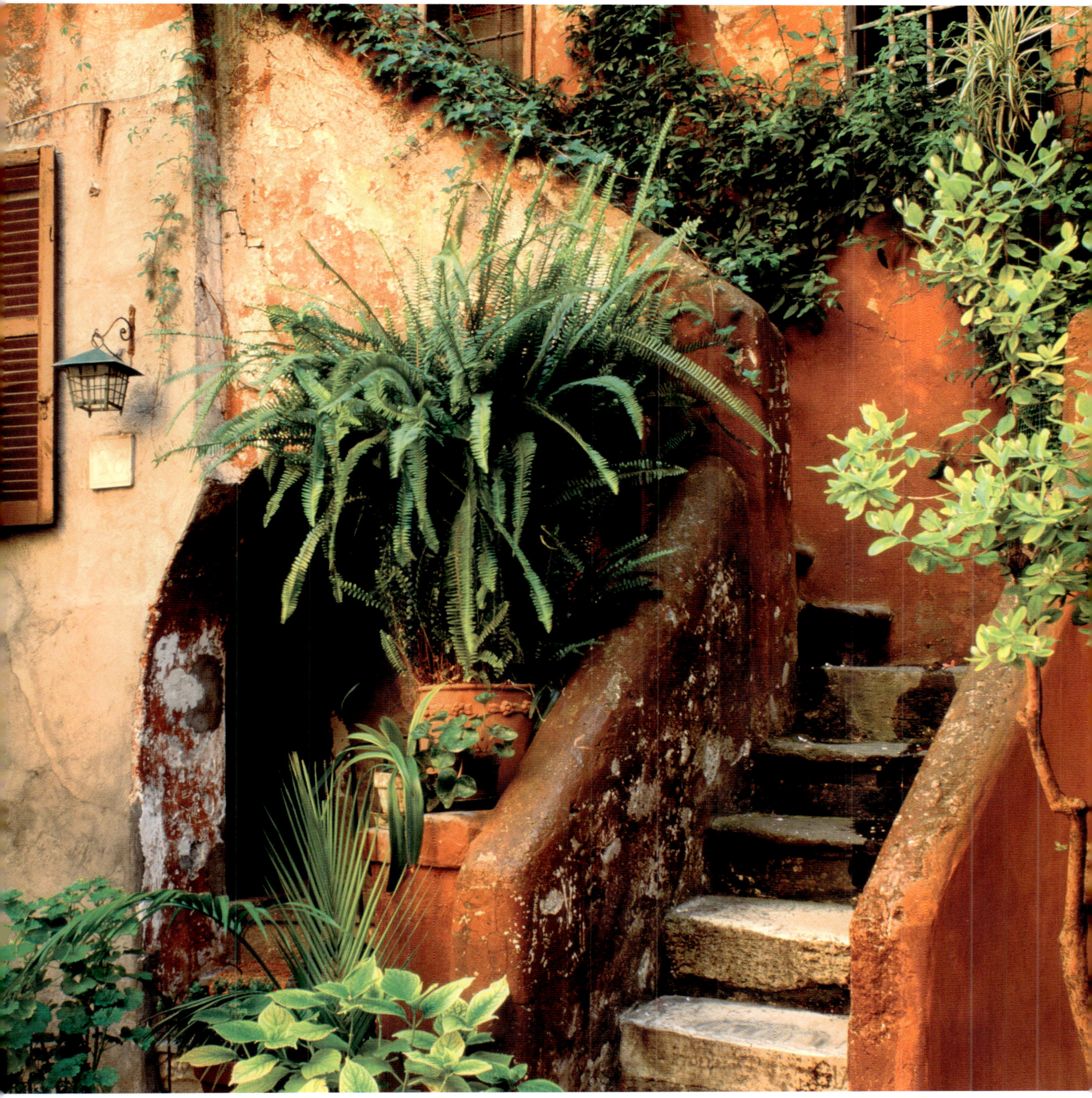

LEFT: Washing strung on a line between houses in a characteristically narrow street in the picturesque Trastevere district of Rome. Trastevere means "across the Tiber" and from the earliest times was the poorer working-class quarter. Today, it is known for its pubs and restaurants, and is home to the John Cabot University, the American Academy in Rome, and the Thomas More College of Liberal Arts. *iStockphoto*

ABOVE: Trastevere city gardening. This rioni (region) of Rome attracts artists: Sergio Leone and Ennio Morricone both went to school here. *Travelpix Ltd/Getty Images*

Right: The Via Veneto runs through the Quirinal and past the late nineteenth century Palazzo Piombino, now the U.S. Embassy. The building was formerly called the Palazzo Margherita after becoming the official residence of Queen Margherita who lived here after the assassination of King Umberto I in 1900. *Dorling Kindersley/Getty Images*

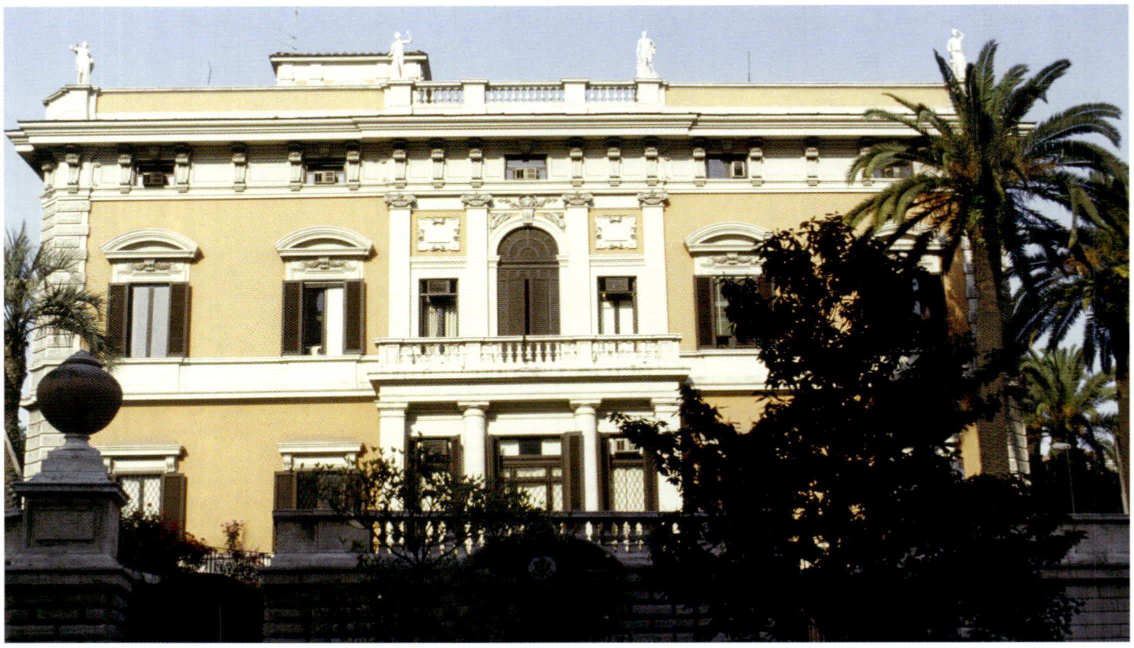

Below right and Far right: Two more views of the EUR—Esposizione Universale Roma—zone created after the Italian government in 1936 made a successful application for hosting the next World Exhibition which was due in 1941. The Exhibition never took place because of the war, but in 1951, the Italian government decided to complete the quarter, relocating public offices there and inviting companies to build their headquarters in the new quarter. The INAIL Tower (**Below right**) is the headquarters of the Istituto Nazionale Assicurazione contro gli Infortuni sul Lavoro, the Italian Workers' Compensation Authority. *Fabio Bianchini/iStockphoto; Enrico Fianchini/iStockphoto*

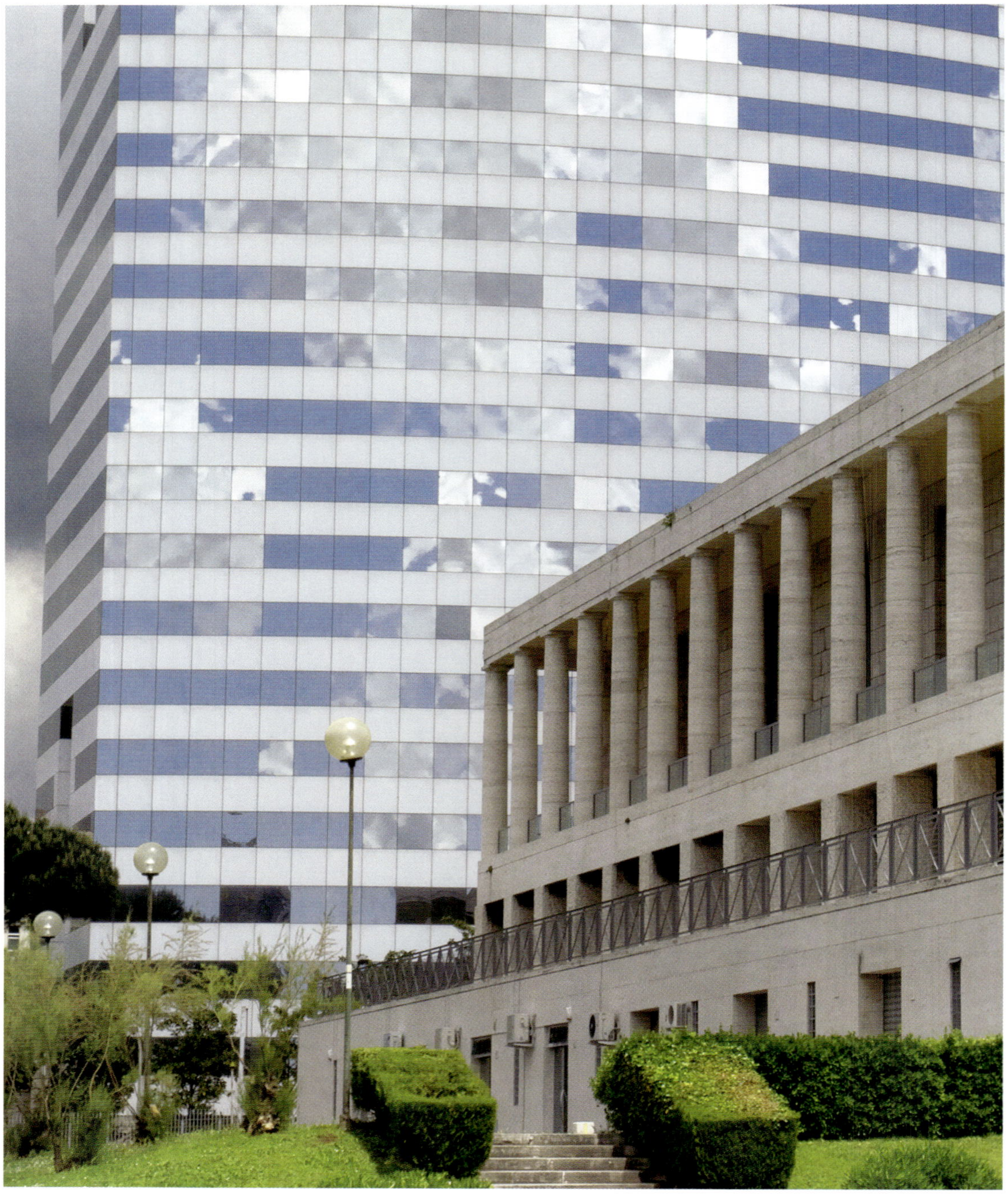

Pages 186–187: As everywhere in Italy, the Romans value good produce and restaurants. There are street vendors evrywhere, but the best known food markets are the Campo dei Fiori, near Piazza Navona, and in the Trastevere, the daily market in the Piazza San Cosimato.

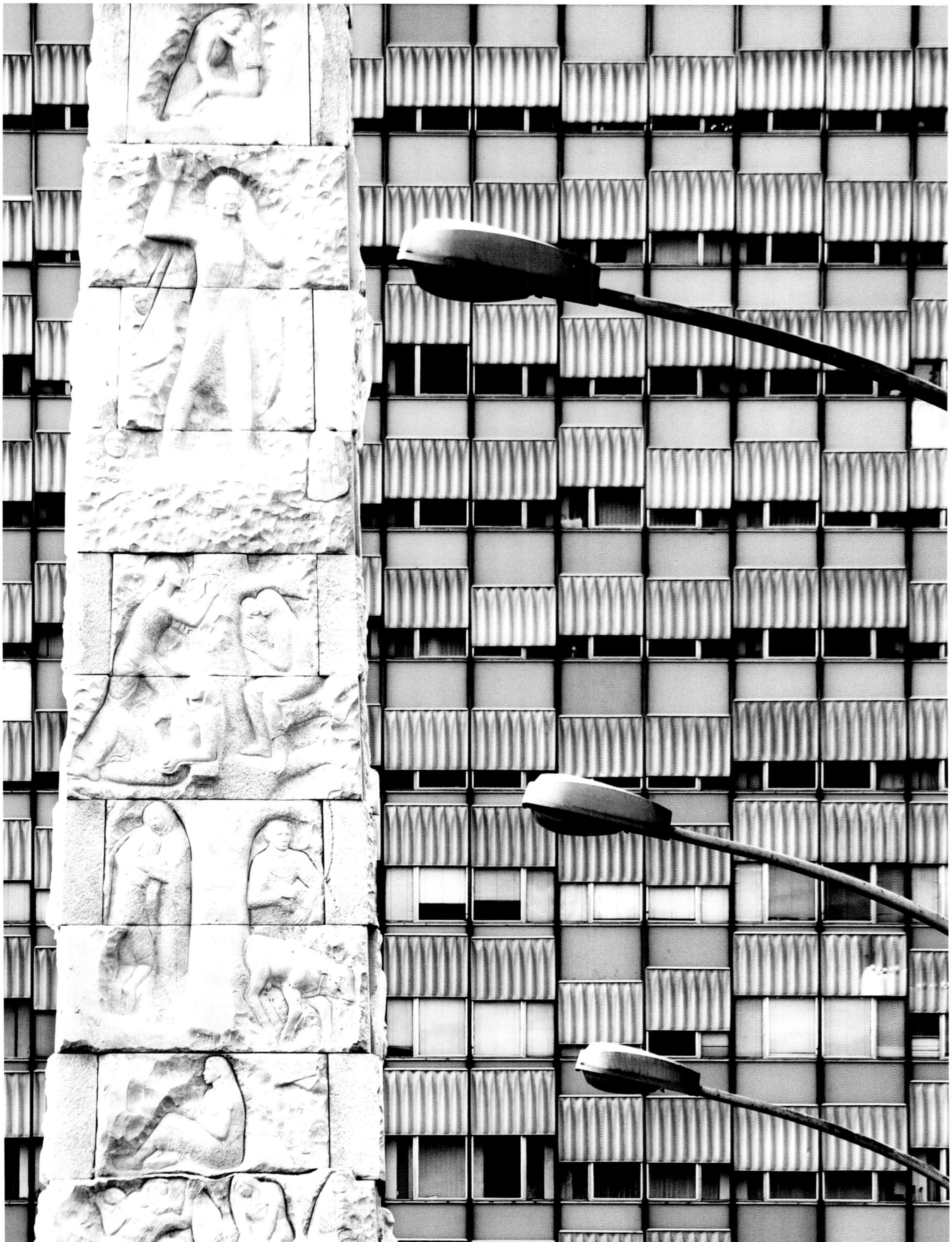

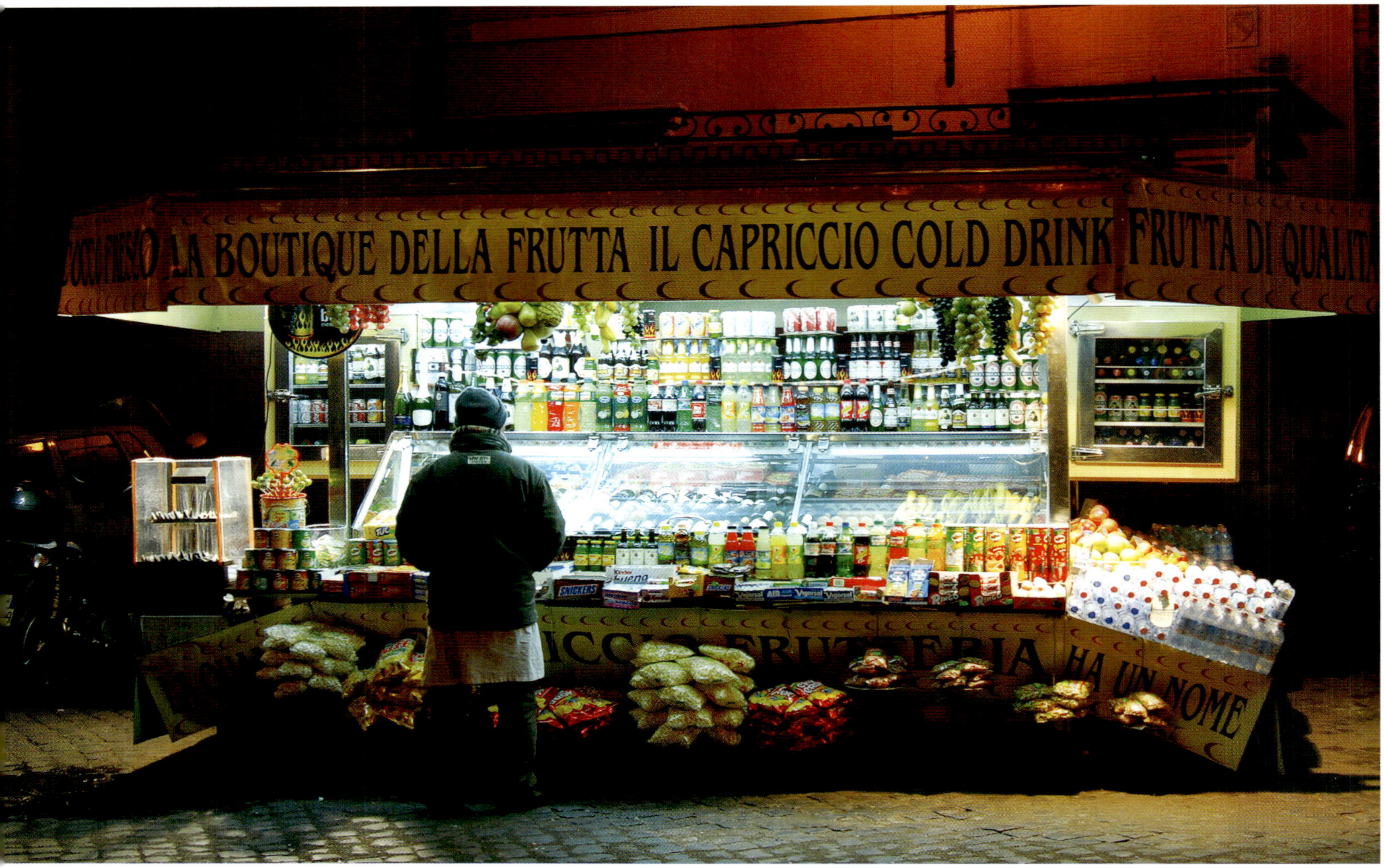
LA BOUTIQUE DELLA FRUTTA IL CAPRICCIO COLD DRINK FRUTTA DI QUALITA
HA UN NOME

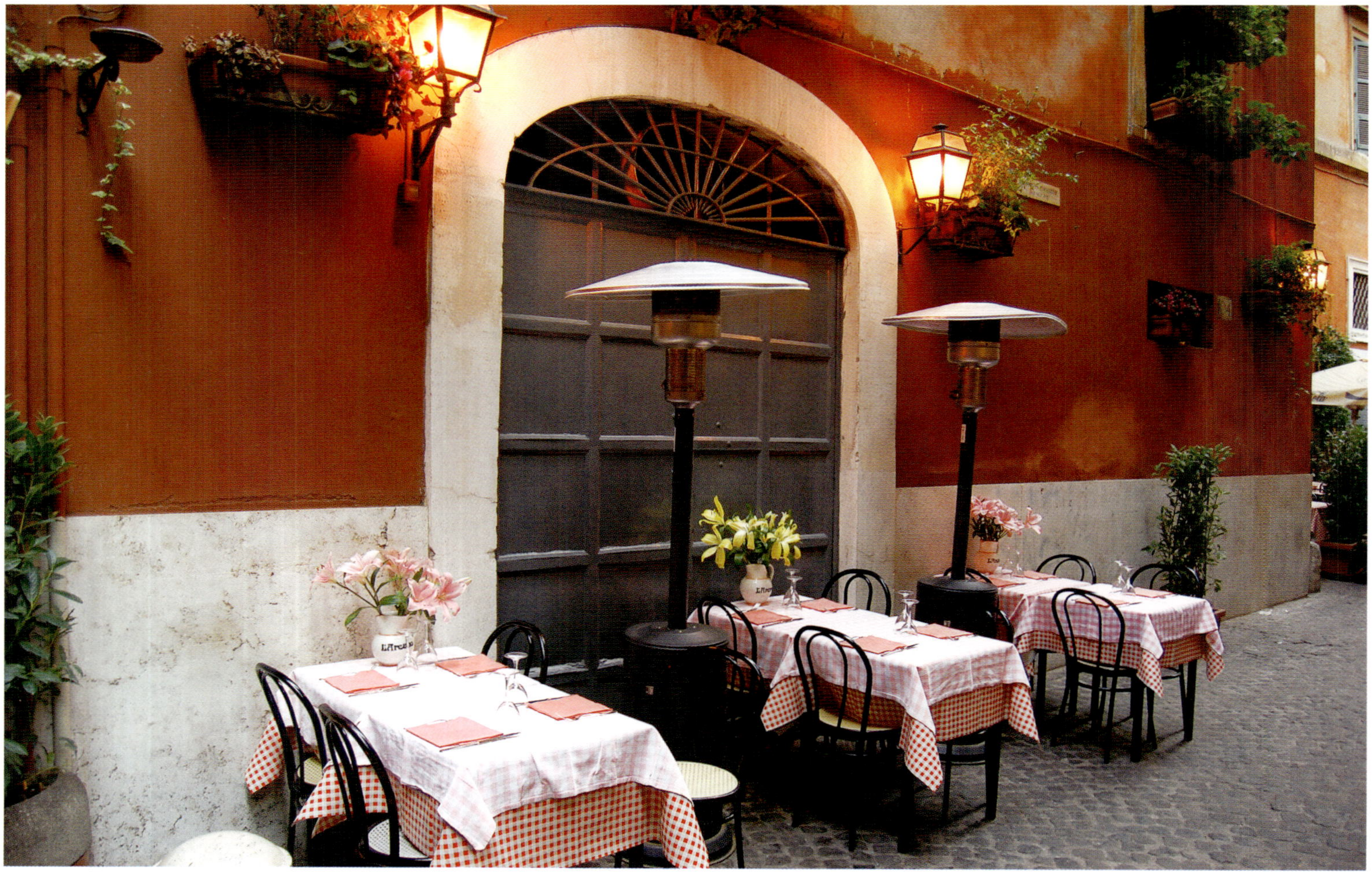

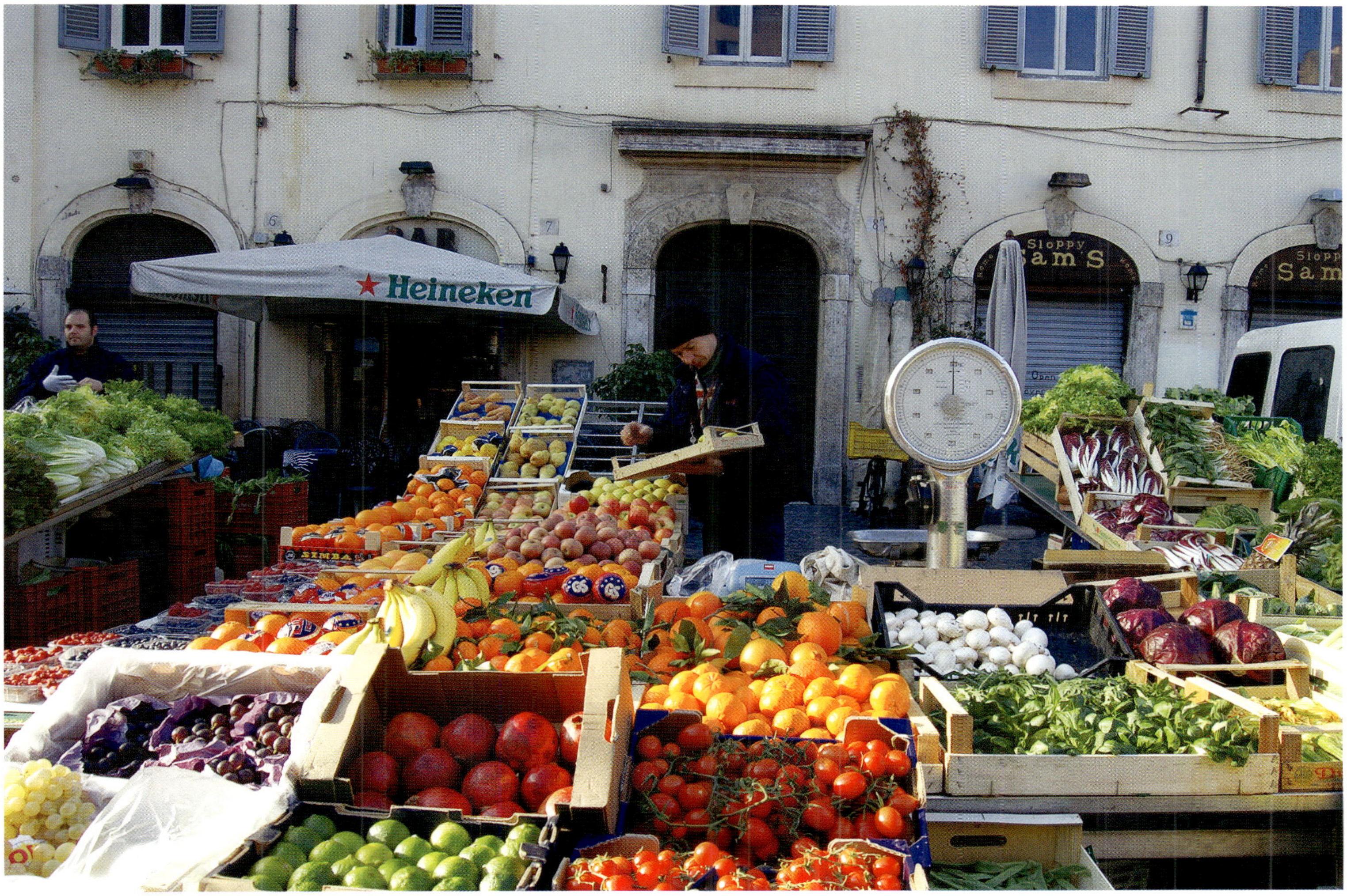
Heineken
Sloppy
Sam's

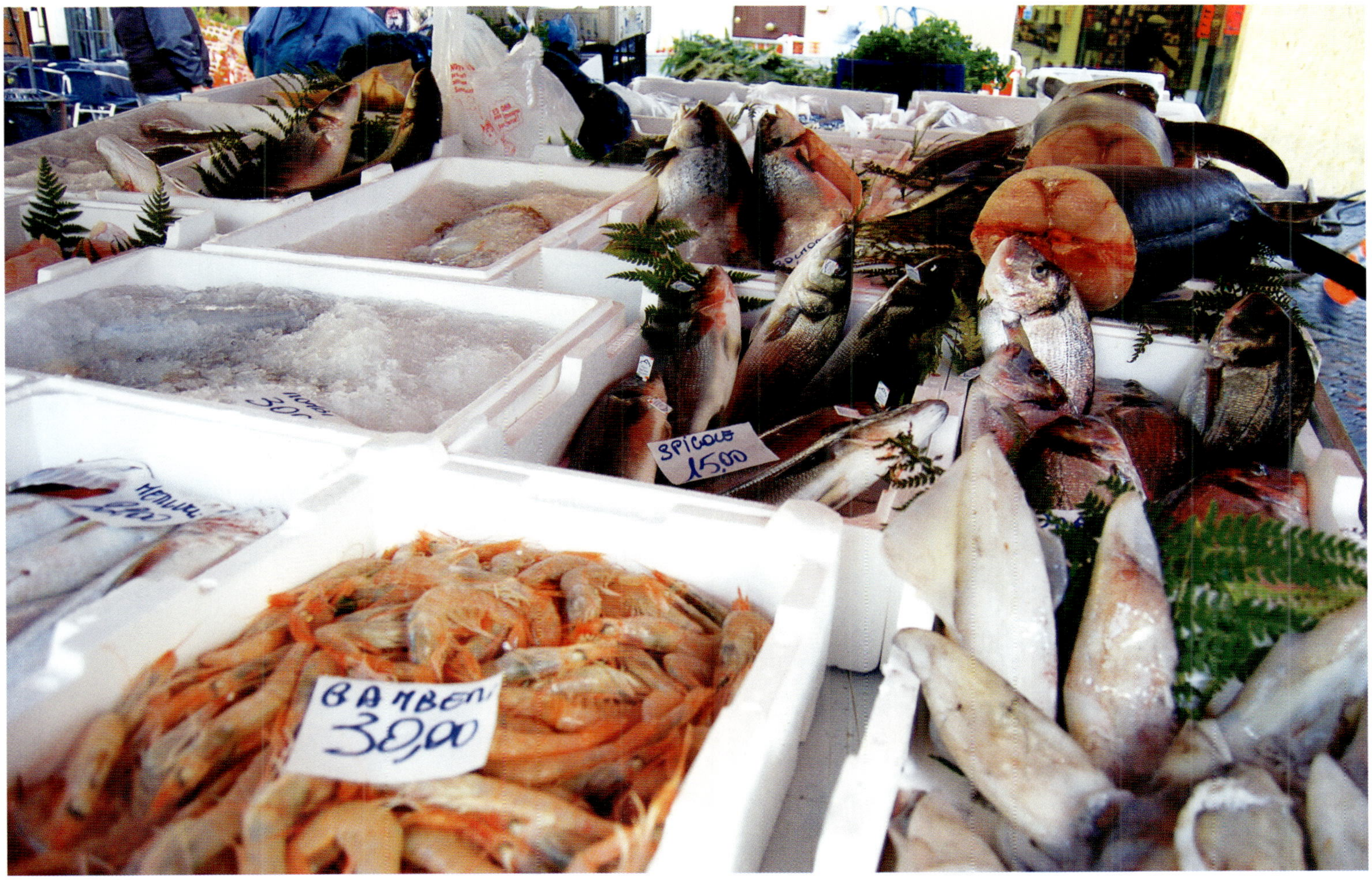

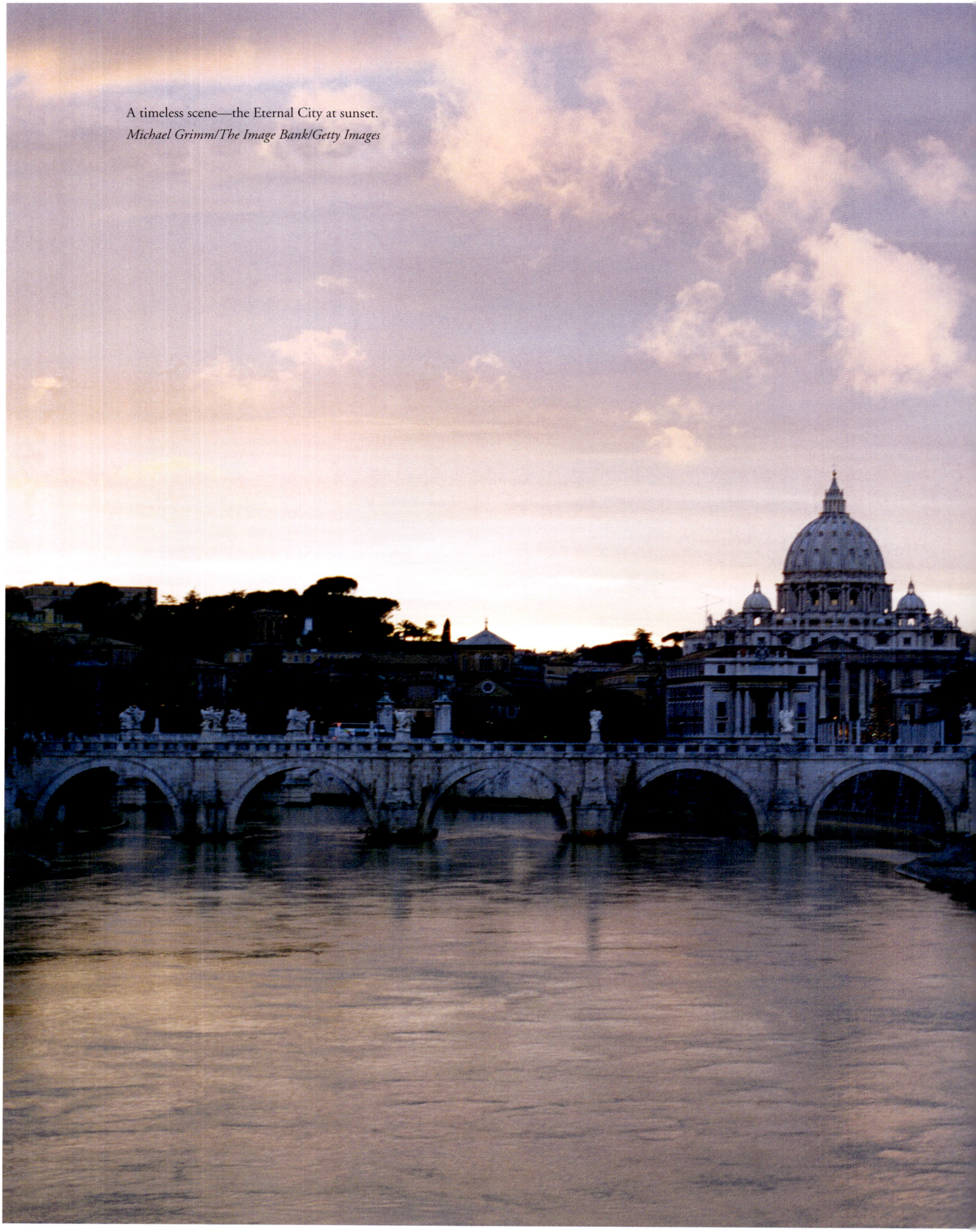

A timeless scene—the Eternal City at sunset.
Michael Grimm/The Image Bank/Getty Images

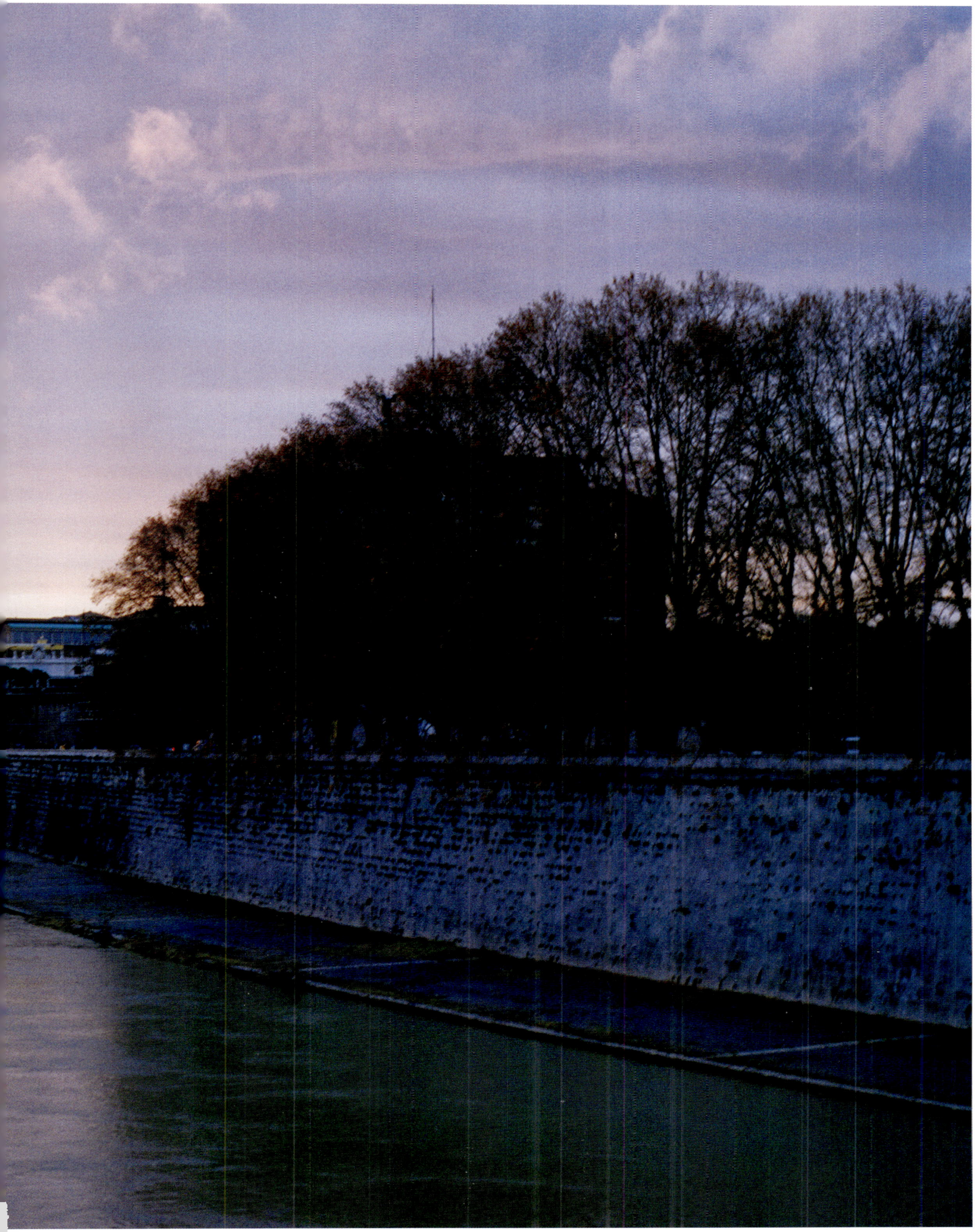

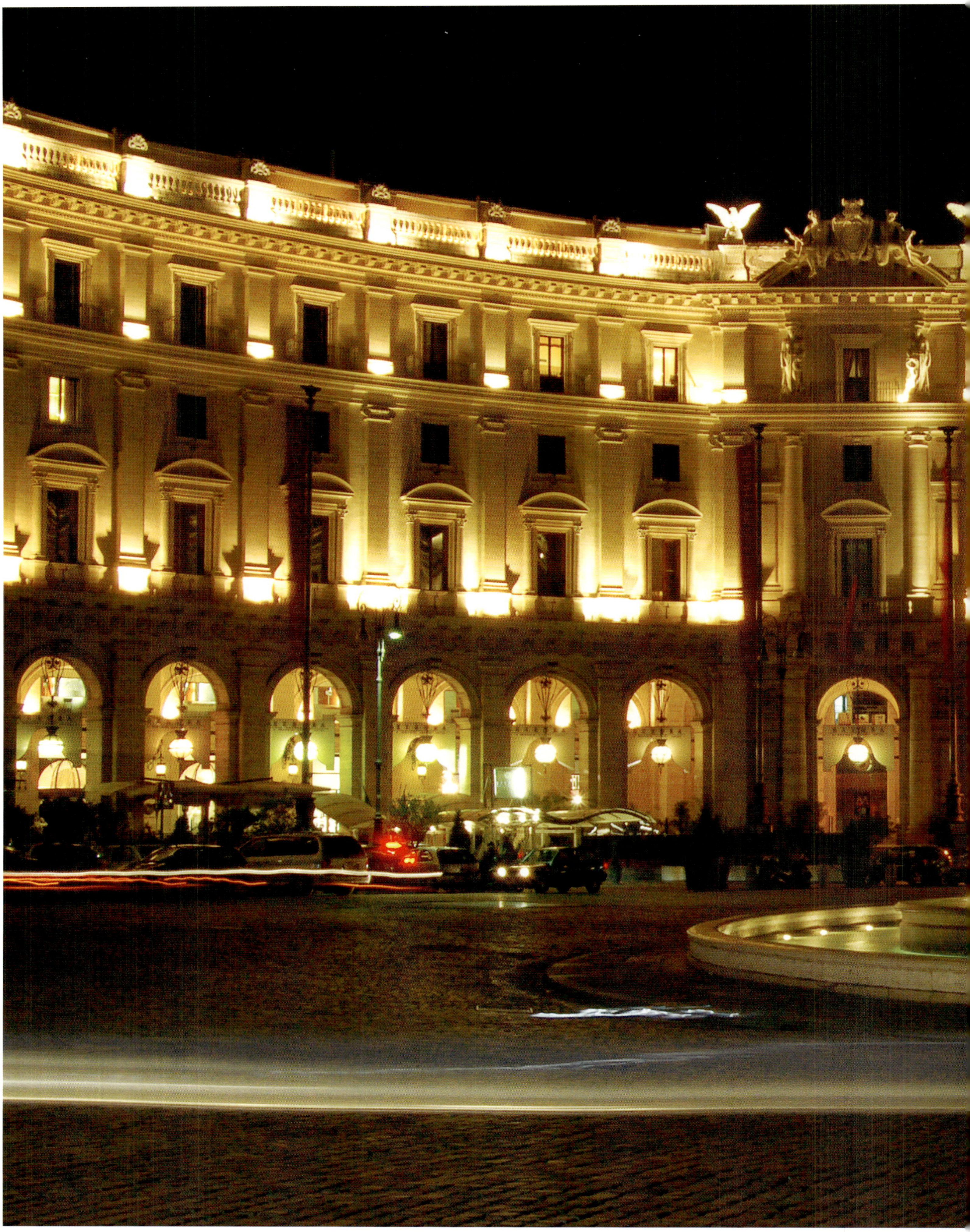

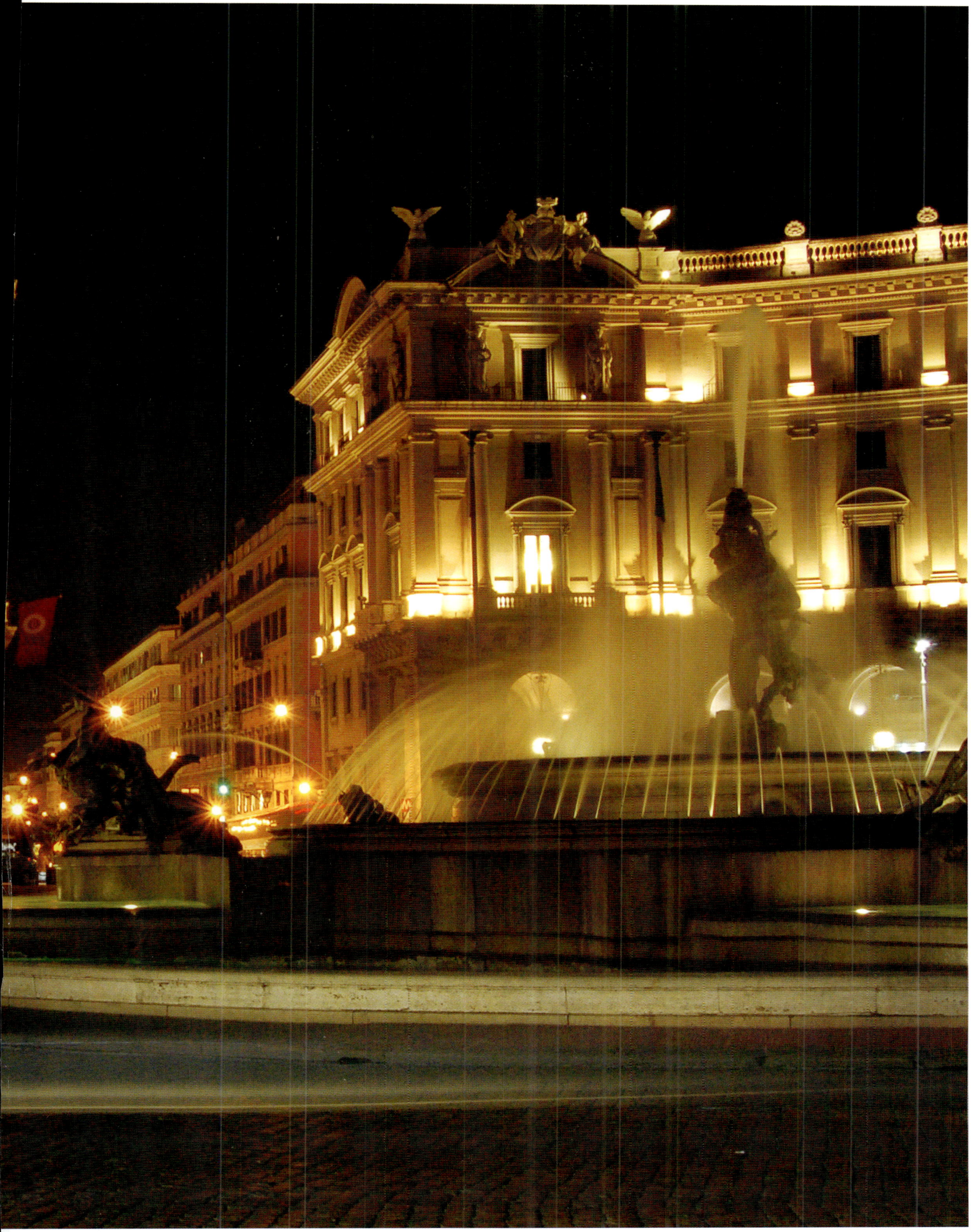